THE 61ST ART DIRECTORS ANNUAL

The 61st Annual of Advertising, Editorial,
and Television Art and Design
Copyright © 1982 by the **Art Directors Club, Inc.**
Published by **A.D.C. Publications**
ISBN 0-937414-02-6

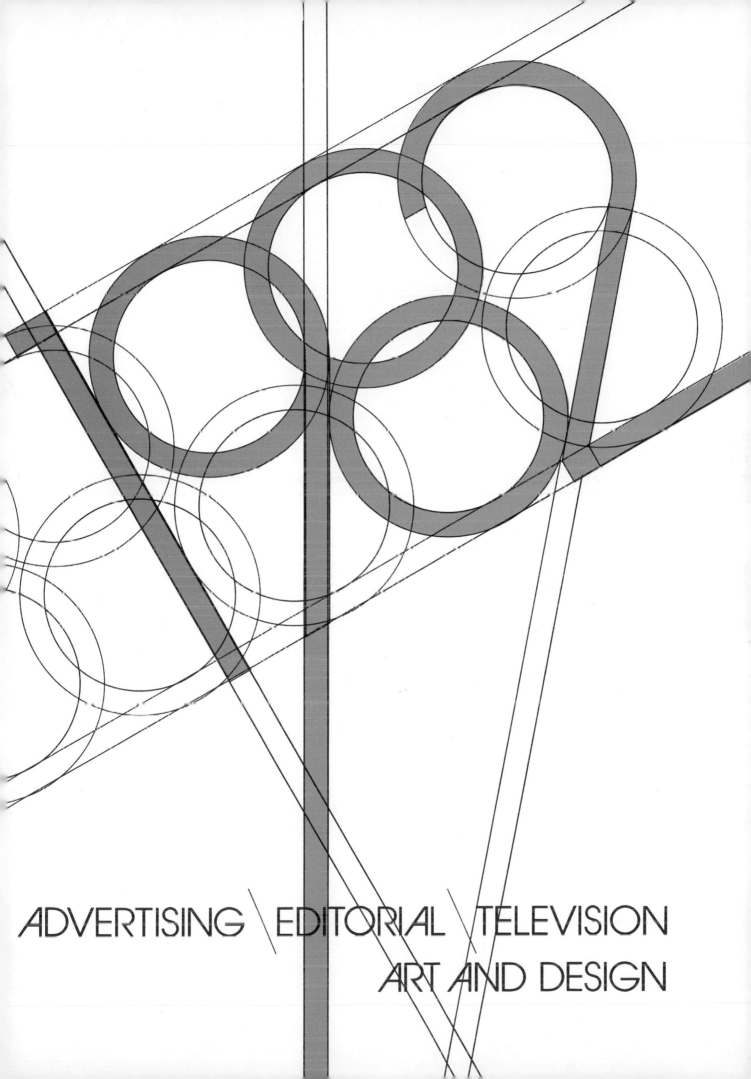

ADVERTISING \ EDITORIAL \ TELEVISION
ART AND DESIGN

CREDITS

Book Division Chairman: **Ernest Scarfone**
Executive Administrator: **Diane Moore**
Editor/Designer: **Otto Storch**
Managing Editor: **Miriam L. Solomon**
Production Coordinator: **Frank DeLuca**
Cover and Section Divider Mechanicals: **William H. Buckley**
Mechanicals: **ARP Graphics Int., Inc., Ralph Smith, Padraic Smith, Mairead Smith**
Club News and Activities Copy Editor: **Jo Yanow**
Club Photographer: **Deborah "Stormy" Weathers**
Exhibition Staff: **Daniel Sheehan, Stephen Hendrix, Michael Chin, Daniel Forte**

Complete Book Packaging Provided by:
Supermart Graphics Inc.
22 East 31st Street
New York, N.Y. 10016
(212) 889-6728

MANUFACTURING

Typesetting: **Gerard Associates Phototypesetting, Inc.**
Paper: **Consolidated, Frostbrite Matte**
supplied by **Marquardt & Co.**
Covers and End Papers: **Lehigh Press, Inc.**
Four Color Separations and Printing: **Toppan Printing Co. (America)**
Camera Work and Stripping: **Jay Publishing Service**
Text Printing and Binding: **Interstate Book Manufacturers**

OTTO STORCH

Otto Storch was born in New York in 1913
and studied at Pratt Institute,
New York University, Art Students League
and with Alexi Brodovitch at the New School workshop.
He is a member of the Society of Illustrators
and a life member of the New York Art Directors Club.
Mr. Storch has been Executive Art Director of Dell Publishing,
Art Editor of Better Living, Art Director and Editor-at-Large of McCall's Magazine
and Vice-President of the McCall Corporation
before forming his own company, Otto Storch, Inc.
He is now a free lance photographer,
designer and consultant Art Director.
Otto Storch has received over 500 awards
for art direction and photography
from the New York A.D.C., ADC of New Jersey, ADC of Philadelphia,
ADC of Los Angeles, The Type Directors Club,
AIGA, Society of Illustrators, C. A. Magazine, Museum of Modern Art,
Society of Publication Designers and others. These awards included 19 gold medals
and best of show awards and 90 awards of distinctive merit.
Other awards are from:
Pratt Institute:
Alumni of the Year
Philadelphia Museum College of Art:
Citation for Outstanding Art Direction
University of Missouri, School of Journalism:
Photography category Award
Rochester Institute of Technology
Brehm Memorial Lecture Medal
New York Art Directors Club Special Medal Award:
for "creative excellence in his art direction of McCall's Magazine"
National Society of Art Directors:
Art Director of the Year
Advertising Women in New York:
Eighth Lively Arts Award in Photography Category
Art Directors Club:
Hall of Fame
Bibliography: a partial list includes Who's Who in America,
Gebrauchgraphic, Graphis, Print, American Artist, Vista U.S.A.,
Printers Ink, Amepnka, Der Spiegel, Time, Advertising Age,
Die Deutsche Sektion Des I.C.T.A. C.A. Magazine
Books include: 4 Graphic Designers in U.S.A., Art Directing,
Art Directors in New York, Photographers in New York,
A History of Graphic Design: Virginia Commonwealth University.

CONTENTS

DISTRIBUTION

Distributors to the book trade
in the United States
Robert Silver Associates
95 Madison Avenue
New York, New York 10016
(212) 686-5630

In Canada
General Publishing Co. Ltd.
30 Lesmill Road
Don Mills, Ont. M3B 2T6

In Europe and the United Kingdom
Graphic Press Corp.
Dufourstrasse 107
CH-8008 Zurich
Switzerland

All other countries
Fleetbooks, S.A.
c/o **Feffer and Simons, Inc.**
100 Park Avenue
New York, New York 10017 U.S.A.

Graphis Press Corp.
Dufourstrasse 107
CH-8008 Zurich
Switzerland

ON REMEMBERING PRINT

I think that we had strong entries in three categories
this year, and quite a surprise in another.
The good news first. Television appeared quite healthy.
A few of last year's campaigns were voted in again
but with some remarkably fresh spots
instead of the usual "poolouts." (Maybe if we eliminate that word,
people won't do them anymore.)
There were also a lot of the quick cut,
"New Wave" commercials for everything from fashion to cars and spas.
I have a feeling that this year's show
will be its saturation point.
The Editorial entries were strong.
I think that many of the magazines
miss the large formats of yesteryear,
but the editorial fellows tell that story better than I can.
Entries in the Promotion and Graphics Category
were generally excellent.
Except for the perennial delinquent,
which is the category of Bookjackets.
Hundreds of beauties seem to peek out from bookshelves all year.
When it's time for the show, nobody shows up.
Again this year, very few entries in this category.
Baffling, but at least consistent.
But the category that stunned me the most in terms of quality
of entries was Advertising Print. Eeegad. Yipes.
One dip into that yellow bin of tearsheets
and you felt like you were stepping off the continental shelf.
I'm not sure why. I have a hunch that more senior people
are doing the television and passing the print on to juniors.
And if that is so I have a question:
What has happened to the taskmasters of yore?
Those people who would look up at an art director
and a writer and say, I know there's a deadline.
Now tear it up and start over again.
Who once told them that a big square halftone that just illustrates
and reiterates the copy is not the path to greatness.
Who once told them that sometimes the best art directing
can be no picture at all if the words are strong.
And that there *is* one creative crime you can commit in our business.
And that's the crime of being dull.
Remember print?
That's the land a lot of us first came from.
HARVEY GABOR, JUDGING CHAIRMAN

GOLD AWARDS

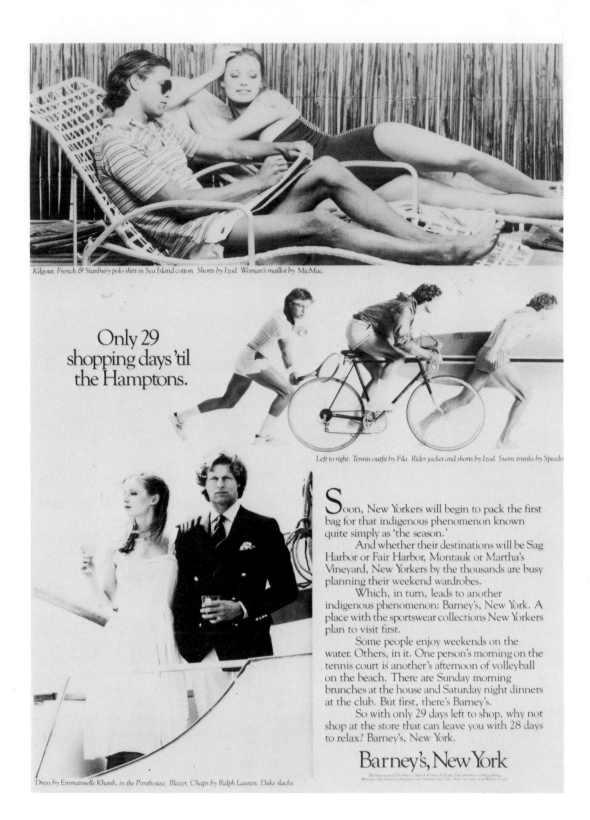

Kilgour, French & Stanbury polo shirt in Sea Island cotton. Shorts by Izod. Woman's maillot by MicMac.

Only 29 shopping days 'til the Hamptons.

Left to right: Tennis outfit by Fila. Rider jacket and shorts by Izod. Swim trunks by Speedo

Soon, New Yorkers will begin to pack the first bag for that indigenous phenomenon known quite simply as 'the season.'

And whether their destinations will be Sag Harbor or Fair Harbor, Montauk or Martha's Vineyard, New Yorkers by the thousands are busy planning their weekend wardrobes.

Which, in turn, leads to another indigenous phenomenon: Barney's, New York. A place with the sportswear collections New Yorkers plan to visit first.

Some people enjoy weekends on the water. Others, in it. One person's morning on the tennis court is another's afternoon of volleyball on the beach. There are Sunday morning brunches at the house and Saturday night dinners at the club. But first, there's Barney's.

So with only 29 days left to shop, why not shop at the store that can leave you with 28 days to relax? Barney's, New York.

Barney's, New York

Dress by Emmanuelle Khanh, in the Penthouse. Blazer, Chaps by Ralph Lauren. Daks slacks.

36   GOLD AWARD
Art Director: **Alex Tsao**
Designer: **Alex Tsao**
Photographers: **Armani: Bruce Lawrence, Hamptons:**
Les Goldberg, Madison Room: Carl Fisher
Writers: **Deborah Polenberg, Mitch Epstein**
Client: **Barney's, New York**
Agency: **Epstein Raboy Advertising**

101   GOLD AWARD
Art Director: **Laura Vergano**
Designer: **Laura Vergano**
Photographers: **Charles Gold** — "Vegetables" &
"**Mussels**," **Phil Marco** — "Coffee"
Writers: **Lynn Stiles, Anne Conlon**
Client: **Hilton International**
Agency: **Lord, Geller, Federico, Einstein Inc.**

Leon Jaworski
on radio, television and
newspapers.

Photograph by Skrebneski

"*Television and radio really whet my appetite for news. Then I turn to a newspaper for the full stories.*
　"*That's because newspapers don't have to squeeze a full day's news* *into a given number of seconds.*
　"*And newspapers don't have to leave out one story in order to give preference to another.*
　"*For as long as I can* *remember, newspapers have been an integral part of my daily routine — whether I'm at work, on my ranch or travelling.*
　"*Without a daily newspaper, my day is incomplete.*"

A lot of powerful people read a newspaper.

In Houston, they read The Chronicle.

More circulation, more $35,000+ readers, more general, retail and classified linage than any other newspaper in the Southwest. Represented nationally by Sawyer Ferguson Walker.

102　GOLD AWARD
Art Director: **Gayl Ware**
Designer: **Gayl Ware**
Photographer: **Victor Skrebnski**
Writers: **Dick Sinreich, Kristy McNichol, Alex Haley,**
Leon Jaworski
Client: **Houston Chronicle**
Agency: **Rives Smith Baldwin & Carlberg / Y&R, Houston**

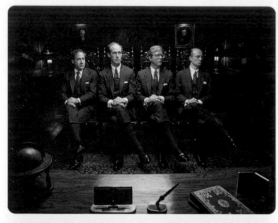

RESTAURANT—BOARDROOM—TENNIS
(MUSIC THROUGHOUT)
Don't you think it's time to change your socks?
To Interwoven.

450　GOLD AWARD
Art Directors: **Jay Loucks, Chris Hill**
Designers: **Chris Hill, Mark Geer**
Photographer: **Gary Braasch**
Writer: **Lee Herrick**
Client: **Compendium**
Agency: **Loucks Atelier, Houston**

618   GOLD AWARD
Art Director: **Lowell Williams**
Designers: **Lowell Williams, Bill Carson, Lance Brown**
Photographers: **Ron Scott, Joe Baraban, Jim Sims**
Artists: **Tom McNeff, Sue Yates**
Writer: **Lee Herrick**
Client: **Oiltools International Ltd.**
Agency: **Lowell Williams Design, Inc.**

852   GOLD AWARD
Art Director: **Peter Windett**
Designer: **Peter Windett**
Artist: **Graham Everden**
Client: **Crabtree & Evelyn, Ltd.**
Agency: **Peter Windett Associates**

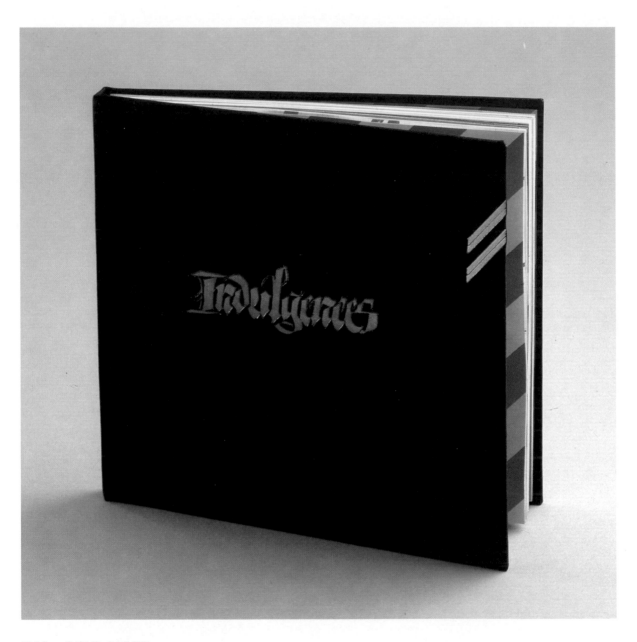

1032 GOLD AWARD
Art Directors: **Judy Anderson, Bill Jackson**
Designers: **Judy Anderson, Bill Jackson**
Artists: **Judy Anderson, Bill Jackson**
Writers: **Judy Anderson, Bill Jackson**
Client: **Self promotion**
Editor: **Max Schaible**
Publisher: **ArtHouse Press**

1033 GOLD AWARD
Art Director: **R.D. Scudellari**
Designer: **R.D. Scudellari**
Photographer: **John Gruen**
Client: **Alfred A. Knopf**
Editor: **R.D. Scudellari**
Publisher: **Alfred A. Knopf**
Director: **Robert Gottlieb**
Producer: **Ellen McNeilly**
Agency: **Corporate Design Staff**

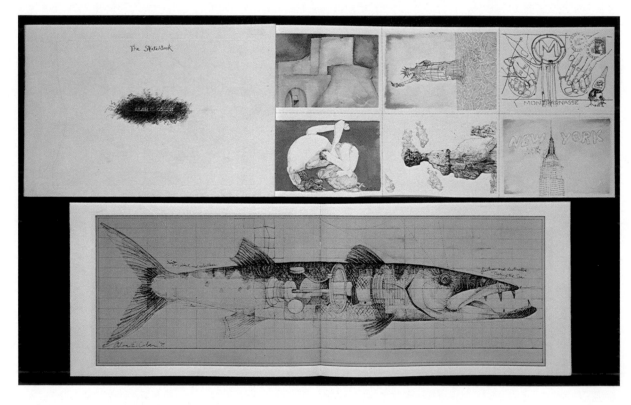

1169　GOLD AWARD
Art Director: **Gordon Fisher**
Designers: **Gordon Fisher, Alan E. Cober**
Artist: **Alan E. Cober**
Writers: **Gordon Fisher, Sue Smith**
Client: **Neenah Paper**
Agency: **Creative Dimensions**

Luis Fuente in
Robert Joffrey's "Postcards."

1245 GOLD AWARD
Art Director: **Robin McDonald**
Designer: **Robin McDonald**
Photographer: **Herbert Migdoll**
Writer: **Judith Jedlicka**
Client: **Horizon Magazine**
Editor: **David Fryxell**
Publisher: **Gray Boone**

1314   GOLD AWARD
Art Director: **Michael Tesch**
Writer: **Patrick Kelly**
Client: **Federal Express**
Editor: **Peggy DeLay/Sedelmaier Films**
Director: **Joe Sedelmaier**
Producers: **Maureen Kearns/A&G,**
Ann Ryan/Sedelmaier
Agency: **Ally & Gargano, Inc.**

PICK UP—PICK UP THE PHONE—FAST PACED
ANNCR (VO): Federal Express is so easy to use, all you
have to do is pick up the phone.
(SFX: RRRRRRRIIIIIIIPPPPPPPPPPPPPP!!!!)
(SFX: WATER)

307 GOLD AWARD
Art Director: **Jerry Pavey**
Designer: **Jerry Pavey**
Artist: **Peter Good**
Writer: **Ronald Erickson**
Client: **The Fiscal Agency for the Farm Credit Banks**
Publisher: **Moore and Moore Inc.**

1332   GOLD AWARD
Art Director: **Joe Sedelmaier**
Writer: **Jeff Gorman**
Client: **Independent Life Insurance**
Editor: **Peggy DeLay**
Director: **Joe Sedelmaier**
Production Co.: **Sedelmaier Film
Productions Inc.**
Agency: **Cecil West**

FAMILY
30-second
ANNCR (VO): You've both worked hard to establish a good way of life for the family.
But what if one of you was no longer in the picture?
Luckily, you have Total Way of Life coverage from Independent Life.
For the kid's all-important education. And Independent Life's Couple Coverage.
So you can continue to live the good life.
When an agent from Independent Life calls, talk to him about Total Way of Life.

1469. GOLD AWARD
Art Director: **Michael Tesch**
Writer: **Patrick Kelly**
Client: **Federal Express**
Editors: **Peggy DeLay/Sedelmaier Films**
Director: **Joe Sedelmaier**
Producers: **Maureen Kearns/A&G,**
Ann Ryan/Sedelmaier
Agency: **Ally & Gargano, Inc.**

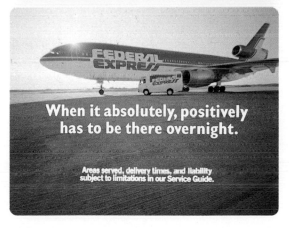

YOU CAN'T COUNT ON ANYTHING
30-second
(MUSIC THROUGHOUT)
(SFX: BIRDS CHIRPING)
(SFX: RATTLE OF ALARM CLOCK)
(SFX: ENGINE)
(SFX: FLAT TIRE)
ANNCR (VO): You can't count on anything these days . . .
(SFX: FOOTSTEPS)
(SFX: TYPING)
MAN (OC): Did you type the letter I told you to type?
SECRETARY (OC): No.
ANNCR (VO): With possibly one exception:
Federal Express.
When it absolutely, positively has to be there overnight.

1561 GOLD AWARD
Art Director: **Michael Tesch**
Writer: **Patrick Kelly**
Client: **Federal Express**
Editor: **Peggy DeLay/Sedelmaier Films**
Director: **Joe Sedelmaier**
Producers: **Maureen Kearns/A&G,**
Ann Ryan, Sedelmaier
Agency: **Ally & Gargano, Inc.**

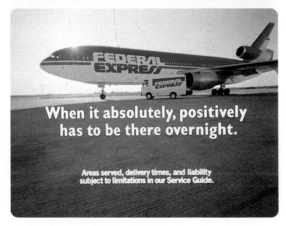

FAST PACED WORLD
60-second
MR. SPLEEN (OC): Okay,Eunice,travelplans.IneedtobeinNew
YorkonWednesday,LAonThursday,NewYorkonFriday.Gotit?
EUNICE (VO): Got it.
MR. SPLEEN (OC):
Soyouwanttoworkhere,wellwhatmakesyou
thinkyoudeserveajobhere?
GUY: Wellsir,Ithinkonmyfeet,I'mgoodwithfiguresandIhavea
sharpmind.
SPLEEN: Congratulations,welcomeaboard.
(SFX)
OC: Wonderful,wonderful,wonderfulAndinconclusion
Jim,Bill,Bob,Paul,Don,Frank,andTed.
Businessisbusinessesandsdweallknowinordertogetsomethingdone
you'vegottodosomething.Inordertodosomethingyou'vegotto
gettoworksolet'sallgettowork.
Thankyouforattendingthismeeting. (SFX)
OC: Peteryoudidabang-upjobI'mputting
youinchargeofPittsburgh.
PETER (OC): Pittsburgh,perfect.
SPLEEN: Iknowit'sperfectPeterthat'swhyIpickedPittsburgh.
Pittsburgh'sperfectPeter.MayIcallyouPete?
PETER: CallmePete.
SPLEEN: Pete.
SECRETARY (OC): There'saMr.Snitlerheretoseeyou.
SPLEEN: Tellhimtowait15seconds.
SECRETARY: Canyouwait15seconds.
MAN: I'llwait15seconds.
SPLEEN (OC): CongratulationsonyourdealinDenverDavid.
I'mputtingyoudowntodealinDallas.Donisitadeal?Dowehaveadeal?
It'sadeal.Ihaveacallcomingin. . .
ANNCR (VO): In this fast moving high pressure, get-it-done
yesterday world.
VO: Aren't you glad that there's one company that can
keep up with it all?
SPLEEN (OC):
Dickwhat'sthedealwiththedeal.Arewedealing?
We'redealing.Daveit'sadealwithDon,DorkandDick.
Dorkit'sadealwithDon,DaveandDick.
Dickit'saDorkwithDonDealandDave.Dave,gotago,disconnecting.
Dorkgottago,disconnecting.Dickgottago,disconnecting. . .
ANNCR (VO): Federal Express. (SFX) When it absolutely,
positively has to be there overnight.

1352 GOLD AWARD
Art Director: **Phil Snyder**
Designer: **Kurt Lundel**
Writer: **Jack Reynolds**
Client: **E.F. Hutton**
Editor: **Bob Lynch/Editors Hideaway**
Agency Producer: **Jane Haeberly**
Director: **Tibor Hirsch**
Production Co.: **THT Productions**
Agency: **Benton & Bowles, Inc.**

ALPHABET/FP
30-second
TEACHER: Alright, children, who's going to be the first one
to recite the alphabet? How 'bout you Ann?
ANN: A . . . b . . . c . . . d . . .
. . . e . . . f . . . e . . . f . . . E.F. Hutton!
ANNCR (VO): When E.F. Hutton talks, people listen.

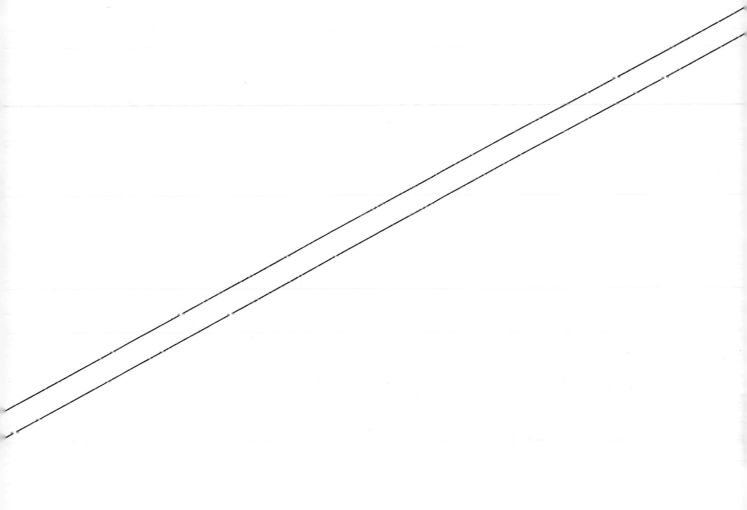

NEWSPAPER ADVERTISING

Easter
Rabbits
$6360

If you've been hunting for the best value in a new car, stop by our showroom before the end of the week. And catch our Easter Week Rabbit Sale. You'll find the room, comfort, quality and handling our Rabbits offer make them a pleasure to own. But one of the best things you'll see at our showroom this week is what our Rabbits are wearing: lower prices.

The Episcopal Church welcomes you. Regardless of race, creed, color or the number of times you've been born.

Whether you've been born once or born again, the Episcopal Church invites you to come and join us in the fellowship and worship of Jesus Christ.
The Episcopal Church

1   SILVER AWARD
Art Director: **Ron A. Louie**
Designer: **Ron A. Louie**
Artist: **Ron A. Louie**
Writer: **David J. Crain**
Client: **Volkswagen of America**
Publisher: **Volkswagen of America**
Agency: **Doyle Dane Bernbach**

2
Art Director: **Nancy Rice**
Designer: **Nancy Rice**
Writer: **Tom McElligott**
Client: **Episcopal Ad Project**
Agency: **Fallon McElligott Rice**

MAKING ABORTION ILLEGAL WON'T MAKE IT UNAVAILABLE. JUST UNSAFE.

Before abortion was legalized in this country, more than 600,000 women each year took their lives into their own hands by having illegal, back-alley abortions.

How many were seriously injured?

How many died?

Right now, there are a handful of U.S. Senators who are determined to bring back those days of dangerous, clandestine abortions.

They are holding the second round of hearings on a proposed statute that would make a fertilized egg a person. If this bill becomes law, any state could outlaw abortion. Overnight.

And this time, it will be even worse than it ever was. Because if you have an abortion it will be considered premeditated murder.

Even a miscarriage could be investigated as manslaughter.

Backing this bill are radical right-wing political and religious forces including New York's very own Senator Alfonse D'Amato. This small but noisy group of people want to impose their beliefs on you. Your friends. Your family.

Don't stand by silently and let outrage become law. Fill out this Planned Parenthood coupon. Give generously of your time and money. With your contributions we can continue our work to preserve safe and legal abortion.

Give now. Before the minority rules.

JOIN PLANNED PARENTHOOD
Planned Parenthood of New York City, Inc.
380 Second Avenue, New York, N.Y. 10010
212/777-2002

☐ I believe that abortion is something personal, not political. Please keep me informed and add me to your mailing list.

☐ I want to keep abortion legal and wish to make a tax-deductible contribution. Here is my check in the amount of $

ABORTION IS SOMETHING PERSONAL. NOT POLITICAL.

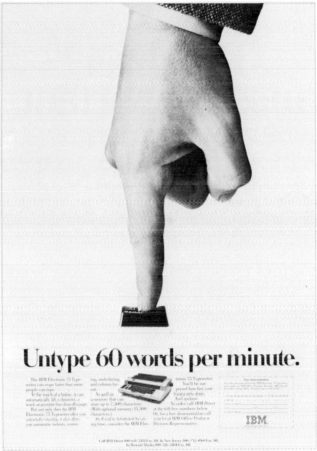

Untype 60 words per minute.

The IBM Electronic 75 Typewriter can erase faster than some people can type.

At the touch of a button, it can automatically lift a character, a word, or an entire line clean off a page.

But not only does the IBM Electronic 75 Typewriter offer you automatic reliability, it also offers you automatic indents, center-

ing, underlining and column layout.

As well as a memory that can store up to 7,500 characters. (With optional memory: 15,500 characters.)

So if you're interested in saving time, consider the IBM Electronic 75 Typewriter.

You'll be surprised how fast your typing gets done.

And unless.

To order call IBM Direct at the toll-free numbers below. Or, for a free demonstration call your local IBM Office Products Division Representative.

IBM

Call IBM Direct 800-631-5582 Ext. 141. In New Jersey 800-352-4960 Ext. 141.
In Hawaii/Alaska 800-526-2484 Ext. 141.

3
Art Director: **Tana Klugherz**
Photographer: **Manny Gonzolez**
Writer: **Debbie Kasher**
Client: **Planned Parenthood of New York City**
Agency: **Levine, Huntley, Schmidt, Plapler & Beaver, Inc.**

4
Art Director: **Rick Elkins**
Photographer: **Jim Young / Hunter Freeman**
Writer: **Rhonda Peck**
Client: **IBM**
Agency: **Doyle Dane Bernbach**

The three most important letters in typing.

IBM

It has a memory like a typewriter.

Not just any typewriter—but an IBM Electronic Typewriter.

The Electronic 75. It has a Jumbo-size memory that can store up to 7,500 characters of whatever you type in. (With its even bigger optional memory: 15,500 characters.)

Now when you have something to retype, the typewriter can type it. Automatically.

And because of its memory, when you have to make changes, you type only the changes. The typewriter types the rest.

It even lets you create new documents by combining stored sentences and paragraphs. Or stored typing with original typing.

The Electronic 60. Its memory is less than Jumbo-size. But it's no peanut.

It can store up to 736 characters of anything you have to type often.

The Electronic 50. It has proportional letter-spacing for a "printed" look.

And it can align numbers in columns automatically—always remembering to put the decimal point in the right place.

All in The Family. Because of their electronics, all three models have automatic margins, tabs, indents, erasing, centering, underlining, and column layout.

They save time. And whatever saves time is more productive. Automatically.

An Element Never Forgets. Not when it's part of an IBM Electronic Typewriter. You get two interchangeable typing elements with each model. And you can choose from over 20 different type styles.

You also get the new combined ribbon and lift-off tape cartridge that snaps in and out of the typewriter. There's no more threading.

Get an IBM Electronic Typewriter. Once you see how much it increases productivity, its cost becomes peanuts.

IBM
Office Products Division

5
Art Director: **Marion Sackett**
Designer: **Marion Sackett**
Writer: **Hal Kaufman**
Client: **IBM**
Agency: **Doyle Dane Bernbach**

6
Art Director: **Roy Grace**
Designer: **Roy Grace**
Artist: **Roy Grace**
Writer: **Tom Yobbagy**
Client: **IBM Office Products Division**
Agency: **Doyle Dane Bernbach**

The only way to describe our new service.

All it took was a couple of miracle workers, a lot of team spirit, a few prayers, and wonder of wonders! Our service is second to none.

In a recent traveler's poll, we ranked first among transatlantic flyers in on-board service, food served and value received.

Just how did we become the chosen airline?

Well our non-stop service from JFK to Ben-Gurion airport could have had something to do with it. And our punctuality certainly didn't hurt. El Al has been coming and going on time more times than ever before. Then there's El Al's hospitality. We have flight attendants who won't

rest until every head is properly propped and everyone has dined on delicious Kosher dinners. Just wait till you try them. But don't wait too long.

Starting April 1st through June 19th, El Al is offering a new, low Miracle Fare. It's only $799** round trip from New York to the Holy Land, and worth every Shekel.

When it comes to great service, El Al reaches for the stars. And gets them.

*"London Daily Mail, August 5, 1980.

**Tickets must be purchased at least 21 days in advance and your stay in Israel must be no less than 10 days, and no more than 60. Prior to 3/31, round trip fare is $699

EL AL אל על
The Airline of Israel

IT'S YOUR FUNERAL. OR IS IT?

THE COMPTON PLAN

7
Art Director: **Jerry Sullivan**
Designer: **Jerry Sullivan**
Photographer: **Allen Matthews**
Writer: **Perry Mitchell**
Client: **The Compton Plan**
Agency: **Jerry Sullivan, Inc.**

8
Art Director: **Ann Pitts**
Designer: **Ann Pitts**
Artist: **Lou Myers**
Writer: **Mimi Chapra**
Client: **El Al Airlines**
Agency: **DDB Group Two**

9
Art Director: **David November**
Designer: **David November**
Client: **CBS News**
Producer: **Mike Spano**

10
Art Director: **Pat Burnham**
Writer: **Phil Hanft**
Client: **Northwestern Bell**
Agency: **Bozell & Jacobs, Inc./Mpls.**

Seen by Gene.

Gene Federico. Art director, creative leader, co-founder of Lord, Geller, Federico, Einstein. Member of the Art Directors Hall of Fame. And a creative does whose career stretches over more than forty years. Here, from a recent conversation, he passes on his observations on advertising, creativity, and America's only national business daily.

On the beginning:
"An art teacher at Pratt called me to tell me I had a job if I wanted it—and I wanted it. It was at the Abbott Kimball Company, an exciting place with young people who learned by doing. We had a great creative group—including Bob Pliskin and later on Bob Gage and some very attractive, very talented young ladies. One became my wife—and a fine artist. Helen and I came together in a sort of a marrying agency; a funny, romantic organization where people loved their work, and loved each other."

On influences:
"I worked at a number of agencies—Doyle Dane Bernbach, Douglas Simon, Benton & Bowles. And I've worked with great people like Pliskin, Gage, Bill Bernbach, Phyllis Robinson, and Bob Larimer. But influences? I'd have to give a lot of credit to a guy who taught art and design at Abraham Lincoln High School in Coney Island where I grew up. Leon Friend didn't tell you how to do things. But he exposed you to a world of ideas. He opened windows for me and all the kids he taught. A fantastic person—and I'd guess the major reason why I became an art director."

On clients:
"The ideal client is smart enough to challenge you to do your best; to push you higher and higher, not necessarily to the highest ... ent and expect you to do better and better work. Good clients don't accept pat answers. They know you have to go beyond the fads and fashions in design, graphics, copy. I think that today's clients recognize these truths—and they help you enormously by encouraging you."

On the creative role:
"It's linked to the entire process of marketing a product. Good creative work can't be generated unless creative people work to gain an understanding of the entire marketing problem, and the marketing environment. People used to talk about 'good designers' and 'good writers' and 'good art directors.' But those crafts are only tools by which you develop advertising which meets marketing objectives."

On creative elegance:
"In my mind, the objective of creative people should be that of coming up with elegant solutions to marketing problems. Elegant may strike you as an odd word. But consider what elegant means. When someone talks about an 'elegant solution to a chess problem,' there's the strong implication of beautiful simplicity. That's true in advertising. Elegant advertising is distinguished by simplicity—and the simplicity makes it effective."

On advertising impact:
"Advertising impact increases as the directness of communication increases. That's the major gain made in our business in recent years; the understanding of how important it is to be direct, to strip away the unnecessary. Art direction and advertising copy ought to reflect the pace of life. Once it was leisurely. Today's pace is far quicker. Copy needs to be terse, direct, concise. The same holds true for art direction. People have neither the time nor inclination to figure out what you're trying to communicate."

On keeping at it:
"This talk about 'burnt-out'—sure, it happens. But the real stars have staying power. In part, it's nothing more than the willingness to keep working, keep involved, keep challenging the standards. In my office the centerpiece is my board. This has been my work. It is my work. It will always be my work. When you focus on your craft, you don't have the time to even consider burning out."

On visibility:
"If an ad isn't seen, it can't be read. And if it isn't seen and read, it won't be believed, and it won't be acted upon. So I begin with the problem of visibility, of working to strip away the nonessentials so that the effect is concentrated and the message stands out in the environment of the medium. Print's more challenging. For a simple reason. It's easier to flip a page than a channel."

On The Wall Street Journal:
"It's an elegant publication—and that's the highest praise I can give any product. We've used The Journal for many of our clients—Tiffany, IBM, Hennessy, and others. The elegance of The Journal provides the sort of media environment that seems instinctively suited for the kind of advertising we try to do. Of course, Tiffany is a retail client—the classiest of all retailers—so we have a good understanding of what a slick and chic doesn't. And, yes, Tiffany ads work in The Journal. I'd hate to see The Journal change. It is elegant. And I think that's good—for the people who read The Journal, and for those who advertise in The Journal."

The Wall Street Journal. It Works.

YOU CAN STILL GET MANHATTAN FOR $24.

UNTIL MAY 31. $24 EACH WAY. 24 HOURS A DAY.

13
Art Director: **Fred DeVito**
Photographer: **Gordon Munroe**
Client: **Bloomingdales**
Creative Director: **John C. Jay**
Agency: **Bloomingdales Adv. Dept.**

14
Art Director: **Nancy Pentecost-Hanover**
Artist: **George Rauch**
Writer: **Mark Goldstein**
Client: **The Washington Post**
Agency: **Earle Palmer Brown**

THE TELEPHONE YOU'LL FLIP OVER.

Get ready to flip again because here comes the new GTE Flip-Phone II telephone. With more colors. And more features. We've added a "Redial" button which automatically redials a busy number. With the "Mute" button you can silence the noise at your end any time you want. And the tone ringer now has three positions—"HI-LO-OFF."

These are all added to its flipped-out, pushbutton, one-piece design. So it's still small. It's still sleek. And, oh yes, it still flips.

So why just call out when you can flip out with the new Flip-Phone II.

FLIP OVER A FREE WALL HOLSTER
(A $7.95 retail value, free with every Flip-Phone II you buy.)

16
Art Director: **Fred DeVito**
Artist: **Michael Van Horn**
Client: **Bloomingdale's**
Creative Director: **John C. Jay**
Agency: **Bloomingdale's Adv. Dept.**

17
Art Director: **Bill Yamada**
Designer: **Bill Yamada**
Photographer: **Rosemary Kait**
Writer: **Joe Nunziata**
Client: **G.T.E.**
Agency: **Doyle Dane Bernbach**

18
Art Director: **Bob Kwait**
Designer: **Bob Kwait**
Artist: **Darrell Milsap / Ron Van Buskirk**
Writer: **Rich Badami**
Client: **Turf Paradise**
Agency: **Phillips-Ramsey Advertising**

19
Art Director: **David Bukvic**
Designer: **David Bukvic**
Photographer: **Michael Caporale**
Writer: **David Bukvic / Steve Thornbury**
Client: **Kenwood Plaza**
Publisher: **Gannet**
Agency: **Horwitz, Mann & Bukvic Advertising**

Welcome home!

Starting today, the only strikes in baseball will be the ones that fly over home plate. Because after 6 long weeks, the baseball strike is finally over.

Who won? Who lost? Who knows and who cares. The only thing that matters is that America's favorite pastime is back in full swing.

And starting today with the All-Star Game, America's number one sports section will bring you all the hits, runs and errors.

Reporters Peter Gammons and Larry Whiteside. Columnists Ray Fitzgerald and Leigh Montville.

They'll be on top of the plays and behind the scenes bringing you all the stories that make up the craziest season in baseball history: 1981 . . . and a half.

"The Globe's here!"

SAMSON
AND
DELILAH

PLACIDO DOMINGO · SHIRLEY VERRETT

When Camille Saint-Saëns brought the Bible's famous story of love and betrayal to life on the stage, he gave the world an immortal work. Now the San Francisco Opera brings you a magnificent new production under the baton of Julius Rudel. With Placido Domingo as Samson, Shirley Verrett as Delilah and Wolfgang Brendel as the High Priest.

Great Performances

EXXON

TONIGHT AT 8:00 ON CHANNEL THIRTEEN PBS
Simulcast on WNCN 104.3 FM

20
Art Director: **David Gardiner**
Photographer: **Frank Foster**
Writer: **Rick Ender**
Client: **Boston Globe**
Agency: **Hill, Holliday, Connors, Cosmopulos**

21
Art Director: **Leslie Singer**
Designer: **Leslie Singer**
Artist: **Michael David Brown**
Client: **McCaffrey & McCall**

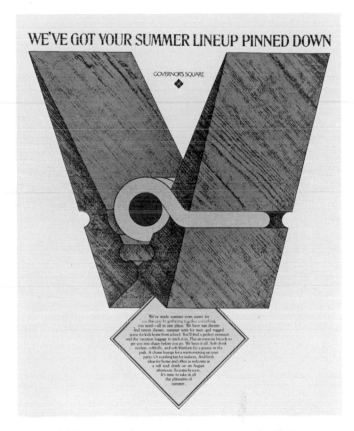

23
Art Director: **Dick Mitchell**
Designer: **Dick Mitchell**
Artist: **Dick Mitchell**
Writer: **Mark Perkins**
Client: **The Rouse Company**
Agency: **Richards, Sullivan, Brock & Assoc/**
The Richards Group

22
Art Director: **Alan Herman**
Designer: **Alan Herman**
Artist: **Alan Herman**
Client: **Messina Sausage Co.**
Agency: **Alan Herman & Assoc. Inc.**

24
Art Director: **Michael Winslow**
Photographer: **Tim Olive**
Writer: **Harriet Frye**
Client: **North Carolina Department of Commerce**
Agency: **McKinney Silver & Rockett**

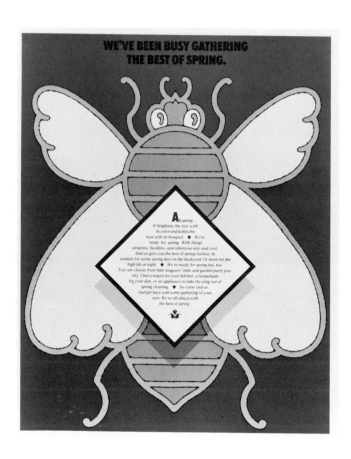

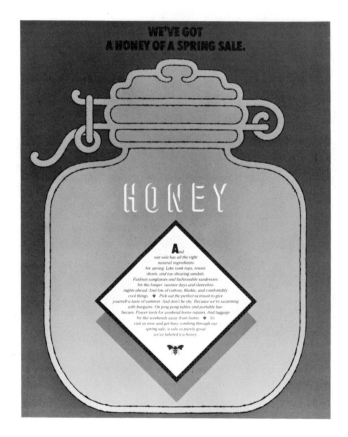

25
Art Director: **Nancy Hoefig**
Designer: **Nancy Hoefig**
Artist: **Nancy Hoefig**
Writer: **Mark Perkins**
Client: **The Rouse Company**
Agency: **Richards, Sullivan, Brock & Assoc/
The Richards Group**

26
Art Director: **Nancy Hoefig**
Designer: **Nancy Hoefig**
Artist: **Nancy Hoefig**
Writer: **Mark Perkins**
Client: **The Rouse Company**
Agency: **Richards, Sullivan, Brock & Assoc/
The Richards Group**

27
Art Director: **Arthur Eisenberg**
Designer: **Linda Eissler**
Artist: **Linda Eissler**
Writer: **Linda Eissler**
Client: **Broadway Square Mall**
Agency: **The Cherri Oakley Company**

28
Art Directors: **Brian Boyd, Ron Sullivan**
Designer: **Brian Boyd**
Artist: **Brian Boyd**
Writer: **Mark Perkins**
Client: **Paul Broadhead & Associates**
Agency: **Richards, Sullivan, Brock & Associates/
The Richards Group**

29
Art Directors: **Brian Boyd, Ron Sullivan**
Designer: **Brian Boyd**
Artist: **Brian Boyd**
Writer: **Mark Perkins**
Client: **Paul Broadhead & Associates**
Agency: **Richards, Sullivan, Brock & Associates/
The Richards Group**

30
Art Directors: **Louis Acevedo, Mike Schroeder**
Designers: **Louis Acevedo, Mike Schroeder**
Artist: **Louis Acevedo**
Writers: **Carol St. George, Louis Acevedo, Lyn Zanville**
Client: **HIDEVCO**
Agency: **Lyn Zanville, Inc.**

31
Art Director: **John Constable**
Designer: **John Constable**
Artist: **Ray Domingo**
Writers: **Steve Laughlin, Karen Ninnemann**
Client: **Regency Mall**
Agency: **Frankenberry, Laughlin & Constable, Inc.**

32
Art Director: **John Constable**
Designer: **John Constable**
Artist: **Ray Domingo**
Writers: **Steve Laughlin, Karen Ninnemann**
Client: **Regency Mall**
Agency: **Frankenberry, Laughlin & Constable, Inc.**

33
Art Director: **Chris Rovillo**
Designer: **Chris Rovillo**
Illustrator: **José Cruz**
Writer: **Mark Perkins**
Client: **The Rouse Company**
Agency: **Richards, Sullivan, Brock & Assoc/**
The Richards Group

34
Art Directors: **Mike Campbell, Steve Gibbs**
Designer: **Steve Gibbs**
Artist: **Steve Gibbs**
Writer: **Mark Perkins**
Client: **The Rouse Company**
Agency: **Richards, Sullivan, Brock & Assoc/**
The Richards Group

35
Art Directors: **Mike Campbell, Steve Gibbs**
Designer: **Steve Gibbs**
Artist: **Steve Gibbs**
Writer: **Mark Perkins**
Client: **The Rouse Company**
Agency: **Richards, Sullivan, Brock & Assoc/
The Richards Group**

36   COLD AWARD
Art Director: **Alex Tsao**
Designer: **Alex Tsao**
Photographers: **Armani: Bruce Lawrence, Hamptons:
Les Goldberg, Madison Room: Carl Fisher**
Writers: **Deborah Polenberg, Mitch Epstein**
Client: **Barney's, New York**
Agency: **Epstein Raboy Advertising**

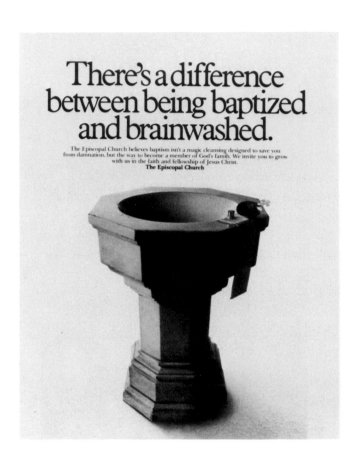

There's a difference between being baptized and brainwashed.

The Episcopal Church believes baptism isn't a magic cleansing designed to save you from damnation, but the way to become a member of God's family. We invite you to grow with us in the faith and fellowship of Jesus Christ.
The Episcopal Church

Removes those unwanted lines in seconds.

When you use an IBM Electronic 75 Typewriter, you'll never be embarrassed by unsightly typing errors again.

At the touch of a button, you can automatically rid yourself of a character, a word, even an entire line—with no tell-tale signs.

But that's not all.

The IBM Electronic 75 also offers you automatic indents, centering, underlining, and column layout.

You also get a memory that can store up to 7,500 characters. (With optional memory: 15,500 characters.)

So when you have something to retype, the typewriter automatically types it.

What do all these features mean to you?

They mean that your work can look perfect in a matter of seconds.

And when your work looks perfect, you can never look bad.

For more information call your local IBM Office Products Division Representative. Or call IBM Direct at the toll-free numbers below.

IBM

37   DISTINCTIVE MERIT
Art Director: **Nancy Rice**
Designer: **Nancy Rice**
Photographer: **Tom Bach**
Artist: **Art Simons**
Writer: **Tom McElligott**
Client: **Episcopal Ad Project**
Agency: **Fallon McElligott Rice**

38   DISTINCTIVE MERIT
Art Director: **Rick Elkins**
Photographers: **Hunter Freeman, Jim Young**
Writer: **Rhonda Peck**
Client: **IBM**
Agency: **Doyle Dane Bernbach**

39   DISTINCTIVE MERIT
Art Director: **Alex Tsao**
Designer: **Alex Tsao**
Photographers: **Bob Brody, Bruce Lawrence**
Writers: **Deborah Polenberg, Mitch Epstein**
Client: **Barney's, New York**
Agency: **Epstein Raboy Advertising**

40
Art Director: **Marvin Mitchneck**
Designer: **Marvin Mitchneck**
Artist: **Barbara Bergman**
Writer: **Jack Keane**
Client: **Johnson & Higgins**
Agency: **Nadler & Larimer, Inc.**

41
Art Director: **Darrell Beasley**
Artist: **Pedro Barrios ("Stripes")**
Client: **Bloomingdales**
Creative Director: **John C. Jay**
Agency: **Bloomingdales Adv. Dept.**

Sociable.

Ants are the most sociable of creatures. Especially when the eats are on you.

Given half a hint, ants — in alarming numbers — will find and contaminate accessible foods. And, they're difficult to discourage— at least with conventional methods.

When ants impose at your house, call Musgrove's Pest Control. They've dealt with these uninvited guests for over 50 years. With services guaranteed effective for 3 months.

Show ants how sociable you can be— invite Musgrove's to *their* party.

Musgrove's PEST CONTROL

Musgrove's Pest Control
Since 1908
903 De La Vina, Santa Barbara, 966-1744
From Santa Ynez (Toll Free) ZE8-0678

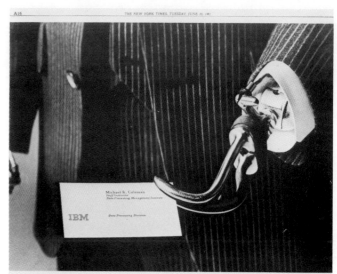

The man behind this hand is Michael Coleman.
The company behind this man is IBM.
There's a story behind both of them.
After the Marines and Vietnam, Coleman earned his MBA and began selling computers for IBM. Promotion followed promotion, and he now teaches our customers how to get the most out of their computers.

His success doesn't surprise us. People with disabilities keep proving that they are as capable as other workers.

As reliable.
As ambitious.
And just as likely to succeed.
At IBM the proof is everywhere, in every part of our business.

The same is true at other companies.
Yet, some people just won't believe that the disabled can do the job.

It has to make you wonder who's handicapped.
And who isn't.

IBM For free information about what disabled persons can do for your company, write: Industry-Labor Council, National Center on Employment of the Handicapped, Human Resources Center, Box 450, Albertson, N.Y. 11507.

42
Art Director: **John M. Alexander**
Designer: **John M. Alexander**
Artist: **Courtlandt Johnson**
Writer: **Richard Barre**
Client: **Musgrove's Pest Control**
Agency: **Barre Advertising Inc.**

43
Art Director: **Seymon Ostilly**
Designer: **Seymon Ostilly**
Photographer: **Henry Wolf** — **"The Handicapped"**
Illustrators: **John Berkey** — **"Mainstreet"**
Richard Hernandez — **"Help Button"**
Client: **IBM Corporation**
Writers: **Bob Higbee** — **"Mainstreet"**
Kevin O'Neill — **"The Handicapped"** & **"Help"**
Agency: **Lord, Geller, Federico, Einstein Inc.**

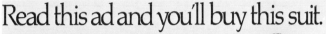

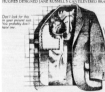

STEPPES IN STYLE

Positively Y.E.S. at
bloomingdale's

We can't reveal
our great
designer names.
Even if
we were so
in Klein'd.

BJ Scott. Discount designer fashions for women.
8807 SW 132 St. Across from the Falls. 235-4768.

46
Art Director: **John C Jay**
Designer: **Charles Banuchi**
Artist: **Antonio Lopez**
Client: **Bloomingdale's**
Creative Director: **John C Jay**
Agency: **Bloomingdale's Adv Dept.**

47
Art Director: **Frank Schulwolf**
Designer: **Frank Schulwolf**
Writer: **Arthur Low**
Client: **B J Scott**
Agency: **Susan Gilbert & Company**
Marketing/Advertising

LAST CHANCE FOR PRE-SEASON FALL FASHION SAVINGS.

Labor Day is the last day to enjoy fabulous pre-season prices on fall fashions at Kelly Kitt. Complete your fall wardrobe now, and save on a wide selection of pure wool skirts, blazers, pants and sweaters, as well as our entire line of coats and suits. And enjoy the helpful and courteous service you've come to expect at Kelly Kitt. But hurry! After Labor Day, these special low prices will be gone with the summer!

AAAH SUMMER!

SAVE 25% TO 33% ON SIZZLING SUMMER SPORTSWEAR!

Temperatures are rising, but prices are falling on summer sportswear at Kelly Kitt. Choose from sporty casuals including blazers, skirts, pants, blouses and shirts, tee shirts, golf skirts and tops, shorts, and jackets. Misses and junior sizes, too. Come in early because the savings are sizzling hot.

PSST! WOOL'S IN!

And Kelly Kitt's got it. So hurry in and put together your wool fashion wardrobe for fall ...before the rush. Our pleasant salespeople will help you select from beautiful suits, skirts, pants, coats, blazers, sweaters, dresses and more. Styled by today's top designers, in luscious wool fabrics. They're the perfect fall fashion for all occasions. Don't wait... because the word's out. And cool weather is just around the corner.

Kelly Kitt

IN 1982, IF YOU HAVE A MISCARRIAGE YOU COULD BE PROSECUTED FOR MURDER.

Last week, right-wing U.S Senators took the first step toward making this nightmare a reality.

They held hearings on a Human Life Statute that would make a fertilized egg a person. If this law is passed, all abortions will be outlawed overnight. Even if the pregnancy is a result of rape. Or incest.

Even a miscarriage could be investigated as a criminal offense. Amazing as it sounds, you could be prosecuted for manslaughter.

Backing this bill are radical right-wing political forces, the right-to-lifers, the Moral Majority, and the electronic churchmen. This handful of people want to impose their religious views on everyone. They will stop at nothing to strip you of your most basic personal rights.

Only you can stop them. But you must begin to fight back now. Before outrage becomes law.

Fill out this Planned Parenthood coupon immediately. We'll advise you as to how you can stop this small group from imposing their beliefs on you. Your friends. Your family. Everyone.

Act now. Before the minority rules.

JOIN PLANNED PARENTHOOD

Planned Parenthood of New York City, Inc.
380 Second Avenue, New York, N.Y. 10010
212-777-2002

☐ I believe that abortion is something personal, not political. Please keep me informed and add me to your mailing list

☐ I want to keep abortion legal and wish to make a tax-deductible contribution. Here is my check in the amount of $

ABORTION IS SOMETHING PERSONAL. NOT POLITICAL.

48
Art Director: **Gary L. Smith**
Designers: **Gary L. Smith, Bob Bender**
Artists: **Gary L. Smith, Bob Bender**
Writers: **Ron Etter, Terry Burrls**
Client: **Kelly Kitt**
Agency: **Lord, Sullivan & Yoder, Inc. Advertising**

49
Art Director: **Tana Klugherz**
Photographer: **Manny Gonzolez**
Writer: **Debbie Kasher**
Client: **Planned Parenthood of New York City**
Agency: **Levine, Huntley, Schmidt, Plapler & Beaver, Inc.**

50
Art Directors: **Bob Needleman, Jamie Seltzer**
Photographers: **Bob Needleman, Steve Meisel**
Writers: **Jamie Seltzer, Bob Needleman**
Client: **Ski Barn**
Agency: **Altschiller, Reitzfeld, Solin/NCK**

51
Art Directors: **Roy Grace, Steve Graff, Marion Sackett**
Designers: **Roy Grace, Steve Graff, Marion Sackett**
Photographer: **Harold Krieger**
Artist: **Roy Grace**
Writers: **Tom Yobbagy, Patty Volk, Hal Kaufman**
Client: **IBM Office Products Division**
Agency: **Doyle Dane Bernbach**

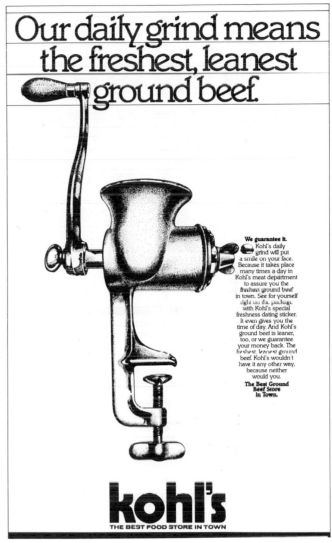

52
Art Director: **Fred DeVito**
Artist: **Michael Van Horn**
Client: **Bloomingdale's**
Creative Director: **John C. Jay**
Agency: **Bloomingdale's Adv. Dept.**

53
Art Director: **Rachel Stephens**
Designer: **Rachel Stephens**
Artist: **Nachreiner Boie Art Factory Ltd.**
Writer: **Effie Meyer**
Client: **Kohl's Food Stores**
Agency: **R.L. Meyer Advertising & Promotions, Inc.**

**Top quality.
We look into it for you.**

When Kohl's receives a shipment of produce, our produce inspector always cuts into a sample to get the inside story on quality. He checks the freshness. Texture. Color. Even the taste. He's very fussy about what Kohl's accepts. Our reputation proves it. Kohl's produce. Quality you can depend on, because we've looked into it for you.

The Best Produce Store in Town.

54
Art Director: **Michael Mazza**
Designer: **Michael Mazza**
Photographers: **Mike Karbelnikoff, Dave Siegel**
Artist: **Howard Post**
Writer: **David O'Hare**
Client: **American Greyhound Racing, Inc.**
Agency: **Winters Franceschi Callahan**

55
Art Director: **Rachel Stephens**
Designer: **Rachel Stephens**
Artist: **Nachreiner Boie Art Factory Ltd.**
Writer: **Effie Meyer**
Client: **Kohl's Food Stores**
Agency: **R.L. Meyer Advertising & Promotions, Inc.**

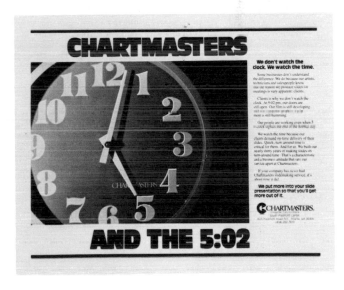

56
Art Directors: **Marty Neumeier, Byron Glaser**
Designer: **Marty Neumeier**
Photographers: **James Chen, Christopher Conrad**
Writer: **Marty Neumeier**
Client: **Cox Cable Santa Barbara**
Agency: **Neumeier Design Team**

57
Art Director: **Wm. Thornburg**
Photographer: **Peter Le Grand**
Writer: **Robert L. Wolf**
Agency: **Robert Wolf & Associates**

MAGAZINE ADVERTISING

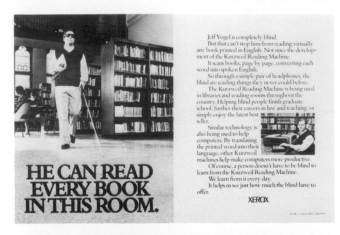

HE CAN READ EVERY BOOK IN THIS ROOM.

Jeff Vogel is completely blind.
But that can't stop him from reading virtually any book printed in English. Not since the development of the Kurzweil Reading Machine.

It scans books, page by page, converting each word into spoken English.

So through a simple pair of headphones, the blind are reading things they never could before.

The Kurzweil Reading Machine is being used in libraries and reading rooms throughout the country. Helping blind people finish graduate school, further their careers in law and teaching, or simply enjoy the latest best seller.

Similar technology is also being used to help computers. By translating the printed word into their language, other Kurzweil machines help make computers more productive.

Of course, a person doesn't have to be blind to learn from the Kurzweil Reading Machine.

We learn from it every day.

It helps us see just how much the blind have to offer.

XEROX

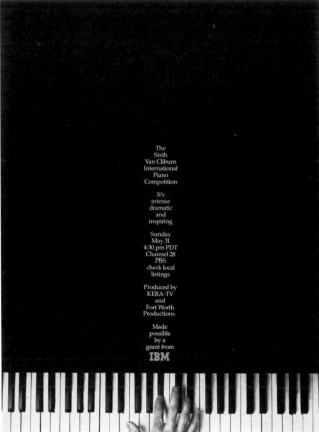

The
Sixth
Van Cliburn
International
Piano
Competition

It's
intense
dramatic
and
inspiring

Sunday
May 31
4:30 pm PDT
Channel 28
PBS
check local
listings

Produced by
KERA-TV
and
Fort Worth
Productions

Made
possible
by a
grant from
IBM

The Eagle and the Goose

Before taking off on his annual winter flight to South America, the Goose stopped by to show the Eagle his vacation wardrobe: white patent leather loafers, purple slacks and silk shirts of all colors.

"These outfits aren't you," said the Eagle, who's a stickler for taste. "It's silly for a goose to try to look like a cockatoo. Stay with what suits you." "Out of the question," said the Goose. "I'm tired of being just one of the flock. This year, I'm going to stand out."

And stand out he did. Somewhere over West Virginia, a hunter selected him out of two thousand other geese and let him have it. In the wing. The Goose crash landed in Wheeling, where he spent the winter in a convalescent home while all the other geese were in Rio, taking Portuguese lessons and drinking Pina Coladas.

MORAL: If you're dressed to kill, somebody may very well take a shot at you.

Mercifully the days of blatant overstatement in men's fashions are gone. Today most men (and women) want what Eagle has been known for through the years: shirts that can become old friends. The colors of our custom-woven fabrics are unusual but never gaudy. Sometimes classic, sometimes bold, but never overwhelming. And because the parts of every Eagle shirt are cut out by hand (at the same time and from the same bolt) the color of each section of an Eagle shirt exactly matches that of every other. That's why, no matter how styles may change, nobody ever shoots down an Eagle.

Now, where to find our shirts. It may be a problem since a lot of fine stores like them so much they have us sew in their labels. Same shirt, different name. If you're dead set on buying an Eagle shirt, with or without a real Eagle label, just drop us a card and we'll let you know where you can.

Miss Afferbach, P.O. Box 580, Quakertown, PA 18951

59
Art Director: **Mike Ciranni**
Photographer: **Howard Menken**
Writers: **Kevin McKeon, Allen Kay**
Client: **Xerox Corporation**
Agency: **Needham, Harper & Steers, Inc.**

60
Art Director: **Mark Hughes**
Designer: **Mark Hughes**
Photographer: **Michael Pruzan**
Writer: **Diane Sinnot**
Client: **IBM**
Agency: **Doyle Dane Bernbach**

61
Art Director: **Sheila McCaffery**
Designer: **William McCaffery**
Artist: **R.O. Blechman**
Writer: **Jay Cheek**
Client: **Eagle Shirtmakers, Inc.**
Agency: **William McCaffery, Inc.**

RESTRAINT WITHOUT CONSTRAINT

(The theory and practice of being at home in the office.)

THE question of whether the restrained business suit is a constraint on one's individuality equal to that of a uniform is a constantly recurring theme with some of our young friends starting out in the business world. We must admit to some impatience, as we fail to see that such a suit is more of a uniform than the ubiquitous blue jeans. No doubt if a dress code were promulgated requiring jeans to be worn to the office they, too, would become symbols of constraint.

But essentially, what we mean by restraint in dressing, and most particularly, in dressing for the office, is a suit that knows its place. It should never distract attention from the wearer, neither in cut, color nor in pattern. Ideally, one would notice the man and receive a general impression that he is well dressed without being able to say exactly what he is wearing.

We believe that the cut of the suit is the most important ingredient of this good impression and makes the greatest contribution to comfort. For that reason we have always stood for the natural shoulder suit that follows the general shape of the man's body, neither shapeless and baggy nor exaggeratedly sharp-shouldered and pinched at the waist.

Of course, even that natural silhouette would fail in its purpose if the suiting were to be loud in pattern or noticeable in color. So we search out suitings that are interesting without being obtrusive, in colors that blend into the office background as quietly as the plumage of the partridge blends into the moor or the meadow.

Finally, since the subtleties of the soft-shoulder silhouette and the niceties of the suiting could be wasted if the workmanship were less, we entrust the making of our suits to men as dedicated to restraint and to excellence as you and we.

This is all very well, this theorizing, but in practice restraint has some very practical advantages. The suit that abjures the eccentricities of fashion will still be in style when fashion changes, as fashion will. The suit that is well made of good quality woolen will, given the care it deserves, serve you well for many years. And if it was a suit that suited you in the first place, the longer you wear it, the more at home in it you'll feel.

Some of our suits are made for us in Canada by our master tailors there, others are tailored here in the U.S. by SOUTHWICK. They're made of woolens and wool worsteds from Scotland, England, France, Italy, from all the great weaving centers of the world. Flannel and gabardine, tweeds and plaids and cheviots and Shetlands, herringbones and nailheads and pin stripes, you'll find them all. You will also be able to find the natural shoulder cut in both single and double breasted suits. The collection, $325. to $478.

Paul Stuart
Madison Avenue at 45th Street, New York. 10017

The Eagle and the Crane

The Eagle and the Crane were spending a long weekend in the Hamptons. The Eagle was happy because he had brought along several books and he was getting a nice tan. But the Crane grew restless.

"Seems like the Peacocks get all the action around here," he said. "I'm going into town and buy some finer feathers."

"How do I look?" he asked upon his return. "Well," said the Eagle, a staunch believer in quiet elegance, "you're colorful, all right, but those feathers just won't fly."

That afternoon at the beach they fell into animated conversation with two attractive birds from Baltimore. It went well until the girls suggested they all go hang-gliding and the Crane crashed into the ocean a few hundred yards from shore.

The Eagle flew on with the birds to their place for a cold-beer-and-steak cookout. The Crane was pulled out of the water by the Montauk Air-Sea Rescue Service and had to hitch a ride home.

One of the first things you'll notice about your Eagle shirt is the fit. Not just collars and sleeves but all-over fit. Roomy enough but never blousy. Tailored but comfortable. An example: our split yoke follows your shoulder contour perfectly.

Eagle shirts have been designed and made in Pennsylvania since 1867. To American figures and tastes. So they feel good when you wear them. And look good. And probably fit you better, whatever your numbers.

Blechman

Now, where to find our shirts. It may be a problem since a lot of fine stores like them so much they have us sew in their labels. Same shirt, different name. If you're dead set on buying an Eagle shirt, with (or without) a real Eagle label, just drop us a card and we'll let you know where you can. Miss Afflerbach, P.O. Box 580, Quakertown, PA 18951

MORAL: There's little good in being dressed to the nines, if you wear an eight.

62
Art Director: **William McCaffery**
Designer: **Rachel Senft**
Artist: **Tony Kokinos**
Writer: **Anne Stegemeyer**
Client: **Paul Stuart**
Agency: **William McCaffery, Inc.**

63
Art Director: **Sheila McCaffery**
Designer: **William McCaffery**
Artist: **R.O. Blechman**
Writer: **Jay Cheek**
Client: **Eagle Shirtmakers, Inc.**
Agency: **William McCaffery, Inc.**

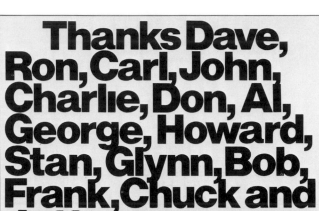

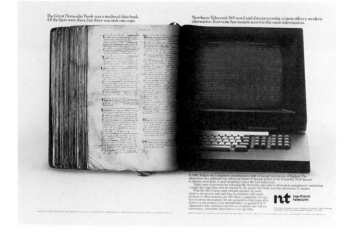

Disappears rather quickly, doesn't it.

(Bet you've opened
an Oreo cookie too.)

Mr. Christie, you make good cookies.

How simple life would be if help were just a push-button away.
It is. On some of IBM's newest computers and office systems.
It's called a HELP button and it's just one of the ways we're making our machines easier to learn and easier to use.
Push it. and our machine will explain itself, flashing easy-to-follow messages on the display screen. It will tell you what other buttons on the keyboard mean. what they do. and how to use them. Instantly.
It's like taking instruction manuals off the shelf and putting them at your fingertip. To teach a beginner. Or refresh the memory of an old pro.
Of course. some people may never need any help.
But it's nice to know it's just a push-button away. **IBM**

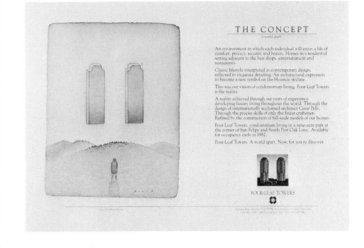

70   DISTINCTIVE MERIT
Art Director: **Seymon Ostilly**
Designer: **Seymon Ostilly**
Illustrator: **Richard Hernandez**
Writer: **Kevin O'Neill**
Client: **IBM Corporation**
Agency: **Lord, Geller, Federico, Einstein Inc.**

71
Art Director: **Mike Anderson**
Designer: **Mike Anderson**
Photographer: **Michael Kluch**
Writer: **Ed Bigelow**
Client: **Haan Motoring Accessories**
Agency: **Klein/Richardson Advertising**

72
Art Director: **Steven Sessions**
Designer: **Steven Sessions**
Artist: **Jean-Michel Folon**
Writer: **Various**
Client: **Four Leaf Towers**
Agency: **Baxter & Korge, Inc.**

73
Art Directors: **Ken Amaral, Joel Baumwoll**
Photographer: **Anthony Edgeworth**
Writers: **Stephen Fenton, Allen Kay**
Client: **AMTRAK, The Nat'l. RR Passenger Corp.**
Agency: **Needham, Harper & Steers, Inc.**

74
Art Director: **Christine Armstrong**
Photographers: **Art Beck, Walter Ioos**
Writer: **Roger Proulx**
Client: **Dr. Fernando Aleu**
Agency: **Ogilvy & Mather, Inc.**

75
Art Directors: **Ken Amaral, Joel Baumwoll**
Photographer: **Anthony Edgeworth**
Writers: **Stephen Fenton, Allen Kay**
Client: **AMTRAK, The Nat'l. RR Passenger Corp.**
Agency: **Needham, Harper & Steers, Inc.**

76
Art Director: **Gail Daniels**
Designer: **Gail Daniels**
Artist: **Eraldo Carugati**
Writer: **Angus McQueen**
Client: **Resistol Hats**
Agency: **Ackerman & McQueen Advertising, Inc.**

77
Art Director: **Ann-Marie Light**
Designer: **Ann-Marie Light**
Photographer: **Anthony Edgeworth**
Writer: **Mitch Epstein**
Client: **Fieldcrest Mills, Inc.**
Editor: **Jan Dwyer**
Agency: **Epstein Raboy Advertising**

78
Art Director: **Steve Ohman**
Designer: **Richard Ferrante**
Photographer: **George Cochran**
Writer: **Larry Vine**
Client: **Johnnie Walker Black Label**
Agency: **Smith/Greenland Inc.**

79
Art Director: **John F. Benetos**
Designer: **John F. Benetos**
Photographer: **Gary Hanlon**
Writer: **Robert M. Solomon**
Client: **Ocean Spray Cranberries, Inc.**
Agency: **Sullivan & Brugnatelli Advertising, Inc.**

80
Art Directors: **Richard Radke, Martin Lipsitt**
Designers: **Richard Radke, Martin Lipsitt**
Photographers: **H. Freeman, J. Standart**
Writer: **Ellen Azorin**
Client: **West Point Pepperell**
Agency: **Calet, Hirsch, Kurnit & Spector, Inc.**

ABOVE AND BEYOND THE CALL OF BEAUTY.

Whoever it was that said that beauty is only skin deep obviously never rested the seat of his pants in a Honda Prelude. And that's a pity. Because here is a car that not only has body. It has soul.

The Honda Prelude is, perhaps, as rare as miracles. On one hand, it is so refined that it can join comfortably in the society of the world's most expensive cars.

On the other hand it is so economical and realistically priced that it can snuggle firmly in with today's concerns. Conservation. And economy.

With front wheel drive, 5 speed transmission, independent suspension on all 4 wheels, electric sun-roof, AM/FM Stereo radio, and full instrumentation all standard, it leaves very little to be desired. Except the desire to own one. Body and soul.

HONDA PRELUDE.

SLICE AND BARBECUE

BEERWURST · SUMMER SAUSAGE · KIELBOSSA · SALAMI · HAM & BACON LOAF · HOT DOG

SWISS CHEESE CRACKERS · RITZ CRACKERS · TRISCUIT WAFFERS · MEALMATES CRACKERS · FRENCH ONION THINS CRACKERS · SOUR CREAM & CHIVES CRACKERS

Barbecued meats meet crunchy Christie crackers.

81
Art Director: **Ken Boyd**
Photographer: **Terry Collier**
Writer: **Douglas Moen**
Client: **Honda Canada Inc.**
Agency: **McCann-Erickson Advertising of Canada Ltd.**

82
Art Director: **Brian Harrod**
Artist: **Tony Kew**
Writer: **Allan Kazmer**
Client: **Christie, Brown and Company Ltd.**
Agency: **McCann-Erickson Advertising of Canada Ltd.**

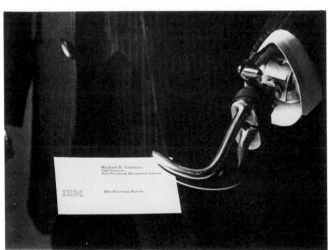

The man behind this hand is Michael Coleman.
The company behind this man is IBM.
There's a story behind both of them.
After the Marines and Vietnam, Coleman earned his MBA and began selling computers for IBM. Promotion followed promotion, and he now teaches our customers how to get the most out of their computers.
His success doesn't surprise us. People with disabilities keep proving that they are as capable as other workers. As reliable. As ambitious. And just as likely to succeed.
At IBM the proof is everywhere, in every part of our business.
The same is true at other companies.
Yet, some people just won't believe that the disabled can do the job. It has to make you wonder who's handicapped.
And who isn't. **IBM**

ABERCROMBIE & FITCH

"We carry within us the wonders we seek without us;
There is all Africa and her prodigies in us." *Sir Thomas Browne.*
Understanding the very spirit of adventure has
been a tradition at Abercrombie & Fitch® for over 90 years.
Whatever your adventure, begin it with
the utmost in sporting equipment, fine clothing and
distinctive gifts from Abercrombie & Fitch.

The adventure goes on.

Limited edition prints available for $100 through Abercrombie & Fitch (800) 231-9715. Beverly Hills, Dallas, Las Vegas, South Coast Plaza.

83
Art Director: **Seymon Ostilly**
Designer: **Seymon Ostilly**
Photographer: **Henry Wolf**
Writer: **Kevin O'Neill**
Client: **IBM Corporation**
Agency: **Lord, Geller, Federico, Einstein Inc.**

84
Art Director: **James Dalthorp**
Designer: **James Dalthorp**
Artist: **Walt Spitzmiller**
Writer: **Priscilla Wallace**
Client: **Abercrombie & Fitch**
Agency: **McCann-Erickson, Inc. (Houston)**

"WE HAVE LIFTOFF."

To be honest, our Columbia isn't exactly like their Columbia. But talk about thrust. Wait until you're atop that refined Air-Sole™. It's not quite the same as 6.65 million pounds of rocket propellant. But it's enough to move you about two percent faster, or two percent farther.*

And the ride. It's awesome.

Even if you don't experience total weightlessness.

Equally important, it's a ride that will last. Because we built this Columbia strictly for training flights. Big, long ones. After more than 800 miles, laboratory tests showed virtually no loss of cushioning. And wear on the new Anatomical outsole — minimal.

We've even come out with a model that has the exact same per-

formance characteristics. The Aurora. For women only.

Now, you don't see NASA doing that.

Naturally, this kind of technology doesn't come cheap. But look at it this way. You can buy one of theirs. Or about 20,000,000 of ours.

NIKE

Benedictine.
The near-perfect mixer.

Club soda.	Tonic.	Eggnog.
Punch.	Cider.	Satchmo.
Bach.	~~Bagels.~~	Seltzer.
Ice cream.	O.J.	
Picnics.	Chess.	
Milk.	Late news.	
Pretzels.	Nuts.	
~~Prunes.~~	Burgers.	
Byron.	Puzzles.	
Espresso.	Chips.	
Vodka.	Cola.	

imported from France by Julius Wile Sons & Co., Lake Success, N.Y. 80 Proof

BENEDICTINE

85
Art Director: **David Kennedy**
Photographers: **Time-Life Staff; Craig Wagner / Studio III**
Writer: **Dan Wieden**
Client: **NIKE, Inc.**
Agency: **William Cain, Inc.**

86
Art Director: **Joseph LaRosa**
Photographer: **Arthur Beck**
Writer: **Joseph LaRosa**
Client: **Julius Wile Sons & Co.**
Agency: **Waring & LaRosa, Inc.**

Take away aluminum and most of America would be dark tonight.

Today, almost 100 percent of our nation's electricity is transmitted over aluminum cross-country lines. Strong and efficient, aluminum is much more abundant than other good conductors like copper, gold and silver. And it's also a lot less expensive.

Alcoa® produced the first aluminum conductor in 1897. And today, aluminum has become the standard throughout the world for the transmission of electrical power.

Aluminum. So much a part of our way of life, we'd be in the dark without it. For more information, write Aluminum Company of America, 519 Alcoa Building, Pittsburgh, PA 15219.

We can't wait for tomorrow.

◇ALCOA

There are two schools of thought on the best way to catch trout.

Some say spinning. Others say spincast. Whichever way you prefer, Daiwa gives you the best of both worlds.

For spin fishermen, there's our new internal trip Regal. It has that same durability at a good price that made our Silver™ Series the most popular skirted spool spinning reels ever made. But Regal has a long-life camera-mat black finish that makes it even better.

For spincasters, our Silvercast makes it easy to go after trout. It'll let you cast far and smooth without leaving you in a jam. And it's built tough, so you'll still be fishing with it years downstream.

Match your Regal or Silvercast with a Daiwa Regal Silver rod. And you'll get a perfect match for trout.

When it comes to choosing the right rod and reel at the right price, you can wind it all up in one word. Daiwa.

Daiwa
NUMBER 1 IN THE WORLD IN DESIGN

The perfect match for every catch.

89
Art Director: **Jim Stein**
Designer: **Jim Stein**
Photographer: **John Naso**
Writer: **Rick St. John**
Client: **ALCOA**
Agency: **Creamer Inc.**

90
Art Director: **Bob Kwait**
Designer: **Bob Kwait**
Photographer: **Chris Wimpey**
Artist: **Ron VanBuskirk**
Writer: **Hal Maynard**
Client: **Daiwa**
Agency: **Phillips-Ramsey Advertising**

91
Art Director: **Bob Kwait**
Designer: **Bob Kwait**
Photographer: **Chris Wimpey**
Artist: **Ron Van Buskirk**
Writer: **Hal Maynard**
Client: **Daiwa**
Agency: **Phillips-Ramsey Advertising**

92
Art Director: **Mas Yamashita**
Designer: **Mas Yamashita**
Photographers: **Carl Furuta, Norman Sugimto**
Writer: **John Annarino**
Client: **Paul Masson Vineyards**
Agency: **Doyle Dane Bernbach / West**

Elizabeth Ashley talks about her 'first time.'

ASHLEY: My first time was on the 'red-eye' from LA to New York.

INTERVIEWER: Gee, I had no idea you could get it on airplanes.

ASHLEY: Well, only on some U.S. airlines. But I'm told you can get it on most European flights. They're really much more cosmopolitan.

INTERVIEWER: Well, what was it like?

ASHLEY: It wasn't sweet. On the other hand, it wasn't really bitter. I guess bittersweet is the only way to describe it.

INTERVIEWER: Really? Tell me the whole story.

ASHLEY: Well, I was restless...couldn't sleep...didn't feel like reading. Then, somewhere over the Rockies, the man next to me turned and said, "Look, as long as you can't sleep, how'd you like to try something really different?"

I figured, oh, what the heck, why not.

So he turned off the reading lamps, called for the flight attendant, and ordered Campari for two.

Let's see. I had Campari and orange juice, and he had Campari and tonic.

INTERVIEWER: You certainly have a memory for detail. Then what?

ASHLEY: I guess I'm known for speaking my mind and about half way through I just had to tell him the truth.

INTERVIEWER: What did you say?

ASHLEY: "Is this it? Is this what all my friends are raving about?"

INTERVIEWER: Was he offended?

ASHLEY: Not at all. He just smiled and said, "Miss Ashley, most people feel that way their first time. But I assure you, it gets better and better."

You know, he was absolutely right. The second time was wonderful. And now I just love it...there are so many interesting ways to enjoy it.

INTERVIEWER: Yes, I'm sure. By the way, whatever happened to the man on the plane?

ASHLEY: That's my one regret. I just wish my second time could have been with him. I feel I owed him that much.

CAMPARI. THE FIRST TIME IS NEVER THE BEST.

Thousands of years from now, they'll know this was a society of good taste.

93
Art Director: **Bill Harris**
Designers: **Bill Harris, Torril Smith**
Photographer: **Barry Seidman**
Writer: **Rudi Seligman**
Client: **Austin Nichols**
Agency: **Compton Advertising**

94
Art Director: **Jerry Prestomburgo**
Designer: **Jerry Prestomburgo**
Photographer: **Arthur Beck**
Writers: **Larry Brown, Jerry Prestomburgo**
Client: **Seagram Distillers Company**
Agency: **Warwick, Welsh & Miller, Inc.**

Patience does have its rewards.

95
Art Director: **Woody Pirtle**
Designer: **Woody Pirtle**
Photographer: **Chuck Untersee**
Writer: **The Adolphus Hotel**
Client: **The Adolphus Hotel**
Agency: **Woody Pirtle, Inc./The Rominger Agency**

96
Art Director: **Bill Gustat**
Designer: **Bill Gustat**
Photographer: **Jim Thomas**
Writer: **Carolyn Gura**
Client: **Brooks Running Shoes**
Agency: **Ingalls Associates Boston**

97
Art Director: **Charles Piccirillo**
Photographer: **Chuck LaMonica**
Writer: **Ted Bell**
Client: **Seagrams**
Agency: **Doyle Dane Bernbach**

YOU DON'T HAVE TO SHELL OUT
A LOT TO SEE THE BEACH

98
Art Director: **Dom Marino**
Designer: **Dom Marino**
Artist: **Jerry Cosgrove**
Writer: **Walt Hampton**
Client: **O.M. Scott & Son**
Agency: **Doyle Dane Bernbach**

99
Art Director: **Don Crum**
Designer: **Don Crum**
Photographer: **Greg Booth**
Writers: **Don Crum, Steve Connatser**
Client: **South Padre Tourist Association**
Agency: **The Williams Group**

100
Art Directors: **Mike Schell, Joe Puhy**
Designers: **Mike Schell, Joe Puhy**
Artists: **cover — Marvin Mattelson,
next page — Dick Meissner**
Writer: **John Nieman**
Client: **Lincoln Mercury**
Agency: **Young & Rubicam**

101 GOLD AWARD
Art Director: **Laura Vergano**
Designer: **Laura Vergano**
Photographers: **Charles Gold — "Vegetables" &
"Mussels," Phil Marco — "Coffee"**
Writers: **Lynn Stiles, Anne Conlon**
Client: **Hilton International**
Agency: **Lord, Geller, Federico, Einstein Inc.**

102 GOLD AWARD
Art Director: **Gayl Ware**
Designer: **Gayl Ware**
Photographer: **Victor Skrebnski**
Writers: **Dick Sinreich, Kristy McNichol, Alex Haley,
Leon Jaworski**
Client: **Houston Chronicle**
Agency: **Rives Smith Baldwin & Carlberg/Y&R, Houston**

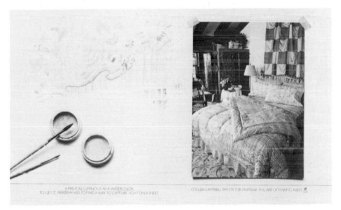

103   SILVER AWARD
Art Directors: **Bruce Bloch, Susan Lloyd**
Designers: **Bruce Bloch, Susan Lloyd**
Photographer: **Ulf Skogsbergh**
Writer: **Patty Rockmore**
Client: **Ron Chereskin**
Agency: **AC&R**

105   DISTINCTIVE MERIT
Art Directors: **Ken Amaral, Mario Giua**
Photographer: **Anthony Edgeworth**
Writers: **Stephen Fenton, Allen Kay**
Client: **AMTRAK, The Nat'l RR Passenger Corp.**
Agency: **Needham, Harper & Steers, Inc.**

104   DISTINCTIVE MERIT
Art Director: **Wally Arevalo**
Designers/Illustrators: **McNamara Associates**
Writer: **Dennis Schmidt**
Client: **B.F. Goodrich Co.**
Agency: **Grey Advertising, Inc.**

106   DISTINCTIVE MERIT
Art Directors: **Richard Radke, Tom Wai-Shek,
Martin Lipsitt**
Designers: **Richard Radke, Tom Wai-Shek, Martin Lipsitt**
Photographers: **Hunter Freeman, Joseph Standart**
Writers: **Ken Majka, Ellen Azorin**
Client: **West Point Pepperell**
Agency: **Calet, Hirsch, Kurnit & Spector, Inc.**

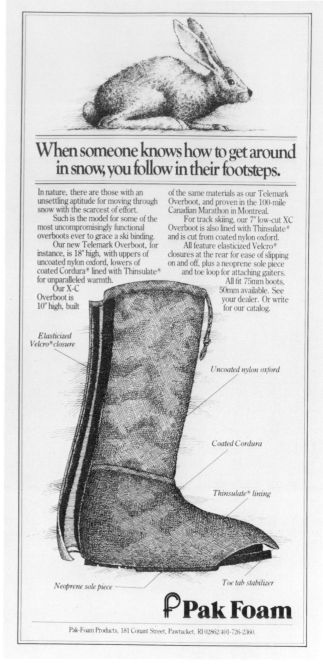

107
Art Directors: **Denis Johnson, Jeff Vetter**
Photographers: **Larry Williams, Phillip Bennett, Raul Vega**
Client: **Anheuser-Busch, Inc.—Budweiser**
Agency: **D' Arcy-MacManus & Masius/St. Louis**

108
Art Director: **Brian McPeak**
Designer: **Brian McPeak**
Artist: **John Burgoyne**
Writer: **Ernie Schenck**
Client: **Pak-Foam**
Agency: **Leonard Monahan Saabye**

THE MOST EXTRAVAGANT SHOES, BOOTS, AND ACCESSORIES IN MANHATTAN
440 PARK AVENUE NEW YORK, NY 10022. (212) 755-4197

SUSAN **BENNIS** WARREN **EDWARDS**

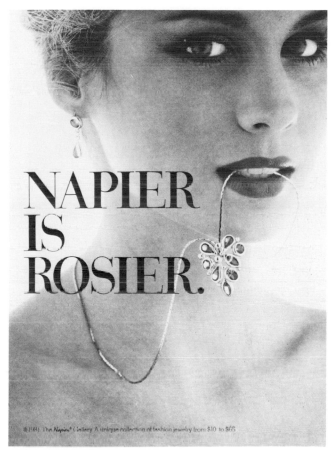

NAPIER
IS
ROSIER.

© 1981 The Napier Company. A unique collection of fashion jewelry from $10 to $65.

109
Art Director: **Stanley Eisenman**
Designers: **Stanley Eisenman, Dennis Dollens**
Photographer: **John Pilgreen**
Writer: **Curvin O'Reilly**
Client: **Susan Bennis/Warren Edwards**
Agency: **Eisenman & Enock**

110
Art Director: **Gene Federico**
Designer: **Gene Federico**
Photographer: **William Helburn**
Writer: **Anne Conlon**
Client: **The Napier Company**
Agency: **Lord, Geller, Federico, Einstein Inc.**

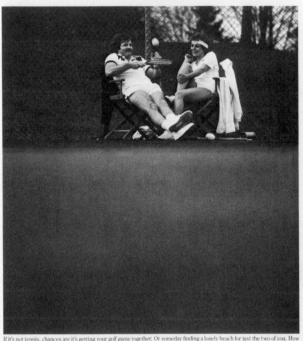

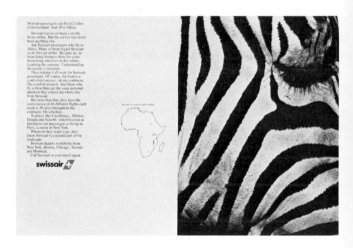

112
Art Director: **Brian Harrod**
Artist: **Kim LeFave**
Writer: **Ian Mirlin**
Client: **Christie, Brown and Company Ltd.**
Agency: **McCann-Erickson Advertising of Canada Ltd.**

111
Art Director: **Bob Tanaka**
Designer: **Bob Tanaka**
Photographers: **Bruce Carroll; Stock Photos Unlimited**
Writer: **Hal Newsom**
Client: **Boeing Commercial Airplane Company**
Production Co.: **Walker Engraving Company**
Agency: **Cole & Weber**

113
Art Directors: **Hubert Graf, Peter Fischer**
Designer: **Peter Fischer**
Photographer: **Werner Zryd, Photo Researchers**
Writer: **Robert Evans**
Client: **Swissair**
Agency: **GrafDesley**

114
Creative Director: **Marion Howington**
Art Director: **John Trusk**
Designer: **John Trusk**
Artist: **John Trusk**
Writers: **Tony Moon, Bill Pittman**
Client: **Hyatt**
Agency: **J. Walter Thompson Co.**

115
Art Director: **Karl Zimmerman**
Photographers: **Bill Silano, Paul Barton**
Writer: **Frederick Johnson**
Client: **Puerto Rico Tourism Company**
Agency: **Tromson Monroe Advertising, Inc.**

116
Art Director: **Tony Carillo**
Designer: **Tony Carillo**
Photographers: **Door: Andy Levin, Ship: Neil Leifer,
Soldier: Mark Meyer**
Writer: **Brian Dillon**
Client: **Time Inc.**
Agency: **Young & Rubicam**

117
Art Director: **Bob Kwait**
Designer: **Bob Kwait**
Photographer: **Chris Wimpey**
Artist: **Ron VanBuskirk**
Writer: **Hal Maynard**
Client: **Daiwa Golf Company**
Agency: **Phillips-Ramsey Advertising**

118
Art Directors: **Sam Minnella, John Broutin**
Photographer: **Ken Stidwill**
Writer: **Bob Paklaian**
Client: **Lincoln Mercury Division**
Agency: **Young & Rubicam**

121
Art Director: **Lester Feldman**
Designer: **Lester Feldman**
Photographer: **Sean Eager**
Writer: **Mike Mangano**
Client: **GTE**
Agency: **Doyle Dane Bernbach**

120
Art Director: **Onofrio Latona**
Artist: **Onofrio Latona**
Writer: **Nelsy Mesdag**
Client: **General Mills — Bacos**
Agency: **Needham, Harper & Steers Inc.**

122
Art Director: **Tony Cappiello**
Designer: **Carol Maisto**
Writer: **Terry Chabrowe**
Client: **John R. Hoffman**
Agency: **Cappiello & Chabrowe, Inc.**

SOME OF OUR BEST CLIENTS HAVEN'T PAID US IN TEN YEARS.

But that's OK with us. Because some things are more important than money.

When HBM was founded 10 years ago, we made a unique commitment. We promised to treat our public service clients like our paying clients.

We actually put our best creative and account people on their accounts. And gave them lots of our time.

And it worked.

We created some very effective and award-winning advertising for the Museum of Science, the New England Aquarium, the MSPCA, the Boys' Club, Franklin Park Zoo and the BSO. In fact, we couldn't have done a better job, if they'd paid us.

Humphrey Browning MacDougall

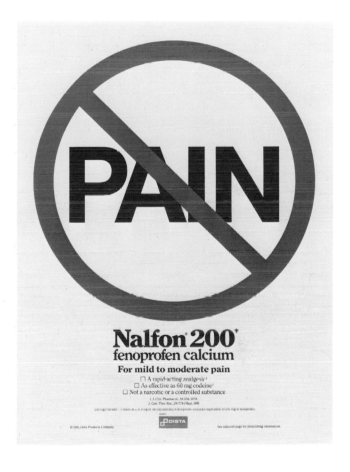

Nalfon®200*
fenoprofen calcium
For mild to moderate pain
☐ A rapid-acting analgesic
☐ As effective as 60 mg codeine
☐ Not a narcotic or a controlled substance

123
Art Director: **Richard Foster**
Designer: **Richard Foster**
Writer: **Gale Litchfield**
Client: **Humphrey Browning MacDougall**
Agency: **Humphrey Browning MacDougall**

124
Art Director: **Robert Talarczyk**
Designer: **Robert Talarczyk**
Writer: **Ned Putnam**
Client: **Eli Lilly & Company, Dista Products**
Agency: **J. Walter Thompson Healthcare Division**

DON'T GET STUCK IN AN AD AGENCY.

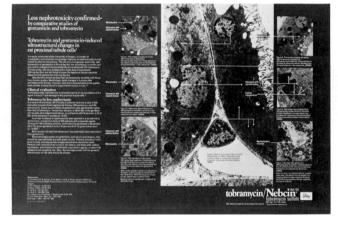

The 4A's and the USC Graduate School of Business Administration are looking for 40 talented young advertising professionals who refuse to stop short of making it big in advertising.

For those determined few, we're offering the 1982 Institute of Advanced Advertising Studies, an intensive 15-week evening course that gives you a comprehensive background in the agency business.

In just one semester, you'll have the opportunity to develop an understanding of media, creative, marketing and client

management that can be the important competitive edge on your way up the corporate ladder.

Best of all, you'll profit from the experience of real ad-stars. People who know what it takes to get to the top—because they did it. John A. Foster, vice president, creative director, Foote, Cone & Belding/Honig; James M. Spero, senior vice president, media director, Doyle Dane Bernbach/West; James B. Helin, senior vice president, manage-

ment supervisor, Dailey & Associates, Inc.; William B. White, professor of marketing, USC Graduate School of Business.

If you work for an agency, client or media organization, you're eligible to enroll. Sessions meet every Wednesday night at 7 p.m. on the USC campus, from January 13 to April 21. Tuition is $600 including materials, books and parking.

So tell your boss you're bound for glory. Then call or write; Bob Stephens, AAAA Western Office, 8500 Wilshire Blvd., Beverly Hills, California 90211. (213) 657-3711.

AAAA

Institute of Advanced Advertising Studies

126
Art Director: **Chris Chaffin**
Designer: **Chris Chaffin**
Writer: **Mary Geilfuss**
Client: **Institute of Advanced Advertising Studies**
Agency: **Cochrane Chase Livingston & Co.**

125
Art Director: **Charles Guarino**
Photographer: **Andrew Unangst**
Writers: **Robert Shaffron, Charles Guarino**
Client: **Smithsonian Magazine**
Agency: **Warwick, Welsh & Miller, Inc.**

127
Art Director: **Robert Talarczyk**
Designer: **Robert Talarczyk**
Photographer: **University of Oregon**
Writer: **Bruce Vardon**
Client: **Eli Lilly & Company**
Agency: **J. Walter Thompson Healthcare Division**

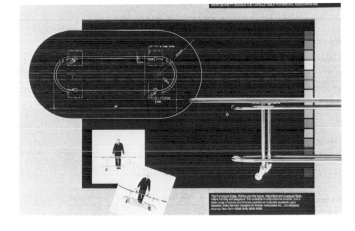

128 GOLD AWARD
Art Director: **Rick Boyko**
Photographer: **Dennis Manarchy**
Writer: **Steve Diamant**
Client: **Handgun Control Inc.**

130
Art Director: **Robert Qually**
Designer: **Robert Qually**
Artist: **Alex Murawski**
Writer: **Ethan Revsin**
Client: **Standard Brands Confectionery**
Agency: **Lee King & Partners**

129
Art Director: **Edward Seymore**
Designer: **Edward Seymore**
Photographer: **Irene Stern**
Writer: **Harry Pesin**
Client: **Cuisine Magazine**
Agency: **Pesin, Sydney & Bernard**

131
Art Director: **Michael Donovan**
Designer: **Michael Donovan**
Photographer: **Michael Pateman**
Writer: **Peter Carlson**
Client: **Brickel Associates, Inc.**
Agency: **Donovan and Green, Inc.**

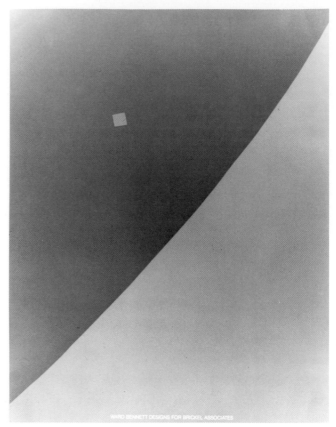

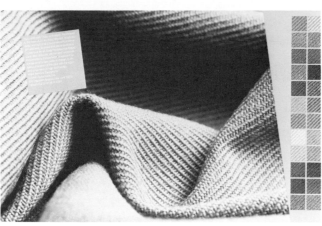

132
Art Director: **Bob Kwait**
Designer: **Bob Kwait**
Photographer: **Chris Wimpey**
Artist: **Ron Van Buskirk**
Writer: **Hal Maynard**
Client: **Daiwa**
Agency: **Phillips-Ramsey Advertising**

133
Art Director: **Michael Donovan**
Designers: **Michael Donovan, Jane Zash**
Photographer: **Steve Ogilvy**
Writer: **Peter Carlson**
Client: **Brickel Associates, Inc.**
Agency: **Donovan and Green, Inc.**

134
Art Director: **Michael Donovan**
Designer: **Michael Donovan**
Client: **Brickel Associates, Inc.**
Agency: **Donovan and Green, Inc.**

135
Art Director: **Anthony A. Macioce**
Writer: **Arthur D. Newell**
Client: **Ex-Cell-O Corporation**
Agency: **Gray & Kilgore, Inc.**

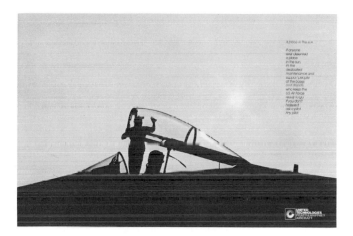

136
Art Director: **Wayne Gibson**
Illustrator: **Edward Sorel**
Writer: **Ed Jones**
Client: **First Colony Coffee & Tea Co.**
Agency: **Finnegan & Agee, Inc.**

140
Art Director: **Joseph Kamuck**
Designer: **Joseph Kamuck**
Artist: **Vero Radu**
Writer: **Jo Dakin**
Client: **Roche Laboratories**
Agency: **William Douglas McAdams Inc.**

137
Art Director: **Leonard Wesley**
Photographer: **Stock**
Writer: **Ted French**
Client: **United Technologies — Pratt & Whitney**
Agency: **Marsteller Inc.**

141
Art Director: **John Muller**
Designer: **John Muller**
Photographer: **R.C. Nible**
Writer: **Rob Price**
Client: **Constable Hodgins Printing**
Publisher: **Kansas City Art Directors Club**
Agency: **Valentine-Radford, Inc.**

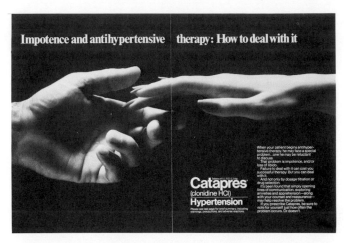

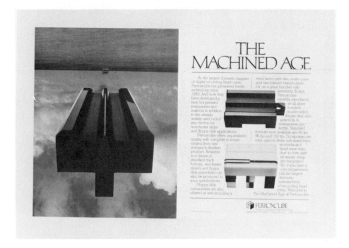

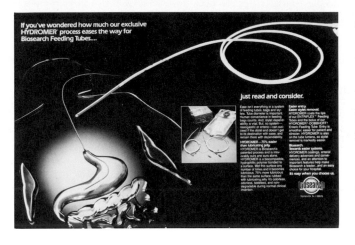

142
Art Director: **Duane Wirak**
Designer: **Duane Wirak**
Photographer: **Frank Miller**
Writer: **Virg Viner**
Client: **3M Copying Products**
Agency: **D'Arcy-MacManus & Masius**

143
Art Director: **Thomas J. Weisz**
Designer: **Thomas J. Weisz**
Photographer: **Donald Dempsey**
Artist: **Michael Lalicki**
Writer: **Thomas E. Greco**
Client: **Ferroxcube Division of Amperex**
Agency: **Weisz/Greco, Inc.**

144
Art Director: **Burt Pollack**
Designer: **Burt Pollack**
Photographer: **Sheldon Secunda**
Writers: **Ivan Manson, Noel Holland**
Client: **Boehringer Ingelheim Ltd.**
Agency: **Barnum Communications, Inc.**

145
Art Director: **Michael Robby**
Designers: **Susan C. Wolff, Michael Robby**
Photographer: **Al Francekevich, Inc.**
Artist—Model Maker: **Mark Yurkiw**
Writer: **Jim Nickel**
Client: **Biosearch**
Agency: **Louis Scott Assoc.**

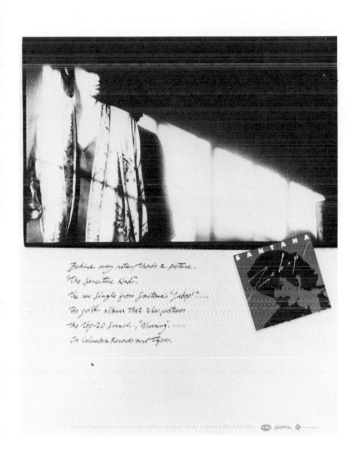

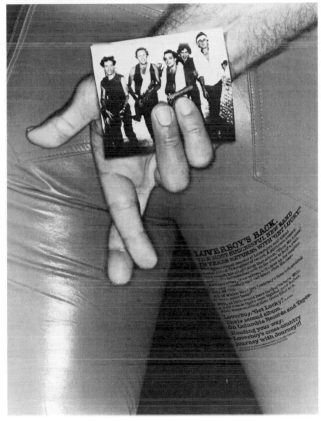

146
Art Director: **Holland S. Macdonald**
Designer: **Holland S. Macdonald**
Photographer: **Cristine Olympia Rodin**
Writer: **Art Fiyalka**
Client: **Columbia Records**

148
Art Director: **Josephine Di Donato**
Photographer: **David Kennedy**
Writer: **Mark Levitt**
Client: **CBS RECORDS**
Agency: **CBS**

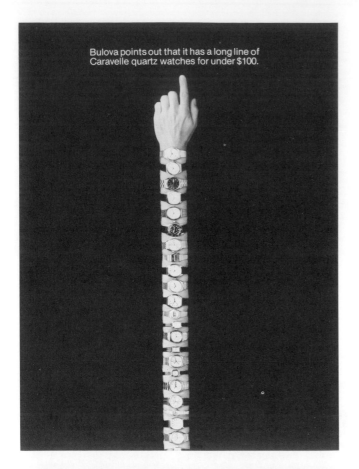

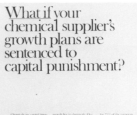

150
Art Director: **Joe DelVecchio**
Designer: **Joe DelVecchio**
Photographer: **David Pruitt**
Writer: **D.J. Webster**
Client: **Bulova**
Agency: **Doyle Dane Bernbach**

152
Art Director: **Tycho Weil**
Designer: **Tycho Weil**
Photographer: **Gordon E. Smith**
Writer: **Edward Butler**
Client: **Olin Chemicals**
Agency: **Marquardt & Roche Inc.**

151
Art Director: **Michael Donovan**
Designers: **Michael Donovan, Clement Mok**
Photographer: **Steve Ogilvy**
Writer: **Tom Bird**
Client: **Litton Business Furniture/LBF**
Agency: **Donovan and Green, Inc.**

153
Art Director: **John Burk**
Designer: **John F. Burk**
Photographer: **Steve Lane**
Artist: **Chris Bartlett**
Writer: **Jim Frost**
Client: **American Cyanamid**
Agency: **Richardson Myers & Donofrio**

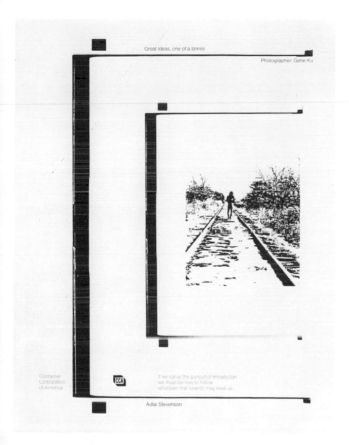

Great ideas, one of a series

Photographer: Gene Ku

Container
Corporation
of America

If we value the pursuit of knowledge
we must be free to follow
wherever that search may lead us.

Adlai Stevenson

HOW DO FINE RESTAURANTS RATE CHAMPION DISHWASHING MACHINES?

"★★★★★"

What do restaurants like New York's Sardi's and Maxwell's Plum and hotel chains like Westin, Marriott and Hilton all have in common? They have the same uncompromising standards in dishwashing machines.

Champion custom-designs dishwashing machine layouts to satisfy any capacity requirement from 1,500 to 13,000 dishes per hour. Our machines have an industry-wide reputation for superior dependability and easy serviceability. In

fact, many of our systems have been on the job for more than 20 years. And we offer a full line of energy-efficient low-temperature machines.

Champion dishwashing machines. For fine restaurants, they're the surest way to keep your reputation spotless. See your Champion dealer. Or write Champion Industries, P.O. Box 4149, Winston-Salem, NC 27105.

Champion

The Providence Gravure Companies

154
Art Director: **John Massey**
Designer: **John Massey**
Photographer: **Gene Ku**
Writer: **Adlai Stevenson**
Client: **Container Corporation of America**
Agency: **Communication Dept. Container Corporation of America**

155
Art Directors: **Bob Saabye, Brian McPeak**
Designers: **Brian McPeak, Bob Saabye**
Photographers: **Clint Clemens, Bob Oliveira**
Writer: **Tom Monahan**
Client: **Providence Gravure**
Agency: **Leonard Monahan Saabye**

156
Art Director: **Jim Mountjoy**
Writer: **Steve Lasch**
Client: **Champion Industries**
Agency: **McConnell & Associates**

This isn't just another middle of the road paint.

Introducing Saf-T-Mark 108™ a new epoxy-based traffic paint that provides 3 to 6 times the life of standard road surface paints. That means reduced labor and material costs for you. And less exposure to traffic hazards for your crew.

Saf-T-Mark 108 is specifically formulated for use in conventional striping equipment.

And because of its unique chemical and physical properties, the epoxy in Saf-T-Mark 108 forms a long lasting bond with glass beads. As a result, it provides reflectivity long after standard paints have faded away.

Unlike other epoxies, Saf-T-Mark 108 has a usable pot life of 10 days. And it can be applied to asphalt or concrete, dry or damp – providing quick,

track-free drying.

So if you've been looking for a traffic paint that's durable, economical and easy to apply, try Saf-T-Mark 108.

For more information, call (214) 597-8121. Or write Saf-T-Mark, P.O. Box 4026, Tyler, Texas 75712.

SAF·T·MARK

Manufactured exclusively for Saf-T-Mark by Bradco Plastics, Inc.

158   SILVER AWARD
Art Director: **Jim Condit**
Photographer: **Phillip Vullo**
Writers: **Marti Spinks, Tommy Thompson**
Client: **Progressive Farmer magazine**
Agency: **Fletcher/Mayo/Associates Inc.**

157
Art Director: **Rob Lawton**
Designer: **Rob Lawton**
Photographer: **Gary Blockley**
Writers: **Ben Vergati, Jim Ferguson**
Client: **Saf-T-Mark**
Creative Director: **Ben Vergati**
Agency: **Crume & Associates, Inc.**

159   DISTINCTIVE MERIT
Art Director: **Sherri Oldham**
Designer: **Sherri Oldham**
Photographers: **Gary Braasch, David Meunch, Jay Maisel**
Writers: **Lee Herrick, Carol Miller**
Client: **Dresser Magcobar**
Agency: **Metzdorf Advertising Agency**

160   DISTINCTIVE MERIT
Art Director: **Arthur Taylor**
Designer: **Ben Kuwata**
Photographer: **Thomas Victor**
Writer: **Robert Phillips**
Client: **Eastman Kodak Company**
Agency: **J. Walter Thompson Company**

162
Art Director: **David Kennedy**
Photographer: **Lamb & Hall**
Writer: **Dan Wieden**
Client: **Louisiana-Pacific Corp.**
Agency: **William Cain, Inc.**

161   DISTINCTIVE MERIT
Art Director: **Jack Mariucci**
Designer: **Jack Mariucci**
Photographers: **Anthony Edgeworth, Jim Canaty,
Oliver Parker, Jack Velter, Jay Maisel, Steve Grohe**
Writers: **Stu Hyatt, Mike Rogers**
Client: **Polaroid**
Agency: **Doyle Dane Bernbach**

163
Art Director: **Ted McNeil**
Designer: **Ted McNeil**
Photographer: **Phil Marco**
Writer: **Paul Diffenderfer**
Client: **Westvaco Corporation**
Agency: **McCaffrey & McCall, Inc.**

164
Art Director: **Nancy Rice**
Designer: **Nancy Rice**
Photographers: **Vern Hammerlund, Charlton Photos, Tom Bach**
Writer: **Tom McElligott**
Client: **Meredith Corporation — Successful Farming**
Agency: **Fallon McElligott Rice**

166
Art Director: **Marvin Mitchneck**
Designer: **Marvin Mitchneck**
Artist: **Barbara Bergman**
Writer: **Jack Keane**
Client: **Johnson & Higgins**
Agency: **Nadler & Larimer, Inc.**

167
Art Director: **George Titonis**
Artist: **Gary Overacre**
Writers: **David Bandler, Chris Labash**
Client: **PPG Industries**
Agency: **Ketchum Advertising, Pittsburgh**

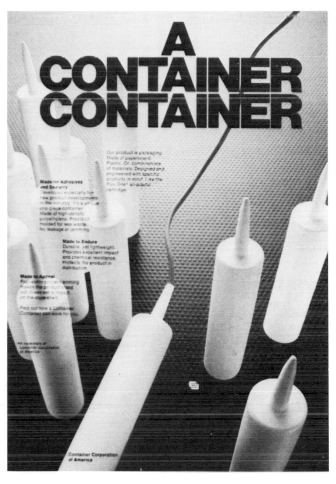

168
Art Director: **Don Putman**
Designer: **Don Putman**
Photographer: **Marty Evans**
Writer: **John van der Zee**
Client: **Wells Fargo Bank**
Agency: **McCann-Erickson, Inc.**

169
Art Director: **Kathy Forsythe**
Designer: **Kathy Forsythe**
Photographers: **(1.) Jim Matusik, (2. & 3.) Robert Keeling**
Writer: **Amy Bacon**
Client: **CCA Marketing Communications**
Publisher: **Various Trade Magazines**
Agency: **CCA Communications Dept.**

Show your good taste.

Don't toss your salad into any old package.

Give your eggs a break.

170
Art Director: **Eric Hanson**
Designer: **Eric Hanson**
Photographer: **Lamb & Hall**
Writer: **Bob Finley**
Client: **A&E Plastics**
Agency: **Sachs, Finley & Company**

We can squeeze the sour out of the sourest crude.

FOSTER WHEELER

FASTER.

MEMOREX

The marketplace demands more productivity.
Manufacturers Hanover maximizes.

MANUFACTURERS HANOVER
The financial source.Worldwide.

171
Art Director: **Robert Martin**
Photographers: **John Olivo, Rick Globus**
Writer: **Carl Walters**
Client: **Foster Wheeler**
Agency: **Muller Jordan Weiss**

172
Art Director: **Mario Giuriceo**
Designer: **Mario Giuriceo**
Photographer: **Marvin Koner**
Writer: **John Williams**
Client: **Manufacturers Hanover**
Agency: **Edwin Bird Wilson**

174
Art Director: **Patrick O'Connell**
Designer: **Patrick O'Connell**
Photographer: **Mark Carry**
Artist: **Dave Jensen**
Writer: **Ernie Brower**
Client: **Memorex**
Agency: **The Advertising Company of Offield And Brower**

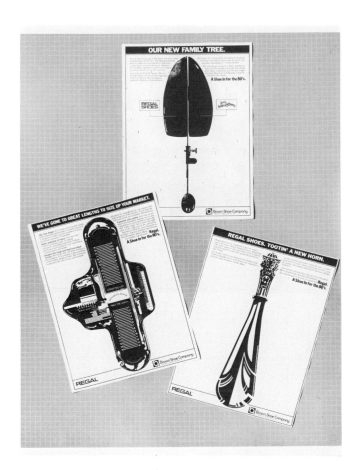

WHY TIMBERLAND HAS TAKEN AN APPROACH TO MAKING SHOES THAT'S YEARS BEHIND OTHER COMPANIES.

Over the years, the shoe industry has seen many changes. Materials that cost less money, machines that turn out more shoes—changes that have enabled manufacturers to make shoes faster and more economically.

But not necessarily better.

At Timberland, we've always believed the only way to make shoes is the way shoes were made years ago.

TIMBERLAND'S HANDSEWN MOCCASIN CONSTRUCTION. THE ART OF HANDSEWING TAKEN TO ITS ULTIMATE.

Consider just the materials:

Where other companies may be satisfied using less expensive leathers, Timberland uses only premium full-grain leathers. In fact, on the average, we believe we invest more money in leathers and soles than any of our competitors.

They cost more in the short run but, because they hold up better, they're worth more in the long run.

We use only solid brass eyelets, so they won't rust. Nylon thread and chrome-tanned rawhide laces because they last longer. And long-wearing rugged Vibram® soles that are unbeatable for resistance to abrasion.

But what we do with these materials is even more impressive.

We all know how comfortable slippers are. Well, before the outer soles are attached, our handsewns are actually leather slippers to which we add full mid-soles. Ours provide excellent support on the bottoms of the shoes, while the tops form molds around the feet. (In other words, our shoes conform to

the feet instead of vice versa.)

Here, Timberland hand-sewers take over.

Where others are often satisfied machine-sewing the vamp and kicker, our handsewers sew every stitch by hand. One at a time.

In addition, unlike machine-sewn shoes, Timberland handsewns are dampened and made on the last. Then, they're allowed to dry on the last, ensuring no wrinkles on the uppers.

But, more important, this total control by man instead of machine results in handsewns that, unequivocably, are the finest, most comfortable shoes in the world.

WE'RE COMBINING OLD WORLD CRAFTSMANSHIP WITH NEW WORLD SELLING.

A lot of companies would be satisfied merely making a product as good as our handsewns.

But Timberland isn't a lot of companies.

Soon, we'll be launching a major advertising campaign for our handsewns.

We'll also supply you with a complete package of p.o.p. material.

The reason for all this? Very simple.

Surely, we take great pride in how well Timberland handsewns are made.

But we take even greater pride in how well they sell.

Timberland
The Timberland Company, P.O. Box 370, Newmarket, New Hampshire 03857.

175
Art Director: **David Bartels**
Designer: **David Bartels**
Artists: **Don Strandell, Cindy Wrobel,
Michael David Brown Inc.**
Writer: **Mark Shapiro**
Client: **Advertising Department, Brown Shoe Company**
Agency: **The Hanley Partnership**

176
Art Director: **Dennis D'Amico**
Photographer: **Hunter Freeman**
Writer: **Ron Berger**
Client: **Timberland**
Agency: **Ally & Gargano, Inc.**

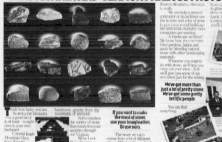

177
Art Director: **Rick St. Vincent**
Designer: **Rick St. Vincent**
Photographer: **Paul Schulz**
Writer: **Charles McGovern**
Client: **L.P. McDonnell**
Agency: **St. Vincent, Milone & McConnells**
Advertising Inc.

178
Art Directors: **Bill Wynne, Jim Brock**
Photographers: **Bob Jones, John Whitehead**
Illustrator: **Charlie Sheffield**
Writer: **Ed Jones**
Client: **Luck Stone Centers**
Agency: **Finnegan & Agee, Inc.**

179
Art Director: **Tom Wood**
Designer: **Tom Wood**
Photographer: **Ford Smith**
Artist—Retoucher: **Davidson & Co.**
Writer: **Sid Schwartz**
Client: **Horizon Carpets**
Agency: **Creative Services Inc.**

NEWSPAPER EDITORIAL

180
Art Director: **Greg Paul**
Designer: **Greg Paul**
Photographer: **Janet Gardner**
Client: **The Plain Dealer Magazine**

181
Art Directors: **Louis Silverstein, Tom Bodkin**
Design Director: **Louis Silverstein**
Photographer/Engraver: **Culver Pictures Inc.**
Writers: **Various**
Client: **The New York Times**
Editor: **Michael Leahy**
Publisher: **The New York Times**

182
Art Director: **Michael Keegan**
Designer: **Michele Chu**
Photographer: **Rob Brown**
Writer: **Aram Bakshian Jr.**
Client: **Los Angeles Herald Examiner**
Editor: **Jim Bellows**

183
Art Director: **Tom Bodkin**
Designer: **Tom Bodkin**
Photographer: **Bottom Photos: Collection of
Virginia Macy, Robert Levin**
Artist: **Joan Hall**
Writers: **Ada Louise Huxtable, Suzanne Slesin,
Maryann Bird**
Client: **The New York Times**
Editor: **Dona Guimaraes**
Publisher: **The New York Times**

184
Art Director: **John Sullivan**
Designer: **Claudia Steenberg-Majewski**
Photographer: **Vincent Maggiora**
Client: **San Francisco Chronicle**
Editor: **Richard Thieriot**
Publisher: **Richard Thieriot**

185
Art Director: **Louis Silverstein**
Design Director: **Louis Silverstein**
Photographers: **Bottom Photos: Jean Gaumy/Magnum, Frank Rich**
Artist: **Leslie Cabarga**
Writers: **Various**
Client: **The New York Times**
Editor: **Michael Leahy**
Publisher: **The New York Times**
Prod'n Co: **The New York Times**

186
Art Director: **Joseph W. Scopin Jr.**
Designer: **Joseph W. Scopin Jr.**
Writers: **Theodore Libbey, David Shribman**
Client: **Washington Star**
Editor: **Jack Schnedler**
Publisher: **Washington Star**

187
Art Director: **Nicki Kalish**
Designer: **Nicki Kalish**
Writers: **Various**
Client: **The New York Times**
Editor: **Bill Honan**
Publisher: **The New York Times**

"I'M SORRY"

Anonymously, they call Apology Line to admit to murder and mayhem, real or imagined. For the man at the other end, it often gets scary.

By David Behrens

LAST FALL, a 36-year-old artist tramped through the streets and parks of New York, literally a Johnny Appleseed of Expiation, distributing 1,500 posters on the trees, walls and subway pillars of the city.

It was a message from Mr. Apology.

His posters urged wrong-doers of every ilk to open their hearts and to dial APOLOGY at (212) 255-2748. It was a way "to apologize for their wrongs against people without jeopardizing themselves." Apology Line, the reader was reassured, was an experiment, unconnected to church or state.

The response was immediate. Within weeks, Mr. Apology recorded calls from people who said they were murderers, rapists, thieves or losers in love and some who were just plain crazy.

They called around the clock, using the telephone booth as a confessional, apologizing with a vengeance, with no fear of punishment.

Anyone could call and be sorry about anything Mr. Apology, genial and non-judgmental, sat beside his phone, promising only anonymity to his callers. "Do not leave your name," they were told.

Since the fall, more than a thousand people have confessed or fussed. Their collective tale of woe adds up to more than 30 hours of tape, including a fair share of threats, warnings and non-apologies of every sort.

Mr. Apology was a name used by some of Apology Line's earliest callers. At first, he was going to call the telephone service, "Confession Line." But Apology Line sounded more gentle, with no hint of punishment or criticism, nothing police-like or priestly. That was what Mr. Apology wanted. Now, he is happy that he, too, has remained anonymous. His life, he thinks, might depend on it.

Someday, Mr. Apology may go public, playing a selection of his tapes in a public hall, with criminals phoning in if they like. Or perhaps, he said, "a sort of Temple of Confession" will emerge in a Times Square storefront. "Just to give people a reading of what's going on in other people's minds."

But for now, someone else can run that storefront. Mr. Apology is staying undercover. When he was younger, he often shoplifted, he said. The experience might have planted a seed, perhaps, to turn confession into a new form of conceptual art. In recent years, Mr. Apology has created several sculptures on the theme of crime and punishment, a subject which haunts him like a recurring dream.

There is no typical caller. He may regret his marital failure or his inability to live up to other people's expectations. He may regret cheating his boss or simply be sorry he just killed someone.

Murder comes up often. There are calls from people claiming they murdered John Kennedy and Sharon Tate. Another man claimed he killed a dope dealer. "I got no need for an apology. I'm the Vigilante of God," he said.

Just another day on Apology Line.

John Lennon's murder also stirred things up. One woman called and said that since John Lennon "was killed by a nut and I'm a nut, that makes me part of what killed John Lennon and I'm sorry."

Mr. Apology has also gotten used to calls that whisper: "I may come and blow you away. I don't like establishments like yours."

Less easy to take is the recurring sense of helplessness. "I'd like to confess," a woman said slowly. "I was into drugs of all sorts and I killed a man, robbing a drugstore with my boyfriend. We didn't mean to. We didn't get caught, but it's on my mind."

And some supposed killers are business-like. "Well, I don't know how to say this but I should apologize for killing someone."

And then there was a call, possibly long distance: "I want everyone down here in Atlanta to catch me," a hoarse voice said. Mr. Apology played the tape for Atlanta police, who are searching for a child killer, "since the guy wanted to be caught."

Others are not apologetic at all. "I just shot a guy in the chest. Now we're gonna beat up some old lady and we're on our way to your mother's house."

And some are genuinely frightening, leaving the listener limp, listening to the tick of a time bomb. "I'm going through so many changes," a voice droned. "I was raised without a mother or father and I have so little. I don't know what to do. I don't want to live. I feel like killing. Who? My loved ones? Who? One day I might explode."

But it is not only murderers—real or imagined—who use Apology Line. Rapists, wife-beaters and people into incest and people out of love also call.

There are calls from non-voters and racists and homosexuals and scared people. Some weep and some talk forever and some threaten to slit the throat of Mr. Apology.

Some call from as far away as the Mideast. Sometimes, Mr. Apology will call them back, collect. But he is careful not to get too involved. One woman wanted him to go to her boyfriend's house and tell him she missed him. Mr. Apology didn't oblige, although from time to time, he is tempted.

Some lives are less inviting. He has played some of his tapes for a psychiatrist. He listened to one of the more manic calls, a man who said he had killed and raped in the past and threatened to kill again.

"The psychiatrist was genuinely concerned about the call. In violent calls like that, he said, you can't be sure every bit is literally true. But he felt the caller was potentially dangerous, even if he was fantasizing. He was still in trouble," Mr. Apology recounted. While some of the calls were obvious put-ons, the psychiatrist said, some fell into a gray area and require subjective judgment.

Apology Line, however, does seem to appeal to all types of troubled people. So it attracts estranged lovers who are sorry for being mean or possessive or abusive. It attracts people who have been unfaithful and people who use one another badly. It attracts students who have been overworking and bosses who have been nasty to their employees.

Some people are not repentant. "I'm not guilty. The state is guilty," one furious caller said. "And you really have nerve. Who set you up anyhow?" The CIA Apologize for what? Who are you?"

But it is the sense of violence and anger that is unrelenting, sometimes approaching virtuous level.

"I'm just sorry," a caller intoned, "that I didn't kick all the people who gave me grief, that I saved Gen. Haig's life in Vietnam and that I didn't wipe out my wife when I had a chance."

Angry wife-beaters provide a recurring theme. "I beat my wife pretty regular," one man said "I feel bad about it but she gets on my nerves. I hit her and I hit her again. I don't know how not to."

A frequent caller phones from Indiana. "Her first husband beat her on her wedding night," Mr. Apology said "Her second husband molested their child. Now she goes out with truck drivers who leave her stranded." He offers no advice.

Rape, incest, sex and love are also interwoven in the tapes. "Hello, I'm a rapist," a voice says, matter of fact. "Women. Little girls. Boys. Society considers it wrong. That's society's problem."

A repentant voice says: "I lied to my girlfriend when I was with another girl," and a woman with a voice that hurts says, "I love a man and we don't know how to get close to each other . . . I'm scared of hurting him and he's scared of hurting me. I don't know what to do. Thank you."

A sad man asks, "Why is it so hard to get along with people you love?" An unfaithful wife joyously announces: "I had an affair with someone without my husband's knowing. But I don't feel guilty about it at all. In fact, I feel rather good about it."

The incest calls are more curious. One worried man called and said "I've had sex with my sister for five or six years. Now she wants to live together." But he didn't want to upset their mother. Another complained that his sister always seduced him. "Disgusting, but I enjoy it," he confessed.

Calls from kids are even more surprising. Mr. Apology says. One said he just killed his mother. "I get a lot like that." And one childlike voice confessed: "There's a kid in school who's 12 and I snap her bra strap." More bizarre was the call from a wronged party that they are sorry or even know to whom to apologize.

He has played some of his tapes for a psychiatrist. He listened to one of the more manic calls, a man who said he had killed and raped in the past and threatened to kill again.

caller who assumed Mr. Apology was Satan. "He wanted me to help find his brother in New Jersey."

Mr. Apology never knows if his callers are killers or remixes or escapees from dreamland. And sometimes he doesn't want to. Perhaps one call caught the spirit of violence more than any other and gave Mr. Apology a genuine chill.

The call came early this year. The caller's name was Bernie and his monologue began innocently enough. Apology Line, he said, was a great service. In the past, he had been feeling guilty about bad things he had done. He sounded almost innocent, at first, a little sheepish. "I guess what I do is say I'm sorry, apologize, and then everything is all right" For the bad things I've done?"

Then the voice sounded manic. Now he said, "I won't feel guilty anymore and I can start doing the same things again? Right? In other words, I can say I'm sorry and that's okay? Then there's no more guilt? I don't have to worry about police or courts or anything? Oh, you're a fantastic person!"

Then came a catalog of crimes. He had raped his cousin when she was 9. "What do I do? Say I'm sorry?"

"I'm sorry, Louise."

Then there was Henry.

"I killed Henry," the caller said. Henry was his neighbor. "I hit him over and over again, with a rock . . . He shouldn't have kept teasing me about the size of my ears . . . I want to say I'm sorry, Henry."

In New York, he had robbed about 15 people. "How do I apologize? What do I have to do? Say it 15 times?" The laugh became more manic. "Oh, I'm getting to feel so much better now . . . I feel a weight lifted from my shoulders. Boy, I can go out tonight and start the mugging again. Doing all those things. Oh, you've changed my whole life."

The operator cut in and asked for money. "Listen, I got to hang up soon but I want to tell you I've never said I'm sorry to someone beforehand. But to the person who's running this service, to the person answering this phone. I will find out who you are and I'm telling you right now: I'm sorry but I'm going to kill YOU."

Laughter again. More sinister. "I'm sorry I'm telling you right now. I'm sorry. So that'll make it all right. There'll be no problem, right? And I'm gonna find out who you are. No problem at all. I have friends in the telephone company. I have friends who are cops, too. They get me information.

"So when you least expect me, when everything seems calm, your death will come. Oh, you'll know that too, Bernie. Telephone call. And you will know, that I've followed through with exactly what I said I'd do, which is your death.

"But I'm sorry. I'm telling you right now. I'm sorry. Because I'm not gonna have time then. I'm saying it now. Okay? Oh, this is a wonderful service. You're a fantastic person and you're gonna make me very very happy when I kill you. Thanks." ∎

189
Art Director: **Lynn Staley**
Designer: **Lynn Staley**
Chart Design: **Deb Perugi**
Artist: **Roger Leyonmark**
Client: **The Boston Globe Calender Section**
Editor: **Jan Shepherd**
Publisher: **The Boston Globe**

191
Art Directors: **Louis Silverstein, Tom Bodkin**
Design Director: **Louis Silverstein**
Photographer: **Engraving/Culver Pictures Inc.**
Client: **The New York Times**
Editor: **Michael Leahy**
Publisher: **The New York Times**

190
Art Director: **Terry Ross Koppel**
Designer: **Terry Ross Koppel**
Artist: **Patrick Blackwell**
Writer: **Bob MacDonald**
Client: **The Boston Globe Calendar Section**
Editor: **Jan Shepherd**
Publisher: **The Boston Globe**
Agency: **T. Ross Koppel Graphics**

192
Art Director: **Roger Dale Rushing**
Designer: **Roger Dale Rushing**
Photographer: **Larry C. Price**
Writer: **Paul Rowan**
Client: **Fort Worth Star-Telegram**
Editor: **Mike Blackman**
Publisher: **Fort Worth Star-Telegram**

MAGAZINE EDITORIAL

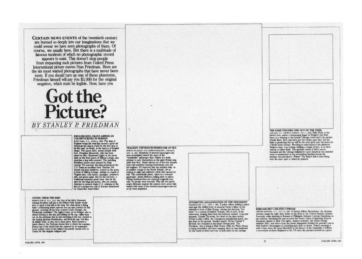

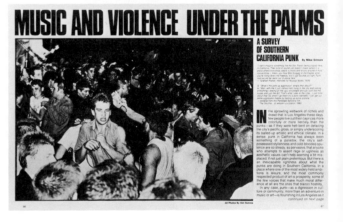

193
Art Director: **Robert Priest**
Designer: **April Silver**
Client: **Esquire**
Editor: **Phillip Moffitt**
Publisher: **Esquire Publishing Co.**

195
Art Director: **Ronn Campisi**
Designer: **Ronn Campisi**
Photographer: **John Goodman**
Editor: **Al Larkin**
Publisher: **The Boston Globe**

194
Art Director: **Howard Shintaku**
Designer: **Howard Shintaku**
Artist: **Jean Francois Allaux**
Writer: **Paul Gillette**
Client: **CalToday Magazine**
Editor: **John Parkyn**
Publisher: **San Jose Mercury News**

196
Art Director: **Sam Holdsworth**
Designer: **Sam Holdsworth**
Photographer: **Anne Summa**
Writer: **Mikal Gilmore and Ken Tucker**
Client: **Musician Magazine**
Editor: **Sam Holdsworth**
Publisher: **Gordon Baird**

197
Art Director: **Joseph Baumer**
Designer: **Joseph Baumer**
Photographer: **Skeeter Hagler**
Writer: **Geoffrey Gould**
Client: **Topic Magazine**
Editor: **Urmila K. Devgon**
Publisher: **United States International
Communication Agency**

198
Art Director: **Eric Keller**
Designer: **Eric Keller**
Photographer: **David Franklin**
Client: **Monthly Detroit Magazine**
Editor: **Robert Pisor**
Publisher: **City Magazines, Inc.**

199
Art Director: **James Hiscott, Jr.**
Designer: **James Hiscott, Jr.**
Photographer: **Bill Horin**
Writer: **Robin Palley**
Client: **Atlantic City Magazine**
Editor: **Donna Andersen**
Publisher: **Frances F. Freedman**

200
Art Director: **Ronn Campisi**
Designer: **Catherine Aldrich**
Artist: **Doug Smith**
Editor: **Al Larkin**
Publisher: **The Boston Globe**

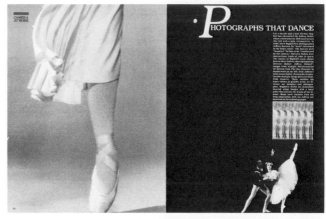

201
Art Director: **David Moore**
Designer: **Patricia Gipple**
Client: **America Illustrated**
Editor: **Robert Poteete**
Publisher: **U.S. International Communication Agency**

202
Art Director: **Ronn Campisi**
Designer: **Ronn Campisi**
Artist: **Vivienne Flesher**
Editor: **Al Larkin**
Publisher: **The Boston Globe**

203
Art Director: **Bob Ciano**
Designer: **Mary K. Baumann**
Photographer: **Herbert Migdol**
Writer: **Harriet Heyman**
Editors: **Philip Kunhardt, Mary Steinbauer**
Publisher: **LIFE Magazine**

204
Art Director: **Frank M. Devino**
Designer: **Margaret Richichi**
Photographer: **Tony Guccione**
Artist: **Nick Aristovulos**
Client: **Omni Publications Int'l Ltd.**
Publisher: **Bob Guccione**

205
Art Director: **Maxine Davidowitz**
Designer: **Joy Toltzis Makon**
Photographer: **Liza Himmel**
Writer: **Marianne Gingher**
Client: **Redbook Magazine**
Editor: **Sey Chassler**
Publisher: **Redbook Magazine**

208
Art Director: **Robin McDonald**
Designer: **Ira Friedlander**
Photographer: **Michael Alexander**
Writer: **Jane Adams**
Client: **Horizon Magazine**
Editor: **David Roberts**
Publisher: **Gray Boone**

206
Art Director: **Caroline Bowyer**
Designer: **Caroline Bowyer**
Photographer: **Granger Collection; Brent C. Broline**
Writer: **Tom Wolfe**
Client: **Book Digest Magazine**
Editor: **Raymond Sokolov**
Publisher: **Dow Jones and Company**

209
Art Director: **John Tom Cohoe**
Designer: **John Tom Cohoe**
Photographer: **Dilip Mehta**
Writer: **Joseph H. Mazo**
Client: **GEO Magazine**
Editor: **David Maxey**
Publisher: **Knapp Communications Corp.**

210
Art Director: **Sam Holdsworth**
Designer: **Sam Holdsworth**
Photographers: **Deborah Feingold, Ric Murray**
Writer: **J.C. Costa**
Client: **Musician Magazine**
Editor: **Sam Holdsworth**
Publisher: **Gordon Baird**

212
Art Director: **Eva Pietrzak**
Designer: **Eva Pietrzak**
Photographer: **Harry Hartman**
Artist: **Tim Girvin — Lettering**
Writer: **Stacey Smith**
Client: **Meredith Corporation**
Publisher: **Meredith Corporation**

211
Art Director: **Frank M. Devino**
Designer: **Margaret Richichi**
Artist: **James Marsh**
Client: **Omni Publications Int'l Ltd.**
Publisher: **Bob Guccione**

213
Art Director: **Frank M. Devino**
Designer: **Margaret Richichi**
Photographer: **Anthony Wolff**
Client: **Omni Publications Int'l Ltd.**
Publisher: **Bob Guccione**

214
Art Director: **Ronn Campisi**
Designer: **Ronn Campisi**
Photographer: **John Goodman**
Editor: **Al Larkin**
Publisher: **The Boston Globe**

216
Art Director: **Sam Holdsworth**
Designer: **Sam Holdsworth**
Photographer: **Deborah Feingold**
Writers: **Mikal Gilmore, David Breskin**
Client: **Musician Magazine**
Editor: **Sam Holdsworth**
Publisher: **Gordon Baird**

215
Art Director: **Frank M. Devino**
Designer: **Elizabeth Woodson**
Artist: **Michael Parkes**
Client: **Omni Publications Int'l Ltd.**
Publisher: **Bob Guccione**

217
Art Director: **Michael R. Dexter**
Designer: **Michael R. Dexter**
Photographer: **Art Pasquali**
Writer: **Mike Reid**
Client: **Living Single Magazine**
Editor: **Robert B. Smith**
Publisher: **The Dispatch Printing Company**

218
Art Director: **Gary Gretter**
Designer: **Carol Rheuban**
Photographer: **Kelly Dean/Photo Researchers, Inc.**
Artist: **Richard Le Fulgham**
Client: **Sports Afield**
Editor: **Tom Paugh**
Publisher: **Alan Waxenberg**
Production Co.: **Hearst Magazines**

219
Art Director: **Maxine Davidowitz**
Designer: **Paula Laniado**
Artist: **Braldt Bralds**
Writer: **Sara Clayton**
Client: **Redbook Magazine**
Editor: **Sey Chassler**
Publisher: **Redbook Magazine**

220
Art Director: **Karen Huber**
Designer: **Karen Huber**
Artist: **Gary Kelley/Hellman Design Associates**
Writer: **Douglas A. Jimerson**
Client: **Ralston Purina**
Editor: **Douglas A. Jimerson**
Publisher: **Meredith Corporation**

221
Art Director: **David J. Talbot**
Designer: **Nina Ovryn**
Photographer: **John Paul Endress**
Writer: **Jane Helsel**
Client: **Cuisine Magazine**
Editor: **Patricia Brown**
Publisher: **Charles D. Coletti**

222
Art Director: **David J. Talbot**
Designer: **Nina Ovryn**
Photographer: **Michel Tcherevkoff**
Writer: **Anne Mendelson**
Client: **Cuisine Magazine**
Editor: **Patricia Brown**
Publisher: **Charles D. Coletti**

223   SILVER AWARD
Art Director: **Shinichiro Tora**
Designer: **Shinichiro Tora**
Photographer: **Edward Cornachio**
Writer: **Edward Cornachio**
Client: **Popular Photography**
Editor: **Nancy T. Engel**
Publisher: **Ziff Davis Publishing Co.**

224   DISTINCTIVE MERIT
Art Director: **Ruth Ansel**
Designer: **Ruth Ansel**
Photographer: **Ernest Hemingway Collection. Photos
copied by Lynn Karlin.**
Writers: **Ernest Hemingway; Cowles Broadcasting, Inc.;
Courtesy Ernest Hemingway Collection/JFK Library**
Client: **The New York Times**
Editor: **Ed Klein**
Publisher: **The New York Times**

226
Art Director: **Bob Ciano**
Designers: **Bob Ciano, Sibbie Chalawick**
Photographer: **Helmut Newton**
Writer: **Jed Horne**
Editors: **Philip Kunhardt, Jim Watters**
Publisher: **LIFE Magazine**

227
Art Director: **Robert Flora**
Designer: **Robert Flora**
Photographers: **Deborah Turbeville, Sharon Schuster**
Client: **Harper's Bazaar**
Editor: **Anthony T. Mazzola**
Publisher: **Martin Schrader**

229
Art Director: **Susanne Walsh**
Designer: **John Tom Cohoe**
Photographer: **Walter Schmitz**
Writer: **Gerald Astor**
Client: **GEO Magazine**
Editor: **David Maxey**
Publisher: **Knapp Communications Corp.**

228
Art Director: **Shinichiro Tora**
Designer: **Shinichiro Tora**
Photographer: **Jack Krawczyk**
Writer: **Jack Krawczyk**
Client: **Popular Photography**
Editor: **Ken Poli**
Publisher: **Ziff Davis Publishing Co.**

230
Art Director: **Bob Ciano**
Designer: **Bob Ciano**
Photographer: **Stephen Green-Armytage**
Writer: **Daphne Hurford**
Client: **Philip Kunhardt**
Editor: **Eleanor Graves**
Publisher: **LIFE Magazine**

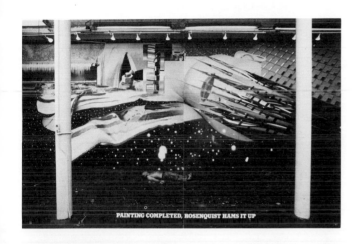

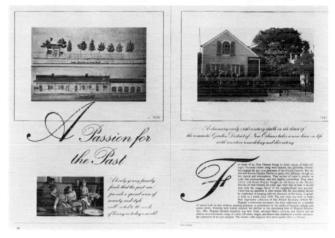

231
Art Director: **Bob Ciano**
Designer: **Bob Ciano**
Photographer: **Bob Adelman**
Writer: **Todd Brewster**
Editors: **Philip Kunhardt, Mary Simons**
Publisher: **LIFE Magazine**

233
Art Director: **Bob Ciano**
Designer: **Bob Ciano**
Photographer: **Annie Leibowitz**
Calligraphy: **Tim Girvin**
Writer: **Harriet Heyman**
Client: **Philip Kunhardt**
Editor: **Loudon Wainwright**
Publisher: **LIFE Magazine**

232
Art Director: **Jim Darilek**
Designer: **Jim Darilek**
Photographer: **Reagan Bradshaw**
Artist: **Janice Ashford**
Client: **Texas Monthly**
Editor: **Greg Curtis**
Publisher: **Mediatex Communications Corp.**

234
Art Director: **Lloyd Ziff**
Designer: **Lloyd Ziff**
Photographer: **Karen Radkai**
Writer: **Martin Filler**
Client: **House & Garden Magazine**
Editor: **Babs Simpson**
Publisher: **Condé Nast Publications Inc.**

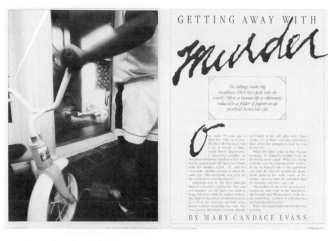

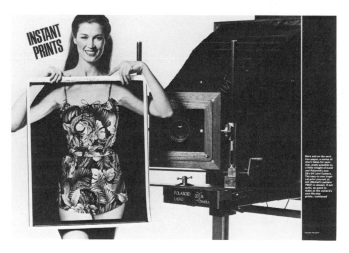

235
Art Director: **Will Hopkins**
Designer: **Louis F. Cruz**
Photographer: **Alan MacWeeney**
Writers: **W.B. Yeats, Kathryn Livingston, Artelia Court**
Client: **CBS Publications**
Editor: **Sean Callahan**
Publisher: **Gary Fisher**

236
Art Director: **Alvin Grossman**
Photographer: **Roger Prigent**
Writer: **Alvin Grossman**
Publisher: **The McCall Publishing Co.**

237
Art Director: **Fred Woodward**
Designer: **Fred Woodward**
Photographer: **Robert Latorre**
Artist: **Don Grimes**
Writer: **Mary Candace Evans**
Client: **D Magazine**
Editor: **Rowland Stiteler**
Publisher: **Bernie Kraft**

238
Art Director: **Fred Woodward**
Designer: **Fred Woodward**
Photographers: **Chuck Untersee, Robert Latorre, Maciej Pinno**
Artist: **Cap Pannell**
Writers: **Amy Cunningham, Chris Wohlwend, Lisa Broadwater**
Client: **D Magazine**
Editor: **Rowland Stiteler**
Publisher: **Bernie Kraft**

239
Art Director: **Thomas Ridinger**
Designer: **Thomas Ridinger**
Photographer: **Antonio Mendoza**
Writer: **Christopher Smart**
Editors: **Jim Hughes; Article editor, Laurance Wieder**
Publisher: **Ziff Davis Publishing Company**

242
Art Director: **Maxine Davidowitz**
Designer: **Paula Laniado**
Photographer: **Liza Himmel**
Artist: **Charles Santore**
Writers: **(1.) Margaret Ellington, (2.) Marjorie Franoo, (3.) Ethan Canin**
Editor: **Sey Chassler**
Publisher: **Redbook Magazine**

240
Art Director: **Mark Borden**
Designer: **Mark Borden**
Photographer: **Alfredo Cella**
Artist: **Marian Chin**
Writer: **Phyllis Schneider**
Client: **Young Miss Magazine**
Editor: **Phyllis Schneider**
Publisher: **Gruner & Jahr, U.S.A.**

244
Art Director: **Greg Paul**
Designer: **Greg Paul**
Artist: **Daniel Maffia**
Client: **The Plain Dealer Magazine**

A SPECIAL SECTION INSIDE: "YOUR HOME"

The Boston Globe Magazine

March 22, 1981

THEY WERE SOLDIERS
of fortune from the United
States, ex-CIA men and
Green Berets who journeyed
to this Libyan palace to
further the
cause of
international terrorism.

A SPOTLIGHT REPORT

BY STEPHEN KURKJIAN AND
BEN BRADLEE

THE PRIVATE HEMINGWAY

From His
Unpublished
Letters
1918 to 1961

Passport photograph of Ernest Hemingway, 1923.

245
Art Director: **Ronn Campisi**
Designer: **Ronn Campisi**
Editor: **Al Larkin**
Publisher: **The Boston Globe**

246
Art Director: **Ruth Ansel**
Designer: **Ruth Ansel**
Photographer: **Ernest Hemingway Collection, Photo
copied by Lynn Karlin**
Writer: **Ernest Hemingway/Cowles Broadcasting
Inc./Courtesy of Ernest Hemingway Collection**
Client: **The New York Times Magazine**
Editor: **Edward Klein**
Publisher: **The New York Times**

247
Art Director: **Terry Ross Koppel**
Designer: **Terry Ross Koppel**
Artist: **Steven Guarnaccia**
Writer: **David Young**
Client: **The Boston Globe**
Editor: **David Young**
Publisher: **The Boston Globe**
Agency: **T. Ross Koppel Graphics**

248
Art Director: **Ronn Campisi**
Designer: **Ronn Campisi**
Photographer: **Anne Sager**
Editor: **Al Larkin**
Publisher: **The Boston Globe**

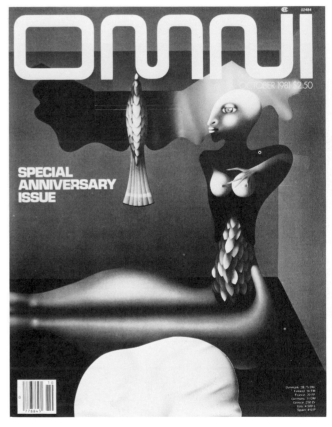

250
Art Director: **Gary Bennett**
Designer: **David Muench**
Photographer: **David Muench**
Writer: **Richard G. Stahl**
Client: **Arizona Highways Magazine**
Editor: **Gary Avey**
Publisher: **Mark Sanders**
Director: **William Ordway**
Production Co.: **Arizona Highways Magazine**

252
Art Director: **Frank M. Devino**
Designer: **Elizabeth Woodson**
Artist: **Paul Wunderlich**
Client: **Omni Publications Int'l Ltd.**
Publisher: **Bob Guccione**

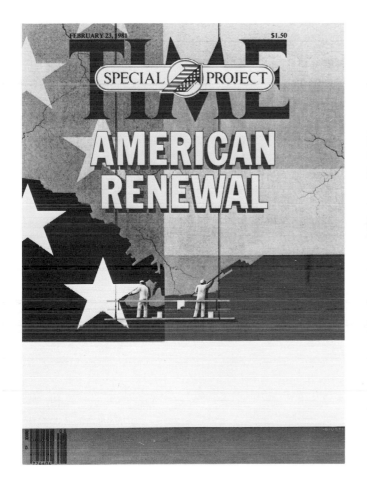

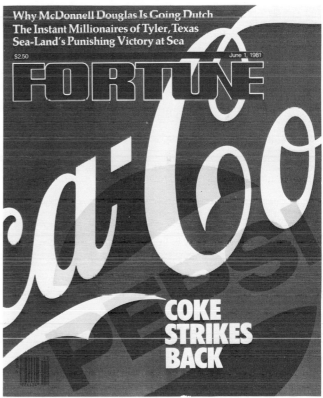

255
Art Director: **Rudolph Hoglund**
Designer: **Irene Ramp**
Artist: **Robert Giusti**
Writers: **Henry Grunwald, Otto Freidrich, Strobe Talbott, Lanoo Morrow**
Editor: **John Elson**
Publisher: **John A. Meyers**

256
Art Director: **Ron Campbell**
Designer: **Ron Campbell**
Client: **Fortune**

258
Art Director: **Kiyoshi Kanai**
Designer: **Kiyoshi Kanai**
Photographer: **David Riley**
Client: **American Craft Council**
Editor: **Lois Moran**
Publisher: **American Craft Council**

257
Art Director: **Tom Page**
Designer: **Tom Page**
Photographer: **John Marshall**
Editor: **Alan Ternes**
Publisher: **American Museum of Natural
History Magazine**

259
Art Director: **Kiyoshi Kanai**
Designer: **Kiyoshi Kanai**
Photographer: **August Riccio, Jr.**
Client: **American Craft Council**
Editor: **Lois Moran**
Publisher: **American Craft Council**

260
Art Director: **Richard Hess**
Designer: **Richard Hess**
Photographer: **Claus Meyer**
Writer: **Stuart I. Frolick**
Client: **Champion International Corporation**
Editor: **Stuart I. Frolick**

261
Art Director: **Jaye Medalia**
Designer: **Jaye Medalia**
Photographer: **Christopher Baker**
Writer: **Barbara Knox**
Client: **Restaurant Design**
Editor: **Regina Baraban**
Publisher: **Bill Communications**

262
Art Director: **Nickolas Dankovich**
Designer: **Nickolas Dankovich**
Artist: **Jim Kingston**
Writer: **William Pat Patterson**
Client: **Industry Week Magazine**
Editor: **Stanley J. Modic**
Publisher: **Patrick B. Keefe**
Producer: **Penton/IPC Publishing Co.**

263
Art Director: **Nickolas Dankovich**
Designer: **Nickolas Dankovich**
Artist: **Robert Crawford**
Writer: **Donald B. Thompson**
Client: **Industry Week Magazine**
Editor: **Stanley J. Modic**
Publisher: **Patrick B. Keefe**
Producer: **Penton/IPC Publishing Co.**

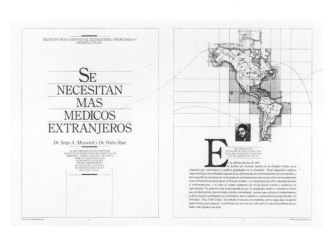

264
Art Directors: **Javier Romero, Rafael Rovira**
Designer: **Javier Romero**
Artist: **Javier Romero**
Client: **Medico Interamericano**
Publisher: **Interamerican Medical Publications**
Agency: **Periscope Studio, Inc.**

266
Art Director: **Charles Curtis**
Designer: **Charles Curtis**
Photographer: **Camille Vickers**
Client: **Peat, Marwick, Mitchell & Co.**
Editor: **Jerry Bowles**

265   DISTINCTIVE MERIT
Art Directors: **Saul Bass, Art Goodman**
Designer: **Saul Bass**
Artists: **Saul Bass, Art Goodman**
Client: **Art/Work**
Publisher: **Art/Work**
Producer: **Saul Bass/Herb Yager & Associates**

267
Art Director: **Jack Lefkowitz**
Designer: **Jack Lefkowitz**
Artists: **Jack Lefkowitz, Jeff Davis**
Writer: **David Ritchey**
Client: **Industrial Launderer Magazine**
Editor: **David Ritchey**
Publisher: **Institute of Industrial Launderers**
Agency: **Jack Lefkowitz, Inc.**

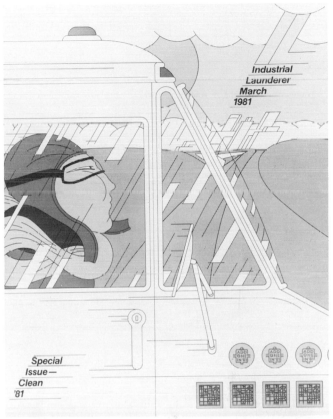

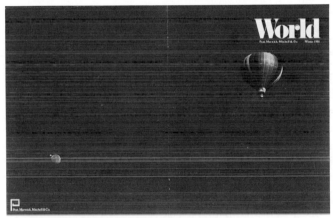

269
Art Director: **Jack Lefkowitz**
Designer: **Jack Lefkowitz**
Artists: **Jack Lefkowitz, Jeff Davis**
Writer: **David Ritchey**
Client: **Industrial Launderer Magazine**
Editor: **David Ritchey**
Publisher: **Institute of Industrial Launderers**
Agency: **Jack Lefkowitz Inc.**

268
Art Director: **M.J. Cody**
Artist: **Marvin Rubin**
Editor: **Constance J. Sidles**
Publisher: **Flowers &**
Director: **Barbara Cady**

270
Art Director: **Charles Curtis**
Designer: **Charles Curtis**
Photographer: **Charles Moore**
Client: **Peat, Marwick, Mitchell & Co.**
Editor: **Jerry Bowles**

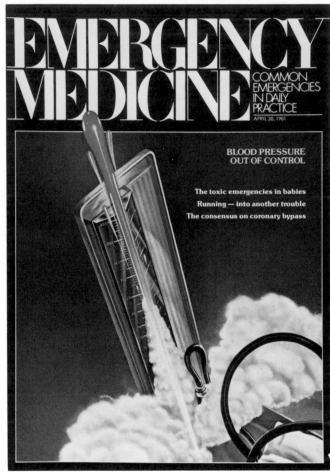

271
Art Director: **Jack Lefkowitz**
Designer: **Jack Lefkowitz**
Artists: **Jack Lefkowitz, Jeff Davis**
Writer: **David Ritchey**
Client: **Industrial Launderer Magazine**
Editor: **David Ritchey**
Publisher: **Institute of Industrial Launderers**
Agency: **Jack Lefkowitz Inc.**

272
Art Director: **Tom Lennon**
Designer: **James T. Walsh**
Artist: **Frank Riley**
Client: **Emergency Medicine**
Publisher: **Fischer Medical Publications**

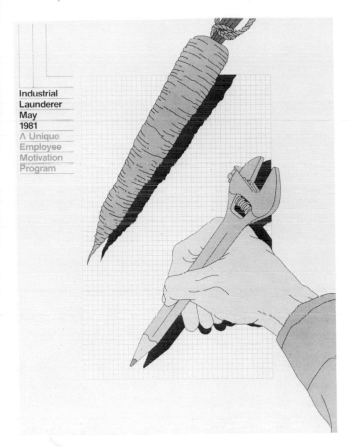

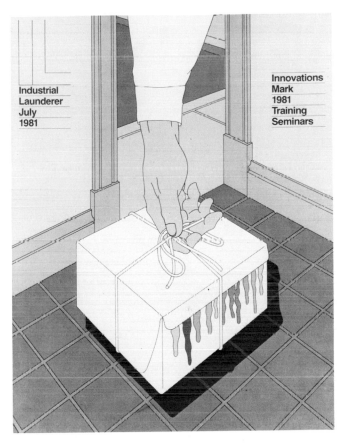

273
Art Director: **Jack Lefkowitz**
Designer: **Jack Lefkowitz**
Artist: **Jack Lefkowitz**
Writer: **David Ritchey**
Client: **Industrial Launderer Magazine**
Editor: **David Ritchey**
Publisher: **Institute of Industrial Launderers**
Agency: **Jack Lefkowitz Inc.**

274
Art Directors: **Craig Bernhardt, Janice Fudyma**
Designer: **Roger Gorman**
Photographer: **Stu Peltz**
Artist: **Nick Fasciano**
Client: **W.R. Grace & Co.**
Editor: **Joyce Cole**
Publisher: **W.R. Grace & Co.**
Agency: **Bernhardt Fudyma Design Group**

275
Art Director: **Jack Lefkowitz**
Designer: **Jack Lefkowitz**
Artist: **Jack Lefkowitz**
Writer: **David Ritchey**
Client: **Industrial Launderer Magazine**
Editor: **David Ritchey**
Publisher: **Institute of Industrial Launderers**
Agency: **Jack Lefkowitz Inc.**

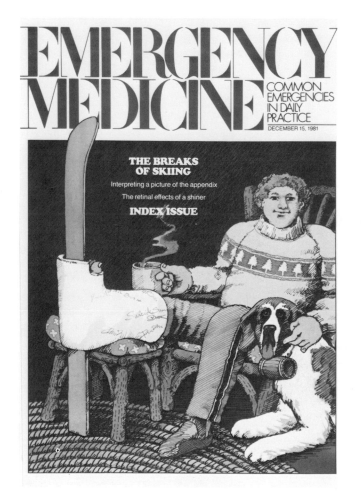

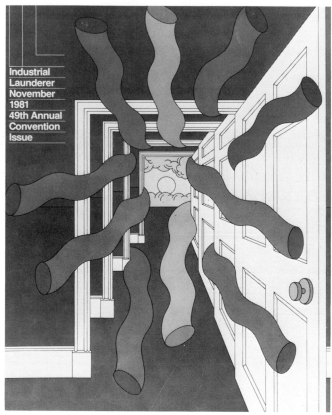

276
Art Director: **Tom Lennon**
Designer: **Tom Lennon**
Artist: **Werner Kappes**
Client: **Emergency Medicine**
Publisher: **Fischer Medical Publications**

277
Art Director: **Jack Lefkowitz**
Designer: **Jack Lefkowitz**
Artists: **Pam and Jack Lefkowitz**
Writer: **David Ritchey**
Client: **Industrial Launderer Magazine**
Editor: **David Ritchey**
Publisher: **Institute of Industrial Launderers**
Agency: **Jack Lefkowitz Inc.**

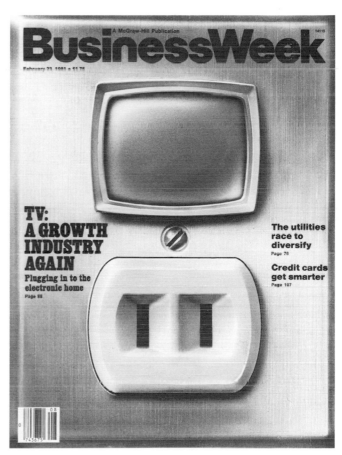

278
Art Director: **Andrew Kner**
Designer: **Dan Weaks**
Photographer: **Dan Weaks**
Client: **Print Magazine**
Editor: **Martin Fox**
Publisher: **R.C. Publications**

279
Art Director: **John R. Vogler**
Designer: **John R. Vogler**
Artist: **Richard Newton**
Client: **McGraw-Hill, Inc.**
Editor: **Lewis H. Young**
Publisher: **Bernard Alexander — Business Week**

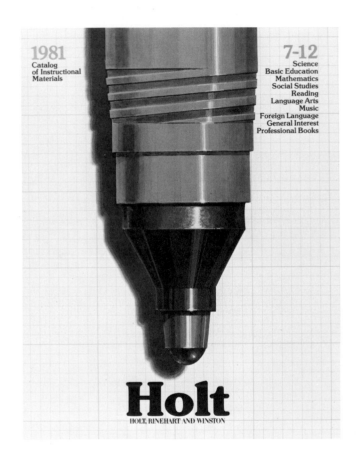

280
Art Director: **Craig Bernhardt**
Designer: **Roger Gorman**
Artist: **Ellen Gavin**
Client: **Holt Rinehart & Winston**
Agency: **Bernhardt Fudyma Design Group**

281
Art Directors: **William J. Kircher, Bobbie Lee**
Designer: **Bobbie Lee**
Artist: **Kevin Chadwick**
Client: **National Association of Elementary School Principals**

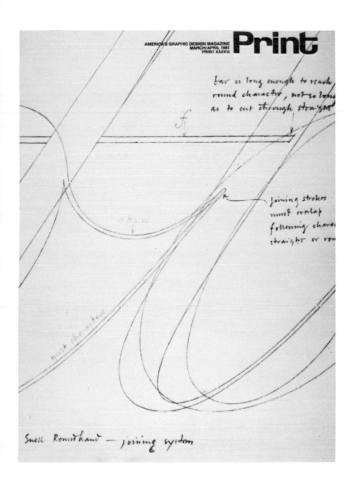

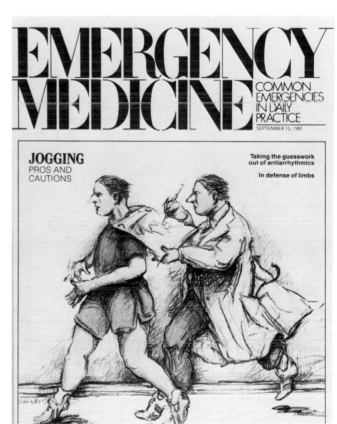

282
Art Director: **Andrew Kner**
Designer: **Andrew Kner**
Artist: **Matthew Carter**
Writer: **Martin Fox**
Client: **Print Magazine**
Editor: **Martin Fox**
Publisher: **R.C. Publications**

283
Art Director: **Richard Hess**
Designer: **Richard Hess**
Photographer: **Tom Hollyman**
Client: **Champion International Corporation**
Editor: **Stuart L. Frolick**

284
Art Director: **Tom Lennon**
Designer: **Tom Lennon**
Artist: **Geoffrey Moss**
Client: **Emergency Medicine**
Publisher: **Fischer Medical Publications**

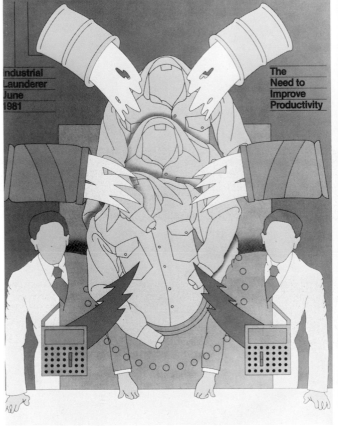

285
Art Director: **Elaine Anderson**
Artist: **Bill Imhoff**
Client: **Teleflora**
Editor: **Constance J. Sidles**
Publisher: **Barbara Cady**
Producer: **Flowers &**

286
Art Director: **Jack Lefkowitz**
Designer: **Jack Lefkowitz**
Artists: **Jack Lefkowitz, Jeff Davis**
Writer: **David Ritchey**
Client: **Industrial Launderer Magazine**
Editor: **David Ritchey**
Publisher: **Institute of Industrial Launders**
Agency: **Jack Lefkowitz Inc.**

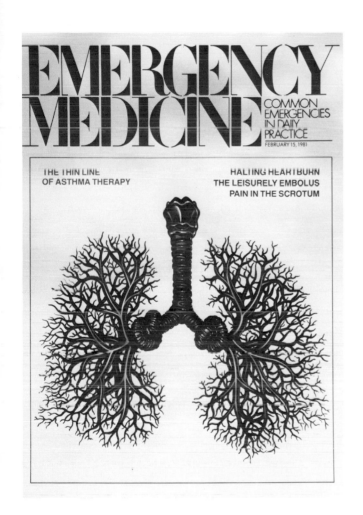

287
Art Director: **Tom Lennon**
Designer: **James T. Walsh**
Artist: **Hovik Dilaklan**
Client: **Emergency Medicine**
Publisher: **Fischer Medical Publications**

288
Art Director: **Richard Hess**
Designer: **Richard Hess**
Artist: **Unknown**
Client: **Champion International Corporation**
Editor: **Stuart I. Frolick**
Director: **David R. Brown**

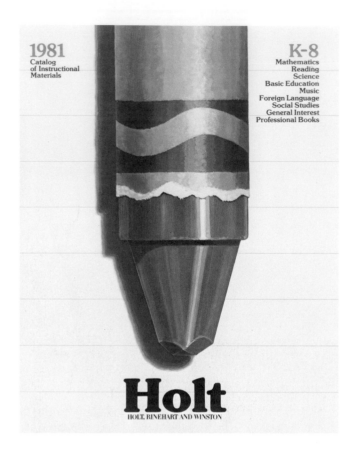

289
Art Director: **Craig Bernhardt**
Designer: **Roger Gorman**
Artist: **Ellen Gavin**
Client: **Holt, Rinehart & Winston**
Agency: **Bernhardt Fudyma Design Group**

290
Art Directors: **Craig Bernhardt, Janice Fudyma**
Designer: **Janice Fudyma**
Artist: **Kimmerle Milnazik**
Client: **W.R. Grace & Co.**
Editor: **Joyce Cole**
Publisher: **W.R. Grace & Co.**
Agency: **Bernhardt/Fudyma Design Group**

291
Art Director: **Everett Halvorsen**
Designer: **Ronda Kass**
Artist: **Kinoku Craft**
Writer: **James Cook**
Client: **Forbes Magazine**
Editor: **James Michaels**
Publisher: **Forbes, Inc.**

292
Art Director: **Thomas Darnsteadt**
Design Director: **John Newcomb**
Photographer: **Stephen Munz**
Artist: **Janice Conklin**
Writers: **Seth L. Haber, M.D., Marcia C. Inhorn**
Client: **MEDICAL LABORATORY OBSERVER** Magazine
Editor: **Robert Fitzgibbon**
Publisher: **H. Mason Fackert**
Designer: **Kathleen Cuddihy**
Production Co.: **Medical Economics Co., Inc.**

293
Art Director: **George Coderre**
Designer: **George Coderre**
Artist: **Mitchell Giurgola Thorp**
Client: **Progressive Architecture**
Editor: **John Morris Dixon**
Publisher: **James J. Hoverman**
Production Co.: **Reinhold Publishing**

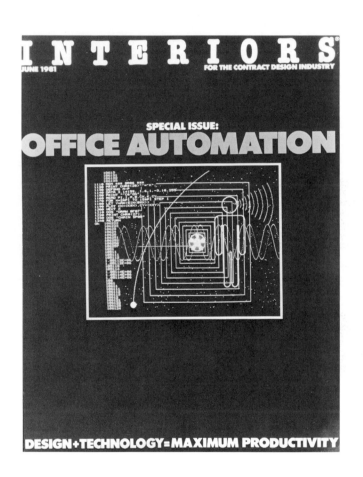

294
Art Director: **Paul Hardy**
Designer: **William H. Work**
Client: **Interiors Magazine**
Editor: **Beverly Russell**
Publisher: **Billboard Publications**

295
Art Director: **George Coderre**
Designer: **George Coderre**
Photographer: **Steve Rosenthal**
Client: **Progressive Architecture**
Editor: **John Morris Dixon**
Publisher: **James J. Hoverman**
Production Co.: **Reinhold Publishing**

296
Art Director: **Susanne Walsh**
Designers: **John Tom Cohoe, Greg Leeds**
Client: **GEO Magazine**
Editor: **David Maxey**
Publisher: **Knapp Communications Corp**

297
Art Director: **Frank M. Devino**
Designers: **Frank M. Devino, Margaret Richichi,
Elizabeth Woodson**
Client: **OMNI Publications Int'l Ltd.**
Publisher: **Bob Guccione**

298
Art Director: **Mauricio Arias**
Designer: **Mauricio Arias**
Photographers: **Light Language, David Madison,
Becker/Bishop, Nick Felicé, Kristin Finnegan,
Stephen Frink, Mark Tuschman**
Sculptor: **Tom Eckert**
Illustrators: **Paul Giovanopoulos, Jim Endicott,
John Mattos, Gary Meyer, Jack Unruh,
Jerry Jeanmard, Don Weller, Saul Bernstein**
Artists (Production): **Michael Chikamura, Diane Keller**
Writers: **Barbara Gibson, Allan Lundell, Tony Dirksen,
Mike Cashman, Dale Archibald, Betsy Gilbert,
Richard Immel, Ray Bradbury, Susan Luttner,
Charlotte K. Beyers, Patty Winter**
Client: **Apple Computer, Inc.**
Editor: **Monte Lorenzet**
Publisher: **Apple Computer, Inc.**
Agency: **Mauricio Arias Design**

299
Art Directors: **Craig Bernhardt, Janice Fudyma**
Designers: **C. Bernhardt, J. Fudyma, D. Duerr, R. Gorman,
K. Thompson**
Photographers: **Various**
Artists: **Various**
Writers: **Various**
Client: **W.R. Grace & Co.**
Editor: **J. Cole**
Publisher: **W.R. Grace & Co.**
Agency: **Bernhardt Fudyma Design Group**

300
Art Director: **Peter Bradford**
Designers: **Peter Bradford, Byron Taylor**
Photographers: **Various**
Writers: **James Roper and various**
Client: **Briggs Associates, Inc.**
Editor: **James Roper**
Publisher: **Porter Briggs**
Agency: **Peter Bradford and Associates**

301
Art Director: **Susanne Walsh**
Designers: **John Tom Cohoe, Greg Leeds**
Client: **GEO Magazine**
Editor: **David Maxey**
Publisher: **Knapp Communications Corp**

302
Art Director: **Richard Hess**
Designer: **Richard Hess**
Photographers: **Claus Meyer, Tom Hollyman**
Writers: **Stuart I. Frolick, Jack Long, David Monagan,
Nancy K. Garfinkel**
Editor: **Stuart I. Frolick**

303
Art Director: **Richard Hess**
Designer: **Richard Hess**
Writers: **H.R. Meier, Jack Long, Eliot Tozer,
Sarah Theurkauf**
Client: **Champion International Corporation**
Editor: **Stuart I. Frolick**
Director: **David R. Brown**

304
Art Director: **Richard Hess**
Designer: **Richard Hess**
Photographer: **Tom Hollyman**
Writers: **H.R. Meier, Sarah Theurkauf, Eliot Tozer,
Jack Long**
Client: **Champion International Corporation**
Editor: **Stuart I. Frolick**

305
Art Director: **Frank M. Devino**
Designers: **Frank M. Devino, Margaret Richichi, Elizabeth Woodson**
Client: **OMNI Publications Int'l Ltd.**
Publisher: **Bob Guccione**

306
Art Director: **Susanne Walsh**
Designers: **John Tom Cohoe, Greg Leeds**
Client: **GEO Magazine**
Editor: **David Maxey**
Publisher: **Knapp Communications Corp**

PROMOTION \ GRAPHIC DESIGN

307 GOLD AWARD
Art Director: **Jerry Pavey**
Designer: **Jerry Pavey**
Artist: **Peter Good**
Writer: **Ronald Erickson**
Client: **The Fiscal Agency for the Farm Credit Banks**
Publisher: **Moore and Moore Inc.**

308 SILVER AWARD
Art Director: **Robert Cipriani**
Designer: **Robert Cipriani**
Photographers: **Al Fisher, Gary Koepke, Pete Turner**
Writer: **Catherine Flannery**
Client: **The Charles Stark Draper Laboratory, Inc.**
Typographer: **Typographic House**
Printer: **Nimrod Press**
Agency: **Robert Cipriani Associates**

309 SILVER AWARD
Art Director: **Ron Sullivan**
Designer: **Ron Sullivan**
Photographer: **Greg Booth**
Writer: **John Stone**
Client: **Lomas & Nettleton Mortgage Investors**
Publisher: **Heritage Press**
Agency: **Richards, Sullivan, Brock & Assoc/
The Richards Group**

310 SILVER AWARD
Art Directors: **Jay Loucks, Chris Hill**
Designers: **Chris Hill, C. Randall Sherman**
Photographers: **Joe Baraban, Ron Scott, Don Glentzer**
Writers: **Richard Jones, Sam Miller**
Client: **Fosti**
Agency: **Miller/Johnston, Inc.**

Boston Edison Company Annual Report 1980

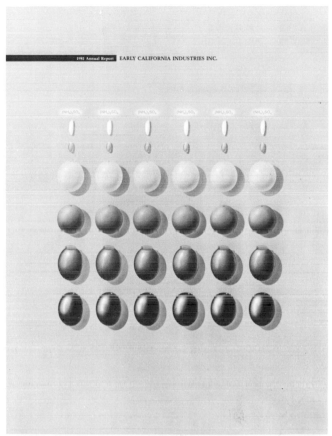

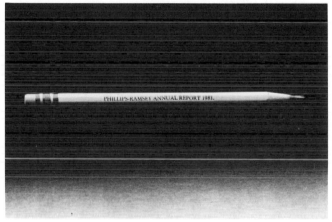

312　DISTINCTIVE MERIT
Art Director: **Robert Miles Runyan**
Designer: **Dennis Tani**
Artist: **Warren Hile**
Writer: **Mary McCarthy**
Client: **Early California Industries**
Agency: **Robert Miles Runyan & Associates**

311　DISTINCTIVE MERIT
Art Director: **Wendy Hilgert**
Designer: **Wendy Hilgert**
Photographer: **Clint Clemens**
Artist: **Oliver Kline**
Writers: **Walt Skowronski, Ann Carter, Steven Ringlee**
Client: **Boston Edison Company**
Printer: **W.E. Andrews**
Agency: **Ingalls Associates**

313　DISTINCTIVE MERIT
Art Director: **Bob Kwait and Bridgit Cody**
Designer: **Bob Kwait and Bridgit Cody**
Photographer: **Chris Wimpey**
Writer: **Rich Badami**
Client: **Phillips-Ramsey Advertising**

314   DISTINCTIVE MERIT
Art Directors: **Jay Loucks, Chris Hill**
Designers: **Chris Hill, Betty Thomas**
Photographer: **Arthur Meyerson**
Writer: **Don Pierce**
Client: **Boy Scouts, Sam Houston Area Council**
Editor: **Leroy Mayne**
Agency: **Loucks Atelier, Houston**

316
Art Director: **Lawrence Bender**
Designers: **Linda Brandon, Lawrence Bender**
Photographer: **Tom Tracy**
Writer: **Anne Peters**
Client: **Cetus Corporation**
Editor: **Anne Peters**
Agency: **Lawrence Bender & Associates**

317
Art Director: **Ron Jefferies**
Designers: **Ron Jefferies, M. Alyce Barker**
Photographer: **William James Warren**
Writer: **Rosanne O'Brien**
Client: **Tiger International**

318
Art Director: **Milton Glaser**
Designer: **Karen Skelton**
Photographers: **Jon Brenneis, Philippe Charliat,
Michel Desjardins, Matthew Klein, Jean Marquis,
Sepp Seitz, Kenneth Siegel**
Writers: **Seth McCormick, Jean Claude Comert**
Client: **Schlumberger, Ltd.**
Agency: **Milton Glaser, Inc.**

319
Art Director: **Alicia Landon**
Designer: **Corpcom Services Inc.**
Artist: **Tom Bazzel**
Writer: **Nicholas Iammartino**
Client: **Celanese Corporation, Mr. Donald Ogilvie**
Agency: **Corpcom Services Inc.**

320
Art Director: **Linda Hinrichs**
Designers: **Linda Hinrichs, Lenore Bartz**
Photographers: **Tom Tracy, John McDermott**
Writer: **Bill McClave**
Client: **Transamerica**
Publisher: **Graphic Arts Center**
Agency: **Jonson Pedersen Hinrichs & Shakery**

321
Art Director: **Nancy Hoefig**
Designer: **Nancy Hoefig**
Photographer: **Gary McCoy**
Writer: **Charlie Allan**
Client: **Ridglea Bank**
Agency: **Richards, Sullivan, Brock & Assoc/
The Richards Group**

322
Art Director: **Bennett Robinson**
Designer: **Bennett Robinson**
Photographer: **Jay Maisel**
Writer: **Austin Mayer**
Client: **Standard Oil Company (Ohio)**
Agency: **Corporate Graphics Inc.**

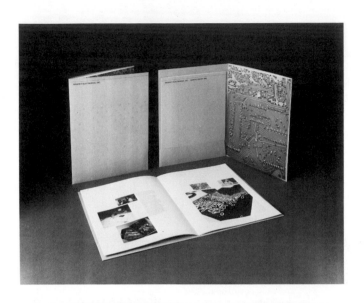

323
Art Director: **Dawn Keller**
Designer: **Dawn Keller**
Photographer: **Richard Spahr**
Writer: **Amy Lincoln/Design Forum**
Client: **Regency Electronics, Inc.**
Agency: **RMS Advertising**

324
Art Director: **Reginald Jones**
Designer: **Ellen Smith**
Photographer: **John Blaustein**
Client: **Victoria Station, Incorporated**

325
Art Director: **Reginald Jones**
Designer: **Ellen Smith**
Photographer: **John Blaustein**
Client: **Reading and Bates**

326
Art Director: **Lella Vignelli**
Designer: **Peter Laundy**
Photographers: **Richard Avedon, Bruce Weber, Uri Rose,**
Alex Chatlain, Peter Aaron
Writer: **Ronald Frankel**
Client: **Puritan Fashions Corporation**

Federal Express Corporation   Annual Report   1981

328
Art Director: **Ken Parkhurst**
Designer: **Peter Sargent**
Photographer: **Tom Tracy**
Client: **National Semiconductor Corp.**

327
Art Director: **Bob Glassman**
Designer: **Dagfinn Olsen**
Photographer: **Dana Duke**
Client: **Federal Express Corporation**
Printer: **Sanders Printing**
Agency: **The Graphic Expression, Inc.**

329
Art Director: **Richard Holmes**
Designers: **Ronald Morris, Connie Simon**
Photographer: **Scott Williamson**
Writer: **Don Burns**
Client: **Newport Harbour National Bank**
Prod'n Co: **Austin Printing**
Agency: **Richard Holmes Advertising & Design**

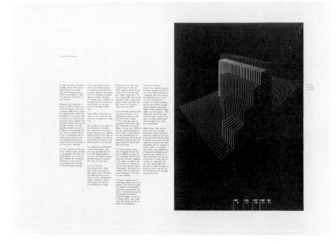

331
Art Director: **Bennett Robinson**
Designer: **Bennett Robinson**
Photographers: **Farrell Grehan, Charles Harbutt, Mattthew Klein, Arthur Lavine**
Artist: **Pierre Le Tan**
Writer: **Judy Mangiero**
Client: **Chase Manhattan Corporation**
Agency: **Corporate Graphics Inc.**

332
Art Director: **Kit Hinrichs**
Designers: **Kit Hinrichs, Lenore Bartz**
Photographer: **John Blaustein**
Writer: **Dave Sanson, Crocker National Corp.**
Client: **Crocker National Corporation**
Publisher: **Graphic Arts Center, Portland**
Agency: **Jonson Pedersen Hinrichs & Shakery**

333
Art Directors: **Jim Berte, Rik Besser**
Designer: **Rik Besser**
Artists: **Paul Rice, Kenji Matsumoto**
Client: **Electro Rent Corporation**
Agency: **Robert Miles Runyan & Associates**

334
Art Director: **Neil Shakery**
Designer: **Neil Shakery**
Photographer: **Jay Freis, Nick Pavlov, Robert Jamieson**
Writer: **Harry Matte, Amfac**
Client: **Amfac**
Publisher: **George Rice & Sons/Edwards Enterprises**
Agency: **Jonson Pederson Hinrichs & Shakery**

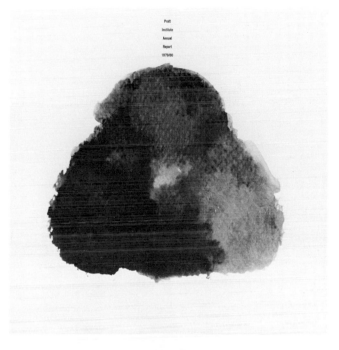

336
Art Director: **Joseph J. Azzinaro**
Designer: **Michael McGinn**
Photographers: **Jeanne Strongin, Marc Weinstein, Doug Wonders**
Artists: **Steve Bennett, Judy Pensky, Sharon Gresh, Scott Menchin**
Writers: **Joseph J. Azzinaro, Marie Avona, Ayana Johnson**
Editor: **Joseph J. Azzinaro**
Publisher/Client: **Division of External Affairs, Pratt Institute**
Agency: **Michael McGinn Inc.**

335
Art Director: **Alan Spaeth**
Designer: **Alan Spaeth**
Photographers: **Bill Crump, Robert Latorre**
Writer: **Robert A. Wilson**
Client: **Texas Industries, Inc.**
Agency: **Robert A. Wilson Associates**

337
Art Director: **Les Silva**
Designers: **Chris Hill, Les Silva**
Photographer: **Arthur Myerson**
Writers: **Ken Bernhardt, Paul MacAlester, Rayna Ware**
Client: **Hillsborough County Aviation Authority**
Agency: **Louis Benito Advertising**

338
Art Director: **Steven Liska**
Designer: **Steven Liska**
Photographers: **various**
Artists: **various**
Writer: **Susan Tash**
Client: **Playboy Enterprises, Inc.**
Publisher: **Playboy Enterprises, Inc.**
Agency: **Liska and Associates**

339
Art Director: **Kit Hinrichs**
Designers: **Kit Hinrichs, Arlene Finger**
Photographer: **Tom Tracy**
Writer: **Delphine Hirasuna**
Client: **Potlatch Corporation**
Printer: **Anderson Lithograph**
Agency: **Jonson Pedersen Hinrichs & Shakery**

340
Art Director: **Lou Silverstein**
Designers: **Philip Gips, Steven Fabrizio**
Photographers: **Duane Michaels, others**
Writer: **Elliott Sanger**
Client: **The New York Times Company**
Editor: **Leonard Harris**

341
Art Director: **Kerry Bierman**
Designers: **David Bates, Kerry Bierman,**
Barbara Wasserman Vinson & Judy Beniot
Writers: **George Couch, Chris Svare, Sandee Carman**
Photographers: **Joe DeNatale, Michael Vollen**
Client: **American Hospital Supply Corporation**
Editor: **George Couch**

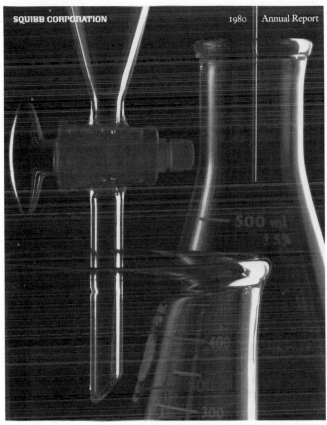

342
Art Director: **Bruce Blackburn**
Designers: **Bruce Blackburn, G. Bruce Johnson**
Photographers: **Eric Meola, D. Kingdon, C. Raymond, R. Doytos, J. Salenetri**
Artists: **Petrea McDonald, Juliet Shen, Phil Goldberg**
Writer: **Squibb Corporation**
Client: **Squibb Corporation**

343
Art Director: **Chris Rovillo**
Designers: **Chris Rovillo, Ron Sullivan**
Illustrator: **Ruth Brunner-Strosser**
Writer: **Dave Smith**
Client: **Centex Corporation**
Agency: **Richards, Sullivan, Brock & Assoc/ The Richards Group**

344
Art Director: **James Borcherdt**
Designer: **James Borcherdt**
Photographer: **Steve Kline**
Writer: **James Richardson**
Client: **U.S. National Bank**
Agency: **Lord, Sullivan & Yoder Advertising, Inc.**

345
Art Director: **Bruce Blackburn**
Designers: **Bruce Blackburn, Stephen Loges**
Photographer: **Jeff Perkel**
Writer: **American District Telegraph Company**
Client: **American District Telegraph Company**

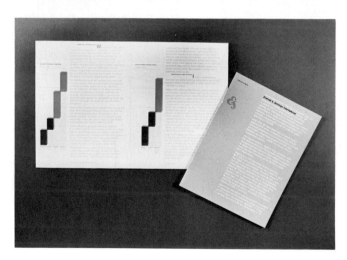

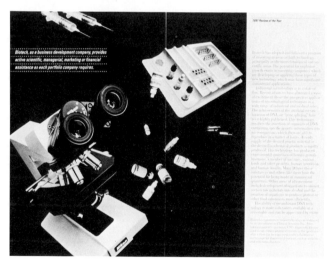

346
Art Director: **Herman L. Vander Berg**
Designers: **Debra Schultz, Herman L. Vander Berg**
Photographers: **John Lewis Stage, Ernst Haas, Bob Day, John Hill**
Client: **The Interpublic Group of Companies**
Agency: **The Marschalk Company, Inc.**

348
Art Director: **Neil Shakery**
Designers: **Neil Shakery, Barbara Vick**
Artist: **Jean Michel Folon**
Writer: **Foremost-McKesson**
Client: **Foremost-McKesson**
Publisher: **Graphic Arts Center, Portland**
Agency: **Jonson Pederson Hinrichs & Shakery**

347
Art Director: **Emmett Morava**
Designer: **Heidi-Marie Blackwell**
Client: **Everest & Jennings**
Agency: **Cross Associates**

349
Art Director: **Randee Rafkin-Rubin**
Designers: **Randee Rafkin-Rubin, George Shakespear**
Photographer: **Paul Elfenbein**
Writer: **Biotech Capitol Corporation**
Client: **Biotech Capitol Corporation**

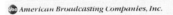

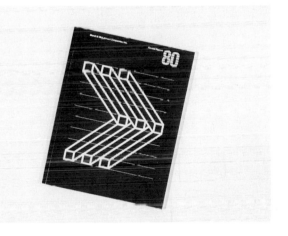

WORK
WORK
WORK

California
Human Development
Corporation

Annual Report
1980

351
Art Directors. **Gene Rosner, Kathleen Sullivan Kaska**
Designer. **Chris Broquet**
Photographers: **Various**
Writer: **James L. Podany**
Client: **Sears-Roebuck Foundation**
Agency: **Brown & Rosner, Inc.**

352
Art Directors: **Philip Gips, Diana Graham**
Designers: **Philip Gips, Diana Graham, Gina Stone**
Photographers: **Steve Fenn, others**
Writer: **Corporate Affairs Department**
Client: **American Broadcasting Companies, Inc.**

353
Art Director: **Wayne D. Gibb**
Designer: **Wayne D. Gibb**
Photographer: **Ken Light**
Writer: **Wayne D. Gibb**
Client: **California Human Development Corporation**
Publisher: **California Human Development Corporation**

354
Art Director: **Karen Kutner Katinas**
Designer: **Karen Kutner Katinas**
Photographer. **Cheryl Rossum**
Artist: **Charles Katinas**
Writer: **Barbara J. Walker**
Client: **Marsh & McLennan Companies, Inc.**
Agency: **Corporate Annual Reports, Inc.**

355
Art Director: **Beverly Schrager**
Designer: **Corporate Annual Reports**
Photographer: **Jay Maisel**
Writer: **Ronald S. Ziemba**
Client: **Chesebrough-Pond's Inc.**
Agency: **Corporate Annual Reports**

356
Art Director: **Tartak/Libera Design, Inc.**
Designers: **Joan D. Libera, Gary Baker**
Photographers: **Steven Kahn, Muench**
Writers: **Eugene Heller, Silverman-Heller**
Client: **Petrominerals Corporation**

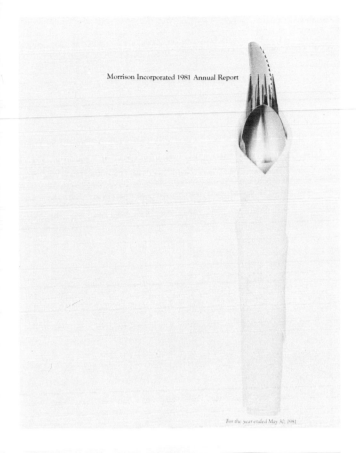

Morrison Incorporated 1981 Annual Report

For the year ended May 30, 1981

Innovation

The pictorial essay on the following pages is about innovation at SCM. We think this is a subject of deep significance for all American industry, not just SCM's small part of it.

It's important to remember that "innovation" isn't limited to glamorous items like computers, lasers and genetic engineering. An innovation is anything new or improved, whether esoteric or mundane. We consider the innovative process so important to SCM's future that it was selected as the theme of our first corporate advertising program, launched earlier this year. Using full-page advertisements in *The Wall Street Journal*, we tell readers that through research and development the people of SCM are constantly working to invent new products and improve existing ones.

Innovation is time-consuming and expensive, but it is a necessary process if SCM is to remain a leader in the five basic businesses in which we are involved. New products and processes are developed to meet a variety of business objectives. Some recent SCM innovations: an electronic office typewriter that sells for less than most clock or office models, a water-based liner for beer and beverage cans that meets environmental standards while saving energy, a new, energy-efficient toaster, an improved liquid shortening that enables bakeries to be more efficient. Most important, each of these products has already made or is soon expected to make an important contribution to SCM profits.

On a larger scale, innovation is vital in all industries if America is to remain at the forefront of technology and maintain its position in world markets that in recent years has been eroded by foreign competition.

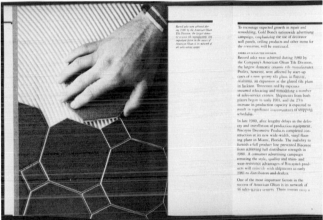

Record sales were achieved during 1980 by the Company's American Olean Tile Division, the largest domestic ceramic tile manufacturer...

To encourage expected growth in repair and remodeling, Gold Bond's nationwide advertising campaign, emphasizing the use of decorative wall panels, ceiling products and other items for the consumer, will be continued.

AMERICAN STOCK EXCHANGE
Since the birth of this nation, the outdoor "Curb" market and its successor, the American Stock Exchange, have funnelled capital into America's emerging enterprises. In this report, we look back at the ingenuity and perseverance that laid the foundation of the people's marketplace of today...and tomorrow.

ANNUAL REPORT
1980

357
Art Director: **Tom Wood**
Designers: **Tom Wood, Susan Templeton**
Photographers: **Charlie Lathem, Graphics
Associates, Inc.**
Writer: **Marc Schenker**
Client: **Morrisons Incorporated**
Agency: **Creative Services, Inc.**

359
Art Director: **Arnold Saks**
Designer: **Robert Jakob**
Photographers: **Gary Gladstone, Peggy Barnett**
Client: **SCM Corporation**
Agency: **Arnold Saks Inc.**

358
Art Director: **Woody Pirtle**
Photographer: **Gary McCoy**
Client: **National Gypsum Company**
Agency: **Arnold Harwell McClain & Assoc., Inc.**

360
Art Director: **David Bloch, Irwin Graulich**
Designer: **Lloyd Miller**
Photographers: **Various**
Client: **American Stock Exchange**
Publisher: **American Stock Exchange**
Agency: **Bloch Graulich Whelan Inc.**

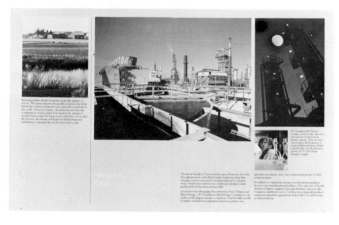

361
Art Director: **Victor Gialleonardo**
Designer: **Patricia Allen**
Photographers: **William Rivelli, Bob Colton**
Artist: **Frank Bozzo**
Client: **French American Banking Corporation**
Agency: **Doremus Design**

362
Art Director: **John Dearlove**
Designer: **Terry Okura**
Photographers: **Alex Bachnick, Robert B. Tolchin**
Writer: **Bob Kolcz**
Client: **CF Industries, Inc.**
Agency: **Creative Directions Inc.**

363
Art Directors: **Steve Bisch, Jeff Jackson**
Designer: **Steve Bisch**
Photographer: **Bob Maxham**
Writers: **Dirk Ronk, David Ham**
Client: **Victoria Bankshares, Inc.**
Agency: **ReedHam Jackson, Inc.**

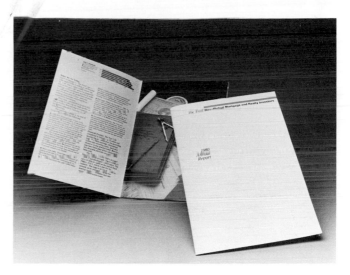

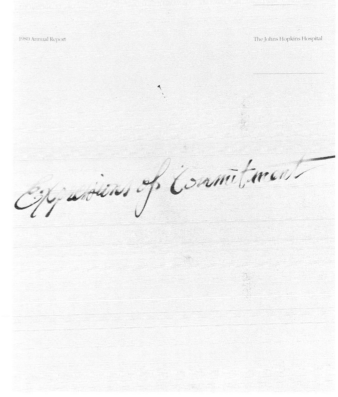

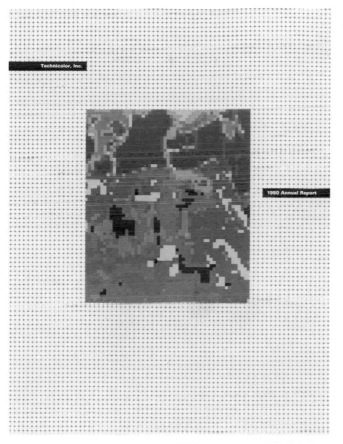

364
Art Director: **Jim Berte**
Designer: **Jim Berte**
Photographer: **Steve Kahn**
Client: **Technicolor, Inc.**
Agency: **Robert Miles Runyan & Associates**

365
Art Director: **Arnold Saks**
Designer: **Ingo Scharrenbroich**
Photographer: **Burk Uzzle/Magnum**
Client: **Northwest Energy Company**
Agency: **Arnold Saks Associates**

366
Art Director: **Arnold Wechsler**
Designer: **Patty Nalle**
Photographer: **Jim Kiernan**
Client: **MassMutual Mortgage and Realty Investors**

367
Art Director: **David A. Ashton**
Designer: **David A. Ashton**
Photographer: **Richard Anderson**
Writer: **Terry Fortunato**
Client: **Johns Hopkins Hospital**
Agency: **Ashton-Worthington, Inc.**

369
Art Director: **Ken Resen**
Designer: **Ken Resen**
Photographers: **Hiro, Chas. Harbutt, etc.**
Writer: **Burt Kaplan**
Client: **Revlon, Inc.**
Editor: **Roger Shelley, Revlon, Inc.**
Publisher: **Revlon, Inc.**
Director of Design: **Martin Stevens, Revlon, Inc.**
Agency: **Page, Arbitrio & Resen**

368
Art Director: **John Milligan**
Designer: **Lynda Fishbourne**
Writer: **Steve Wallis**
Client: **Alpha Industries**

370
Art Director: **Wes Keebler**
Designers: **B.K. Hughes, Wes Keebler**
Photographer: **Richard Clark**
Writer: **Lou Loeb**
Client: **Countrywide Credit Industries, Inc.**
Agency: **The Webb Silberg Company**

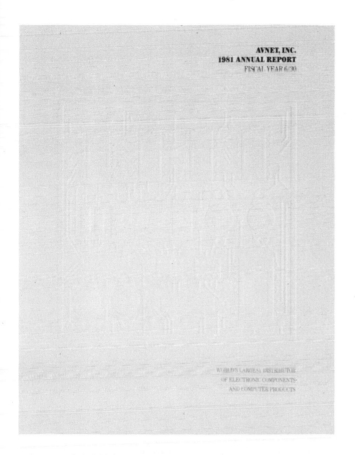

AVNET, INC.
1981 ANNUAL REPORT
FISCAL YEAR 600

WORLD'S LARGEST DISTRIBUTOR
OF ELECTRONIC COMPONENTS
AND COMPUTER PRODUCTS

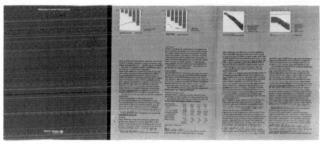

371
Art Director: **Herb Lubalin**
Designer: **Mike Aron**
Artist: **Mike Aron**
Editor: **Avnet, Inc.**
Client: **Avnet, Inc.**
Publisher: **Avnet, Inc.**
Production Co.: **Konner Printing Co.**

372
Art Director: **Dick Mitchell**
Designer: **Dick Mitchell**
Photographer: **Greg Booth**
Writers: **A.C. Greene, John Stone**
Client: **Mercantile Texas Corporation**
Agency: **Richards, Sullivan, Brock & Assoc./
The Richards Group**

373
Art Director: **Loren Weeks**
Designer: **Loren Weeks**
Photographers: **Jerome Hart, Louis Bencze**
Artist: **Dan Mandish**
Writers: **Tim Leigh, Nancy Hearon**
Client: **Cascade Steel Rolling Mills**
Publisher/Printer: **Schultz/Wack/Weir**
Agency: **Bronson Leigh Weeks**

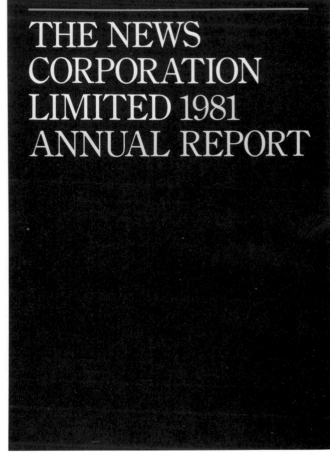

374
Art Director: **Alan Fletcher**
Designers: **Alan Fletcher, Paul Anthony**
Photographer: **Brian Duffy**
Artist: **Wolf Spoerl**
Agency: **Pentagram Design**

375
Art Director: **Peter Harrison**
Designer: **Susan Hochbaum**
Photographers: **Neil Selkirk, Mickey Kaufman, George Bennett**
Writer: **John Berendt**
Client: **The News Corporation Limited**
Agency: **Pentagram Design**

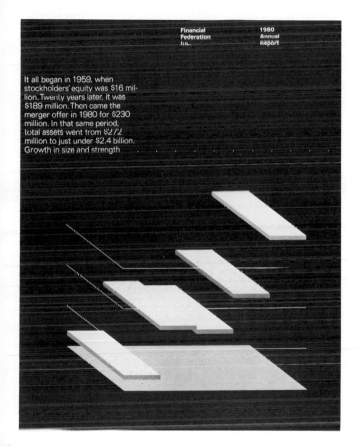

Financial Federation Inc.

1980 Annual Report

It all began in 1959, when stockholders' equity was $16 million. Twenty years later, it was $189 million. Then came the merger offer in 1980 for $230 million. In that same period, total assets went from $272 million to just under $2.4 billion. Growth in size and strength

THE E.F. HUTTON GROUP INC. ANNUAL REPORT 1980

"Hutton's 77 years of uninterrupted profits are unmatched in the securities industry"

376
Art Director: **Thomas D. Ohmer**
Designer: **Koji Takei**
Artist: **Koji Takei, Don Oka**
Writer: **Robert Wolcott**
Client: **Financial Federation, Inc.**
Agency: **Advertising Designers, Inc.**

377
Art Director: **Robin Davis**
Designer: **Robin Davis**
Photographer: **Cheryl Rossum**
Writer: **E.F. Hutton**
Client: **Robert Fomon C.E.O.**
Publisher: **E.F. Hutton**

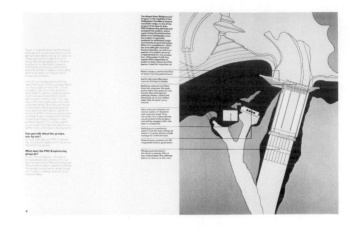

379
Art Director: **Don Ervin**
Designer: **John Laughlin**
Artist: **Nick Fasciano**
Writer: **David Boorstin**
Client: **Planning Research Corporation**
Agency: **Siegel & Gale**

378
Art Director: **Jeff Moriber**
Designer: **Jeff Moriber**
Writer: **Hill and Knowlton, Inc.**
Client: **Rabobank**
Agency: **Hill and Knowlton, Inc.**

380
Art Director: **Jeffrey Moriber**
Designer: **Jeffrey Moriber**
Photographers: **H. Clay White, Dave Mjolsness**
Writer: **David Satterfield**
Client: **A.E. Staley**
Agency: **Hill and Knowlton, Inc.**

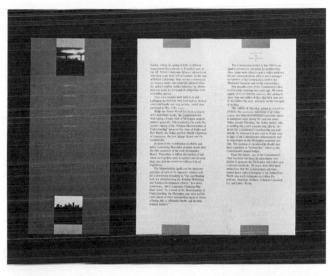

381
Art Director: **Randee Rafkin-Rubin**
Designer: **Randee Rafkin-Rubin**
Photographer: **Paul Elfenbein**
Writer: **Jack Galub**
Client: **Marubeni America Corporation**

383
Creative Director: **Bob Dennard**
Art Director: **Rex Peteet**
Designer: **Rex Peteet**
Photographer: **Gary McCoy**
Writer: **Dudley Lynch**
Client: **North Texas Commission**
Agency: **Dennard Creative, Inc.**

382
Art Director: **Reginald Jones**
Designer: **Dawson Zaug**
Photographer: **John Blaustein**
Client: **Homestake Mining Company**

384
Art Director: **Eugene J. Grossman**
Designer: **Eugene J. Grossman**
Client: **Aero-Flow Dynamics, Inc.**
Agency: **Anspach Grossman Portugal Inc.**

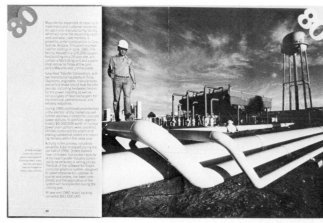

386
Art Director: **Peter Harrison**
Designer: **Randee R. Rubin**
Photographer: **Dick Durrance II**
Writer: **Ogden Corporation**
Client: **Ogden Corporation**

385
Art Director: **Richard Hess**
Designer: **Richard Hess**
Photographer: **Tom Hollyman**
Artist: **Mark Hess**
Client: **Champion International Corporation**
Publisher: **Case-Hoyt Rochester**

387
Art Director: **Jay Loucks**
Designers: **Jay Loucks, C. Randall Sherman**
Photographer: **Joe Baraban**
Client: **Industrias CM**
Agency: **Loucks Atelier, Houston**

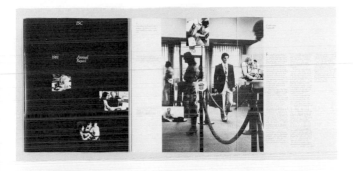

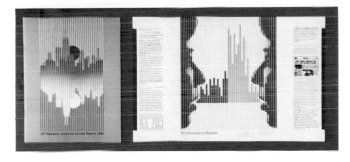

388
Art Director: **Lee Beggs**
Designer: **Lee Beggs**
Photographers: **Paul Ambrose, Casey Mallough**
Writer: **John Lindeblad/ISC Systems Corp.**
Client: **ISC Systems Corporation**
Agency: **Paul Ambrose Studios**

389
Art Directors: **Philip Gips, Aubrey Balkind**
Designer: **Jane Cullen**
Photographer: **John Hill**
Writer: **Peter Hauk**
Client: **Macmillan, Inc.**

390
Art Directors: **Herb Lubalin, Alan Peckolick**
Designers: **Herb Lubalin, Alan Peckolick**
Client: **Touche Ross**
Publisher: **Touche Ross**
Production Co.: **Sanders Printing Co.**

391
Art Director: **Gene Rosner**
Designer: **Gene Rosner**
Photographer: **Don Anderson**
Artist: **George Panfil**
Writer: **Paula Norton**
Client: **IIT Research Institute**
Agency: **Brown & Rosner, Inc.**

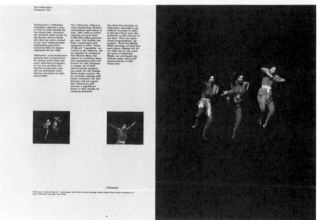

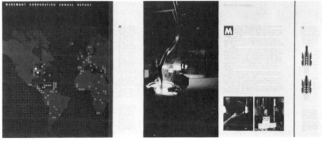

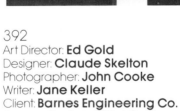

392
Art Director: **Ed Gold**
Designer: **Claude Skelton**
Photographer: **John Cooke**
Writer: **Jane Keller**
Client: **Barnes Engineering Co.**
Agency: **Barton-Gillet Co.**

393
Art Director: **Gene Rosner**
Designer: **Rachel Schreiber Levitan**
Photographer: **Bruce Thomas**
Artist: **George Panfil**
Writer: **Jane Ranshaw**
Client: **Maremont Corporation**
Editor: **M. Robert Wolfson**
Agency: **Brown & Rosner, Inc.**

394
Art Director: **Judy Anderson**
Designer: **Judy Anderson**
Photographer: **Allen Birnbach**
Client: **Baldwin-United**
Publisher: **Printing Service Company**

395
Art Director: **Jim Berte**
Designer: **Jim Berte**
Photographer: **Steve Kahn**
Client: **Technicolor, Inc.**
Agency: **Robert Miles Runyan & Associates**

Pension Investment Management

1981 Report
Pooled Separate Accounts
Ætna Life Insurance Company
Group Pension Department

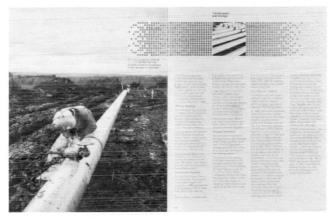

396
Art Director: **Sande Bristol**
Designers: **Sande Bristol, Stan Domian**
Photographers: **Al Ferreira, Mark Sitkin, Jack McConnell**
Writer: **Theresa Carpentieri**
Client: **Max Smith, AVP, Employee Benefits Division**
Editor: **Karen Avery**
Publisher: **Aetna Life & Casualty**
Director: **Jack Mastrianni**
Production Co.: **The Waverly Printing Co.**
Agency: **Creative Services; Corporate Communications**

397
Art Director: **Robert Meyer**
Designer: **Robert Meyer**
Photographer: **Ted Kawalerski**
Artist: **Chris Duke**
Client: **Gannett Co., Inc.**
Agency: **Robert Meyer Design, Inc.**

398
Art Director: **Bob Pellegrini**
Designer: **Ed Broderick**
Photographer: **Camille Vickers**
Artist: **Enno Poersch**
Client: **Peabody International Corp.**
Agency: **Pellegrini and Associates, Inc.**

399
Art Director: **Diane Wasserman**
Designer: **Diane Wasserman**
Artist: **Eric Goto**
Writer: **Bruce Quayle**
Client: **Columbia Gas System**
Agency: **Hill and Knowlton, Inc.**

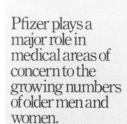

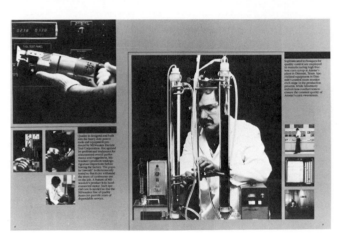

400
Art Director: **Alan Peckolick**
Designer: **Alan Peckolick**
Photographer: **Frank Moscati**
Artist: **Fred Otnes**
Writers: **Grupo Industrial Alfa, Rita Gurbert, Mark Strage**
Client: **Jesus Guzman**
Agency: **Corporate Annual Reports, Inc.**

401
Art Director: **Bob Pellegrini**
Designer: **Ed Broderick**
Photographer: **Cheryl Rossum**
Client: **Amstar Corporation**
Agency: **Pellegrini and Associates, Inc.**

402
Art Director: **Bennett Robinson**
Designer: **Naomi Burstein**
Photographers: **Ian Berry, Elliott Erwitt, Matthew Klein**
Client: **Pfizer Inc.**
Agency: **Corporate Graphics Inc.**

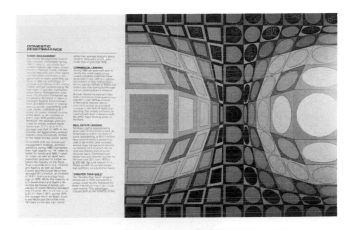

403
Art Director: **Bennett Robinson**
Designer: **Naomi Burstein**
Photographers: **Ian Berry, Matthew Klein**
Client: **Consolidated Foods Corporation**
Agency: **Corporate Graphics Inc.**

405
Art Director: **Joseph Piatti**
Designer: **Daniel Terdoslavich**
Photographer: **Ray Fisher**
Artist: **Vasarely**
Writers: **Alex Benet, Penny Lambeth**
Client: **First National Bank of Greater Miami**
Agency: **Piatti/Wolk Design Associates, Inc.**

404
Art Director: **Ron Jefferies**
Designer: **Claudia Jefferies**
Photographer: **William James Warren**
Writer: **Frederick J. Fajardo**
Client: **Fluor Corporation**
Agency: **The Jefferies Association**

406
Art Director: **Richard Foy**
Designer: **Julie Gerblick**
Photographer: **The Photo Works/Richard Foy**
Writer: **Paul Harris**
Client: **NBI, Inc.**
Agency: **Communication Arts Inc.**

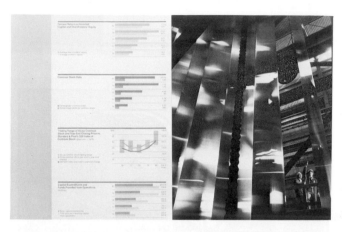

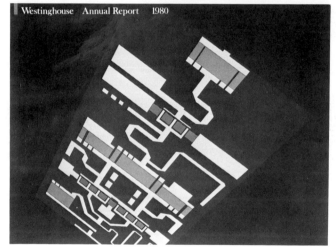

413
Art Director: **Arnold Wechsler**
Designer: **Patty Nalle**
Photographers: **Burt Glinn, Dick Frank**
Client: **Scott Paper Company**
Agency: **Mayo-Infurna Design Inc.**

415
Art Director: **Arnold Saks**
Designer: **Robert Jakob**
Photographer: **Burk Uzzle, Magnum**
Client: **Aluminum Company of America**
Agency: **Arnold Saks Inc.**

414
Art Directors: **Martin Bennett, Randall Hensley**
Designers: **Martin Bennett, Randall Hensley**
Photographer: **Doug Barber**
Writer: **Bernice A. Thieblot**
Client: **Allentown & Sacred Heart Hospital Center**
Agency: **The North Charles Street Design Organization**

416
Art Director: **Benjamin R. Larrabee**
Photographers: **Jack Merhaut, Dick Luria**
Artists: **Peter Wing, Mark Fainstein, Toby Seger**
Writer: **Patricia Shields**
Client: **Westinghouse Electric Corporation**
Agency: **Westinghouse Corporate Graphic Design**

F.W. Woolworth Co.
Annual Report

1980

*Warner Communications Inc.
Annual Report
1980*

417
Art Director: **James N. Miho**
Designers: **James N. Miho, Berenice Abbott,
Jane Evelyn Atwood**
Photographers: **Eisenstaedt, Gerda Taro, David
Seymour, Bill Jones, Roland I. Freeman, Lou Bernstein,
Herbert List, Don McCullin, Frederick Sommer**
Writers: **Jacob Riis, John Abrams, Stephen Singer,
Ann Doherty**
Client: **International Center of Photography**
Director: **Cornell Capa**

418
Art Director: **Richard J. Whelan**
Designers: **Richard J. Whelan, Carol Grasmehr**
Photographers: **Matthew Klein, Skip Hine**
Client: **F.W. Woolworth Co.**
Agency: **The Whelan Design Office Inc.**

419
Art Director: **Reginald Jones**
Designer: **Dawson Zaug**
Photographers: **Paul Fusco, Rudy Legname**
Client: **Monogram Industries, Inc.**
Agency: **Unigraphics**

420
Art Director: **Peter Harrison**
Designer: **Susan Hochbaum**
Photographers: **Neil Selkirk, Neil Slavin, Joel Sternfeld,
Mickey Kaufman, Arnold Newman**
Writers: **John Berendt, Kon Platnick, Paul Duffy**
Client: **Warner Communications Inc.**
Agency: **Pentagram Design**

422
Art Director: **Eugene J. Grossman**
Designer: **Sandra Meyers**
Photographer: **Arthur Beck**
Writer: **Eliot Tozer**
Client: **Alghanim Industries**
Production Co.: **Sanders Printing**
Agency: **Anspach Grossman Portugal Inc.**

421
Art Director: **Margie Coates**
Designer: **Margie Coates**
Artist: **Margie Coates**
Writer: **The Hanley Partnership, Inc.**
Client: **Anheuser-Busch, Inc.**
Agency: **The Hanley Partnership, Inc.**

423
Art Director: **Eugene J. Grossman**
Designers: **Ken Godat, Don Burg**
Photographer: **Arnold Newman**
Client: **Peat, Marwick, Mitchell & Co.**
Production Co.: **Crafton Graphics Company, Inc.**
Agency: **Anspach Grossman Portugal Inc.**

424
Art Directors: **Craig Bernhardt, Janice Fudyma**
Designers: **C. Bernhardt, J. Fudyma, D. Duerr, R. Gorman, K. Thompson**
Photographers: **Various**
Artists: **Various**
Writers: **Various**
Client: **W.R. Grace & Co.**
Editor: **J. Cole**
Publisher: **W.R. Grace & Co.**
Agency: **Bernhardt Fudyma Design Group**

425
Art Director: **Ted Nagata**
Designer: **Ted Nagata**
Photographer: **Grant Heaton**
Artists: **Eric Robinson, D.J. Hutchinson, Jillaire Robinson, Mark Hess, Ted Nagata, Brent Croxton, Greg Erickson, Paul Seo, Cal Nez**
Client: **Art Directors Salt Lake City**

GRACE HAS BIRDS IN ITS PARADISE
Phosphate mines are transformed into animal and people havens in south-central Florida.

When Grace runs into a sailor—or a relative of one—from old shipping days, the company always treats him well. Even if he happens to be a double-crested cormorant. This marine bird thrives in south-central Florida on Grace's phosphate fertilizer mine property which the company is reclaiming for animal habitats, cattle ranches, housing subdivisions, orange groves, industrial parks and shopping centers. By coincidence, the cormorant's cousin, the guanay cormorant on the Chincha and Ballestas Islands off the Peruvian coast, helps produce guano fertilizer, which gave Grace its business start more than 125 years ago.

Egrets nestle in water recirculating area, courtesy of Grace.

In its way, this odd partnership—the cormorant and the corporation—keynotes Grace's environmental philosophy: that business, animals, plants and people are family partners in the Peaceable Kingdom.

Family ties extend to the company's other Florida friends: wood storks, alligators, armadillos and cabbage palms. Grace identifies these and hundreds more wild neighbors on its phosphate properties before its Agricultural Chemicals dragline sinks iron teeth into each new phosphate mine. Never a ruin-and-run operator, Ag Chem has been rehabilitating land since its mining start near Lakeland 27 years ago—when today's government regulations did not exist. "We always thought reclamation

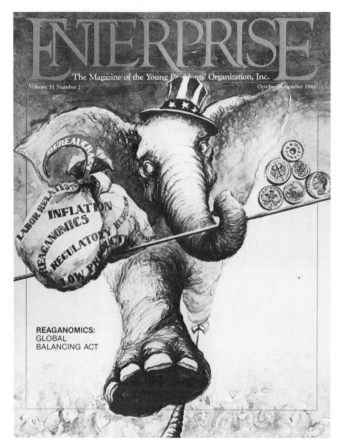

REAGANOMICS:
GLOBAL
BALANCING ACT

426
Art Director: **Victor Cevoli**
Designer: **Victor Cevoli**
Client: **Polaroid**
Editor: **Marnie Samuelson**

427
Art Directors: **Craig Bernhardt, Janice Fudyma**
Designers: **C. Bernhardt, J. Fudyma, D. Duerr, R. Gorman, K. Thompson**
Photographers: **Various**
Artists: **Various**
Writers: **Various**
Client: **W.R. Grace & Co.**
Editor: **Joyce Cole**
Publisher: **W.R. Grace & Co.**
Agency: **Bernhardt Fudyma Design Group**

428
Art Director: **Lori Barra**
Designer: **Lori Barra**
Artist: **Kimberely Belger**
Writers: **Various**
Client: **Young Presidents Organization**
Editor: **Alice B. Berkowitz**
Publisher: **William E. Havemeyer**

429
Art Director: **Don Johnson**
Designer: **Bonnie Berish**
Photographers: **George Mattei & Robert Schlegel**
Writer: **Melvin J. Grayson**
Client: **Nabisco Brands, Inc.**
Editor: **M. Virginia McLeod**
Agency: **Johnson & Simpson Graphic Designers**

430
Art Director: **Linda Hinrichs**
Designer: **Linda Hinrichs**
Artists: **John Hayatt, Paul Fusco, Ward Schumaker,
Philipe Weisbecker**
Writer: **Delphine Hirasuna, Potlatch Corp.**
Client: **Potlatch Corp.**
Publisher: **George Rice & Sons**
Agency: **Jonson Pedersen Hinrichs & Shakery**

431
Art Director: **Eugene J. Gossman**
Designer: **Ken Godat, Sandra Meyers**
Writer: **Anspach Grossman Portugal Inc.**
Client: **Peat, Marwick, Mitchell & Co.**
Production Co.: **Craflon Graphic Company, Inc.**
Agency: **Anspach Grossman Portugal Inc.**

432
Art Director: **Brian Boyd**
Designers: **Brian Boyd, Scott Eggers**
Artists: **Various**
Writer: **Joel Sarrett**
Client: **Muscular Dystrophy Association**
Agency: **Richards, Sullivan, Brock & Assoc./
The Richards Group**

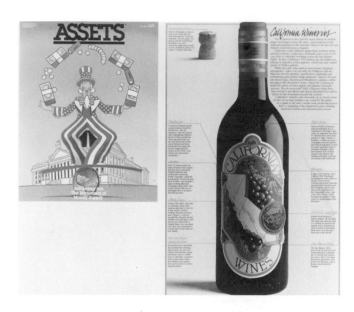

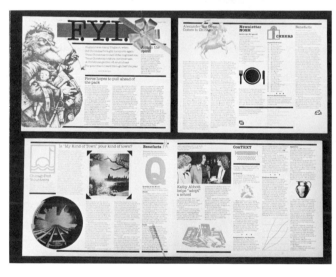

433
Art Director: **Kit Hinrichs**
Designers: **Kit Hinrichs, Barbara Vick**
Photographers: **Tom Tracy, Armando Diaz, George Hall**
Artists: **Everett Peck, Dennis Ziemienski, Steve Gerber**
Writer: **Dave Sanson, Crocker National Corp.**
Client: **Crocker National Corporation**
Editor: **Peterson & Dodge**
Publisher: **Graphic Arts Center**
Agency: **Johnson Pedersen Hinrichs & Shakery**

434
Art Director: **Kathy Forsythe**
Designers: **(1) Bill McDowell, (2) Caroline Hartwell,
(3) Kathy Forsythe**
Writers: **Marge Tresley, Dan Kubera, Diana Ichkoff**
Client: **CCA Employee Communications**
Editor: **Marge Tresley**
Agencies: **(1&2) Cagney & McDowell, (3) CCA
Communications**

435
Art Directors: **Robert Petrocelli, Michael Bracco**
Designers: **Robert Petrocelli, Michael Bracco**
Photographer: **Grant Roberts**
Artists: **Ivan Powell (inside), Bob Bidner (cover)**
Client: **Ted Bates Worldwide, Inc.**
Editor: **Jeanne Delsener**
Production Co.: **Sterling Regal Graphics**
Agency: **Ted Bates Worldwide, Inc.**

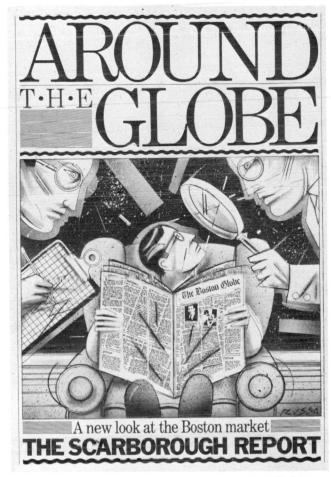

436
Art Director: **John Muller**
Designers: **John Muller, Mary Stanley**
Photographers: **Hartzell Grey, R.C. Nible**
Writers: **Rob Price, Jerry Schleicher**
Client: **Valentine-Radford, Inc.**
Editor: **Rob Price**
Publisher: **Valentine-Radford, Inc.**
Agency: **Valentine-Radford, Inc.**

437
Art Director: **Kit Hinrichs**
Designers: **Kit Hinrichs, Gillian Smith**
Photographers: **John Blaustein, Tom Tracy**
Writer: **Russom & Leeper**
Client: **Hills Bros.**
Publisher: **Pacific Rotaprinting**
Agency: **Jonson Pedersen Hinrichs & Shakery**

438
Art Director: **Terry Ross Koppel**
Designer: **Terry Ross Koppel**
Artist: **Anthony Russo**
Client: **The Boston Globe**
Editor: **Mary Jane Patrone**
Publisher: **The Boston Globe**
Agency: **T. Ross Koppel**

439
Art Director: **Harold Matossian**
Designer: **Steven Schnipper**
Client: **Knoll International**
Agency: **Knoll Graphics**

440
Art Director: **Kit Hinrichs**
Designers: **Kit Hinrichs, Barbara Vick**
Photographer: **John Blaustein**
Artists: **Steve Gerber, Tim Lewis, John Mattos,
Hank Osuna**
Writer: **Dave Sanson, Crocker National Corp.**
Client: **Crocker National Corporation**
Editor: **Peterson & Dodge**
Publisher: **Graphic Arts Center**
Agency: **Johnson Pedersen Hinrichs & Shakery**

441
Art Director: **Patrick Louden**
Designer: **Patrick Louden**
Artist: **Patrick Louden**
Client: **Pratt & Whitney Aircraft — Media
Communications**
Editor: **Steve Lokker**

442
Art Director: **Barry Bomzer**
Designers: **Barry Bomzer, Patrick McDonough**
Photographers: **Richard Wood, Jonathan Rawle,
Ted Polumbaum, Barry Bomzer, Arthur Leipzig**
Writers: **Julian Weiss, Fred Pillsbury, Margaret A. Bengs,
Maury Breecher, Jack Denton Scott, Robert Suarez**
Editor: **Robert Suarez**
Agency: **Bomzer Associates, Inc.**

443
Art Director: **Kit Hinrichs**
Designers: **Kit Hinrichs, Barbara Vick**
Artist: **John Mattos**
Writer: **Dave Sanson, Crocker National Corp.**
Client: **Crocker National Corporation**
Editor: **Peterson & Dodge**
Publisher: **Graphic Arts Center**
Agency: **Jonson Pedersen Hinrichs & Shakery**

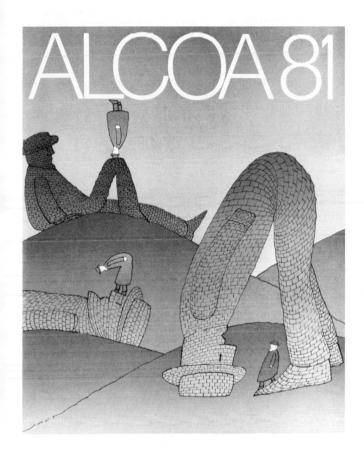

444
Art Director: **Barton Denmarsh Esteban**
Designer: **Barton Denmarsh Esteban**
Photographers: **Coz Zacharria, Clyde Hare**
Artists: **Folon, Robert Pryor, Dan Bridy**
Writers: **John Wright, Kathy Buechel, William Ochl,**
Yankelovich & Kaagan
Client: **John Wright—Mgr. Corporate Information—Alcoa**
Editor: **Kathy Buechel**
Publisher: **Aluminum Company of America**
Agency: **Barton Denmarsh Esteban**

445
Creative Director: **Robert E. Cargill**
Art Director: **Inge Fox**
Designers: **Inge Fox, Bonnie Lovell**
Photographers: **Neal Higgins (cover), various**
Artist: **Philip Wende**
Writers: **Various**
Client: **IBM—General Systems Division**
Editor: **Rosalind Ayres**
Publisher: **IBM**
Agency: **Cargill and Associates, Inc.**

446
Art Directors: **Mort Kallan, Michael Bracco**
Designers: **Mort Kallan, Michael Bracco**
Photographers: **Grant Roberts (inside),
Bjorn Winses (cover)**
Artist: **Norm Doherty**
Client: **Ted Bates Worldwide, Inc.**
Editor: **Jeanne Delsener**
Production Co: **Sterling Regal Graphics**
Agency: **Ted Bates Worldwide, Inc.**

447
Art Director: **James Jarratt**
Designers: **J.C. Almquist, Dana Jones**
Photographers: **Burgess Blevins, Ed Eckstein**
Project Managers: **Stephen Smiley, Jane Shannon**
Client: **Citibank**
Agency: **The Creative Department, Inc.**

448
Art Directors: **Mort Kallan, Michael Bracco**
Designers: **Mort Kallan, Michael Bracco**
Photographers: **Grant Roberts (inside),
Phil Marco (cover)**
Artist: **Teresa Fasolino**
Client: **Ted Bates Worldwide, Inc.**
Editor: **Jeanne Delsener**
Production Co: **Sterling Regal Graphics**
Agency: **Ted Bates Worldwide, Inc.**

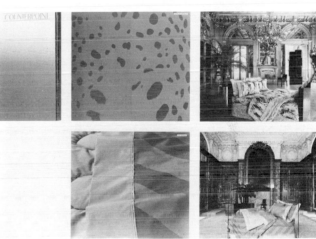

449
Art Director: **Bruce Blackburn**
Designers: **Bruce Blackburn, Stephen Loges**
Photographer: **Burt Glinn**
Writer: **IBM Corporate Personnel Communications**
Client: **IBM Corporation**
Editor: **Jerry Blood**

450   GOLD AWARD
Art Directors: **Jay Loucks, Chris Hill**
Designers: **Chris Hill, Mark Geer**
Photographer: **Gary Braasch**
Writer: **Lee Herrick**
Client: **Compendium**
Agency: **Loucks Atelier, Houston**

451   SILVER AWARD
Art Director: **Arthur Congdon**
Designer: **Arthur Congdon**
Photographer: **CBS Entertainment Division, Photo Unit**
Writer: **Barbara Coulter Cox**
Client: **CBS Television Network/Sales/Marketing
Services**
Editor: **Donald W. Evers, Jr.**
Publisher: **CBS Inc.**
Printer: **Eastern Press, Inc.**
Design Firm: **Congdon Macdonald Inc.**

452   DISTINCTIVE MERIT
Art Director: **James Sebastian**
Designers: **James Sebastian, Michael Lauretano**
Photographers: **Joe Standart, Elizabeth Heyert**
Writer: **Ralph Caplan**
Client: **MARTEX/West Point Pepperell**
Agency: **Designframe, Incorporated**

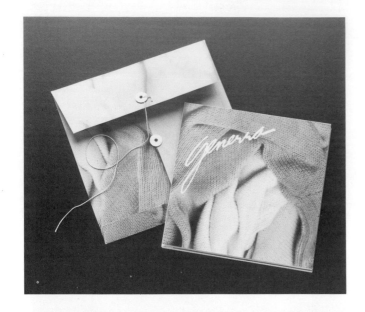

453
Art Directors: **David Eldelstein, Nancy Borin,
Lanny French**
Designers: **Wilkins & Peterson, Edelstein/Borin**
Photographer: **Mary Kay Bernitt**
Writer: **Ron Koliha**
Client: **Generra Sportswear**
Production Co.: **United Graphics**
Agency: **Edelstein/Borin Advertising**

454
Art Director: **Joseph M. Essex**
Designer: **Joseph M. Essex**
Photographers: **Eric Futran, Joseph M. Essex**
Artist: **Judith Austin Essex**
Writer: **Judith Austin Essex**
Client: **Judith Austin Essex/SX Design**
Agency: **Burson•Marsteller Design Group**

455
Art Director: **Barbara Shimkus**
Designer: **Barbara Shimkus**
Photographer: **Swain Edens**
Artist: **Diane McMurry**
Writer: **Ann Eklund-Phillips**
Client: **Guido Brothers Construction Co.**
Agency: **Barbara Shimkus/Graphic Design**

456
Art Director: **Marie Avona**
Designer: **Marie Avona**
Photographer: **Jeanne Strongin**
Artist: **Jeanine Colini**
Writer: **Admissions & Financial Aid Staff**
Client: **Pratt Institute**
Editor: **Marie Avona**
Publisher: **Marie Avona**

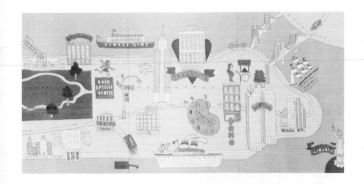

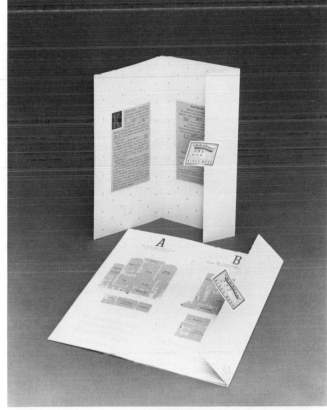

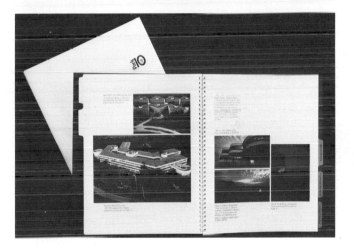

157
Art Directors: **Toshiko Mori, Jeffrey Blonde**
Designers: **Toshiko Mori, Jeffrey Blonde**
Photographer: **Robert Murray**
Artist: **Seymour Chwast**
Writers: **Kristin Joyce, Abbie Simon**
Client: **Greenwood Consultants**

459
Art Directors: **Marty Neumeier, Sandra Higashi**
Designers: **Sandra Higashi, Byron Glaser, Rikki Conrad**
Writers: **Marty Neumeier, Rikki Conrad**
Client: **C-D Investment Company**
Agency: **Neumeier Design Team**

458
Art Directors: **Harold Burch, Ken White**
Designer: **Harold Burch**
Artist: **Harold Burch**
Writer: **Art Paquette**
Client: **Aldus Type Studio, Ltd.**
Editor: **Art Paquette**
Agency: **Ken White Design Office, Inc.**

460
Art Director: **Jay Loucks**
Designers: **Jay Loucks, Betty Thomas**
Photographer: **Joe Baraban**
Artist: **Larry Olez**
Writers: **Paul Meyer, Roy Binion**
Client: **Wolff Morgan**
Agency: **Loucks Atelier, Houston**

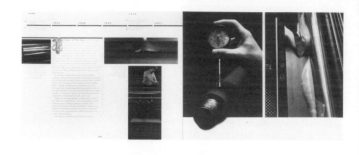

THESE TIMES DEMAND MORE OF AMERICA'S LEADERS

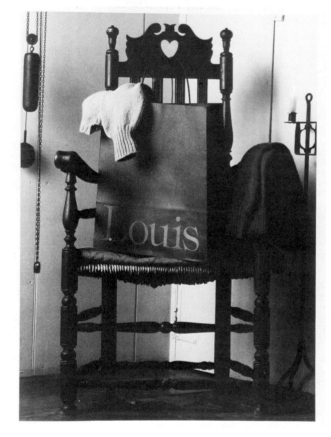

461
Art Director: **Andrew Kner**
Designer: **Peter Schaefer**
Artist: **Istvan Ventilla**
Writer: **Shep Conn**
Client: **The New York Times**
Publisher: **The New York Times**

462
Art Director: **Thom La Perle**
Designer: **Thom La Perle**
Photographer: **Tom Tracy**
Artist: **Rick Von Holdt**
Writer: **Stuart Nixon**
Client: **James H. Barry, Co.**
Editor: **William H. (Bud) Barry, Jr.**
Publisher/Production Co.: **James H. Barry, Co.**
Director: **Leslie Ferroggiaro**
Agency: **La Perle/Assoc., Inc.**

463
Art Director: **Tyler Smith**
Designer: **Tyler Smith**
Photographers: **Clint Clemens, Myron Taplin**
Writer: **Geoff Currier**
Client: **Louis (Boston)**
Producer: **Tyler Smith, Art Direction Inc.**
Agency: **Welch Currier Smith**

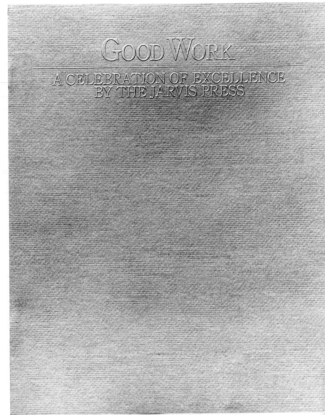

464
Art Directors: **Linda Lane, Paul Hawken**
Designer: **Linda Lane**
Photographer: **Sylvia Johnson (Cover Photo)**
Artist: **Mimi Osborne**
Writer: **Paul Hawken**
Client: **Smith & Hawken Tool Company**
Editor: **Paul Hawken**

466
Art Director: **Dennis Benoit**
Designer: **Dennis Benoit**
Photographer: **Gary Blockley**
Writer: **Bill Baldwin**
Client: **The Jarvis Press**
Agency: **Ben-Wah Design, Inc.**

465
Art Directors: **Joel Howard, Cliff Gillock**
Designers: **Joel Howard, Wayne Franks**
Photographer: **Frank Cruz**
Writer: **Wayne Franks**
Client: **Goodwin, Dannenbaum, Littman & Wingfield**
Agency: **Goodwin, Dannenbaum, Littman & Wingfield**

467
Art Director: **Holley Flagg**
Designer: **Holley Flagg**
Artist: **Holley Flagg**
Writer: **Kathy Petersen**
Client: **TIME Inc.**
Editor: **Marjorie Rafael**
Director: **Marjorie Rafael**

THERE'S NO OTHER MAGAZINE LIKE IT.

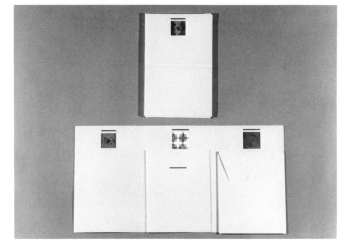

468
Art Director: **Anthony W. Rutka**
Designer: **Anthony W. Rutka**
Photographer: **Doug Barber**
Client: **The Madeira School**
Editor: **Joan Lee Weadock**
Agency: **The North Charles Street Design Organization**

469
Art Director: **Andrew Kner**
Designer: **Andrew Kner**
Photographer: **Howard Whitely**
Writer: **Louise Francke**
Client: **The New York Times**
Publisher: **The New York Times**

470
Art Director: **Bill Sontag**
Designer: **Bill Sontag**
Photographer: **Corson Hirshfeld**
Artist: **Bill Sontag**
Writer: **Kirby Sullivan**
Client: **Murray Ohio Manufacturing Company**
Agency: **Sive Associates**

471
Art Director: **Steve Connatser**
Designer: **Steve Connatser**
Photographer: **Kenn Berry**
Writer: **Bill Baldwin**
Client: **Casolar/Grupo Industrial Alfa**
Agency: **Steve Moi & Assoc.**

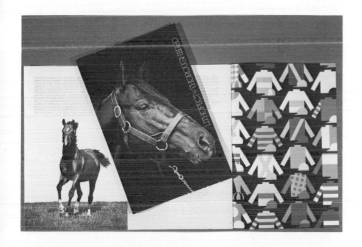

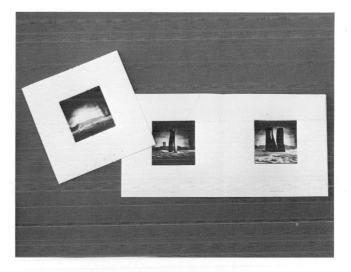

472
Art Director: **Russ Luedke**
Designer: **Russ Luedke**
Photographers: **John Noye, Tony Leonard**
Writer: **Russ Luedke**
Client: **Midtec Paper Corporation**
Production Co.: **Winnebago Corporation**
Agency: **Media House Inc.**

473
Art Directors: **Douglas Boyd, Scott A. Mednick**
Designer: **Gordon Tani**
Writers: **Nancy Goliger, Iris Zurawin, Scott A. Mednick**
Client: **Polygram Pictures**
Agency: **Douglas Boyd Design and Marketing**

474
Art Director: **Virginia A. Clarke**
Designer: **Virginia A. Clarke**
Photographer: **Mark Packo**
Writer: **Virginia A. Clarke**
Client: **Acorn Press**

475
Art Director: **Bart Ivic**
Designer: **Chip Cappelucci**
Writer: **Peter Jones**
Client: **Loctite Corporation**

476
Art Director: **Jay Loucks**
Designer: **C. Randall Sherman**
Photographers: **Arthur Meyerson, Tom Payne,
Michael Von Helms**
Writer: **JoAnn Stone**
Client: **Cadillac Fairview**
Agency: **Loucks Atelier, Houston**

477
Art Director: **Woody Pirtle**
Designer: **Woody Pirtle**
Photographer: **Mike Haynes**
Writer: **Mary Keck/Corgan Associates**
Client: **Corgan Associates AIA/American Airlines**
Agency: **Woody Pirtle, Inc.**

478
Art Director: **Dick Lemmon**
Photographer: **Dennis Manarchy**
Writer: **Jan Zechman**
Client: **Midland Hotel**
Agency: **Zechman and Associates**

479
Art Director: **John Casado**
Designer: **John Casado**
Photographer: **Oliviero Toscani**
Writer: **Esprit De Corp**
Client: **Esprit De Corp**
Publisher: **Esprit De Corp**

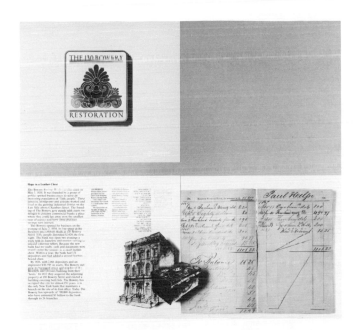

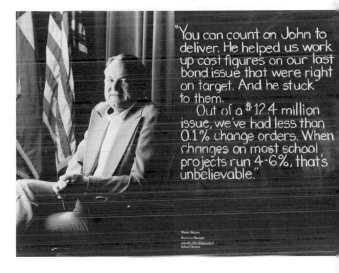

480
Art Director: **Jesse Califano**
Designer: **Johannes Regn**
Photographer: **Bob Day**
Artist: **Johannes Regn**
Client: **The Bowery Savings Bank**

481
Art Director: **David Martino**
Designer: **David Martino**
Writer: **Russell H. Irving**
Client: **Phoenix Mutual Life Insurance Co.—
Group Pensions**

482
Art Director: **Lowell Williams**
Designer: **Lance Brown**
Photographer: **Jim Sims**
Artist: **Tom McNeff**
Writer: **Lee Herrick**
Client: **John Perry Associates**
Agency: **Lowell Williams Design, Inc.**

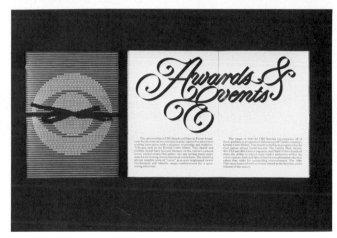

484
Art Director: **John deCesare**
Designer: **John deCesare**
Artists: **Various**
Writer: **Beryl Bridges**
Client: **The Illustrators Workshop**
Publisher: **Lindenmeyr Paper Company**
Agency: **deCesare Design Associates**

483
Art Director: **Lowell Williams**
Designer: **Bill Carson**
Photographer: **Jim Sims**
Artist: **Tom McNeff**
Writer: **Lee Herrick**
Client: **Serv-Rigs, Inc.**
Agency: **Lowell Williams Design, Inc.**

485
Art Directors: **David November,**
Marie-Christine Lawrence
Designers: **Marie-Christine Lawrence, Clement Mok,**
Noel Werrett
Artist: **Tom Carnase**
Writer: **Francis Piderit**
Producer: **Tom Rinaldi**

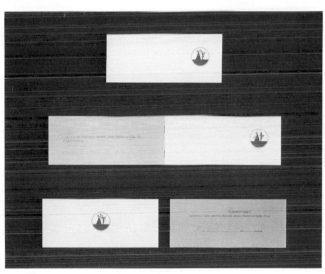

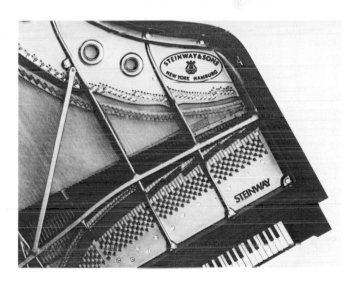

486
Art Directors: **John Hornall, Jack R. Anderson**
Designers: **Jack R. Anderson, John Hornall, Rey Sabado**
Photographer: **John Terance Turner**
Writers: **Rachel Bard, Debbie Tonkovich**
Client: **Westin Hotels**
Production Co.: **Print Northwest**
Agency: **Cole & Weber Design Group**

487
Art Director: **Rex Peteet**
Designer: **Rex Peteet**
Artist: **Rex Peteet**
Writer: **Rex Peteet**
Client: **Stan Fichelbaum**
Agency: **Dennard Creative, Inc.**

488
Art Directors: **Frank Ombres, Flavian Cresci**
Designer: **Flavian Cresci**
Photographer: **Brian Kosoff**
Writer: **Stephen DeGange**
Client: **Atalanta Corporation**
Production Co.: **Starkman & Company**
Agency: **Promotion Alley, Inc.**

489
Art Director: **Harvard Toback**
Designer: **Harvard Toback**
Photographer: **David Langley**
Artist: **Charles E. Chambers**
Writer: **Arthur Einstein**
Client: **Steinway & Sons**
Agency: **Lord, Geller, Federico, Einstein**

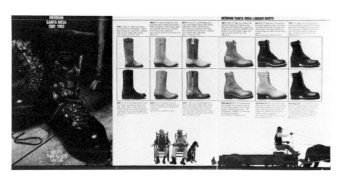

490
Art Director: **Michael Diliberto**
Designer: **Michael Diliberto**
Artist: **Jim Butcher**
Writer: **Rail Company Staff**
Client: **Rail Company**
Agency: **Mathis, Burden & Charles, Inc.**

491
Art Director: **Cheryl Heller**
Designers: **Cheryl Heller, Sandy Runnion**
Photographers: **Jim Wood, Geoff Stein**
Writers: **Marc Deschenes, Jeff Billig**
Client: **Joseph M. Herman Company**
Agency: **Humphrey Browning MacDougall**

492
Art Director: **David Broom**
Designer: **Broom & Broom, Inc.**
Artist: **Hank Osuna**
Writer: **Peterson & Dodge**
Client: **Pacific Telephone**
Agency: **Broom & Broom, Inc.**

494
Art Director: **John F. Burk**
Designer: **John F. Burk**
Photographer: **Steve Longley**
Artist: **Graphics Group**
Writer: **Burke Walker**
Client: **T. Rowe Price**
Agency: **Richardson, Myers & Donofrio**

493
Art Director: **Gary Gukeisen**
Designer: **Gary Gukeisen**
Photographer: **Peter Samerjan**
Artist: **David Hessemer (National Meeting Co.)**
Writer: **Patti McGrath**
Client: **Jantzen Inc.**
Agency: **Jantzen Ad Dept. Inc.**

495
Art Director: **Jim Jacobs**
Designer: **Jim Jacobs**
Photographer: **Bob Shaw**
Artist: **Sean Early**
Writer: **Jim Jacobs**
Client: **Broyles & Broyles, Inc.**

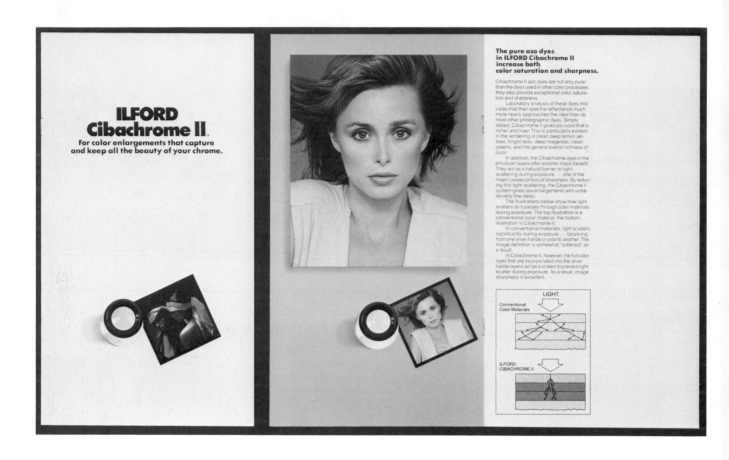

496
Art Director: **Dick Grider**
Designer: **Dick Grider**
Photographers: **Lisl Dennis, David Muench,**
Andrew Unangst
Writer: **Jack Warner**
Client: **Ilford**
Agency: **Warner, Bicking & Fenwick Inc.**

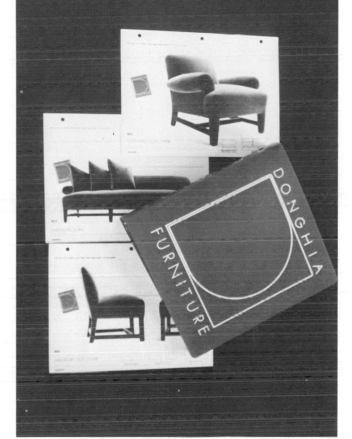

497
Art Directors: **David November,
Marie-Christine Lawrence**
Designers: **David November,
Marie-Christine Lawrence, Vanya Akraboff**
Artists: **Tom Carnase, Marty Norman**
Producer: **Mike Dunn**

499
Art Director: **Harvard Toback**
Designer: **Don Buckler**
Photographer: **Pete Scolamiero**
Artists: **Larry Ottino, Peter Taylor**
Writer: **Gilbert Ziff**
Client: **Steinway & Sons**
Agency: **Lord, Geller, Federico, Finstein Inc.**

498
Art Director: **Jeff Barnes**
Designer: **Jeff Barnes**
Photographers: **Various (Dennis Manarchy shown
in photos)**
Writer: **Paul Casper**
Client: **Chicago Talent**
Publisher: **Chicago Talent, Inc.**
Agency: **Alexander Communication**

500
Art Director: **Martha Voutas**
Designers: **June Robinson, Martha Voutas**
Photographer: **Harve Bergman**
Artists: **Martha Voutas, Diana Huff**
Writer: **Peter Alexander**
Client: **Donghia Furniture Company, Residential Div.**
Editor: **John Hutton**
Agency: **Martha Voutas Productions, Inc.**

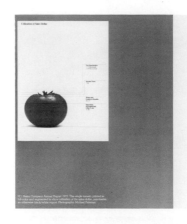
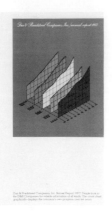

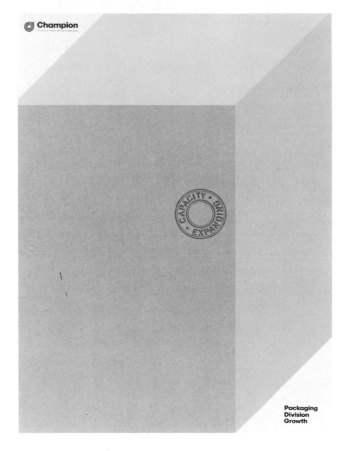

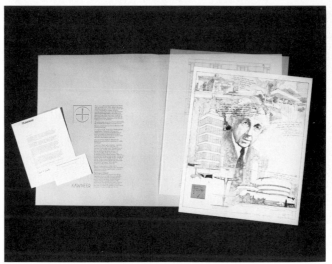

501
Art Director: **Bennett Robinson**
Designer: **Bennett Robinson**
Photographers: **Various**
Artists: **Various**
Writers: **Adrienne Claiborne, Bennett Robinson**
Client: **Corporate Graphics Inc.**
Agency: **Corporate Graphics Inc.**

502
Art Director: **Philip Gips**
Designers: **Philip Gips, Denys Gustafson**
Photographer: **Tom Hollyman**
Writer: **Michael Steinberg**
Client: **Champion International Corporation**
Agency: **Gips & Balkind & Associates, Inc.**

503
Art Director: **Warren Hanson**
Designers: **Warren Hanson, Joan Clothier**
Photographer: **Rick Dublin**
Artist: **Warren Hanson**
Writer: **Warren Hanson**
Client: **Webster Lumber Company**

504
Art Director: **Steve Miller**
Designer: **Steve Miller**
Photographer: **Tom Casalini**
Writer: **Jerry Steadham**
Client: **Garrison, Jasper, Rose & Company**
Agency: **Garrison, Jasper, Rose & Company**

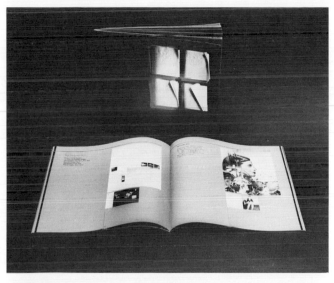

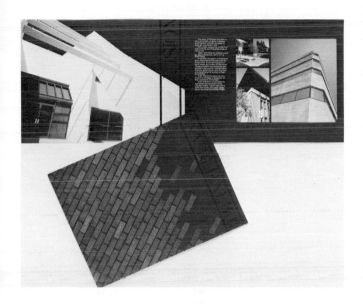

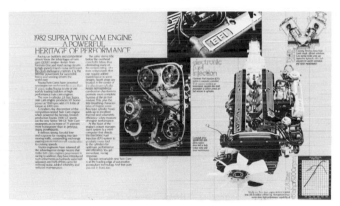

505
Art Director: **Dennis Caldwell**
Designer: **Dennis Caldwell**
Photographer: **Mert Carpenter**
Writer: **Mark Aulman**
Client: **RJB/Interland**
Production Co: **Pacific Rotoprinting**
Agency: **Carter, Callahan & Associates**

506
Art Director: **Jim Doyle**
Designer: **Jim Doyle**
Photographer: **Mickey McGuire/Boulevard Photographic Inc.**
Artist: **Konrad Kahl**
Writer: **Jim Lodge**
Client: **Toyota Motor Sales, U.S.A., Inc.**
Publisher: **Anderson Litho Co. Los Angeles, CA.**
Creative Director: **Sean K. Fitzpatrick**
Agency: **Dancer Fitzgerald Sample, Inc./S. Calif.**

507
Art Director: **Jann Church Adv. & Graphic Design, Inc.**
Designer: **Jann Church Adv. & Graphic Design, Inc.**
Photographer: **Cover: Walter Urie Photography, Annual Spreads: Schwartz Studios**
Writer: **Jann Church Adv. & Graphic Design, Inc.**
Client: **The Mead Paper Co./The Mead Library of Ideas**
Editor: **Jann Church Adv. & Graphic Design, Inc.**
Printer: **The Hennegan Company**
Typography: **Headliners of Orange County**

508
Art Director: **Adler-Schwartz Graphics, Inc.**
Designer: **Adler-Schwartz Graphics, Inc.**
Photographer: **Steve Longley**
Writer: **Bob Cooke**
Client: **Perfect Books (Bindery)**
Publisher: **Wolk Press, Inc.**
Production Co: **Wolk Press, Inc. & Adler-Schwartz**

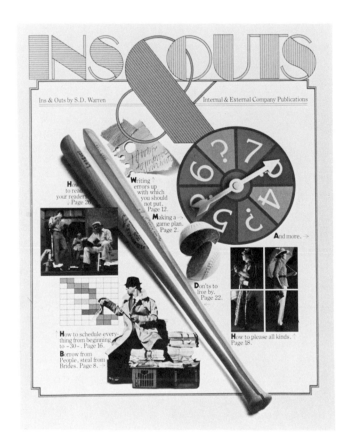

509
Art Director: **Robert Cipriani**
Designer: **Robert Cipriani**
Photographer: **Clint Clemens**
Artist: **John Gatie**
Writers: **Mark Myers, Judy Myers, Christine Flouton**
Client: **S.D. Warren Paper Company, Inc.**
Typographer: **Typographic House**
Printer: **Lebanon Valley Offset**
Production Managers: **Andre Cordello, David Lopes**
Agencies: **Robert Cipriani Associates,
Gunn Associates, Myers & Myers**

510
Art Director: **Jann Church Advertising &
Graphic Design, Inc.**
Designer: **Jann Church Advertising &
Graphic Design, Inc.**
Photographer: **Cover: "4 x 5" & photobank duotone:
Walter Urie Photography**
Artist: **Graphics: Jann Church Advertising &
Graphic Design, Inc.**
Writer: **Jann Church Advertising & Graphic Design, Inc.**
Client: **Signal Landmark**
Editor: **Jann Church Advertising & Graphic Design, Inc.**
Printer: **Hutton/Roach Lithography**
Typography: **Headliners of Orange County**

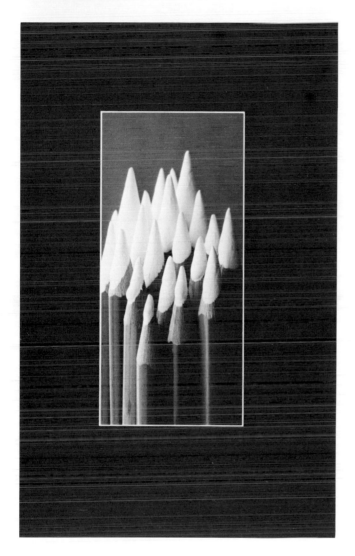

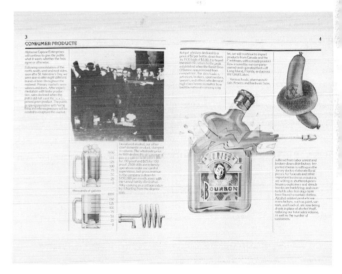

511
Art Director: **Stephen Miller**
Designer: **Stephen Miller**
Photographer: **Michael Haynes**
Writer: **John Stone**
Client: **Missouri-Kansas-Texas Railroad**
Agency: **Richards, Sullivan, Brock & Assoc./
The Richards Group**

514
Art Director: **Loren Weeks**
Designer: **Loren Weeks**
Artist: **Loren Weeks**
Writer: **Dave Bronson**
Client: **Packouz & Steinberg**
Printer: **Key Lithograph**
Agency: **Bronson Leigh Weeks**

513
Art Directors: **Mikio Osaki, Jon Anderson, Don Weller**
Designer: **Don Weller**
Photographers: **Stan Caplan, Mark Wagner**
Artist: **Everett Peck**
Writer: **Bob Porter**
Client: **TDCTJHTBIPC**
Editor: **Jon Anderson**
Publisher: **TDCTJHTBIPC**
Agency: **The Weller Institute for the Cure of Design, Inc.**

515
Art Director: **Steven Jacobs**
Designer: **Steven Jacobs**
Artists: **Dennis Zaminski, John Mattos, Ed Jaciow,
Norman Orr**
Writer: **Maxwell Arnold**
Client: **Simpson Paper Company**

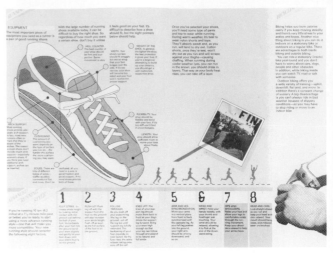

516
Art Director: **Peter Windett**
Designer: **Peter Windett**
Photographer: **Tessa Traeger**
Writer: **Cyrus Harvey**
Client: **Crabtree & Evelyn, Ltd.**
Production Co: **Van Dyck Printing, Inc.**
Agency: **Peter Windett Associates**

517
Art Director: **Charles Fillhardt**
Designer: **Cathy Danzeisen**
Photographers: **Becker Bishop, Pete Turner**
Writer: **Lynne Bowman**
Client: **Calma**
Agency: **Bergthold, Fillhardt & Wright, Inc.**

518
Art Director: **Robert J. Warkulwiz**
Designer: **Robert J. Warkulwiz**
Photographer: **Thad Richardson**
Artist: **Michael Rogalski**
Writer: **Alan Turetz**
Client: **Citicorp**
Agency: **Warkulwiz Design**

519
Art Director: **Bruce Blackburn**
Designer: **Bruce Blackburn**
Photographer: **Alan Orling**
Writer: **Champion Corporate Creative Services**
Client: **Champion International Corporation**

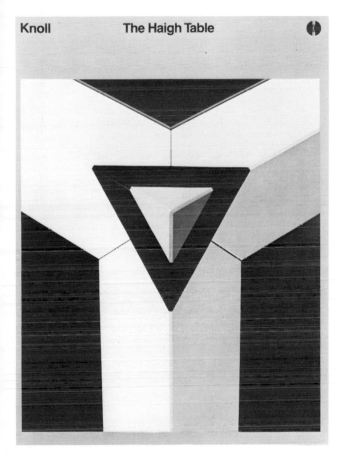

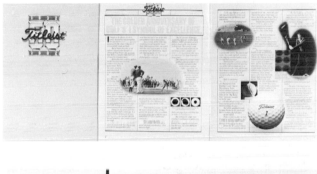

520
Art Directors: **David November,**
Marie-Christine Lawrence
Designers: **David November, Douglas Grimett**
Artist: **Ted Andresakes**
Writer: **David November**
Client: **CBS Television Network**
Producer: **John Smith**

521
Art Director: **Harold Matossian**
Designer: **Steven Schnipper**
Photographer: **Mario Carrieri**
Client: **Knoll International**
Agency: **Knoll Graphics**

522
Art Director: **Nick deSherbinin**
Designer: **Nick deSherbinin**
Photographer: **Stein-Mason Studio**
Artist: **Roger Huyssen**
Writer: **Chuck Matzell**
Client: **Acushnet Company**
Agency: **Humphrey Browning MacDougall**

523
Art Director: **Jay Loucks**
Designer: **Chris Hill**
Photographer: **Joe Baraban**
Artist: **Tom Bailey**
Writer: **Lee Herrick**
Client: **Gerald D. Hines Interests**
Editor: **Susan Scace**
Agency: **Loucks Atelier, Houston**

OCTOBER 24, 1979, President Spencer W. Kimball dedicated a beautiful garden on the Mount of Olives in Jerusalem to the memory of Orson Hyde, the early LDS Apostle who offered a dedicatory prayer of the land of Israel on that site in 1841.

The Orson Hyde Memorial Garden is a part of the Jerusalem National Park and is not owned by the Church.

524
Art Director: **Ian Barribal**
Designer: **Ian Barribal**
Photographer: **Bill Farrell**
Writer: **Gene Plotnik**
Client: **Ted Colangelo Associates**
Production Co.: **Sanders Printing**
Agency: **Ted Colangelo Associates**

526
Art Director: **Bryan L. Peterson**
Designers: **Bryan L. Peterson, Thomas W. Pratt**
Artist: **McRay Magleby**
Writer: **Paul Schneiter**
Client: **Brigham Young Univ. Travel Studies**
Editor: **Paul Schneiter**
Producer: **Brigham Young University**
Agency: **Graphic Communications**

525
Art Director: **Andrew Kner**
Designer: **Scott Menchin**
Photographer: **Leonard Nones**
Writer: **Neil Leonard**
Client: **The New York Times**

527
Art Director: **Hayward R. Blake**
Designer: **Rebecca Michaels**
Photographers: **Rhodes Patterson, Dave Jordano**
Writer: **Donald Phillips**
Client: **Bang & Olufsen of America, Inc.**
Editor: **Daniel Radecki**
Publisher: **Jack Trux, Bang & Olufsen**
Director: **Hayward R. Blake**
Production Co.: **Bruce Offset**
Agency: **Hayward Blake & Company**

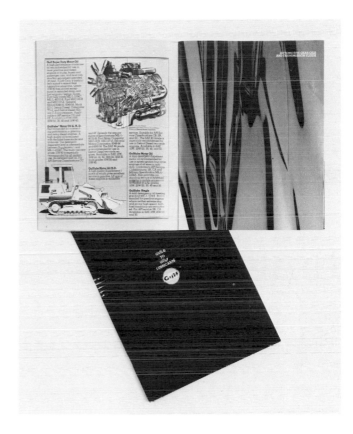

528
Art Director: **David A. Ashton**
Designer: **David A. Ashton**
Photographer: **Don Carstens**
Writer: **AIA Research Corporation**
Client: **American Institute of Architects**
Agency: **Ashton-Worthington, Inc.**

529
Art Director: **Jud Smith**
Photographer: **Dennis Manarchy**
Artist: **McNamara & Associates/Conrad Fialkowski**
Writer: **Ron Sackett**
Client: **Harley-Davidson Motor Company**
Agency: **Carmichael-Lynch, Inc.**

530
Art Director: **Dick Baker**
Designers: **Jack Amuny, Dick Baker**
Photographers: **Bob Gomel, Harry Seawell, Dick Baker**
Artist: **Larry McEntire**
Writer: **Pat Carrithers**
Client: **Gulf Oil Corporation**
Agency: **Ketchum Communications**

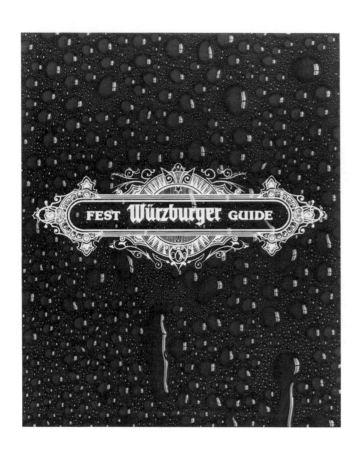

531
Art Director: **David Bartels**
Designer: **David Hencke**
Photographer: **Dale Taylor**
Artists: **Bettman Archives, St. Louis Library/**
Lance Jackson, Dave Hencke
Writer: **Maurice Wright**
Client: **Anheuser-Busch, Inc.**
Agency: **The Hanley Partnership, Inc.**

532
Art Director: **David A. Ashton**
Designer: **Elizabeth Nead**
Photographer: **Richard Anderson**
Writer: **Douglass Forsyth**
Client: **Chapel Valley Landscaping Co.**
Agency: **Ashton-Worthington, Inc.**

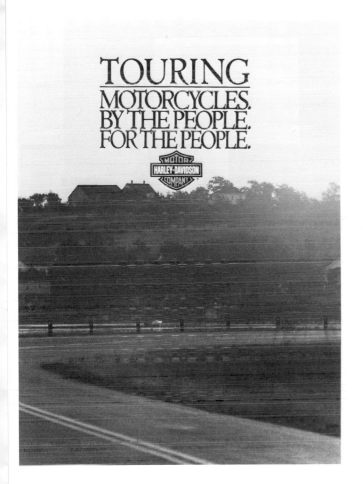

533
Art Director: **Jud Smith**
Photographer: **Dennis Manarchy/Image Bank**
Artist: **McNamara & Associates/Conrad Fialkowski**
Writer: **Ron Sackett**
Client: **Harley-Davidson Motor Company**
Agency: **Carmichael-Lynch, Inc.**

534
Creative Director: **Charles V. Blake**
Art Directors: **E. Zeitsoff, V. Kalayjian, T. Matsuura**
Designer: **Tetsuya Matsuura**
Photographers: **Various**
Writer: **Hal Alterman**
Client: **NBC Marketing**
Production Co.: **Jurist Co., Inc.**

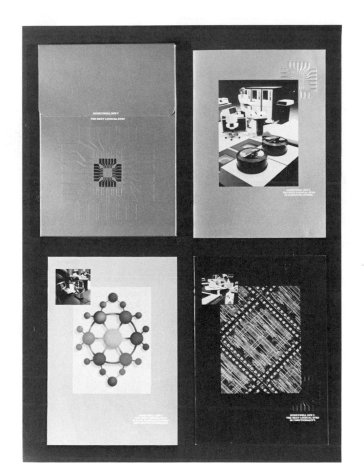

543
Art Director: **Robert Cipriani**
Designer: **Robert Cipriani**
Artist: **Janis Plauger**
Writers: **Peter Stavropulos, Maura Milden, Bill Manning**
Client: **Honeywell Information Systems**
Typographer: **Typographic House**
Printer: **Congraf Printing Co.**
Agency: **Robert Cipriani Associates**

544
Art Director: **Jud Smith**
Photographer: **Dennis Manarchy**
Artist: **McNamara & Associates/Conrad Fialkowski**
Writer: **Ron Sackett**
Client: **Harley-Davidson Motor Company**
Agency: **Carmichael-Lynch, Inc.**

546
Art Director: **Dabni Harvey**
Designer: **Dabni Harvey**
Photographer: **Roger Bell**
Artist: **Gordon Bellamy**
Writer: **Cindy Ferrell**
Client: **Texas Scottish Rite Hospital**
Agency: **The Collateral Group**

545
Art Director: **John P. Traynor/Studio West**
Designer: **John P. Traynor/Studio West**
Photographer: **Al Bonanno**
Writer: **Betsy Lee**
Client: **Conklin Company, Inc./Nexus**
Printer: **Bolger Publications**
Director: **Tom Misurek**
Typographer: **Great Faces**
Agency: **Studio West**

547
Art Director: **Lowell Williams**
Designers: **Lowell Williams, Bill Carson, Lance Brown**
Photographers: **Joe Baraban, Jim Sims**
Artists: **Tom McNeff, Sue Yates**
Writer: **Jo Ann Stone**
Client: **Cadillac Fairview Urban Development, Inc.**
Agency: **Lowell Williams Design, Inc.**

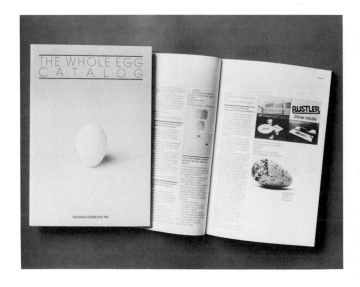

557
Art Director: **Robert Miles Runyan**
Designer: **Dennis Tani**
Photographer: **Ken Whitmore**
Writer: **Elizabeth Handler**
Client: **Pharmavite Corporation**
Agency: **Robert Miles Runyan & Associates**

558
Art Director: **Lorraine Freeman**
Designer: **Lorraine Freeman**
Photographer: **Kazu**
Writer: **Beth Collins**
Client: **Everett Piano Company**
Agency: **L F&C Associates, Inc.**

559
Art Director: **Muts Yasumura**
Designers: **Hau Chee Chung, Richard Hsiung**
Photographers: **Dean Chamberlain, Fuji**
Writers: **David McGee, Vally Chamberlain**
Client: **Young & Rubicam, Inc.**
Agency: **Yasumura & Associates**

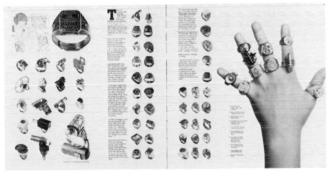

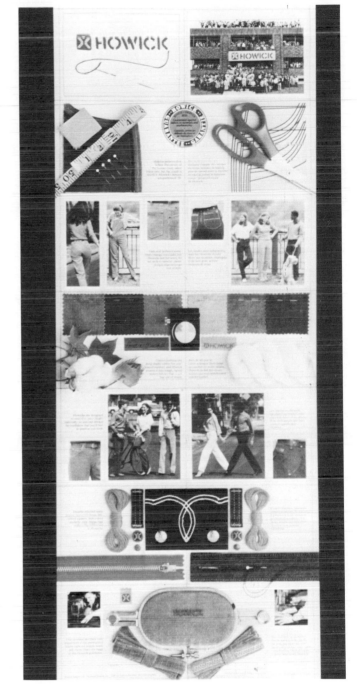

560
Art Director: **Claude Skelton**
Designer: **Amy Knoell**
Photographer: **Shorty Wilcox**
Writer: **David Treadwell**
Client: **Pine Manor College**
Agency: **Barton-Gillet Co.**

561
Art Director: **Richard Hess**
Designer: **Richard Hess**
Photographer: **Arthur Maillet**
Artist: **Richard Hess**
Writer: **Jo Durden-Smith**
Client: **Westvaco Corporation**

562
Art Directors: **Robert Burns, Heather Cooper**
Designer: **Dawn Cooper**
Photographers: **Jeremiah Chechik, Peter Christopher,
Tim Saunders**
Artist: **Dawn Cooper**
Writer: **Jim Hynes**
Client: **Howick Apparel**
Agency: **Burns, Cooper, Hynes Limited**

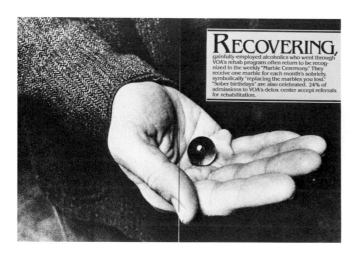

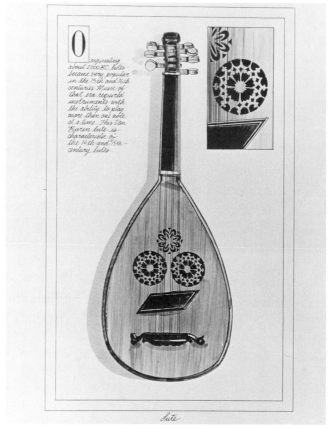

563
Art Director: **Jorge Alonso**
Designer: **Jorge Alonso**
Photographers: **Paul Cleveland, Roger Marshutz**
Writer: **Farida Fotouhi**
Client: **Volunteers of America**
Agency: **Fotouhi Alonso**

564
Art Director: **McRay Magleby**
Designer: **McRay Magleby**
Artist: **McRay Magleby**
Writer: **Norman A. Darais**
Client: **Brigham Young University**
Editor: **Norman A. Darais**
Producer: **Brigham Young University**
Agency: **Graphic Communications**

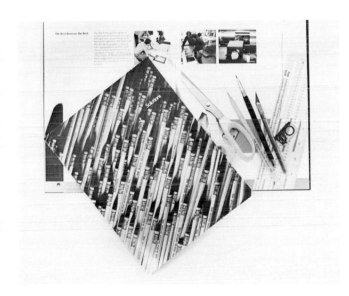

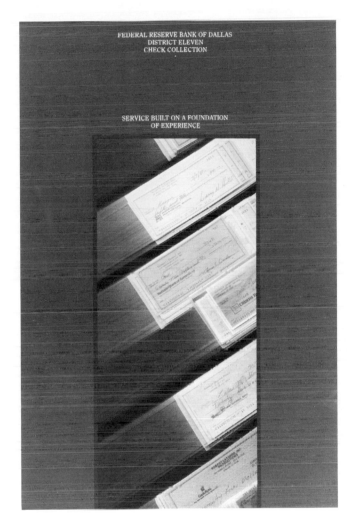

565
Art Director: **Jerry Blank**
Designers: **Jerry Blank, Alice Baker, Linda Degastaldi**
Photographer: **Judson Allen**
Writer: **Jerry Blank**
Client: **The Blank Design Group**
Production Co.: **House of Printing**
Agency: **The Blank Design Group**

566
Art Director: **Alan Spaeth**
Designer: **Alan Spaeth**
Photographer: **Robert Latorre**
Writer: **Barry Wells**
Client: **Federal Reserve Bank of Dallas**
Agency: **Robert A. Wilson Associates**

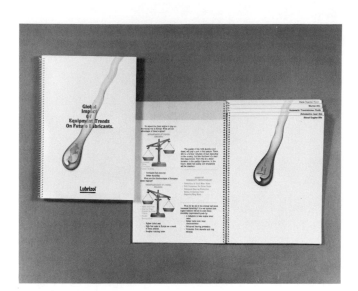

567
Art Directors: **Joseph Toth, David Hlebcar**
Designer: **Joseph Toth**
Artists: **John Chuldenko, Dorothy Wozniak,**
Elaine Wozniak
Writer: **Technology & Product Planning Div.**
Lubrizol Corp.
Client: **The Lubrizol Corporation**
Agency: **Kalman, Hlebcar & Kuhns**

568
Art Directors: **John Luckett, Susan Slover**
Designer: **Susan Slover**
Photographer: **Jerry Friedman**
Writers: **John Luckett, Ralph Destino,**
Barbara Ajmone-Marsan
Client: **Cartier**
Agency: **Luckett & Slover Inc.**

569
Art Director: **Peter Bradford**
Designers: **Peter Bradford, Alexandra Snyder**
Photographers: **Michael Pateman, Frank Chaney**
Artist: **Antonio Goldmark**
Writer: **David Goodman**
Client: **Grow Tunneling Corp.**
Editor: **David Goodman**
Publisher: **Grow Tunneling Corp.**
Agency: **Peter Bradford and Associates**

570
Art Director: **Wayne C. Roth**
Designer: **Wayne C. Roth**
Photographer: **Jeff Smith**
Writer: **Pat Flanagan**
Client: **RKD Oil, Inc.**
Production Co.: **Corpcom New Jersey**
Agency: **Roth + Associates**

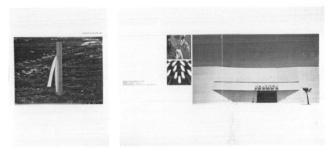

571
Art Director: **Keith Sheridan**
Designers: **Keith Sheridan, Jouk van der Werff**
Photographers: **Steven Caras, Paul Kolnik**
Writer: **Nancy Norman Lassalle**
Client: **New York City Ballet, Inc.**
Editor: **Nancy Norman Lassalle**
Publisher: **New York City Ballet, Inc.**
Agency: **Keith Sheridan Associates, Inc.**

573
Art Director: **Janis Koy**
Designer: **Janis Koy**
Photographer: **Joe Baraban**
Writer: **Bill Pettus**
Client: **Durden & Fulton, Inc., General Contractors**
Agency: **Pettus Advertising**

572
Creative Director: **Charles V. Blake**
Art Directors: **Elaine Zeitsoff, Vasken Kalayjian**
Designer: **Steve Gansl**
Writer: **Hal Alterman**
Client: **NBC Marketing**
Production Co.: **Crafton Printers**

574
Art Director: **Bill Bonnell/Bonnell & Associates**
Designer: **Bill Bonnell/Bonnell & Associates**
Writer: **Michael Steinberg**
Client: **Champion International Corporation**
Editor: **Marian Jill Sendor**
Publisher: **Champion International Corporation**
Director: **Marian Jill Sendor**
Production Co.: **Herbick & Held Printing Company**
Agency: **Bonnell & Associates**

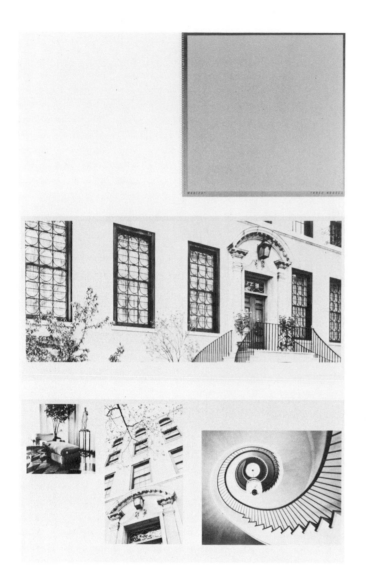

575
Art Director: **James Sebastian**
Designers: **James Sebastian, Michael Lauretano**
Photographer: **Joe Standart**
Client: **MARTEX/West Point Pepperell**
Agency: **Designframe, Incorporated**

576
Art Director: **Alex Tsao**
Designer: **Alex Tsao**
Photographer: **Mario Carrieri**
Writer: **Dick Raboy**
Client: **Knoll International**
Agency: **Epstein Raboy Advertising**

577
Art Director: **Karen Kutner Katinas**
Designer: **Karen Kutner Katinas**
Photographer: **Ed Gallucci and Image Bank**
Artist: **Charles Katinas**
Writer: **Jane Keen**
Client: **Merrill Lynch, Pierce, Fenner & Smith, Inc.**
Agency: **Katinas Design**

578
Art Director: **Gene Rosner**
Designers: **Gene Rosner, Kathleen Sullivan Kaska**
Photographer: **Don Anderson**
Artists: **Various**
Writers: **Peg Wander, Bob Levi**
Client: **IIT Research Institute**
Agency: **Brown & Rosner, Inc.**

579
Designer: **Bill Bonnell**
Photographers: **Gerhard Gscheidle, Rudolph Janu**
Writer: **Michael Steinberg**
Client: **R/Greenberg Associates, Inc.**
Editor: **Sandra Payne**
Publisher: **R/Greenberg Associates, Inc.**
Producer: **Robert M. Greenberg**

580
Art Director: **Stephen Miller**
Designer: **Stephen Miller**
Photographers: **Various**
Artist: **Stephen Miller**
Writer: **Howard Sutton**
Client: **Vecta Contract**
Agency: **Richards, Sullivan, Brock & Assoc/
The Richards Group**

581
Art Director: **Christina Rubin**
Photographer: **Sepp Seitz**
Client: **Peat, Marwick, Mitchell & Co.**

584
Art Director: **Larry G. Clarkson**
Designer: **Larry G. Clarkson**
Photographer: **Brent Herridge**
Artist: **Larry G. Clarkson**
Writers: **Larry G. Clarkson, Murray McInnes**
Client: **Sutton Place East**
Agency: **Smith & Clarkson Design**

583
Art Directors: **Jeff Laramore, David Young**
Designer: **Jeff Laramore**
Photographer: **Dick Spahr**
Writers: **David Young, Jim Crahan**
Client: **Federal Chemical**
Agency: **Pearson Group Advertising**

585
Art Director: **Wes Keebler**
Designers: **B.K. Hughes, Wes Keebler**
Photographer: **Richard Clark**
Writer: **Wendy Tigerman**
Client: **RFC Intermediaries, Inc.**
Agency: **The Webb Silberg Company**

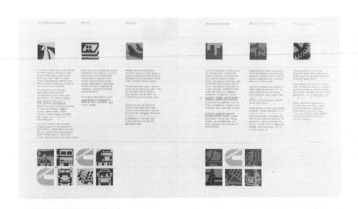

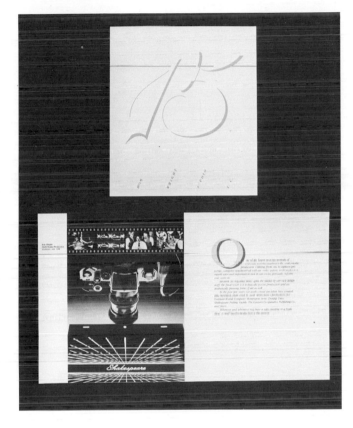

586
Art Director: **Robert M. Halliday**
Designer: **Robert M. Halliday**
Artists: **Keith Spears, Robert Halliday**
Client: **Cummins Engine Company**
Agency: **Halliday & Associates**

587
Art Director: **Robert L. Whiting**
Designer: **Richard Wehrman**
Photographer: **David Sachter**
Artists: **Richard Wehrman, David Buck, Robert Whiting, Dale Campbell**
Writer: **Rick McLay**
Client: **Bob Wright Studio, Inc.**

588
Art Directors: **Doug Akagi, Richard Burns**
Designers: **Doug Akagi, Steve Bragato**
Photographers: **George Selland, Bill Arbogast**
Artist: **Steve Bragato**
Writers: **John Easton, Doug Taylor**
Client: **Peterbilt Motors Company**
Agency: **The GNU Group/Sausalito, Houston**

589
Art Director: **Barbara Balch**
Designer: **Barbara Balch**
Artist: **Rebecca Archey**
Writer: **Lee Edward Stern**
Client: **The Upjohn Company**
Printer: **The Press of A. Colish**
Agency: **Manning, Selvage & Lee**

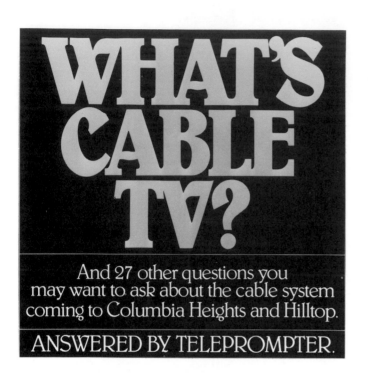

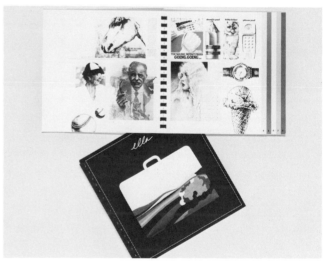

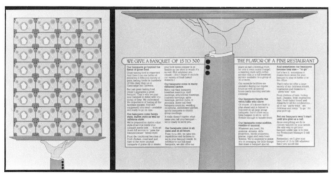

590
Art Director: **Mike Murray**
Designer: **Mike Murray**
Artist: **Anne Egan/Spectrum Studios**
Writer: **Jim Moore**
Client: **Teleprompter/Westinghouse**
Agency: **Chuck Ruhr Advertising, Inc.**

591
Art Director: **David Young**
Designer: **David Young**
Artist: **David Young**
Writer: **Larry Fletcher**
Client: **Cambridge Inn**
Agency: **Pearson Group Advertising**

592
Art Director: **Carl T. Herrman**
Designers: **Carl T. Herrman, Michael David Brown**
Artist: **Michael David Brown**
Client: **San Francisco Theological Seminary**

593
Art Director: **Ken Silvia**
Designer: **Ken Silvia**
Photographer: **Ted Gee**
Artist: **Anna Davidian**
Client: **Ella**
Agency: **Ken Silvia Design Group**

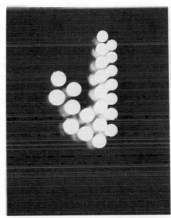

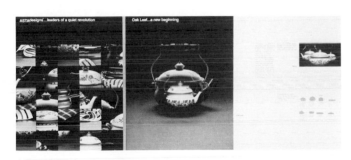

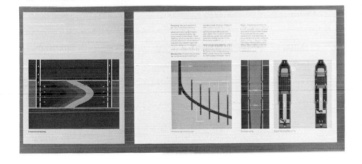

594
Art Director: **John deCesare**
Designers: **Connie Huebner, John deCesare**
Photographer: **Michael Waine**
Writer: **Ciaran McCabe**
Client: **Asta Designs**
Agency: **deCesare Design Associates**

596
Designer: **Ford, Byrne & Associates**
Photographer: **Dan Moerder**
Client: **Insurance Company of North America**
Agency: **Ford, Byrne & Associates**

595
Art Director: **Richard Kilmer**
Designer: **Richard Kilmer**
Artist: **Richard Kilmer**
Writer: **Peter Heyne**
Client: **Hemisphere Licensing Corp.**
Agency: **Ben Carter & Associates**

597
Art Director: **Robert Cuirlinger**
Designer: **Mark Riedy**
Photographer: **Spectrum, Division of Swink**
Artists: **John Maggard, Mark Riedy**
Writers: **Don Folger, Dale Kaiser**
Client: **Prestolite Electronics Division**
Agency: **Howard Swink Advertising**

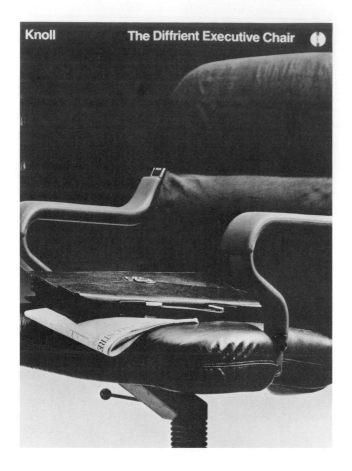

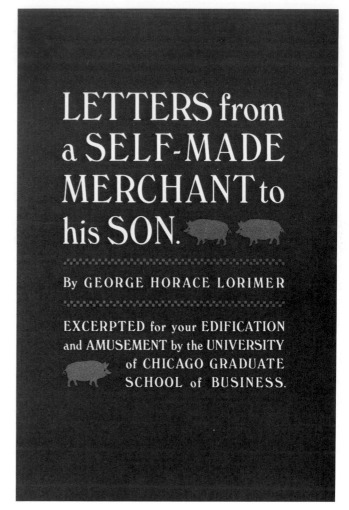

598
Art Director: **Harold Matossian**
Designer: **Steven Schnipper**
Photographer: **Mario Carrieri**
Client: **Knoll International**
Agency: **Knoll Graphics**

599
Art Director: **Jeff Barnes**
Designer: **Jeff Barnes**
Artist: **Bettmann Archive**
Writer: **Sharyn Woods**
Client: **Washington Park Zoo**
Agency: **CCA Communications**

600
Art Director: **Carol Gerhardt**
Designer: **Carol Gerhardt**
Artists: **Carol Gerhardt, Kristie Clemons**
Writer: **George Horace Lorimer**
Client: **Graduate School of Business
University of Chicago**
Editor: **Elizabeth McGuire**
Publisher: **Graduate School of Business
University of Chicago**
Agency: **Gerhardt & Clemons**

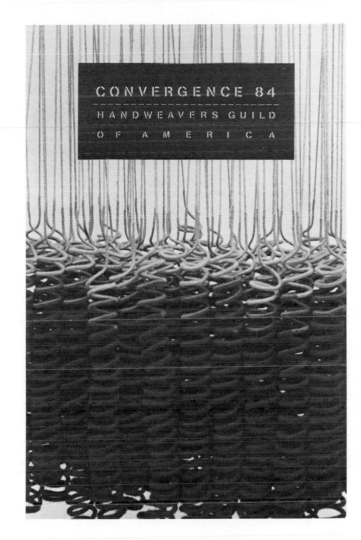

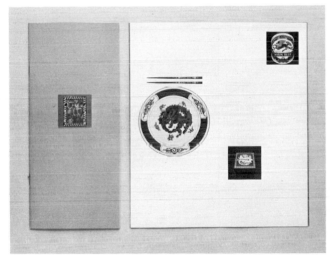

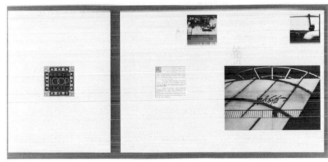

602
Art Director: **Woody Pirtle**
Designer: **Woody Pirtle**
Photographer: **The Handweavers Guild of America**
Writer: **The Handweavers Guild of America**
Client: **The Handweavers Guild of America**
Agency: **Woody Pirtle, Inc.**

601
Art Director: **Cap Pannell**
Designer: **Cap Pannell**
Photographer: **Philip Branner**
Artist: **Cap Pannell**
Writer: **Cap Pannell**
Client: **John A. Williams, Printer**
Production Co: **John A. Williams, Printer**
Agency: **Cap Pannell & Company, Dallas**

603
Art Director: **Mark Geer**
Designer: **Mark Geer**
Photographer: **Jim Sims**
Writer: **Lee Herrick**
Client: **Regency Development Company**
Agency: **Ben Carter & Associates**

Savin 895 Copier

604
Art Director: **Robert A. Monize**
Designer: **Robert A. Monize**
Photographer: **Martin Tornallyay Associates**
Client: **Savin Corporation**
Production Co.: **Adder Printing** ·

605   SILVER AWARD
Art Director: **David November,**
Marie-Christine Lawrence
Designers: **Marie-Christine Lawrence, David**
November, Katsumi Komagata
Artist: **Marie-Christine, Tom Carnase**
Writer: **Sherman Adler**
Producer: **Herman Aronson**

606
Art Director: **Debby Duncan**
Designer: **Bill Kumke**
Artist: **Bill Kumke**
Writer: **Marilyn Popovich**
Client: **Buster Brown Sales Division**
Production Co.: **Blake Graphics**
Agency: **Brown Shoe Company**
Advertising Department

607
Art Director: **W. Lee Einhorn**
Designers: **W. Lee Einhorn, Ron Morgan, Stu Nickerson,**
Paul Michaels
Writer: **Stu Nickerson**
Client: **Volvo of America, Corp.**
Agency: **RMI Advertising/Sales Promotion Agency**

609
Art Director: **Andrew Kner**
Designer: **Arnold Kushner**
Artist: **Tom Carnase**
Writer: **John Schenck**
Client: **The New York Times**

608
Art Director: **Tom Manning**
Designers: **Kim Rothstein, Jo David**
Writers: **Kim Rothstein, Jo David**
Client: **The Clorox Company**
Production Co.: **Marx/David Advertising, Inc.**
Agency: **Marx/David Advertising, Inc.**

610
Art Director: **David Arnold**
Designer: **David Arnold**
Artist: **Whole Hog Studios**
Writers: **Ward Wixon, Julie Manis**
Client: **Amoco Foam Products**

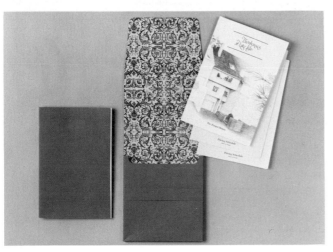

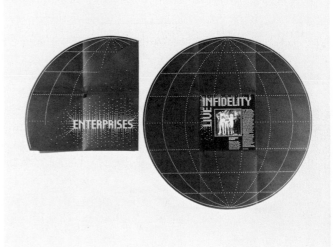

611
Art Director: **Kathy Filter**
Designer: **Kathy Filter**
Artists: **Advertising Arts, JK Art Directions**
Writers: **Dennis Frankenberry, Steve Laughlin**
Client: **Manpower, Inc.**
Producer: **Kris Kagelmann-Holtz, Manpower, Inc.**
Agency: **Frankenberry, Laughlin & Constable, Inc.**

612
Art Director: **Frank C. Lionetti**
Designers: **Frank C. Lionetti, Ann Clementino**
Artist: **Deborah Howland**
Client: **Lusk Corporation**
Agency: **Frank C. Lionetti Design**

613
Art Director: **James Sebastian**
Designers: **James Sebastian, Michael Lauretano**
Photographer: **Joe Standart**
Client: **MARTEX / West Point Pepperell**
Agency: **Designframe, Incorporated**

614
Art Directors: **David November,
Marie-Christine Lawrence**
Designers: **David November,
Marie-Christine Lawrence, David Rosen**
Artist: **David Rosen**
Producer: **Herman Aronson**

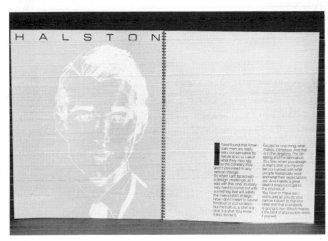

615
Creative Director: **Charles V. Blake**
Art Directors: **Elaine Zeitsoff, Vasken Kalayjian**
Designer: **Steve Gansl**
Artist: **Ray Barber**
Writer: **Steve Jaffe**
Client: **NBC Marketing**
Production Co.: **Jurist Co. Inc.**

617
Art Director: **Carlos J. Darquea**
Designer: **Carlos J. Darquea**
Photographer: **Hunter Freeman**
Artist: **Kenneth Paul Block**
Writer: **Larry Miller**
Client: **The Designer Group "Halston"**
Agency: **Sacks & Rosen Adv.**

618   GOLD AWARD
Art Director: **Lowell Williams**
Designers: **Lowell Williams, Bill Carson, Lance Brown**
Photographers: **Ron Scott, Joe Baraban, Jim Sims**
Artists: **Tom McNeff, Sue Yates**
Writer: **Lee Herrick**
Client: **Oiltools International Ltd.**
Agency: **Lowell Williams Design, Inc.**

619
Art Director: **Susan Hoffman**
Designer: **Susan Hoffman**
Artist: **Mike Carpenter**
Writer: **Mark Silveira**
Client: **Louisiana-Pacific Corp.**
Producer: **Dennis Fraser**
Agency: **William Cain, Inc.**

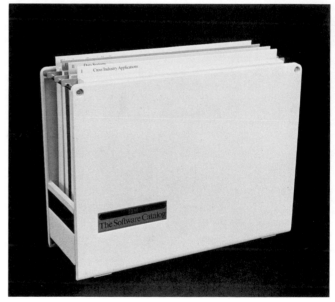

621
Art Directors: **Bill Wynne, Jim Brock**
Designer: **Bill Wynne**
Photographer: **Bob Jones**
Writer: **Ed Jones**
Client: **Luck Stone Centers**
Production Co: **Commonwealth Packaging Corporation**
Agency: **Finnegan & Agee, Inc.**

620
Art Director: **Brooke Kenney**
Designer: **Brooke Kenney**
Artist: **John Alcorn**
Writer: **Terry Bremmer**
Client: **Minnesota Zoological Society**
Agency: **Laughing Graphics**

622
Art Director: **Theo Welti**
Designer: **Jacqueline Rose**
Artist: **Robert Conrad**
Client: **IBM Corporation, National Accounts Division**
Editor: **Martha Hoch**
Production Cos.: **S.D. Scott Printing Co., Inc., Herst Litho Inc., Fanplastic Molding Co.**

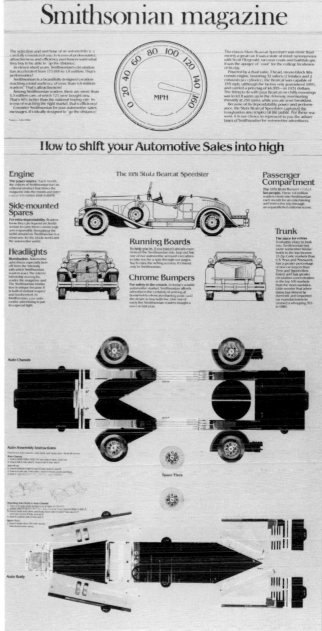

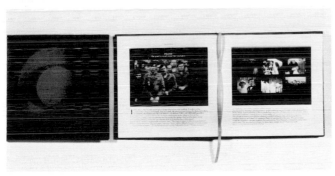

623
Art Director: **Danny Boone**
Designer: **Danny Boone**
Photographer: **Jamie Cook**
Writer: **Mike Hughes**
Client: **Mobil Chemical**
Agency: **The Martin Agency**

624
Art Directors: **David November, Marie-Christine Lawrence**
Designers: **Marie-Christine Lawrence, David November, Georgina Leaf**
Photographer: **CBS News**
Artist: **Gabor Kiss**
Writers: **Nancy Mendleson, Francis Piderit**
Client: **CBS Television Network**
Editor: **Nancy Mendleson**
Producer: **Herman Aronson**
Agency: **CBS Entertainment**

625
Art Director: **Mark Greitzer**
Designer: **Marie Loeber**
Artist: **Bill Wilkinson**
Writer: **Richard Dee**
Client: **Smithsonian Magazine**
Agency: **Millennium Design Communications, Inc.**

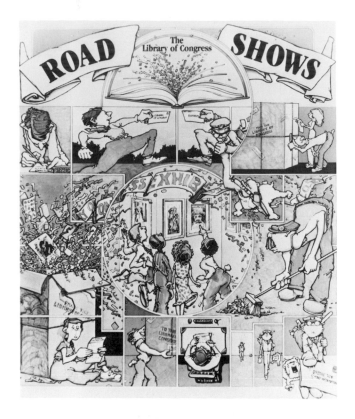

626
Art Directors: **Bobbie Lee, Robert Kircher**
Designer: **Bobbie Lee**
Artist: **Kevin Chadwick**
Client: **Library of Congress**

627
Art Directors: **Cheryl Heller, Jim Witham**
Designers: **Cheryl Heller, Jim Witham**
Photographer: **Tony Petrucelli**
Writer: **Peter Caroline**
Client: **S.D. Warren**
Agency: **Humphrey Browning MacDougall**

628
Art Director: **Ina Kahn**
Designer: **Victor Liebert**
Photographer: **Knut Brut**
Writer: **Lesley Teitelbaum**
Client: **Trevira®**
Agency: **Trevira® (In-House)**

629
Art Director: **Henry Wolf**
Designer: **David Blumenthal**
Photographer: **Henry Wolf**
Writer: **Ken Hall**
Client: **After Six**
Production Co.: **Henry Wolf Productions**

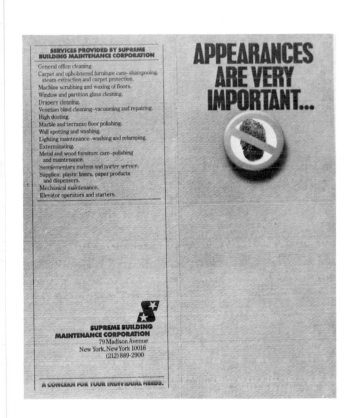

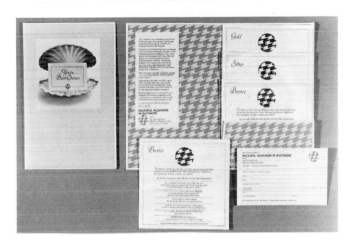

631
Art Director: **Mark Shap**
Designer: **Mark Shap**
Writer: **Mark Shap**
Client: **Ogilvy & Mather Advertising**
Publisher: **Ogilvy & Mather Advertising**
Agency: **Ogilvy & Mather Advertising**

630
Art Director: **Peter Rauch**
Designer: **Peter Rauch**
Artist: **Carol M. Wendling**
Writer: **Helayne Spivak**
Client: **Supreme Building Maintenance Corp.**
Agency: **Peter Rauch Design**

632
Art Director: **Barbara Lebow**
Designer: **Barbara Lebow**
Photographer: **Lee Britz**
Writer: **Ken Fitzgerald**
Client: **National Aquarium in Baltimore**
Agency: **Trahan/Burden/ & Charles**

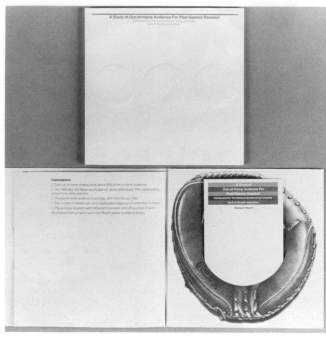

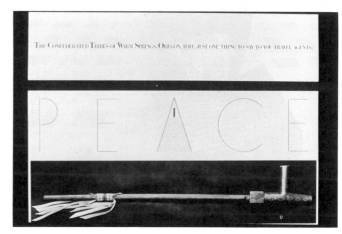

640
Art Directors: **Don Crum, Steve Connatser**
Designers: **Steve Connatser, David Kampa**
Artist: **Bettman Archives**
Writers: **Judy Anderton, Steve Connatser**
Client: **Texas Homes Magazine**
Agency: **Connatser & Crum**

642
Creative Director: **Charles V. Blake**
Art Directors: **E. Zeitsoff, V. Kalayjian, T. Matsuura**
Designer: **Tetsuya Matsuura**
Writer: **Dr. Tom Coffin**
Client: **NBC Research**
Production Co.: **Crafton Printers**

641
Art Director: **Don Lais**
Designer: **Don Lais**
Photographer: **Stock**
Artist: **Jim Heiman**
Writer: **Linda Chandler Frohman**
Client: **PM Magazine**
Agency: **Abert, Newhoff & Burr, Inc.**

643
Art Director: **Ed Tajon**
Designer: **Ed Tajon**
Photographer: **Pete Stone**
Artist: **Ford Gilbreath**
Writer: **Dave Newman**
Client: **Kah-Nee-Ta Resort**
Agency: **Borders, Perrin and Norrander, Inc.**

644
Art Director: **Marianne Gladych**
Designer: **Marianne Gladych**
Photographer: **Kenro Izu**
Writer: **Jack Aaker**
Client: **Litho-Art, Inc.**
Design Firm: **M. Gladych Design**
Agency: **Charle John Cafiero Associates**

645
Art Director: **Jim Jacobs**
Designer: **Jim Jacobs**
Artist: **Jim Jacobs**
Client: **NEH Learning Library/Dallas Public Library**

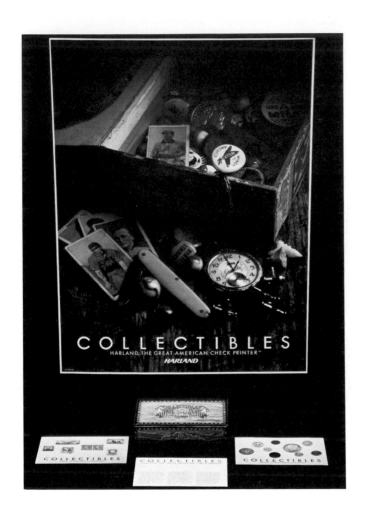

646
Art Directors: **Art Riser, Danny Strickland**
Designers: **Danny Strickland, Judith Martens**
Photographer: **Jamie Cook**
Artist: **Janie Wright**
Writer: **Maria Mackas**
Client: **John H. Harland Co.**
Agency: **John H. Harland Co.**

647
Art Director: **Richard Holmes**
Designer: **Ronald Morris**
Photographer: **Scott Williamson**
Artist: **Kevin Davidson**
Writer: **Jack Marble**
Client: **Mrs. Gooch's Ranch Markets**
Production Co.: **Litho Sales**
Agency: **Richard Holmes Advertising & Design**

648
Art Director: **John Casado**
Designer: **John Casado**
Photographer: **Oliviero Toscani**
Writer: **Esprit De Corp**
Client: **Esprit De Corp**
Publisher: **Esprit De Corp**

649
Art Directors: **Bill Wynne, Jim Brock**
Designer: **Jim Brock**
Photographers: **Bob Jones, John Whitehead**
Writer: **Ed Jones**
Client: **Luck Stone Centers**
Production Co.: **Commonwealth Packaging Corporation**
Agency: **Finnegan & Agee, Inc.**

650
Art Director: **Steve Connatser**
Designers: **David Kampa, Steve Connatser**
Writers: **Judy Anderton, Steve Connatser**
Client: **Texas Homes**
Agency: **Connatser & Crum**

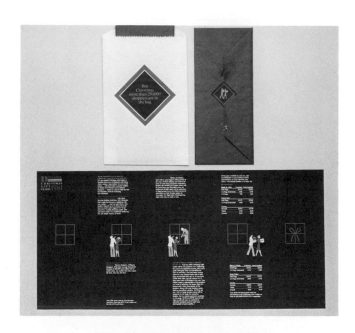

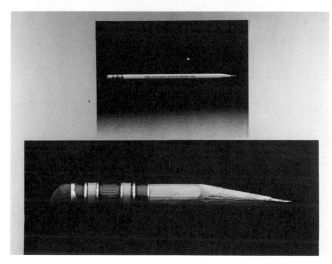

651
Art Director: **Cerita Smith**
Designer: **Cerita Smith**
Artist: **Cerita Smith**
Writer: **Debra Patterson**
Client: **D Magazine and Houston City**
Agency: **Cap Pannell & Company, Dallas**

652
Art Directors: **Bob Kwait, Bridgit Cody**
Designers: **Bob Kwait, Bridgit Cody**
Photographer: **Chris Wimpey**
Writer: **Rich Badami**
Client: **Phillips-Ramsey Advertising**

653
Art Directors: **David Deutsch, Rocco Campanelli**
Writer: **John Clarkson**
Client: **The P.H. Glatfelter Company**
Agency: **David Deutsch Associates, Inc.**

654
Art Director: **Bobbie Lee**
Designer: **Bobbie Lee**
Artist: **Dorothy Rudzik**
Client: **American Council of Life Insurance**
Agency: **William J. Kircher & Associates, Inc.**

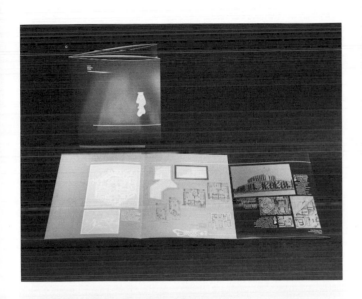

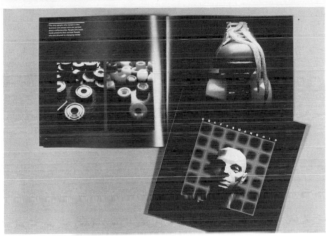

655
Art Director: **Jann Church Adv. & Graphic Design, Inc.**
Designer: **Jann Church Adv. & Graphic Design, Inc.**
Graphics: **Jann Church Adv. & Graphic Design, Inc.**
Writer: **Jann Church Adv. & Graphic Design, Inc.**
Client: **Fujiken Kogyo Co. Ltd./Japan**
Editor: **Jann Church Advertising & Graphic Design, Inc.**
Printer: **Walker Color Graphics**
Typography: **Headliners of Orange County**

656
Art Director: **Craig Frazier**
Designer: **Craig Frazier**
Photographers: **Mark Gottlieb, Rudi Legname, Don Shapero, Tom Tracy**
Writer: **John Frazier**
Client: **Solzer & Hail, Inc.**
Agency: **Jorgensen/Frazier, Inc., Jaciow Kelley Organization**

657
Art Director: **Danny Boone**
Designer: **Danny Boone**
Photographer: **Jamie Cook**
Writer: **Mike Hughes**
Client: **Mobil Chemical**
Agency: **The Martin Agency**

658
Art Director: **Jeffrey Abbott**
Designer: **Jeffrey Abbott**
Photographer: **Pat Pollard**
Writer: **Philip H. Clement**
Client: **Ad Club of Greater Hartford**
Agency: **Creamer, Inc.**

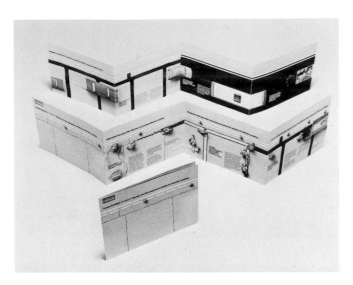

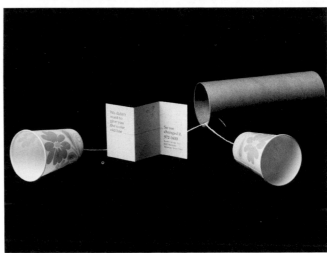

659
Art Director: **Bryon Weeks**
Designer: **Bryon Weeks**
Illustrator: **Stanislaw Fernandes**
Writer: **Jennifer Knox**
Client: **Owens-Corning Fiberglas**
Agency: **Muir Cornelius Moore**

661
Art Director: **Joseph Hutchcroft**
Designer: **Joseph Hutchcroft**
Photographer: **Allan Bruce Zee**
Writers: **Robert Best, Margaret Tresley**
Client: **Container Corporation of America**
Agency: **CCA Communication Dept.**

660
Art Director: **Anne Shaver**
Artist: **Wayne Carey**
Writer: **Mike Gaffney**
Client: **Charleston National Bank**
Agency: **Cargill, Wilson & Acree Inc.**

662
Art Director: **John Ziegmann**
Designers: **Steven Sessions, Alisa Bales**
Writer: **Bruce Huninghake**
Client: **Baxter & Korge, Inc.**
Agency: **Baxter & Korge, Inc.**

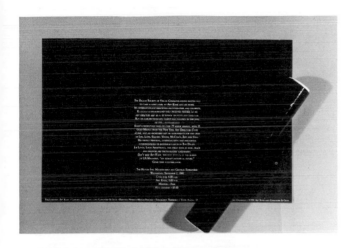

663
Art Director: **Steve Connatser**
Designer: **Steve Connatser**
Photographer: **Art Kane**
Writer: **Steve Connatser**
Client: **Dallas Society of Visual Communications**
Agency: **Connatser & Crum**

664
Art Director: **Carlton Gunn**
Designer: **Carlton Gunn**
Writer: **Carlton Gunn**
Client: **Advertising Club of Richmond**
Agency: **The Paxton Group**

665
Art Director: **Tom Davis**
Designer: **Tom Davis**
Writer: **Gene Gilmore**
Client: **Nashua Corporation**
Production Co.: **MGR-Mike Keannely**
Agency: **Arnold & Company, Inc.**

666   SILVER AWARD
Art Director: **Allen Weinberg**
Designer: **Allen Weinberg**
Artist: **David Wilcox**
Client: **CBS Records**

667
Art Director: **Paula Scher**
Artist: **David Wilcox**
Client: **CBS Records**

668
Art Director: **Gary Gukeisen**
Designers: **Gary Gukeisen, Paul Clark**
Photographers: **Tom Stewart, Craig Fineman**
Writer: **Michael Reed**
Client: **Jantzen Inc.**
Producer: **Roger W. Yost**
Agency: **Jantzen Ad Dept. Inc.**

669
Art Director: **John Berg**
Artist: **Gerard Huerta**
Client: **CBS Records**

670
Art Director: **John Berg**
Artist: **Roger Huyssen**
Client: **CBS Records**

672
Art Director: **Paula Scher**
Client: **CBS Records**

671
Art Director: **Sandi Young**
Designer: **Sandi Young**
Artist: **Leslie Cabarga**
Client: **Atlantic Records**

673
Art Director: **John Berg**
Photographer: **David Michael Kennedy**
Client: **CBS Records**

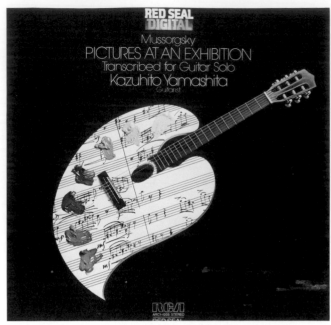

674
Art Director: **Dian-Aziza Ooka**
Designer: **Dian-Aziza Ooka**
Photographer: **Paddy Reynolds**
Client: **Adolescent Records**
Publisher: **Adolescent Records**
Executive Producers: **Eric Paul Fournier,
P. Spencer Gomez**

676
Art Director: **Joseph Stelmach**
Designer: **Joseph Stelmach**
Photographer: **Nick Sangiamo**
Artist: **Ralph Keefe**
Client: **RCA Records**

675
Art Director: **Virginia Team**
Photographer: **Beverly Parker**
Client: **CBS Records**

677
Art Director: **Henrietta Condak**
Artist: **David Wilcox**
Client: **CBS Records**

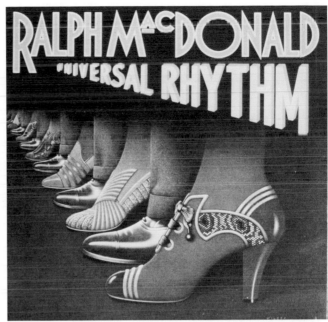

678
Art Director: **Karen Katz**
Photographer: **Joseph Abeles Collection**
Client: **CBS Records**

680
Art Director: **Paula Scher**
Artist: **David Wilcox**
Client: **CBS Records**

679
Art Director: **Ron Kellum**
Designer: **Ron Kellum**
Photographer: **Nick Sangiamo**
Client: **Millennium Records**

681
Art Director: **Karen Katz**
Photographer: **Duane Michals**
Client: **CBS Records**

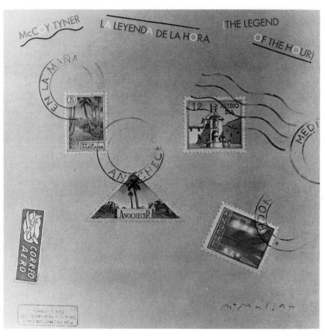

682
Art Directors: **Ron Coro, Kristen Kasell Nikosey**
Artist: **Tom Nikosey**
Client: **Elektra / Asylum / Nonesuch Records**

684
Art Director: **Carin Goldberg**
Artist: **Robert Weaver**
Client: **CBS Records**

683
Art Director: **Carin Goldberg**
Artist: **James McMullan**
Client: **CBS Records**

685
Art Director: **Ron Coro**
Designer: **Kristen Kasell Nikosey**
Artist: **James McMullan**
Client: **Elektra / Asylum / Nonesuch Records**

686
Art Director: **Tony Lane**
Photographer: **Welden Andersen**
Client: **CBS Records**

688
Art Director: **Nancy Donald**
Artist: **Eraldo Carugati**
Client: **CBS Records**

687
Art Directors: **Ron Coro, Norm Ung**
Photographer: **Beverly Parker**
Artist: **Neke Carson**
Client: **Elektra/Asylum/Nonesuch Records**

689
Art Director: **Karon Katz**
Artist: **Bob Felsenstein**
Client: **CBS Records**

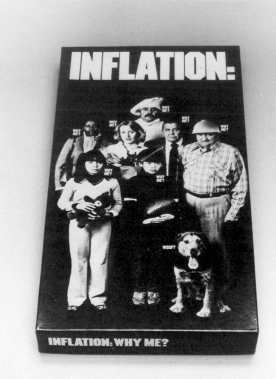

690
Art Director: **Terry Schneider**
Designer: **Terry Schneider**
Photographer: **Jim Piper**
Client: **Mayflower Farms**
Agency: **Gerber Advertising Agency**

692
Art Director: **Ed Brodsky**
Designer: **Ed Brodsky**
Photographer: **Steve Eisenberg**
Writer: **Ellen Emery**
Client: **J.C. Penney Company Inc.**
Publisher: **J.C. Penney Company Inc.**
Production Co: **Raleigh Lithography**
Agency: **Brodsky Graphics Inc.**

691
Art Directors: **Douglas Hoppe Stone, Eric Gardner**
Designers: **Eric Gardner, Stan Evenson**
Artist: **Stan Evenson**
Writer: **Gillen Stone**
Client: **Ganahl Lumber Company**
Agency: **Gillen Stone, Inc.**

693
Art Director: **Richard Kelly**
Designer: **William Miller III**
Client: **Frank S. Owens/F.X. Matt Brewing, Co.**
Agency: **Image Communications**

694
Art Directors: **Herman Davis, Ared Spendjian**
Designers: **Herman Davis, Ared Spendjian**
Writers: **Frankie Cadwell, Michael Delaney**
Client: **Conde Nast Publications**
Agency: **Cadwell Davis Savage**

696
Art Director: **Zengo Yoshida**
Designer: **Zengo Yoshida**
Artist: **Zengo Yoshida**
Client: **Neo-Art Inc.**
Agency: **Zenn Graphics**

695
Creative Director: **Bob Dennard**
Art Director: **Rex Peteet**
Designer: **Rex Peteet**
Artist: **Rex Peteet**
Writers: **Bob Dennard, George Toomer, Rex Peteet,
Glyn Powell**
Client: **Bennigan's Tavern**
Agency: **Dennard Creative, Inc.**

697
Art Director: **Raymond Waites**
Designer: **Jeffrey H. Morris**
Artists: **Jeffrey H. Morris, Katrina Blumenstock**
Client: **Hartstone Inc.**
Agency: **Gear Inc.**

698
Art Director: **Phil Gips**
Designer: **Gerard Huerta**
Artist: **Gerard Huerta**
Client: **Fearon O'Leary/Old Tyme Ginger Beer**
Agency: **Gips & Balkind**

699
Art Director: **Richard Hsiung**
Designer: **Richard Hsiung**
Artist: **Richard Hsiung**
Client: **Brewmaster's Corporation**
Production Co.: **Reynolds Metals, Co.**
Agency: **Yasumura & Associates/CYB**

700
Art Director: **Reinhold Schwenk**
Designers: **Reinhold Schwenk, David Garner**
Artist: **Gene Case**
Client: **Lorillard**
Agency: **Jordan, Case & McGrath**

701
Art Director: **Barry Deutsch**
Designer: **Myland McRevey**
Artist: **Myland McRevey**
Client: **Beach Street Baking Company**
Agency: **Steinhilber, Deutsch & Gard**

702
Art Director: **Johanna Bohoy**
Designers: **Johanna Bohoy, Andy Chulyk**
Artist: **Johanna Bohoy**
Client: **Charrette**
Agency: **Charrette**

703
Art Director: **Barbara Shimkus**
Designer: **Barbara Shimkus**
Artist: **Mark Weakley**
Client: **Glasscock Vineyards**
Agency: **Barbara Shimkus/Graphic Design**

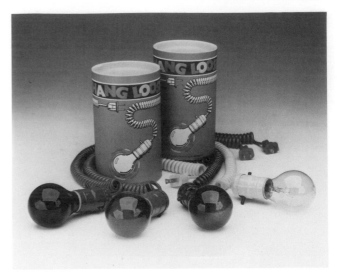

712
Art Director: **Hal Frazier**
Designer: **Hal Frazier**
Artist: **John Vince**
Client: **Vin Baker: Womens Retail Shoe Store**
Agency: **Frazier Design Consultancy**

714
Art Director: **Zengo Yoshida**
Designer: **Zengo Yoshida**
Artist: **Sen Maruyama**
Client: **Neo-Art Inc.**
Agency: **Zenn Graphics**

713
Art Director: **Keith Bright**
Designers: **Ray Wood, Peter Sargent**
Client: **Olympia Brewing Company**
Agency: **Bright & Associates, Inc.**

715
Art Director: **Ferris Crane**
Designer: **Ferris Crane**
Client: **"City Slickers" Maker of raincoats for Adults and Children**
Agency: **Ferris Crane Graphic Design**

/16
Art Director: **Wayne Krimston**
Designer: **Wayne Krimston**
Writer: **Wayne Krimston**
Client: **Murrie, White, Drummond, Lienhart, Assoc.**

717
Art Director: **John Flesch**
Designer: **John Flesch**
Artist: **Don Tate**
Calligrapher: **Horst Mickler**
Client: **The Quaker Oats Company**
Agency: **Murrie, White, Drummond, Lienhart & Assoc.**

718
Art Director: **Lynn Hollyn**
Designer: **Lyn Hollyn Associates**
Artist: **Lowell Herrero**
Writers: **Anitra Frazier, Norma Eckroate**
Client: **Harbor Publishers**
Editor: **Bill Alexander**
Publisher: **Jack Jennings/Harbor Publishers**

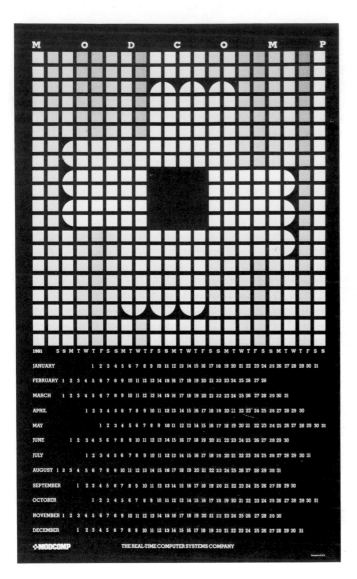

720
Art Director: **Andrew Kner**
Designer: **Andrew Kner**
Artists: **Various, cover: Pierre LeTan**
Writer: **Neil Leonard**
Client: **The New York Times**
Publisher: **The New York Times**

719
Art Director: **Jacques Auger**
Designer: **Jacques Auger**
Artist: **Jacques Auger**
Client: **Modular Computer Systems, Inc.**
Agency: **MODCOMP Corporate Communications**

721
Art Directors: **David November, Marie-Christine Lawrence**
Designers: **Marie-Christine Lawrence, David November, Georgina Leaf**
Photographer: **CBS News**
Artist: **Gabor Kiss**
Writers: **Nancy Mendleson, Francis Piderit**
Client: **CBS Television Network**
Editor: **Nancy Mendleson**
Producer: **Herman Aronson**
Agency: **CBS Entertainment**

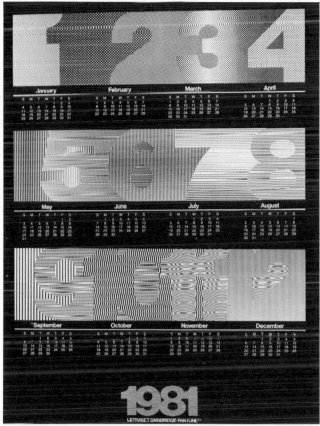

722
Art Director: **Keith Bright**
Designer: **Julie Riefler**
Photographer: **Bret Lopez**
Writer: **Debbie Schwartz**
Client: **Saga Corporation**
Agency: **Bright & Associates, Inc.**

723
Art Director: **Bob Kwait**
Designer: **Bob Kwait**
Photographer: **Chris Wimpey**
Artist: **Ron Van Buskirk**
Writer: **Hal Maynard**
Client: **Daiwa**
Agency: **Phillips-Ramsey Advertising**

724
Art Director: **Rob Silio**
Designers: **Rob Silio, Bob Gagauf**
Artist: **Ron Fiorelli**
Client: **Letraset USA Inc.**
Agency: **Letraset Design Group**

725
Art Director: **Robert S. Todd**
Designer: **Robert S. Todd**
Artist: **Robert S. Todd**
Writer: **Robert S. Todd**
Client: **Union Camp Corporation**
Cover Lettering: **Robert Fernandez—Union Camp Corporation**

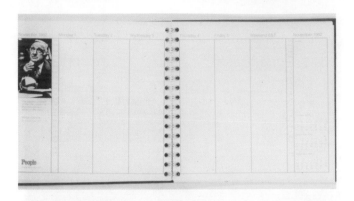

726
Art Directors: **Richard Martell, Liza Greene**
Designer: **Liza Greene**
Photographers: **Various**
Client: **PEOPLE Magazine**
Editor: **Rachel Gelin**
Publisher: **TIME Inc.**
Director: **Liza Greene**
Producer: **Liza Greene**

727
Art Director: **Marianne Gladych**
Designer: **Marianne Gladych**
Photographer: **Kenro Izu**
Writer: **Jack Aaker**
Client: **Litho-Art, Inc.**
Design Firm: **M. Gladych Design**
Agency: **Charle John Cafiero Associates**

728
Art Director: **Tom Schwartz**
Designer: **Tom Schwartz**
Photographers: **Various**
Writer: **Nancy Stevens**
Client: **Nikon Inc.**
Editor: **Nancy Stevens**
Agency: **Scali, McCabe, Sloves, Inc.**

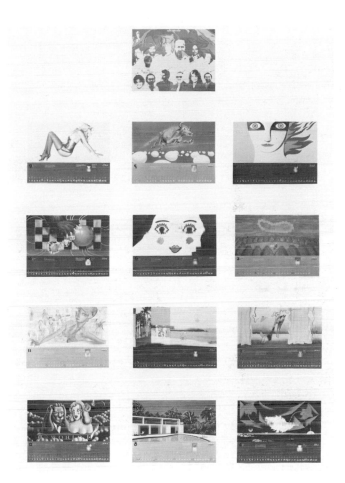

/29
Art Director: **Richard Foy**
Designer: **Richard Foy**
Photographer: **Edward S. Curtis**
Client: **Signature Publications**
Agency: **Communication Arts Inc.**

730
Art Directors: **Shinichiro Tora/U.S. & Yasuharu Nakahara,
Mitsutoshi Hosaka/Japan**
Designer: **Mitsuo Katsui**
Artists: **Shinta Cho, Makoto Wada Haruo, Kazuo Aoki,
Sorayama, Hiroshi Nagai, Japan. George Giusti,
James McMullan, Robert Grossman, Bob Cuningham,
Barbara Nessim, Roger Huyssen, U.S.A.**
Client: **Hotel Barmens Association**
Production Co.: **Dai Nippon Printing Co.**
Agency: **Dai Nippon Printing Co. CDC**

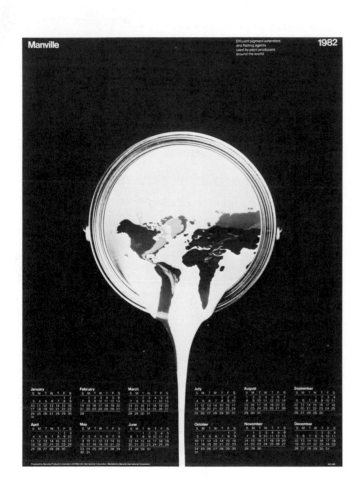

731
Art Director: **Robert W. Taylor**
Designer: **Robert W. Taylor**
Photographer: **Howard Sokol**
Artist: **Robert W. Taylor**
Writer: **Earnst Wehausen**
Client: **Manville International Corporation**

732
Art Director: **Mark Ulrich**
Designer: **Mark Ulrich**
Photographer: **Staff**
Artist: **Staff**
Writer: **Lorraine Wales**
Client: **Denison University**
Editor: **Ellen Kraft**
Publisher: **Denison University**
Agency: **Salvato & Coe Associates, Inc.**

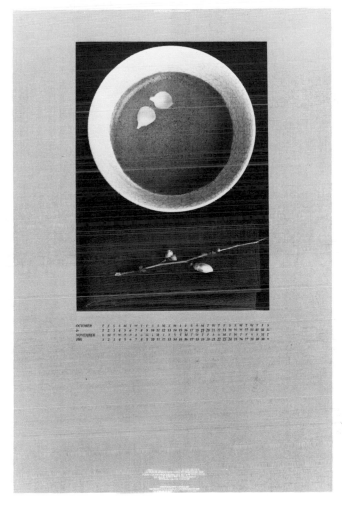

733
Art Directors: **Randall Swatek, David Romanoff**
Designers: **Randall Swatek, David Romanoff**
Client: **Swatek Romanoff Design Inc.**

734
Art Director: **Marianne Gladych**
Designer: **Marianne Gladych**
Photographer: **Kenro Izu**
Writer: **Jack Aaker**
Client: **Litho-Art, Inc.**
Design Firm: **M. Gladych Design**
Agency: **Charle John Cafiero Associates**

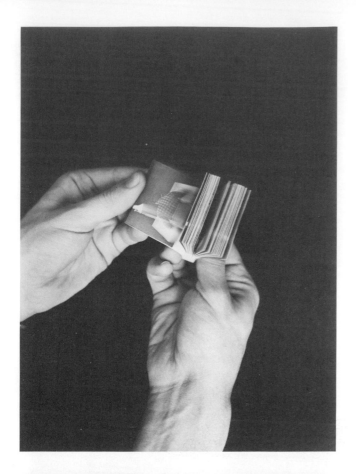

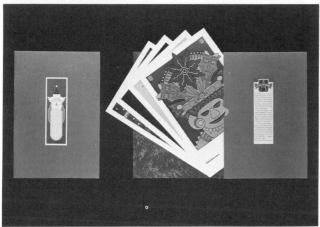

735   SILVER AWARD
Art Director: **Jerry Ketel**
Designer: **Jerry Ketel**
Photographer: **Michael Casey**
Client: **Bernard Jerome Ketel**

737
Creative Director: **Bob Dennard**
Art Director: **Don Sibley**
Designer: **Don Sibley**
Artist: **Don Sibley**
Writer: **Don Sibley**
Client: **Paul Broadhead & Associates, Inc.**
Agency: **Dennard Creative, Inc.**

736   DISTINCTIVE MERIT
Creative Director: **Bob Dennard**
Art Directors: **Don Sibley, Bob Dennard**
Designer: **Don Sibley**
Artists: **Bob Dennard, Don Sibley, Rex Peteet, Tom Curry, Greg King, Sue Llewelyn, Jerry Jeanmard**
Writers: **Bob Dennard, Don Sibley, Cody Newman**
Client: **Heritage Press**
Agency: **Dennard Creative, Inc.**

738
Art Director: **Lou Portuesi**
Designer: **Lou Portuesi**
Artist: **George Beckstead**
Writer: **Don Horton**
Publisher: **Reader's Digest**

739
Art Director: **Jim Hackley**
Designer: **Pete Traynor**
Artist: **Jim Hackley**
Writer: **Pete Traynor**
Client: **Agnihotra Press; Woods Group; Characters**

740
Art Directors: **Kathy Filter, Jay Filter**
Designer: **Kathy Filter**
Artist: **Art Factory**
Writers: **Dennis Frankenberry, Steve Laughlin**
Client: **Manpower, Inc.**
Production Co.: **Jay Filter, Kris Kagelmann-Holtz**
Agency: **Frankenberry, Laughlin & Constable, Inc.**

741
Creative Director: **Bob Dennard**
Art Director: **Rex Peteet**
Designer: **Rex Peteet**
Artist: **Rex Peteet**
Writer: **Rex Peteet**
Client: **Paul Broadhead & Associates, Inc.**
Agency: **Dennard Creative, Inc.**

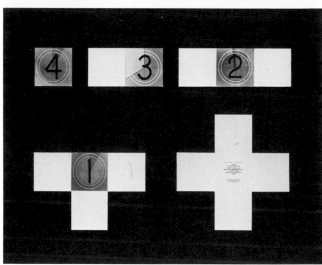

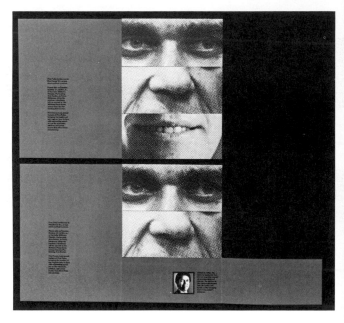

742
Art Director: **Wayne Burkart**
Designer: **Tom Sizemore**
Writer: **John Gerstner**
Client: **Deere & Company, JD Journal**

744
Art Directors: **Warren W. Langston, Carolyn Wade Frazier**
Designer: **Carolyn Wade Frazier**
Artist: **Carolyn Wade Frazier**
Client: **Langston/Frazier Design Associates**
Agency: **Langston/Frazier Design Associates**

743
Art Director: **Sandi Young**
Designer: **Sandi Young**
Client: **Atlantic Records**

745
Art Directors: **Mark Perkins, Steve Gibbs**
Designer: **Steve Gibbs**
Photographers: **Various**
Writer: **Mark Perkins**
Client: **First Tulsa Bank**
Agency: **Richards, Sullivan, Brock & Assoc./
The Richards Group**

747
Art Director: **Harold Matossian**
Designer: **Leslee Ladds**
Client: **Knoll International**
Agency: **Knoll Graphics**

749
Art Director: **Albert Greenberg**
Designer: **Albert Greenberg**
Writer: **Mrs. Gerald Van der Kemp**
Client: **Claude Monet/Giverny Foundation**
Publisher: **Quality Offset Corp.**
Agency: **Wells, Rich, Greene, Inc.**

748
Art Director: **Jack Evans**
Designer: **Craig DuCharme**
Artist: **Craig DuCharme**
Client: **All of the 11th Floor of World Trade Center**
Agency: **Unigraphics, Inc.**

750
Art Directors: **Craig Frazier, Conrad Jorgensen**
Designers: **Conrad Jorgensen, Craig Frazier**
Artist: **Conrad Jorgensen**
Writers: **Conrad Jorgensen, Craig Frazier**
Client: **Jorgensen/Frazier, Inc.**
Agency: **Jorgensen/Frazier, Inc.**

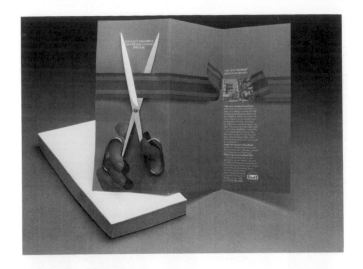

758
Art Director: **Dave Rogers**
Photographer: **Frank White**
Writer: **Pat Carrithers**
Client: **Gulf Oil Chemicals Company**
Agency: **Ketchum Advertising/Houston**

759
Art Director: **Ted Nagata**
Designer: **Ted Nagata**
Artist: **Paul Seo**
Writer: **Ted Nagata**
Client: **Art Directors Salt Lake City**

760
Art Directors: **Richard Martell, Liza Greene**
Designer: **Liza Greene**
Writer: **Gail Duncan**
Client: **PEOPLE Magazine**
Editor: **Gail Duncan**
Publisher: **TIME Inc.**
Director: **Liza Greene**
Producer: **Liza Greene**

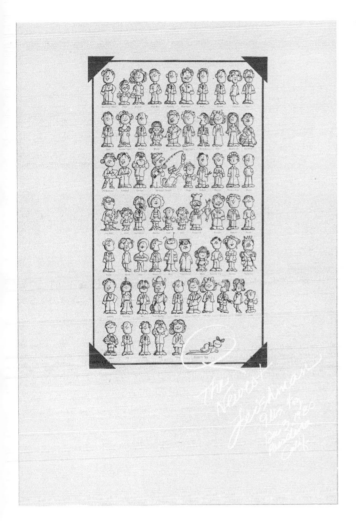

761
Art Director: **Jann Church Advertising &**
Graphic Design, Inc.
Designer: **Jann Church Advertising &**
Graphic Design, Inc.
Artists: **Jann Church, Paula Kretchmeyer**
Writer: **Jann Church Advertising & Graphic Design, Inc.**
Client: **The Leishman's**
Editor: **Jann Church Advertising & Graphic Design, Inc.**
Printer: **MD Silkscreen**

762
Art Director: **Jann Church Advertising &**
Graphic Design, Inc.
Designer: **Jann Church Advertising &**
Graphic Design, Inc.
Artist: **Lea Pascoe, Marilynn Bleck**
Writer: **Jann Church Advertising & Graphic Design, Inc.**
Client: **Kathy Dalzen & Robert Klotz**
Editor: **Jann Church Advertising & Graphic Design, Inc.**
Printer: **MD Silkscreen**

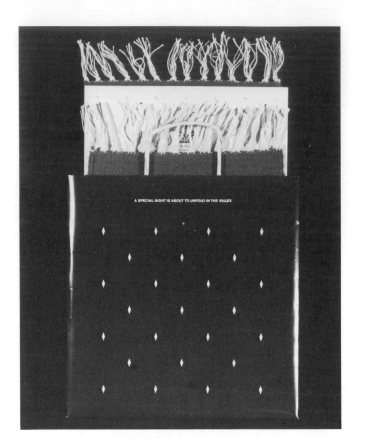

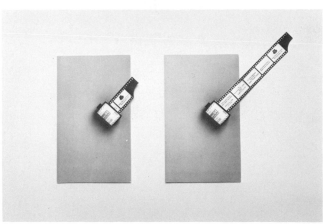

763
Art Directors: **Brian Boyd, Ron Sullivan**
Designer: **Brian Boyd**
Artist: **Brian Boyd**
Writer: **Mark Perkins**
Client: **Paul Broadhead & Associates**
Agency: **Richards, Sullivan, Brock & Assoc./ The Richards Group**

764
Art Director: **Jack Evans**
Designer: **Alberto Tomas**
Photographer: **John Harvey**
Writer: **Bonnie Evans**
Client: **John Harvey & Assoc. Photography Inc.**
Agency: **Unigraphics, Inc.**

765
Art Director: **Woody Pirtle**
Designer: **Woody Pirtle**
Photographer: **Steve Brady**
Writer: **Woody Pirtle**
Client: **Marsha and Steve Brady**
Agency: **Woody Pirtle, Inc.**

766
Art Director: **Eugene J. Grossman**
Designer: **Sandra Meyers**
Client: **American Institute of Graphic Arts**
Production Co.: **S.D. Scott Printing**
Agency: **Anspach Grossman Portugal Inc.**

James Scherzi Photography has left the nest it was born in.
And moved to: 116 Town Line Road, Syracuse, New York 13211. 315/455-7961

767
Art Director: **Don Trousdell**
Designer: **Don Trousdell**
Artist: **Larry Emard**
Writer: **Virgil Shutze**
Client: **McDonald & Little**
Agency: **McDonald & Little**

769
Art Director: **Garry Frankoff**
Photographer: **James Scherzi**
Writer: **Paul J. Bihuniak**
Client: **James Scherzi Photography**
Agency: **Paul, John & Lee, Adv., Inc.**

768
Art Director: **Mike Quon**
Designers: **Anne Twomey, Mike Quon**
Artist: **Mike Quon**
Writers: **Anne Twomey, Mike Quon**
Client: **Mike Quon Design Office**

770
Creative Director: **Bob Dennard**
Art Director: **Rex Peteet**
Designer: **Rex Peteet**
Artist: **Rex Peteet**
Writers: **Bob Dennard, Rex Peteet**
Client: **Federated Stores Realty, Inc.**
Agency: **Dennard Creative, Inc.**

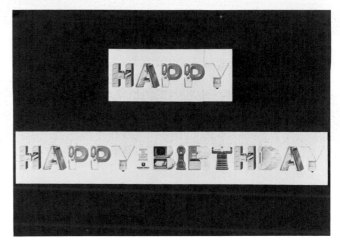

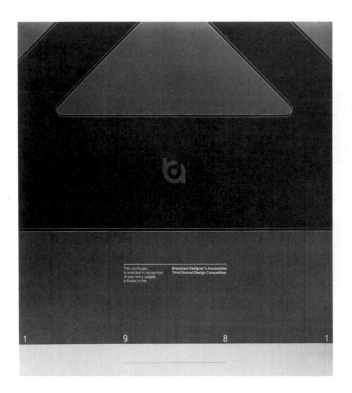

772
Art Director: **Woody Pirtle**
Designer: **Woody Pirtle**
Photographer: **Mike Haynes**
Writer: **The Sherrill Co.**
Client: **Amfac Hotels**
Agency: **Woody Pirtle, Inc./The Sherrill Co.**

771
Art Director: **James A. Houff**
Designer: **James A. Houff**
Client: **Broadcast Designers Association**

773
Art Director: **John Constable**
Designer: **McDill Advertising Design**
Artist: **Art Factory**
Writers: **Dennis Frankenberry, Steve Laughlin**
Client: **Manpower, Inc.**
Production Co.: **Kris Kagelmann-Holtz, Manpower, Inc.**
Agency: **Frankenberry, Laughlin & Constable, Inc.**

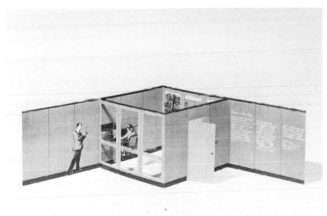

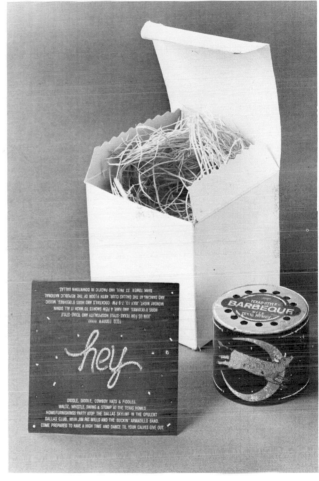

774
Art Directors: **Suzanne Bates, Wes Massey**
Designer: **Wes Massey**
Artist: **Dover Archives**
Writer: **Sam Harrison**
Client: **John H. Harland Co.**
Agency: **John H. Harland Co.**

775
Art Director: **Massimo Vignelli, Peter Laundy**
Designer: **David Dunkelberger**
Artist: **David Dunkelberger**
Writer: **JoAnne Durante**
Client: **E.F. Hauserman**

776
Art Director: **Steve Connatser**
Designers: **Steve Connatser, David Kampa**
Artists: **Steve Connatser, David Kampa**
Writers: **Judy Anderton, Steve Connatser**
Client: **Texas Homes Magazine**
Agency: **Connatser & Crum**

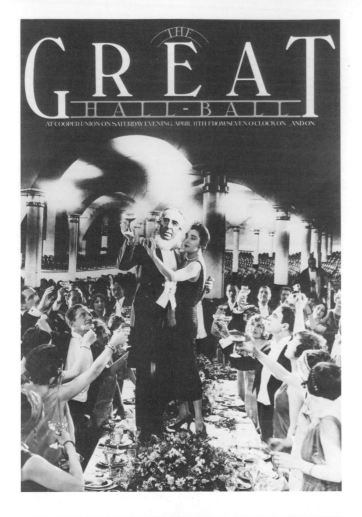

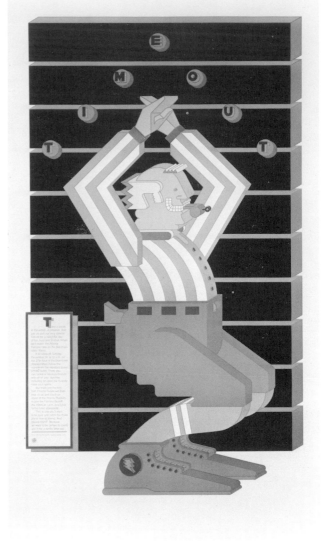

777
Art Directors: **Henrietta Condak, Marilyn Hoffner**
Designer: **Henrietta Condak**
Photographer: **Cooper Union Archive Photo &
Old Movie Still**
Writer: **Marilyn Hoffner**
Client: **The Cooper Union Alumni Association**

778
Art Director: **Frank Roth**
Designer: **Gary Karpinski**
Writer: **Norton Cohen**
Client: **Paragon Group, Inc.**
Agency: **Frank/James Productions**

779
Creative Director: **Bob Dennard**
Art Director: **Rex Peteet**
Designer: **Rex Peteet**
Artist: **Rex Peteet**
Writer: **Rex Peteet**
Client: **Paul Broadhead & Associates, Inc.**
Agency: **Dennard Creative, Inc.**

780
Art Director: **Brian Stewart**
Designer: **Brian Stewart**
Artist: **Brooke Kenny**
Client: **Barry Rubin, C.P.A.**
Agency: **Stewart & Stewart**

781
Art Director: **Robert J. Warkulwiz**
Designer: **Robert J. Warkulwiz**
Artist: **Jeanne Derderian**
Client: **Warkulwiz Design**
Agency: **Warkulwiz Design**

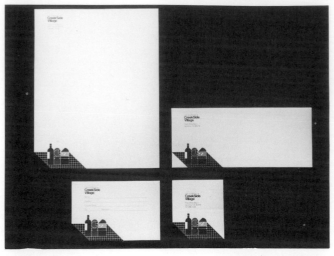

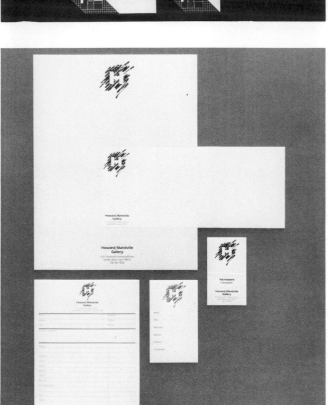

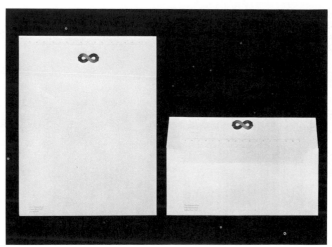

782
Art Director: **Harry Murphy**
Designers: **Harry Murphy, Sheldon Lewis**
Artist: **Sheldon Lewis**
Client: **Fisher Development**
Agency: **Harry Murphy & Friends**

784
Art Directors: **Doug Akagi, Richard Burns**
Designer: **Doug Akagi**
Artist: **Ken Andreotta**
Client: **Society of Environmental Graphics Designers**
Agency: **The GNU Group/Sausalito, Houston**

783
Art Director: **Jack R. Anderson**
Designers: **Jack R. Anderson, Carole Jones**
Client: **Howard/Mandville Gallery**
Production Co: **Frank Potter & Associates Printers**
Agency: **John Hornall Design Works**

785
Art Director: **Woody Pirtle**
Designer: **Woody Pirtle**
Artists: **Woody Pirtle, Frank Nichols**
Client: **The Glenwood School**
Agency: **Woody Pirtle, Inc.**

Fine Grain Films
111 Ainslie Street
Brooklyn, NY 11211

Tucson Museum of Art

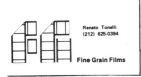

Renato Tonelli
(212) 625-0394

Fine Grain Films

Pardee & Fleming
Landscape Design

614 Palisades Avenue
Santa Monica, CA 90402
213 277-8044
213 451-2470

Residential
Commercial
Landscape
Design
Installation
& Construction

Fine Grain Films   111 Ainslie Street   Brooklyn, NY 11211

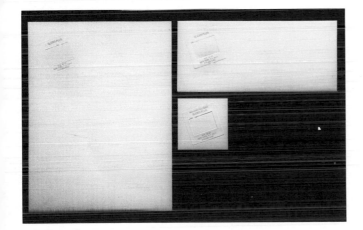

786
Art Director: **Jitsuo Hoashi**
Designer: **Jitsuo Hoashi**
Artist: **Jitsuo Hoashi**
Client: **Fine Grain Films**
Printer: **Erin Malloy**
Director: **Dork Forkle**
Production Co.: **Fine Grain Films**
Agency: **Stellagachi & Ralph, Inc.**

788
Art Director: **Kurt Gibson**
Designer: **Kurt Gibson**
Artist: **Kurt Gibson**
Client: **Tucson Museum of Art**
Director: **R. Andrew Maass**
Agency: **IBM Tucson Design Center**

787
Art Director: **Patrick Florville**
Designer: **Patrick Florville**
Client: **Slides Plus**
Agency: **Florville Design and Analysis**

789
Art Director: **Paul Pruneau**
Designer: **Paul Pruneau**
Artist: **Paul Pruneau**
Client: **Pardee & Fleming Landscape Design**

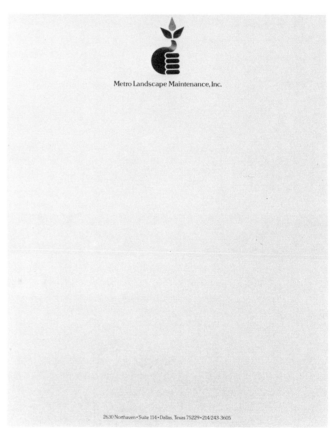

790
Art Director: **David Wojdyla**
Designer: **David Wojdyla**
Artist: **David Wojdyla**
Client: **David Wojdyla**
Agency: **De Krig Advertising, Inc.**

791
Art Director: **Jack Evans**
Designer: **Don Fischer**
Artist: **Bill Carpenter**
Client: **Metro Landscape Maintenance**
Agency: **Unigraphics, Inc.**

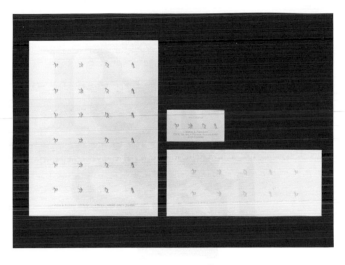

792
Art Director: **Dennis Merritt**
Designer: **Dennis Merritt**
Photographer: **Mike Karbelnikoff**
Artist: **Dennis Merritt**
Client: **Callahan & Associates**

793
Art Directors: **Ben Carter, Mark Geer**
Designer: **Mark Geer**
Artist: **Mark Geer**
Client: **Ben Carter & Associates**
Agency: **Ben Carter & Associates**

794
Art Director: **Lucas R. Visser**
Designer: **Bradley Graham**
Artist: **Bradley Graham**
Client: **Patty's Slim Cooking**
Agency: **Design Communications, Inc.**

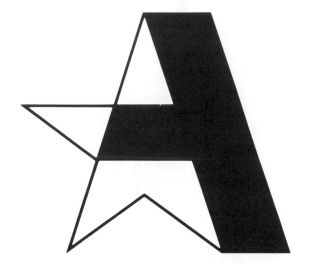

804
Art Director: **Yoshi Sekiguchi**
Designer: **Yoshi Sekiguchi**
Client: **IL Professional Writers Assoc.**
Agency: **Rising Sun Design**

806
Art Director: **Alan Peckolick**
Designer: **Alan Peckolick**
Artist: **Tony DiSpigna**
Client: **American Savings Bank**
Publisher: **American Savings Bank**

805.
Designer: **Marty Neumeier**
Client: **Arntz Cobra (car manufacturer)**
Agency: **Neumeier Design Team**

807
Art Director: **Mark S. Thompson**
Designer: **Mark S. Thompson**
Artist: **Mark S. Thompson**
Client: **Cooper Gaskets & Stampings**
Agency: **AdMark Advertising Marketing Services**

808
Art Director: **Timothy J. Park**
Designer: **Timothy J. Park**
Artist: **Anne O. Walker**
Client: **Tennessee Valley Authority**
Agency: **Park & Stidham Inc.**

810
Art Director: **Marty Neumeier**
Designer: **Sandra Higashi**
Client: **U.S. Invest**
Agency: **Neumeier Design Team**

809
Art Director: **Don Clark**
Designer: **Pam Jones**
Client: **Colorado Ice Hockey Referees Association**
Agency: **Don Clark Design Office**

811
Art Directors: **Doug Akagi, Richard Burns, Jeffry Corbin**
Designers: **Doug Akagi, Richard Burns, Jeffry Corbin**
Artist: **Doug Akagi**
Client: **Society of Enviromental Graphics Designers**
Agency: **The GNU Group/Sausalito, Houston**

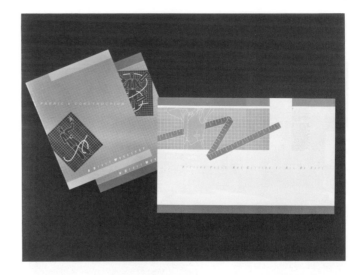

820
Art Director: **Jim Begany**
Designer: **Jim Begany**
Photographers: **Bert McNomee, Ignazio Ruggieri, Bill Begany**
Artist: **Gene Papi**
Writer: **Stu Nickerson**
Client: **Volkswagen of America**
Agency: **RMI, Inc.**

821
Art Director: **Peter Perry**
Designers: **Peter Perry, Peter Erickson**
Photographers: **Jim Thomas, Phil Porcella**
Writers: **Rick Goldberg, Jane Goldman**
Client: **Digital Education Computer Systems**

822
Art Director: **Michael Cronan**
Designer: **Michael Cronan**
Artists: **Michael Cronan, Helene Schaffer, Hockwah Yeo, Carol Kramer**
Writer: **Lon Clark Associates, Inc.**
Client: **Levi Strauss & Company**
Agency: **The Office of Michael Manwaring**

823
Art Director: **Jud Smith**
Photographers: **Dennis Manarchy, Image Bank**
Artists: **McNamara & Associates, Conrad Fialkowski**
Writer: **Ron Sackett**
Client: **Harley-Davidson Motor Company**
Agency: **Carmichael-Lynch, Inc.**

1982 CRESSIDA   1982 CORONA

FOUR!

Release No. 4 from Atlantic, Atco, Cotillion and Custom Labels.

825
Art Director: **Bob Defrin**
Designer: **Bob Defrin**
Photographers: **Allen Levine, David Kennedy, Stock**
Client: **Atlantic Records**

824
Art Directors: **Supra—Jim Doyle, Cressida—Brad Neeley, Corona—Jim Doyle**
Designer: **Jim Doyle**
Photographers: **Supra—Mickey McGuire, Cressida—Dick James, Corona— Marshall Lefferts**
Artist: **Konrad Kahl**
Writers: **Supra—Jim Lodge, Cressida—Bill Brooke, Corona—Bill Brooke**
Client: **Toyota Motor Sales, U.S.A., Inc.**
Publisher: **Supra—Anderson Litho Co., Cressida/Corona Joffries Litho Co.**
Creative Director: **Sean K. Fitzpatrick**
Agency: **Dancer Fitzgerald Sample, Inc./S. Calif**

826
Art Director: **Judy Anderson**
Designer: **Judy Anderson**
Photographer: **Larry Laszlo**
Client: **Colorado Council on the Arts and Humanities**
Editor: **Juliet Wittman**
Publisher: **Intermountain Color**

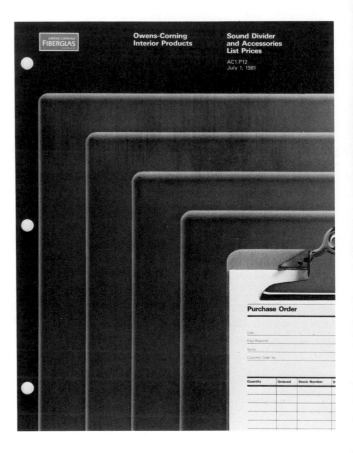

827
Art Director: **Anthony W. Rutka**
Designer: **Anthony W. Rutka**
Photographer: **Doug Barber**
Writer: **Joan Lee Weadock**
Client: **Rider College**
Agency: **The North Charles Street Design Organization**

828
Art Directors: **Terry Lesniewicz, Al Navarre**
Designers: **Terry Lesniewicz, Al Navarre**
Photographer: **Jim Rohman/Owens-Corning Photographic Services**
Writer: **Jim Hynes**
Client: **Owens-Corning Fiberglas Corporation**
Agency: **Lesniewicz/Navarre**

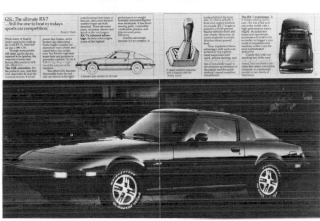

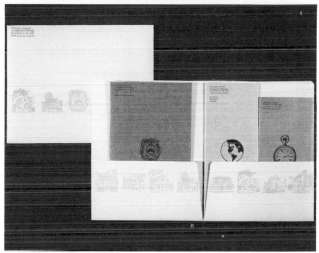

829
Art Director: **Ted Clark**
Designer: **Ted Clark**
Photographers: **Dick James, Gerry Trafficanda**
Artist: **Dave Kimble**
Writer: **Steve Kaplan**
Client: **American Honda Motor Co., Inc.**
Publisher: **Anderson Litho.**
Agency: **Needham, Harper & Steers**

830
Art Director: **Gene Despard**
Writer: **Bo Moroz**
Client: **Mazda Motors of America**
Producer: **Charlie Bungert**
Agency: **Foote, Cone & Belding/Honig**

831
Art Director: **Bennet, Menchin, Robertson**
Designer: **Bennett, Menchin, Robertson**
Artists: **S.A. Menchin (March), Lauren Vram (April), Steve Bennett (May)**
Writer: **Mercedes Sandoval**
Client: **WBGO Jazz Radio**
Editor: **Mercedes Sandoval**
Publisher: **WBGO Jazz Radio**

832 DISTINCTIVE MERIT
Art Director: **Karen Kutner Katinas**
Designer: **Karen Kutner Katinas**
Writer: **Nancy Garfinkel**
Client: **Champion International Corporation**
Agency: **Katinas Design**

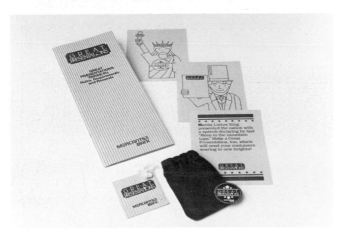

833
Art Directors: **David November, Marie-Christine Lawrence, John LeProvost**
Designer: **Marie-Christine Lawrence**
Artists: **John LeProvost, Jim Deesing**
Writers: **Don Evers, Sherman Adler**
Client: **CBS Television Network**
Producers: **Herman Aronson, Tina Dakin, David Zinzi, Chris Mazzariello**

834
Art Director: **Frank Roth**
Designer: **Gary Karpinski**
Artist: **Linda Solovic**
Writer: **Carol Ansehl**
Client: **Mercantile Bank**
Agency: **Frank/James Productions**

835   DISTINCTIVE MERIT
Art Director: **Kathy Moon**
Designer: **Kathy Moon**
Artist: **Janice Ashford**
Writer: **Becky Benavides**
Client: **San Antonio Convention & Visitors Bureau**
Agency: **Ed Yardang & Associates**

836
Art Directors: **Steve Miller, Joe Smith**
Designer: **Sara Love**
Artists: **Fred Otnes, Wilson McLean, Allan Mardon**
Writer: **Tom Robb**
Client: **Kawneer Architectural Products**
Agency: **Garrison, Jasper, Rose & Company**

837
Art Directors: **Terry McCoy, Paula Andell**
Designers: **Terry McCoy, Paula Andell**
Artist: **Peggy Sue McDaniel**
Writer: **Penny Holme**
Client: **Hilton Inn at Inverrary**
Agency: **Savage Design Group, Inc.**

839
Art Director: **Danny Boone**
Designer: **Danny Boone**
Photographer: **Jamie Cook**
Writer: **Mike Hughes**
Client: **Mobil Chemical**
Agency: **The Martin Agency**

838
Art Directors: **Terry McCoy, Paula Andell**
Designers: **Terry McCoy, Paula Andell**
Photographer: **Jim Lemoine**
Writer: **Penny Holme**
Client: **Hilton Inn at Inverrary**
Agency: **Savage Design Group, Inc.**

840
Art Director: **Richard Nava**
Designers: **Richard Nava, Marla Rosenfeld**
Photographer: **Norman Snyder**
Artist: **Jerry Zimmerman**
Writer: **Jean Zorrios**
Client: **Abbott Shilling/DuPont Company**
Agency: **Image Communications Inc.**

Keeping a clean house can lead to a rash of problems.

841
Art Director: **Jann Church Adv. & Graphic Design Inc.**
Designer: **Jann Church Adv. & Graphic Design Inc.**
Photographer: **Walter Urie/Urie Photography**
Writer: **Jann Church Advertising & Graphic Design, Inc.**
Client: **Mead Paper Co. - The Mead Library of Ideas**
Editor: **Jann Church Advertising & Graphic Design, Inc.**
Printer: **George Rice and Sons**
Typography: **Headliners of Orange County**
Production Co.: **Paper: Mead Black & White**

842
Art Director: **Laurie Carver**
Designer: **Laurie Carver**
Artist: **Jack Stockman**
Writers: **Leo Parenti, Ted Horne**
Client: **Dorsey Laboratories**
Agency: **Sieber & McIntyre, Inc.**

843
Art Director: **Hal Florian**
Designer: **Hal Florian**
Artist: **Ed Acuna**
Writers: **Paul Abrams, Robert Lonergan,
Frank O'Handley**
Client: **Schering Corporation**
Agency: **Ketchum Advertising/New York**

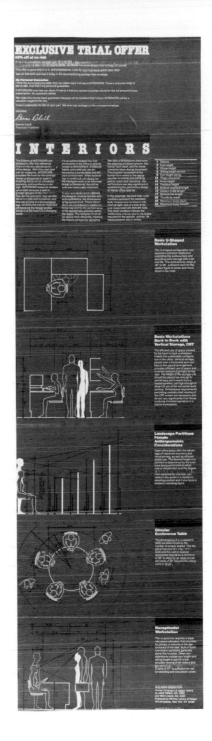

844
Art Director: **Laurie Carver**
Designer: **Laurie Carver**
Artist: **Bill Sanders**
Writer: **Ted Horne**
Client: **Dorsey Laboratories**
Agency: **Sieber & McIntyre, Inc.**

845
Art Director: **Michael Donovan**
Designer: **Michael Donovan**
Artists: **Jim Silks, Randy Lieu**
Client: **Interiors Magazine**
Publisher: **Interiors Magazine**
Agency: **Donovan and Green, Inc.**

846
Art Directors: **Rick Vaughn, Steve Wedeen,
Tadd Johnson**
Designers: **Steve Wedeen, Tadd Johnson, Rick Vaughn**
Photographer: **Steve Wedeen**
Artists: **Tadd Johnson, Rick Vaughn, Steve Wedeen**
Writers: **Rick Vaughn, Steve Wedeen, Tadd Johnson,
Will Sherwood, Maggie Lawrence-McPhee**
Client: **The Design Group**
Printer: **McLeod Printing, Starline Creative Printing**
Typesetting: **Optext Design Typography, Typography
Unlimited**
Lithography: **Arnold Litho.**
Agency: **The Design Group**

847
Art Director: **Richard Nava**
Designer: **Richard Nava**
Photographer: **Norman Snyder**
Artist: **Jerry Zimmerman**
Writer: **Susan MacMurchy**
Client: **Citrus Central Inc.**
Agency: **Image Communications Inc.**

848
Art Director: **George MacFail**
Designer: **George MacFail**
Photographer: **Jon Silla**
Artist: **Marsha Jessup**
Writers: **Tamar Small, Shelley Laurin**
Client: **Geometric Data, a SmithKline Beckman Co.**
Agency: **Cummins, MacFail & Nutry, Inc. Advertising**

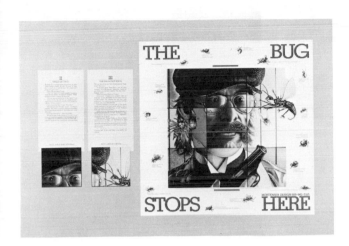

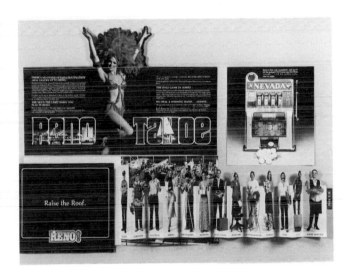

849
Art Director: **Gordon Mortensen**
Designer: **Gordon Mortensen**
Illustrators: **Charles Shields, Eraldo Carugati, Ed Soyka, Cristine Mortensen, John Lykes, Franz Altschuler, Ignacio Gomez, Jósef Sumichrast, Roger Huyssen**
Writer: **Colin Campbell**
Client: **Mortensen Design**
Agency: **Mortensen Design**

850
Art Director: **Stan Dunlap**
Designer: **Stan Dunlap**
Photographers: **John Curtis, Just Loomis**
Artist: **Stan Dunlap**
Writer: **Dean Graves**
Client: **Reno Convention Bureau**

851
Art Director: **Carol Carson**
Designer: **Carol Carson**
Artist: **Manny Schongut**
Client: **Scholastic Early Childhood Program**
Agency: **Push Pin Studios**

852   GOLD AWARD
Art Director: **Peter Windett**
Designer: **Peter Windett**
Artist: **Graham Everden**
Client: **Crabtree & Evelyn, Ltd.**
Agency: **Peter Windett Associates**

853   SILVER AWARD
Art Directors: **Paul Port, Ralph Miolla, Bert Fischer**
Designers: **Paul Port, Ralph Miolla, Karin Kaplan**
Artists: **Christoph Blumrich, Brian Sheridan**
Client: **General Foods, Corporate Design Center**
Agency: **Port Miolla Associates, Incorporated**

855
Art Directors: **Ralph Miolla, Paul Port**
Designers: **Ralph Miolla, Paul Port**
Artist: **Nancy Stahl**
Client: **The Nestle' Corporation**
Agency: **Port Miolla Associates, Incorporated**

854   DISTINCTIVE MERIT
Art Director: **Seymour Chwast**
Designer: **Seymour Chwast**
Artist: **Seymour Chwast**
Client: **PushPinoff Productions**
Agency: **Push Pin Studios**

856
Art Directors: **Jerry Deibert, Steven Mitsch, Samuel Rivman**
Designers: **Jerry Deibert, Steven Mitsch, Samuel Rivman**
Artist: **Bill Mayer**
Writers: **Thomas Davey, Jim Bouton**
Client: **The Jim Bouton Corporation**
Agency: **303 Studio, Inc.**

858
Art Director: **Ross Carron**
Designer: **Ross Carron**
Client: **J.W. Morris Wineries**
Agency: **Ross Carron Design**

860
Program Design & Direction: **Robert P. Gersin**
Graphic Design Direction: **David Curry**
Product Design: **Daniel Murphy**
Photographers: **Dianne Baasch, Dan Kozan**
Artists: **V. Young, L. Chrisman, S. Springer, A. Stewart, G. Kibbee, Fu Lin Hsin**
Writers: **T. Clymer, R. Venezky**
Record Producer: **Erica Malarek**
Client: **Ginn & Company**
Editors: **R. Campanella, K. Baker**
Publisher: **Ginn & Company**
Production Direction: **P. Maka, L. Peabody**
Production Co.: **The Banta Media Group**
Design Agency: **Robert P. Gersin Associates Inc.**

859
Art Director: **Howard Grant**
Designers: **Howard Grant, Leslie Hayes, Scott Feuer**
Photographer: **Leonard Cohen**
Writer: **Jeff Cramp**
Client: **Faber-Castell Corporation**
Agency: **Grant Marketing Communications, Inc.**

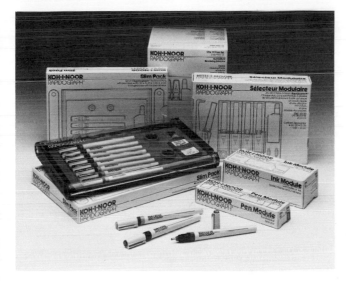

861
Art Director: **Cinda Katz Bonk**
Designers: **Rachel Schreiber Levitan,**
Kathleen Sullivan Kaska
Artist: **Jozef Sumichrast**
Client: **Magicolor**
Producer: **Jeanine Handley**
Agency: **Brown & Rosner, Inc.**

862
Art Director: **Frederick D. Hadtke, Sr. Vice Pres.**
Designer: **Jay Robert Wells, Dir. Graphic Design**
Client: **Koh-I-Noor Rapidograph**
Agency: **Robert Hain Associates, Inc.**

863
Art Directors: **Hal Riney, Gerry Andelin**
Designer: **Barry Deutsch/Steinhilber, Deutsch & Gard**
Artists: **Myland McRevey, James S. Schlesinger**
Client: **Pabst Brewing Company**
Agency: **Ogilvy & Mather, San Francisco**

864
Art Director: **Charles Hively**
Designers: **Lance Brown, Lyle Metzdorf, Charles Hively**
Artists: **Richard Hess, Al Bates**
Writer: **Carol Miller**
Client: **Blue Bell Creameries**
Agency: **Metzdorf Advertising Agency**

865
Art Directors: **Chris Holland, Rob Leyko**
Designers: **Chris Holland, Rob Leyko**
Client: **Audio Dynamics Corp.**
Agency: **Holland Advertising Inc.**

866
Art Director: **Peter Windett**
Designer: **Peter Windett**
Artist: **Tony Meeuwissen**
Client: **Crabtree & Evelyn, Ltd.**
Agency: **Peter Windett Associates**

867
Art Director: **Steve Cloutier**
Designer: **Steve Cloutier**
Artist: **Ed Lindlof**
Writer: **Ed Lindlof**
Client: **McDonald's**
Agency: **Bernstein-Rein Advertising, Inc.**

868
Art Director: **Chris Rovillo**
Designer: **Chris Rovillo**
Artists: **Chris Rovillo, Dick Mitchell**
Writer: **Tom's Foods**
Client: **Tom's Foods**
Agency: **Richards, Sullivan, Brock & Assoc./
The Richards Group**

870
Art Director: **Mario L. Cruz**
Designer: **Mario L. Cruz**
Photographer: **Henry Mills**
Artist: **Chris Daniels**
Writer: **Judy Anderson**
Client: **IBM Charlotte, NC**

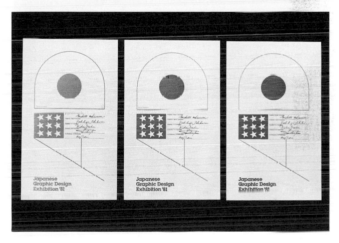

869   SILVER AWARD
Art Director: **Heather Cooper**
Designer: **Heather Cooper**
Artist: **Heather Cooper**
Client: **Ruby Street, Inc.**
Agency: **Burns, Cooper, Hynes Limited**

871
Art Director: **Jitsuo Hoashi**
Designers: **Veena Mattewson, Judy Chan**
Writer: **Meg Crane**
Client: **Japanese Graphic Idea Exhibition '81 Committee**

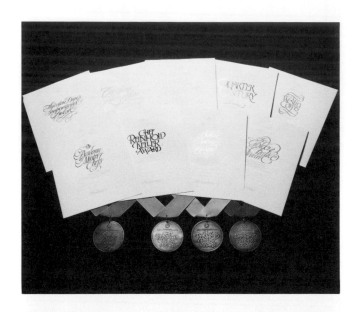

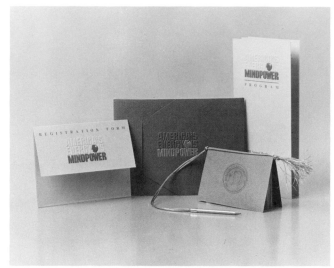

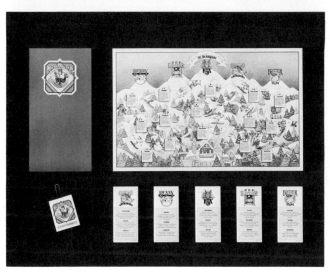

872
Art Directors: **John Hornall, Jack R. Anderson**
Designers: **Jack R. Anderson, John Hornall**
Artist: **Tim Girvin**
Writer: **Rachel Bard**
Client: **Westin Hotel**
Production Co.: **Waller Printing and Lithograph Co.**
Agency: **Cole & Weber Design Group**

874
Art Director: **Stan Gellman**
Designer: **Stan Gellman**
Photographer: **Chartmasters, Inc., Chicago, Illinois**
Writer: **Jim Gobberdiel**
Client: **University of Illinois Foundation**
Agency: **Stan Gellman Graphic Design, Inc.**

873
Creative Director: **Bob Dennard**
Art Director: **Don Sibley**
Designer: **Don Sibley**
Artists: **Don Sibley, Jerry Jeanmard, Rex Peteet**
Writers: **Bob Dennard, Don Sibley**
Client: **Bennigan's Taverns**
Agency: **Dennard Creative, Inc.**

875
Creative Director: **Bob Dennard**
Art Director: **Don Sibley**
Designer: **Don Sibley**
Artists: **Don Sibley, Greg King**
Writers: **Bob Dennard, Don Sibley**
Client: **Paul Broadhead & Associates, Inc.**
Agency: **Dennard Creative, Inc.**

876
Creative Director: **Bob Dennard**
Art Director: **Don Sibley**
Designers: **Don Sibley, Rex Peteet**
Artists: **Don Sibley, Rex Peteet**
Client: **Bennigan's Taverns**
Agency: **Dennard Creative, Inc.**

877
Art Directors: **John Luckett, Susan Slover**
Designer: **Susan Slover**
Writer: **John Luckett**
Client: **Response Concepts/Case-Hoyt**
Agency: **Luckett & Slover Inc.**

878
Art Directors: **Martha Langford, George Nitefor**
Designer: **George Nitefor**
Photographers: **Plane—James Martin
Field—Mary E. Neuseld
Blanket—Len Chatwin**
Writer: **Martha Langford**
Client: **National Film Board of Canada**
Production Co.: **Still Photography Division**

POSTERS

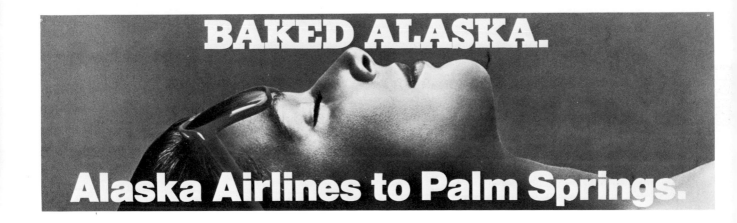

889
Art Director: **Bill Sweney**
Photographer: **Chuck Kuhn**
Client: **Alaska Airlines**
Agency: **Chiat/Day/Seattle**

Saratoga Performing Arts Center, Saratoga Springs, New York

890
Art Director: **Lars Anderson**
Designer: **Lars Anderson**
Photographer: **Steve Steigman**
Writer: **Peter Levathes**
Client: **Maxell Corporation of America**
Agency: **Scali, McCabe, Sloves, Inc.**

891
Art Director: **Tom Yerxa**
Designers: **Russ Almquist, Vic Luke**
Photographer: **Vic Luke**
Costume Designer: **Rudi Gernreich**
Client: **Lewitzky Dance Company**
Production Co.: **Atlantic Richfield Company**
Agency: **In-House**

892
Art Director: **Milton Glaser**
Designer: **Milton Glaser**
Artist: **Milton Glaser**
Client: **Saratoga Performing Arts Center**
Agency: **Milton Glaser, Inc.**

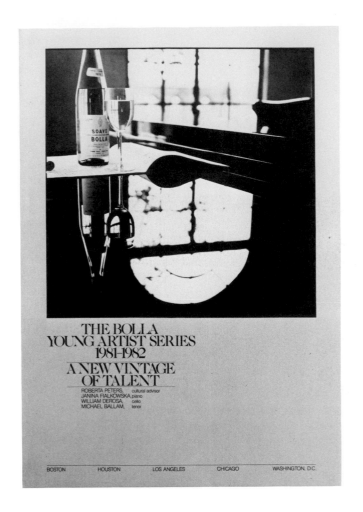

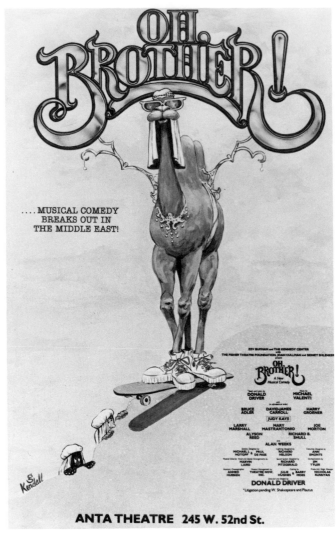

893
Art Director: **Katsuji Asada**
Designer: **Katsuji Asada**
Photographer: **Yuji Sawa**
Client: **Jos. Garneau, Co./Bolla Wine**
Agency: **Ketchum Public Relations**

894
Art Director: **Gary Kendall**
Designer: **Gary Kendall**
Artist: **Gary Kendall**
Client: **Zev Bufman**
Agency: **Ash/LeDonne, Inc.**

895
Art Director: **Jay Morales**
Designer: **Jay Morales**
Photographer: **Sean Eager**
Writer: **Giff Crosby**
Client: **American Airlines**
Agency: **Doyle Dane Bernbach**

896
Art Director: **Irene Ramp**
Designer: **Michael Doret**
Artist: **Michael Doret**
Client: **Peregrine, Inc.**
Agency: **Michael Doret, Inc.**

897
Art Directors: **Art Goodman, G. Dean Smith**
Designers: **Saul Bass, Herb Yager**
Photographer: **John Livzey**
Client: **Filmex**
Agency: **Saul Bass/Herb Yager & Associates**

898
Art Director: **Duncan Milner**
Designer: **Duncan Milner**
Artist: **Torres-Krief Design Assoc./Ron VanBuskirk**
Writer: **Courtney Scott**
Client: **National University**
Agency: **Phillips-Ramsey Advertising**

900
Art Director: **Gerry Gentile**
Photographer: **Carl Furuta**
Writer: **Peter Brown**
Client: **Volkswagen of America**
Agency: **Doyle Dane Bernbach/West**

899
Art Director: **Gerry Gentile**
Photographer: **Carl Furuta**
Writer: **Peter Brown**
Client: **Volkswagen of America**
Agency: **Doyle Dane Bernbach/West**

901
Art Director: **Steven Zwillinger**
Designer: **Steven Zwillinger**
Writer: **Steven Zwillinger**
Client: **N.Y. Dept. of Environmental Protection**

902
Art Directors: **Bill Schwartz, Ed Ward**
Designer: **Bill Schwartz**
Photographer: **Charlie Coppins**
Writers: **Bill Schwartz, Ed Ward**
Client: **Greater Cleveland Boy Scout Council**
Agency: **Meldrum and Fewsmith, Inc.**

903
Art Director: **Joe Shyllit**
Designer: **Joe Shyllit**
Photographer: **Gillian Proctor**
Writer: **Jerry Kuleba**
Client: **Dominion Dairies**
Agency: **Enterprise Advertising Associates, Ltd.**

904
Art Director: **Alan Peckolick**
Designer: **Alan Peckolick**
Artist: **Tony DiSpigna**
Client: **Mobil Corporation**
Agency: **Lubalin, Peckolick Assoc. Inc.**

905
Art Director: **Phil Silvestri**
Writer: **Rita Senders**
Client: **WABC-TV (Eyewitness News)**
Agency: **Della Femina, Travisano & Partners, Inc.**

906
Art Director: **Wayne Salo**
Designer: **Wayne Salo**
Photographer: **Mort Engel**
Artist: **Paul Crifo**
Writer: **Tom Callahan**
Client: **Paramount Pictures**
Agency: **Diener/Hauser/Bates**

907
Art Director: **Richard Radke**
Designer: **Richard Radke**
Artist: **Nick Facciano**
Writer: **Martin Cooke**
Client: **Cointreau America**
Agency: **Intermarco Advertising**

908
Art Director: **Philip Gips**
Designers: **Philip Gips, David Palladini**
Artist: **David Palladini**
Client: **Mobil Oil Corporation**
Agency: **Gips + Balkind Assoc., Inc.**

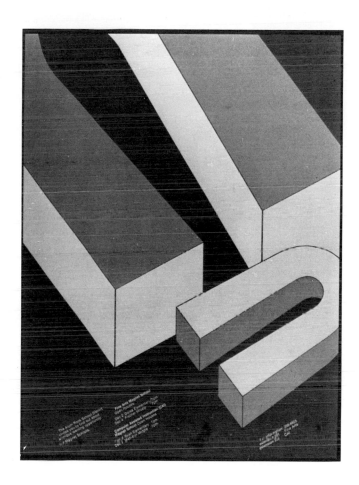

909
Art Directors: **Mark Moffett, Katherine Palladini**
Photographer: **Michael Harris**
Writer: **Confidence Stimpson**
Client: **Buckingham Corporation**
Agency: **Scali, McCabe, Sloves, Inc.**

910
Art Director: **Paige Johnson**
Designer: **Paige Johnson**
Writer: **Barbara Snyder**
Client: **Alum Rock School District**

911
Art Director: **Jimmy Johnson**
Designer: **Jimmy Johnson**
Artist: **Chuck Abraham**
Writer: **Harry Brown**
Client: **First Mississippi National Bank**
Agency: **Maris, West & Baker Advertising**

912
Art Director: **Randy Groft**
Designer: **Randy Groft**
Artist: **Randy Groft**
Client: **Community Gallery**
Agency: **Kelly Advertising, Inc.**

913
Art Director: **George Tscherny**
Designer: **George Tscherny**
Artist: **George Tscherny**
Client: **The Tyler School of Art**
Agency: **George Tscherny, Inc.**

914
Art Director: **George Tscherny**
Designer: **George Tscherny**
Photographer: **George Tscherny**
Artists: **Various**
Client: **Goethe House, New York**
Agency: **George Tscherny, Inc.**

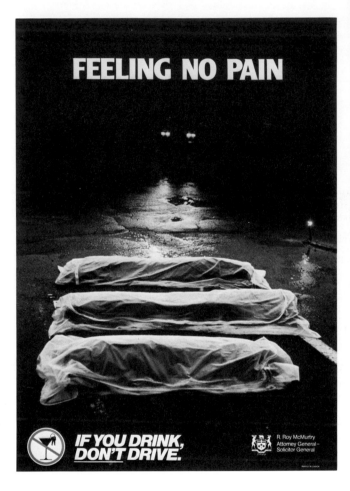

915
Art Director: **Toshiaki Ide**
Designer: **Seymour Chwast**
Artist: **Seymour Chwast**
Client: **New York City Department of Cultural Affairs**

916
Art Director: **Arnold Wicht**
Photographer: **Rudi von Tiedemann**
Writer: **Tim Heintzman**
Client: **Ontario Ministry of the Attorney General**
Agency: **Camp Associates Advertising**

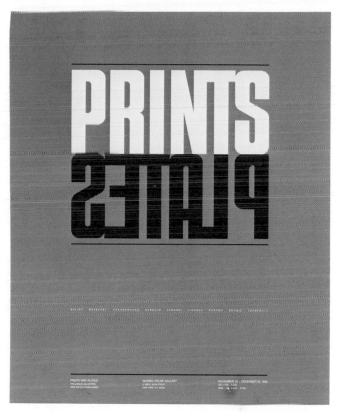

CITY SCAPE

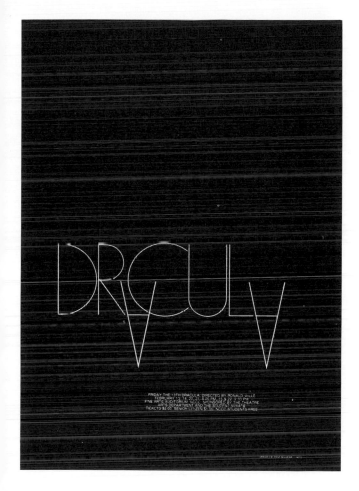

918
Art Director: Nelu Wolfensohn
Designer: Joseph Saleh
Writer: Leo Rosshandler
Client: Lavalin Inc.

917
Art Director: Rand Schuster
Designer: Rand Schuster
Client: Niagara County Community College
Theatre Arts Department

919
Art Director: Peter Rauch
Designer: Peter Rauch
Artist: John Alcorn
Writer: Peter O. Price
Client: Young Presidents' Organization
Agency: Peter Rauch Design

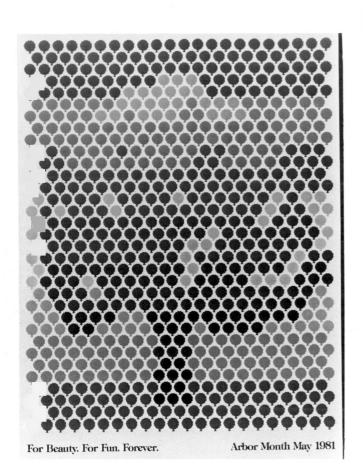

For Beauty. For Fun. Forever.   Arbor Month May 1981

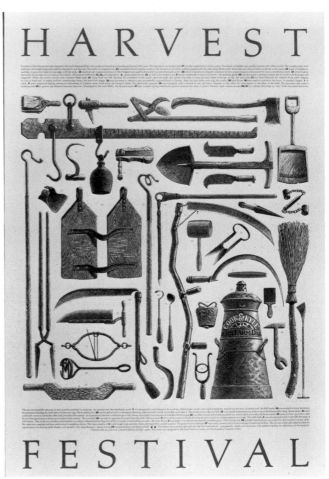

920
Art Directors: **Hideki Yamamoto, Miranda Moss**
Designers: **Hideki Yamamoto, Miranda Moss**
Client: **Minnesota Dept. of Agriculture/
Shade Tree Program**
Agency: **Seitz Graphic Directions Inc.**

921
Art Director: **Michael Cronan**
Designer: **Michael Cronan**
Artist: **Lawrence Duke**
Writer: **Karin Hibma**
Client: **General Exhibitions Corporation**
Agency: **Michael Patrick Cronan**

922
Art Director: **Jan Boleto**
Designer: **Jan Boleto**
Typography Design: **Michael Simpson**
Artist: **Jan Boleto**
Client: **The Repertory Theatre of St. Louis**
Printer: **Silkscreen Products, Inc.**

923
Art Director: **Leslie Tryon Tatoian**
Designer: **Don Weller**
Artist: **Don Weller**
Writer: **Leslie Tryon Tatoian**
Client: **Society of Illustrators of Los Angeles**
Publisher: **Society of Illustrators of Los Angeles**
Agency: **The Weller Institute for the Cure of Design, Inc.**

"Ladies and gentlemen, you have had twelve months to prepare for this examination.

"Those of you who do well can look forward to brilliant careers. Those of you who do not, should seriously consider another profession."

BORROMINI PIRANDELLO BARBERINI VIGNELLI
MORAVIA BOCCIONI COLOMBO PUCCINI RADICE
CROCE DE CARLO PERUZZI CIMABUE PALLADIO
AULENTI GALILEO BRAMANTE BALLA ARMANI
RAGGI MENOTTI FELLINI MENDINI PININFARINA
PAGANINI GIORGIONE NOORDA BERNINI VASARI
CARAVAGGIO BURRI PIRANESI PIERO GIUGIARO
MADERNO NERVI NERONE PASOLINI DONIZETTI
ROSSI TOSCANINI LEOPARDI AGNELLI FERRARI
ORSINI VERDI DONATELLO CENCI SAVONAROLA
FIORUCCI ZEFFIRELLI LIPPI GREGOTTI GUCCI
MAZZEI BRION CERATTO VOLTA SPQR ZANUSO
STRADIVARI GIURGOLA VALENTINO PETRARCA
BRUNELLESCHI BOTTICELLI SCOLA BOCCACCIO
MODIGLIANI CARUSO MANGIONE DE BENEDETTI
GRUCCI CASTAGNOLI PIANO LEONARDO CELLINI
SOTTSASS BERTOLUCCI FERMI CHIGI CASANOVA
BORGIA MARINETTI VALLE ANTONIONI MEDICI
MASACCIO ZEVI ALBERTI WOJTYLA CICERONE
CESARE GARIBALDI BELLINI RESPIGHI MAZZINI
SARTOGO VESPUCCI BENE FALLACI BORGHESE
MACHIAVELLI BARZINI CANOVA SOAVI NICOLAO
FARNESE GIOTTO LOLLOBRIGIDA ECO ROSSINI
CASSINA MARCONI TIZIANO MISSONI ARBASINO
TINTORETTO VILLAGIO VIVALDI QUILICI PESCE
BUGATTI LIONNI BILLESI PECCEI MONTESSORI
RAFFAELLO BODONI OLIVETTI MICHELANGELO
DANTE ETCETERA ETCETERA THE ITALIAN IDEA

INTERNATIONAL DESIGN CONFERENCE IN ASPEN 1981 | JUNE 14 TO 19

924
Art Director: **Dick Pantano**
Photographer: **John Houseman's The Acting Co.**
Writers: **Jay Hill, Jack Wallwork**
Client: **Advertising Club of Boston**
Agency: **Hill, Holliday, Connors, Cosmopulos**

925
Art Director: **George Sadek**
Designers: **George Sadek, Tom Kluepfel**
Client: **International Design Conference—Aspen**
Publisher: **The Center for Design & Typography,
The Cooper Union**
Production Co.: **The Center for Design & Typography,
The Cooper Union**

926
Art Director: **Tom Layman**
Designer: **Tom Layman**
Writer: **Barbara Ford**
Client: **Westminster-Canterbury**
Agency: **The Martin Agency**

927
Art Director: **Clarence Poisson**
Writer: **Clarence Poisson**
Client: **American Cancer Society**
Agency: **Hill, Holliday, Connors, Cosmopulos**

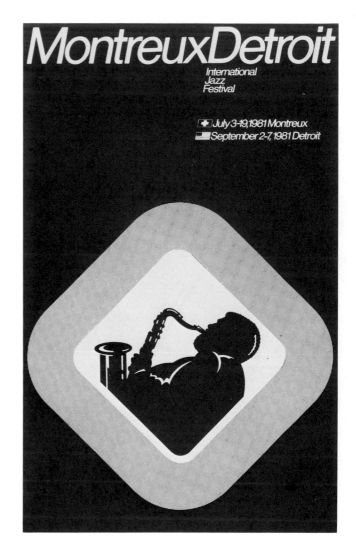

939
Art Directors: **Greg Wilder, Don Weller**
Designer: **Don Weller**
Artist: **Don Weller**
Writer: **Don Weller**
Client: **Sun Graphics**
Publisher: **Sun Graphics**
Agency: **The Weller Institute for the Cure of Design, Inc.**

940
Art Directors: **Greg Moy, Colleen Leonhard**
Designer: **Gary Shortt**
Client: **Detroit Renaissance Foundation**
Agency: **Young & Rubicam**

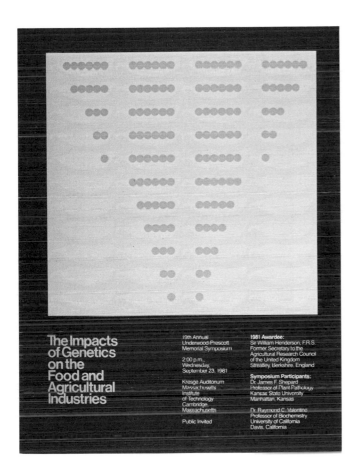

941
Art Director: **Andreé Cordella**
Designer: **Andreé Cordella**
Artists: **Andreé Cordella, Sam Petrucci**
Writer: **Sandy Weistopf**
Client: **Wm. Underwood Canning Company**
Production Co.: **Gunn Associates**

942
Art Director: **Alan E. Cober**
Designer: **John deCesare**
Artist: **Alan E. Cober**
Writer: **Alan E. Cober**
Client: **Alan E. Cober**

943
Art Director: **Michael Williams**
Designer: **Michael Williams**
Photographer: **Anthony Garner**
Writer: **Judy O. Williams**
Client: **Shreveport Advertising Federation**
Production Co.: **Hurst Printing Company**

958
Creative Director: **Bob Dennard**
Art Director: **Rex Peteet**
Designer: **Rex Peteet**
Artist: **Rex Peteet**
Writers: **Bob Dennard, Glyn Powell**
Client: **Bennigan's Taverns**
Agency: **Dennard Creative, Inc.**

959
Art Director: **Don Lynn**
Designers: **Charles R. Gailis, John Pack**
Artist: **John Pack**
Writer: **John Pack**
Client: **IRS Taxpayer Service**
Publisher: **Internal Revenue Service**
Agency: **IRS Design Group**

Purr-fect. Porringer in silverplate. Fantasy spoon in stainless. Complete services at fine stores.

ΞONEIDA

CHRISTEN EAGLE II

961
Art Director: **David Deutsch**
Photographer: **George Ratkai**
Writer: **John Clarkson**
Client: **Oneida Silversmiths**
Agency: **David Deutsch Associates, Inc.**

960
Art Directors: **Nancy Skolos, Thomas Wedell**
Designer: **Nancy Skolos**
Photographer: **Thomas Wedell**
Writer: **Peter DeWalt**
Client: **Reynolds DeWalt Printing, Inc.**
Publisher: **Reynolds-DeWalt Printing, Inc.**
Production Co: **Skolos, Wedell & Raynor**
Agency: **Skolos, Wedell & Raynor**

962
Art Director: **Barry Deutsch**
Designers: **Karen Tainaka, Myland McRevey**
Artist: **Ivan Clede**
Client: **Christen Industries, Inc.**
Agency: **Steinhilber, Deutsch & Gard**

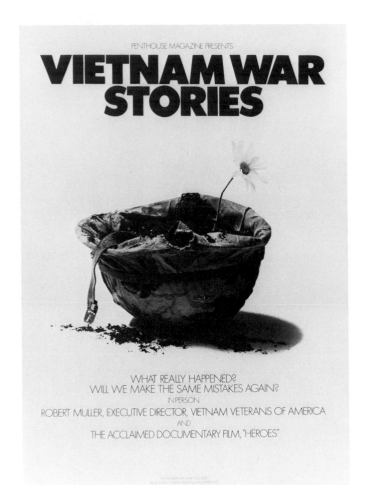

963
Art Director: **Frank M. Devino**
Designers: **Regina Dombrowski, Paul Slutsky**
Photographer: **Tony Guccione**
Client: **Penthouse International, Ltd.**

964
Art Directors: **Rudi Legname, Craig Frazier**
Designers: **Craig Frazier, Conrad Jorgensen**
Photographer: **Rudi Legname**
Client: **Rudi Legname**
Agency: **Jorgensen/Frazier, Inc.**

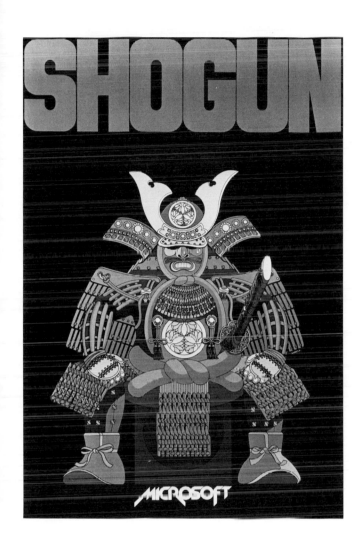

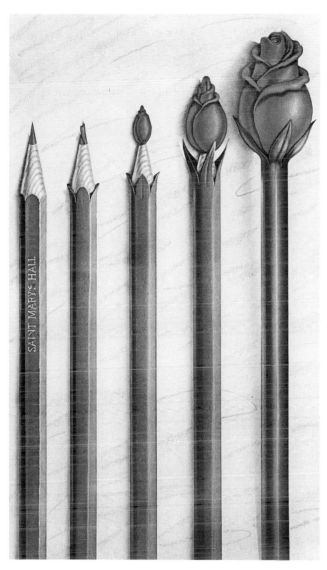

965
Art Director: **Patrick O'Connell**
Designer: **Tom Kamifuji**
Artist: **Tom Kamifuji**
Client: **Microsoft Consumer Products**
Agency: **The Advertising Company ot Offield
And Brower**

966
Art Director: **Barbara Shimkus**
Designer: **Barbara Shimkus**
Artist: **Mark Weakley**
Client: **Saint Mary's Hall**
Agency: **Barbara Shimkus/Graphic Design**

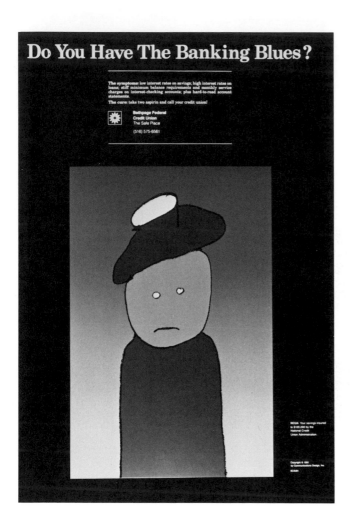

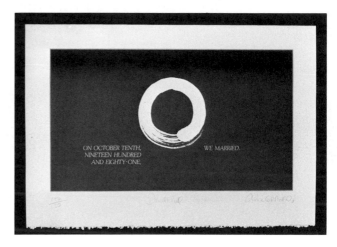

968
Art Directors: **Richard Martell, Liza Greene**
Designer: **Liza Greene**
Artist: **Liza Greene**
Writer: **Gail Duncan**
Client: **PEOPLE Magazine**
Editor: **Gail Duncan**
Publisher: **TIME Inc.**
Director: **Liza Greene**
Producer: **Liza Greene**

967
Designer: **Michael Souter**
Artist: **Michael Souter**
Writer: **Susann Jarvis**
Client: **Bethpage Federal Credit Union**
Agency: **Communications Design**

969
Designer: **Alex Granado**
Writer: **Deborah L. Ball**
Client: **Granado/Ball**

970
Art Director: **Nick Pappas**
Designer: **Nick Pappas**
Artists: **Nick Pappas, Dick DiMaggio**
Client: **Nick Pappas Graphics**
Publisher: **Bon-R Reproductions**

971
Art Director: **George Tscherny**
Designer: **George Tscherny**
Artist: **George Tscherny**
Client: **W.R. Grace & Co.**
Agency: **George Tscherny, Inc.**

972
Art Director: **James Lienhart**
Designer: **James Lienhart**
Artist: **James Lienhart**
Writer: **James Lienhart**
Client: **James Lienhart**

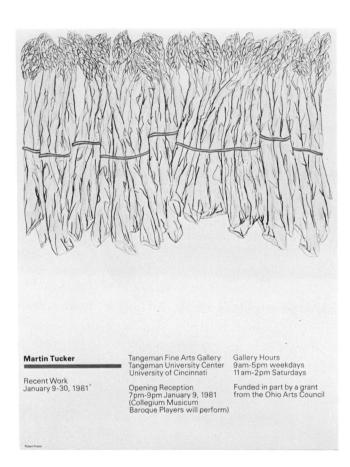

Martin Tucker

Recent Work
January 9-30, 1981*

Tangeman Fine Arts Gallery
Tangeman University Center
University of Cincinnati

Opening Reception
7pm-9pm January 9, 1981
(Collegium Musicum
Baroque Players will perform)

Gallery Hours
9am-5pm weekdays
11am-2pm Saturdays

Funded in part by a grant
from the Ohio Arts Council

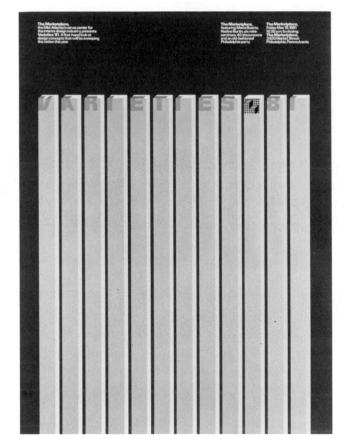

973
Art Director: **Robert Probst**
Designer: **Robert Probst**
Artist: **Martin Tucker**
Client: **Tangeman Fine Arts Gallery, Cincinnati**
Production Co.: **Berman Printing Company**

974
Art Director: **Robert Cooney**
Designer: **Gregg Sibert**
Artist: **Gregg Sibert**
Client: **Philadelphia Market Place**
Agency: **R.A. Cooney Inc./Creative Systems Group**

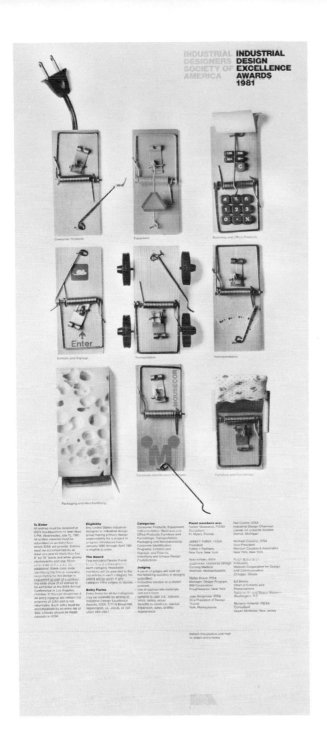

975
Art Director: **Bart Crosby**
Designer: **Bart Crosby**
Photographer: **Georg Bosek**
Client: **Industrial Designers Society of America**
Agency: **Crosby Associates Inc.**

976
Art Director: **Bart Crosby**
Designer: **Bart Crosby**
Photographer: **Georg Bosek**
Client: **Consolidated Foods Corporation**
Agency: **Crosby Associates Inc.**

978
Art Directors: **Rafael Rovira, Javier Romero**
Designers: **Rafael Rovira, Javier Romero**
Photographer: **Lucien Clergue**
Client: **HMK Fine Arts Inc.**
Publisher: **HMK Fine Arts Inc.**
Agency: **Periscope Studio, Inc.**

977
Art Director: **Dick Krogstad**
Designer: **Dick Krogstad**
Artist: **Dick Krogstad**
Writer: **Dick Krogstad**
Client: **Alphagraphics One**
Agency: **Gulick & Henry, Inc.**

979
Art Director: **Robert Burns**
Designer: **Will Novosedlik**
Photographer: **Paul Orenstein**
Client: **Academy of Canadian Cinema**
Agency: **Burns, Cooper, Hynes Limited**

980
Art Director: **McRay Magleby**
Designer: **McRay Magleby**
Artists: **McRay Magleby, JoAnne Verville**
Client: **Brigham Young Univ. Wrestling**
Producer: **Brigham Young University**
Agency: **Graphic Communications**

981
Art Director: **McRay Magleby**
Designer: **McRay Magleby**
Artist: **McRay Magleby**
Writer: **Norman A. Darais**
Client: **Salt Lake City Art Directors Club**
Producer: **Brigham Young University**
Agency: **Graphic Communications**

WARD BENNETT DESIGNS FOR BRICKEL ASSOCIATES

982
Art Director: **Michael Donovan**
Designer: **Michael Donovan**
Client: **Brickel Associates, Inc.**
Agency: **Donovan and Green, Inc.**

983
Art Director: **Gary Kelley**
Designer: **Gary Kelley**
Artist: **Gary Kelley**
Writers: **Clarence Alling, Gary Kelley**
Client: **Waterloo Municipal Galleries**
Publisher: **Waterloo Recreation and Arts Center**
Agency: **Hellman Associates, Inc.**

A New Dimension In Full Color Printing

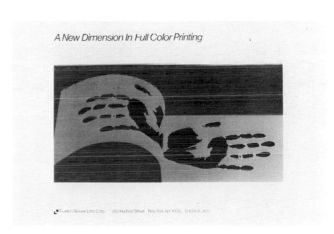

984
Art Director: **Nathan Felde**
Designer: **Nathan Felde**
Photographer: **Warren Lynch**
Writers: **Judy Glasser, Larry Rosenblum**
Client: **Boston Redevelopment Authority**
Publisher: **Boston Redevelopment Authority**

985
Art Director: **Laura Torrisi Goldsmith**
Designer: **Laura Torrisi Goldsmith**
Artist: **Laura Torrisi Goldsmith**
Client: **Froelich/Greene Litho Corp.**
Agency: **Laura Torrisi Goldsmith Graphic Design**

987
Art Director: **Joan Niborg**
Designer: **Joan Niborg**
Photographer: **Michael Geiger**
Writer: **Judi Goldstein**
Client: **Chain Bike Corporation**
Agency: **DDB Group Two**

986
Art Director: **Richard Perlman, Inc.**
Designer: **Susan Schatz**
Artist: **Susan Schatz**
Client: **Sterling-Roman Press, Inc.**
Production Co.: **Sterling-Roman Press, Inc.**

988
Art Director: **Mel Sant**
Designer: **Mel Sant**
Photographer: **Jim Miller**
Writer: **Paul Keye**
Client: **Lone Star Brewing Co.**
Publisher: **Lone Star Brewing Co.**
Agency: **Keye, Donna, Pearlstein Inc.**

989
Art Director: **Bob Young**
Designer: **Bob Young**
Artist: **Chuck Hart**
Writer: **Diane Fannon**
Client: **Nichols Kusan, Old Jacksonville Ceiling Fans**
Agency: **Tracy-Locke/BBDO**

990
Art Directors: **Richard Burns, Doug Akagi, Sarah Nugent**
Designers: **Jim Gray, Sandy Short**
Artists: **Jim Gray, Sandy Short, Ken Andreotta,
Peggy Kamei**
Client: **The GNU Group**
Agency: **The GNU Group/Sausalito, Houston**

Solar Energy

SIXTH VAN CLIBURN INTERNATIONAL PIANO COMPETITION
MAY 17 TO 31, 1981 FORT WORTH TEXAS

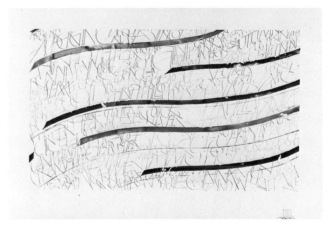

992
Art Directors: **Duane Wiens, Carl Baden**
Designer: **Carl Baden**
Client: **Colorado National Bank**
Printer: **Frederic Printing Company**
Production Co.: **Matrix Design Inc.**

991
Art Directors: **Warren Wilkins, Tommer Peterson**
Designers: **Warren Wilkins, Tommer Peterson**
Client: **The Van Cliburn Foundation**
Production Co.: **Heath Printers**
Agency: **Wilkins & Peterson**

993
Art Director: **Russ Hirth**
Designer: **Tim Girvin**
Artist: **Tim Girvin**
Client: **BF Goodrich**
Agency: **Carr Liggett**

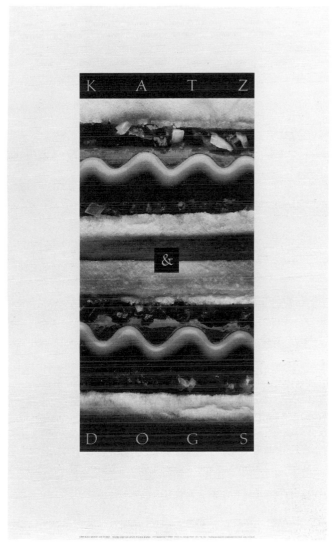

994
Art Directors: **Duane Wiens, Carl Daden**
Designer: **Arvid Wallen**
Client: **Beaver Creek Resort Company**
Printer: **L&M Printing Company**
Production Co: **Matrix Design Inc.**

995
Art Director: **Woody Pirtle**
Designer: **Woody Pirtle**
Photographer: **John Katz**
Writer: **Woody Pirtle**
Client: **John Katz Photography**
Agency: **Woody Pirtle, Inc.**

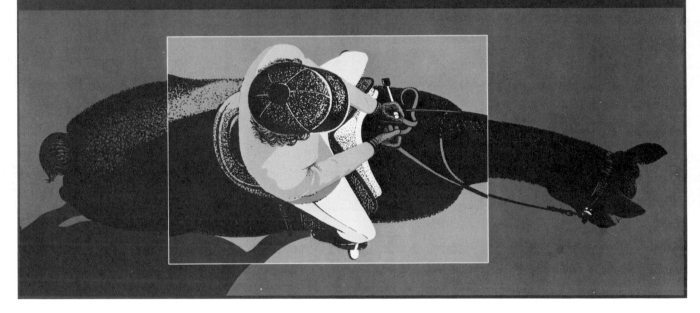

the 60th annual children's horse show

Three days of fun and excitement in a country atmosphere. Acapulco Mexican Food, Hamburgers, Wines, Soft Drinks, Sweets and Treats, Yogurt, Ice Cream and Homemade Desserts, Plants, and a Country Store. Friday Night Steak Buffet catered by the Los Angeles Athletic Club, including an evening horse show, for only $15.50 per person. □ Send reservations to Post Office Box 563, La Canada Flintridge, CA 91011. General Admission—$1.50. Children under 12—50¢ □ The Public is Welcome □ Flintridge Riding Club, 4625 Oak Grove Drive, La Canada Flintridge, California □ Friday through Sunday, May 29, 30, 31, 1981. Sponsored by the Flintridge La Canada Guild of the Huntington Memorial Hospital.

996
Art Director: **Dennis S. Juett**
Designer: **Jeffrey D. Lawson**
Artist: **Jeffrey D. Lawson**
Writer: **Dorothy A. Juett**
Client: **Flintridge La Canada Guild of the Huntington Memorial Hospital**
Agency: **Dennis S. Juett & Associates Inc.**

997
Art Director: **David Wachter**
Designer: **David Wachter**
Photographer: **Cosimo Zaccaria**
Writer: **Paul Adomites**
Client: **Westinghouse Credit Corp.**
Agency: **Ketchum Advertising, Pittsburgh**

998
Art Directors: **Paige Johnson, Steve Zeifman**
Designer: **Paige Johnson**
Photographer: **Peter Gerba**
Client: **Peter Gerba**

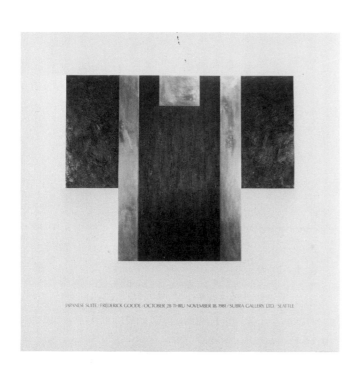

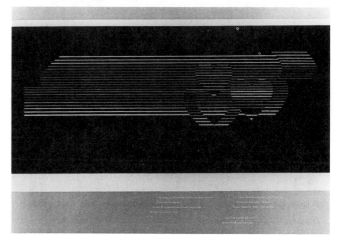

999
Art Director: **Randi Harper Jorgenson**
Designer: **Randi Harper Jorgenson**
Client: **Subra Gallery Ltd.**
Agency: **Harper and Associates**

1001
Art Director: **Richard Holmes**
Designer: **Britt Saunders**
Photographer: **Robert Elias**
Writer: **Richard Holmes**
Client: **Britt Associates**
Production Co.: **Walker Color Graphics**
Agency: **Richard Holmes Advertising & Design**

1000
Art Director: **Joe Toto**
Artist: **Mark Hess**
Writer: **Carol Ogden**
Client: **AMF Voit**
Agency: **Benton & Bowles, Inc.**

1002
Art Director: **Jann Church Advertising & Graphic Design, Inc.**
Designer: **Jann Church Advertising & Graphic Design, Inc.**
Writers: **Jann Church Advertising & Graphic Design, Inc. & Keats**
Client: **Jann Church Advertising & Graphic Design, Inc.**
Printer: **Hutton Roach Lithographers**
Typography: **Headliners of Orange Co.**
Paper: **Mead Black & White**

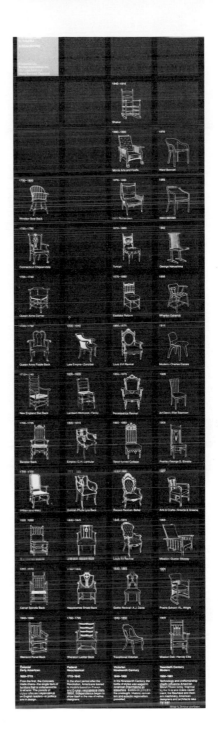

1003
Art Director: **William Brennan**
Designer: **William Brennan**
Client: **Panasonic**
Agency: **Sommer, Inc.**

1004
Art Director: **Michael Donovan**
Designer: **Michael Donovan**
Artists: **Jim Silks, Randy Lieu**
Writer: **C. Ray Smith**
Client: **Brickel Associates Inc.**
Agency: **Donovan and Green Inc.**

1005
Art Directors: **Phil Toy, Keilani Tom**
Designers: **Keilani Tom, Phil Toy**
Photographer: **Phil Toy**
Writer: **Kathryn Van Dyke**
Client: **Phil Toy Photography**
Agency: **Communikations**

1006
Art Director: **Tyler Smith**
Designer: **Tyler Smith**
Photographer: **Myron Taplin**
Writer: **Geoff Currier**
Client: **Southwick**
Producer: **Tyler Smith , Art Direction Inc.**
Agency: **Welch Currier Smith**

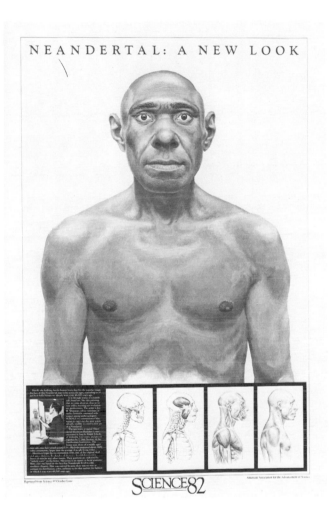

1007
Art Director: **Rodney C. Williams**
Designer: **Wayne Fitzpatrick**
Artist: **Jay Matternes**
Writer: **Boyce Rensberger**
Client: **American Association for the Advancement of Science**
Editor: **Allen Hammond**
Publisher: **William D. Carey**

1008
Art Director: **Linda Powell**
Designer: **Linda Powell**
Artist: **Barb Herman**
Writer: **Nancy Green**
Client: **Herman Miller, Inc.**

Ice Cream Eaters Delight

DesignersChoice

1009
Art Director: **Keith Bright**
Designer: **Kara Blohm**
Artist: **John Bright**
Client: **Self-promotion**
Agency: **Bright & Associates**

1010
Art Director: **Larry S. Paine**
Designer: **Larry S. Paine**
Photographer: **Fred Kligman**
Client: **Stephenson, Inc.**
Publisher: **Stephenson, Inc.**
Agency: **LP&A Design Studio**

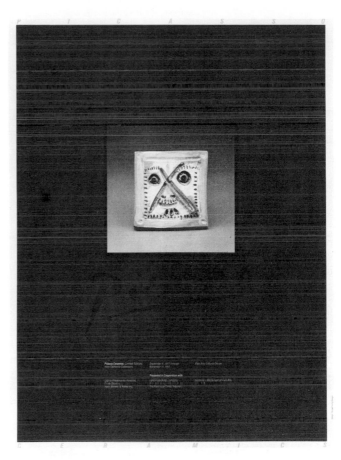

1012
Art Director: **Russell K. Leong**
Designer: **Russell K. Leong**
Photographer: **Alvin Tanabe**
Artist: **Barb Koehn**
Writer: **Linda Langston**
Client: **Palo Alto Cultural Center**
Agency: **Russell Leong Design**

1011
Designer: **Alicia Landon Design**
Client: **Champion International Corporation**
Publisher: **Scott Printing Company**

1013
Art Director: **Dan Bogosh**
Designer: **Dan Bogosh**
Artist: **Fred Hilllard**
Writers: **Jon Bell, Terri Small**
Client: **Western Washington Fair**
Production Co.: **Keogh & Co.**
Agency: **Cole & Weber**

1014
Art Director: **Milton Glaser**
Designer: **Milton Glaser**
Artist: **Milton Glaser**
Client: **New York State Dept. of Commerce**
Agency: **Milton Glaser, Inc.**

1015
Art Director: **John Garr**
Designer: **Seymour Chwast**
Artist: **Seymour Chwast**
Writer: **Warren Watwood**
Client: **Doremus Inc.**
Agency: **Doremus Inc.**

WHEN ABORTION BECOMES ILLEGAL, MAYBE WOMEN WILL FINALLY LEARN TO TAKE CARE OF THEMSELVES.

ABORTION RIGHTS COUNCIL OF MINNESOTA

1016
Art Director: **Phil Silvestri**
Writer: **Rita Senders**
Client: **WABC-TV (Eyewitness News)**
Agency: **Della Femina, Travisano & Partners, Inc.**

1017
Art Director: **Marsha Stone**
Designer: **Marsha Stone**
Photographer: **Tom Berthiaume**
Writer: **Jo Marshall**
Client: **Abortion Rights Council of Minnesota**

1018
Art Director: **Don Price**
Designers: **Don Price, Tim Girvin, Rick Lindberg, Pat Rooney**
Artist: **Tim Girvin**
Writer: **Brian Duffy**
Client: **Art Directors & Artists Club of Sacramento**

1019
Art Director: **Bill Caldwell**
Designers: **Bill Caldwell, Terry Dale, Ethel Kessler**
Artists: **Web Bryant, Bill Caldwell, Ethel Kessler, Ken Krafchek, Paul Salmon, Libby Dorsett Thiel**
Writer: **Victor Hirst**
Client: **International Communications Agency**
Editors: **Victor Hirst, Martha Williams**
Publisher: **International Communications Agency**
Director: **Bill Caldwell**
Agency: **International Communication Agency**

1020
Art Director: **Dennis Merritt**
Designer: **Dennis Merritt**
Photographer: **Rick Gayle**
Artist: **Ken Fritz**
Writer: **Dennis Merritt/Jamie Nichols**
Client: **Public Service**
Agency: **Phillips-Ramsey Advertising**

1021
Art Directors: **Stephen Frykholm, Barbara Loveland**
Designers: **Stephen Frykholm, Barbara Loveland**
Photographers: **Earl Woods, John Boucher**
Writer: **Nancy Green**
Client: **Herman Miller, Inc.**

Very elegant, in basic black

chaise

designed by Charles Eames

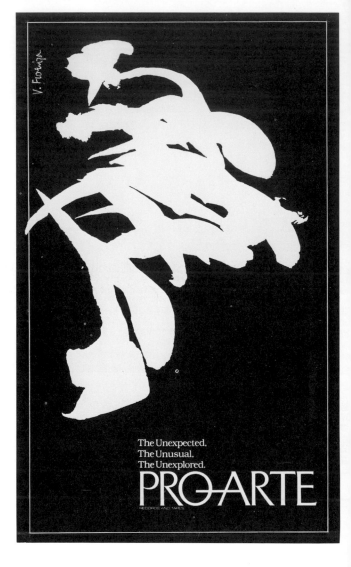

V. Fiorenza

The Unexpected.
The Unusual.
The Unexplored.
PRO-ARTE
RECORDS AND TAPES

1022
Art Directors: **Tom Kamifuji, June Vincent, Alan Drucker**
Designer: **Tom Kamifuji**
Client: **Drucker/Vincent, Inc.**
Publisher: **Drucker/Vincent, Inc.**
Production Co.: **The W.O.R.K.S**
Agency: **H. Tom Kamifuji & Associates**

1023
Art Director: **Barbara Loveland**
Designer: **Barbara Loveland**
Artist: **Kathy Stanton**
Writer: **Nancy Green**
Client: **Herman Miller, Inc.**

1024
Art Director: **Vito Fiorenza**
Designer: **Vito Fiorenza**
Artist: **Vito Fiorenza**
Writer: **Jay K. Hoffman**
Client: **Pickwick/Pro-Arte Records**

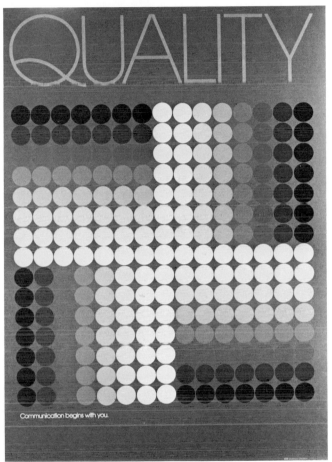

1025
Art Director: **Karen Gourley Lehman**
Designer: **Karen Gourley Lehman**
Writer: **Public Relations Dept.**
Client: **Hewlett-Packard, Waltham Division**
Production Co.: **Fahey Exhibits**

1026
Art Director: **Karen Gourley Lohman**
Designer: **Karen Gourley Lehman**
Writers: **John Young, Neil Duane**
Client: **Hewlett-Packard, Waltham Division**
Production Co.: **Fahey Exhibits**

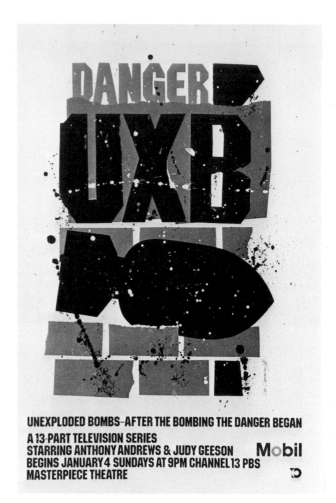

1027
Art Director: **McRay Magleby**
Designer: **McRay Magleby**
Artist: **McRay Magleby**
Writer: **Norman A. Darais**
Client: **Brigham Young Univ.—Registration**
Producer: **Brigham Young University**
Agency: **Graphic Communications**

1028
Art Director: **Ivan Chermayeff**
Designers: **Karen Lewis, Ivan Chermayeff**
Artist: **Ivan Chermayeff**
Client: **Mobil Oil Corporation**
Agency: **Chermayeff & Geismar Associates**

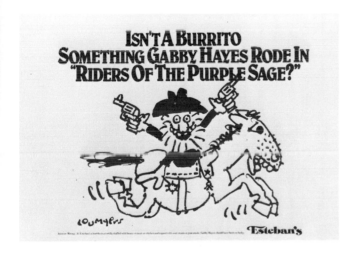

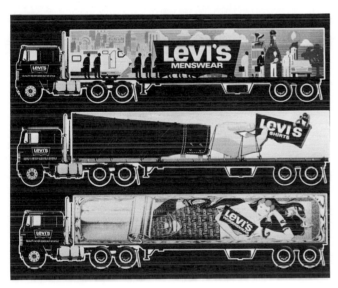

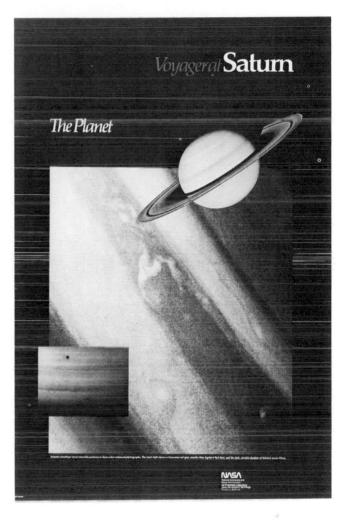

1029
Art Director: **Ron Anderson**
Designer: **Ron Anderson**
Artist: **Lou Myers**
Writer: **Tom McElligott**
Client: **Esteban's**
Agency: **Fallon McElligott Rice**

1030
Art Director: **Chris Blum**
Designer: **Chris Blum**
Artists: **(1)Greg Thomas, (2)Bruce Wolfe,
(3)Tony Naganuma**
Client: **Levi Strauss & Co.**
Printer: **Pacific Lithograph Co.**
Agency: **Foote, Cone & Belding/Honig**

1031
Art Directors: **Ken White, Tak Kiriyama**
Designer: **Ken White**
Photographer: **NASA**
Artist: **Ken White**
Writers: **Ken White, Andrea Stein**
Client: **NASA/JPL**
Editor: **Mary Fran Buehler**
Publisher: **NASA/JPL**
Director: **John Kempton**
Agency: **Ken White Design Office, Inc.**

BOOKS \ JACKETS

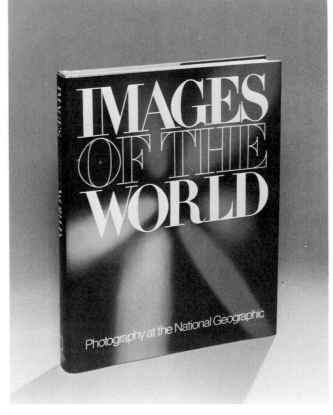

1032   GOLD AWARD
Art Directors: **Judy Anderson, Bill Jackson**
Designers: **Judy Anderson, Bill Jackson**
Artists: **Judy Anderson, Bill Jackson**
Writers: **Judy Anderson, Bill Jackson**
Client: **Self promotion**
Editor: **Max Schaible**
Publisher: **ArtHouse Press**

1033   GOLD AWARD
Art Director: **R.D. Scudellari**
Designer: **R.D. Scudellari**
Photographer: **John Gruen**
Client: **Alfred A. Knopf**
Editor: **R.D. Scudellari**
Publisher: **Alfred A. Knopf**
Director: **Robert Gottlieb**
Producer: **Ellen McNeilly**
Agency: **Corporate Design Staff**

1034   DISTINCTIVE MERIT
Art Director: **David M. Seager**
Designer: **David M. Seager**
Photographer: **Jim Sugar (Cover)**
Client: **National Geographic Society**
Editor: **Thomas B. Allen**
Publisher: **National Geographic Society**
Director: **Charles O. Hyman, Book Service**

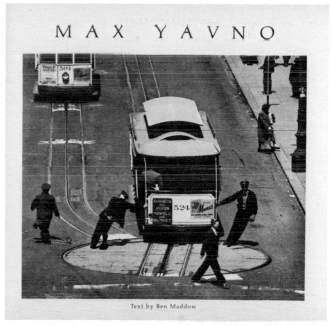

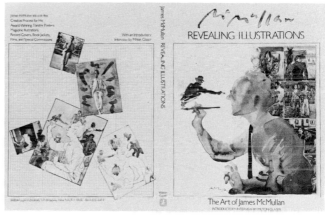

1036
Art Director: **Chet Grycz**
Designer: **Carl Seltzer**
Photographer: **Max Yavno**
Publisher: **University of California Press**

1035
Art Director: **Arnold C. Holeywell**
Designer: **Donald S. Komai**
Artists: **Frank Wootton, John Batchelor**
Writer: **Ralph Barker**
Client: **TIME-LIFE Books, Inc.**
Publisher: **TIME-LIFE Books, Inc.**

1027
Designer: **James McMullan**
Artist: **James McMullan**
Writer: **James McMullan**
Editors: **Michael McTwigan, Betty Vera**
Publisher: **Watson-Guptill Publications**

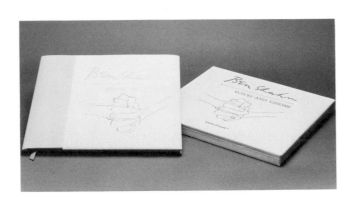

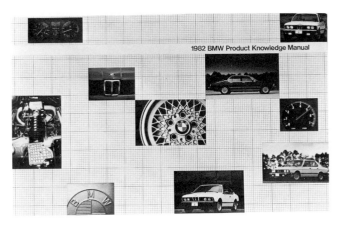

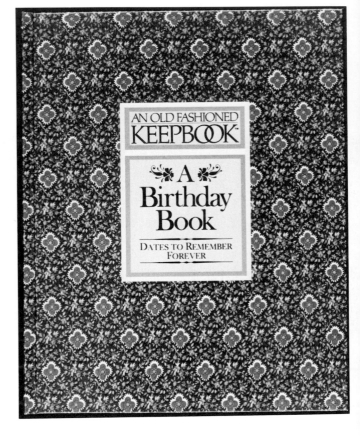

1038
Art Director: **Mina Yamashita**
Designer: **Alma King**
Client: **Santa Fe East Galleries**
Editors: **Alma King**
Publisher: **Santa Fe East Galleries**
Production Co: **Sunstone Corporation/Sunstone Press**
Agency: **Sunstone Press**

1039
Art Director: **John D'Almeida**
Designer: **John D'Almeida**
Photographer: **Greg Jarem**
Writer: **Tom Knighten**
Client: **BMW of North America, Inc.**
Agency: **Senektik Graphiks**

1040
Art Director: **Ronald Gross**
Designer: **Sara Brown**
Writer: **Linda Campbell Franklin**
Client: **Tree Communications, Inc.**
Editor: **Linda Campbell Franklin**
Publisher: **Tree Communications, Inc.**

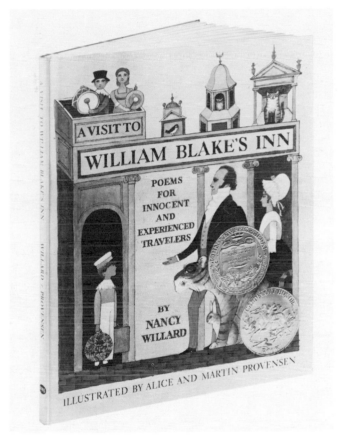

1041
Designers: **Jak Katalan, Alyssia Lazin**
Photographer: **Jak Katalan**
Editor: **Paul Lytle**
Publisher: **The MIT Press**

1042
Art Director: **Barbara Knowles**
Artists: **Alice and Martin Provensen**
Writer: **Nancy Willard**
Client: **Harcourt Brace Jovanovich, Publishers**
Editor: **Anna Bier**
Publisher: **Harcourt Brace Jovanovich, Publishers**

There's a Train Going by My Window

by Wendy Kesselman
pictures by Tony Chen

1043
Art Directors: **Diana Klemin, Douglas Bergstreser**
Designer: **Katharine von Mehren**
Artist: **Tony Chen**
Writer: **Wendy Kesselman**
Editor: **Joanna Cole**
Publisher: **Doubleday & Company, Inc.**

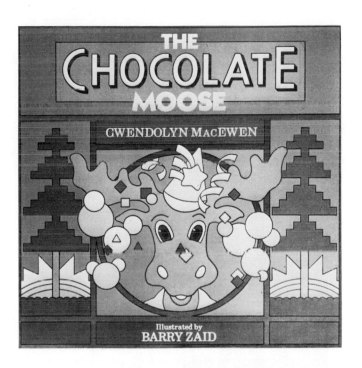

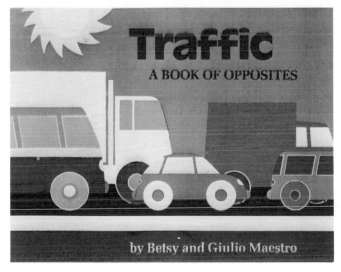

1044
Art Director: **Barry Zaid**
Designer: **Barry Zaid**
Artist: **Barry Zaid**
Writer: **Gwendolyn Macewen**
Client: **N.C. Press**
Editor: **Carolyn Walker**
Publisher: **N.C. Press**
Director: **Carolyn Walker**

1045
Art Director: **Julie Quan**
Designers: **Betsy and Giulio Maestro**
Artist: **Giulio Maestro**
Writer: **Betsy Maestro**
Client: **Crown Publishers, Inc.**
Editor: **Norma Jean Sawicki**
Publisher: **Crown Publishers, Inc.**

1046
Art Director: **Ursula P. Vosseler**
Designer: **Beth Molloy**
Picture Editor: **Alison Wilbur**
Artists: **Barbara Gibson, Robert E. Hynes**
Client: **National Geographic Society**
Editor: **Pat Robbins**
Publisher: **National Geographic Society**
Director: **Donald J. Crump**

1047
Artist: **John Lim**
Writer: **John Lim**
Publisher: **Tundra**

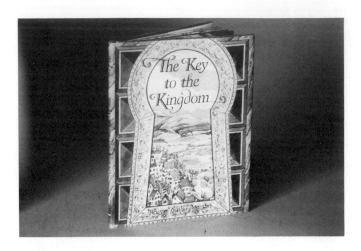

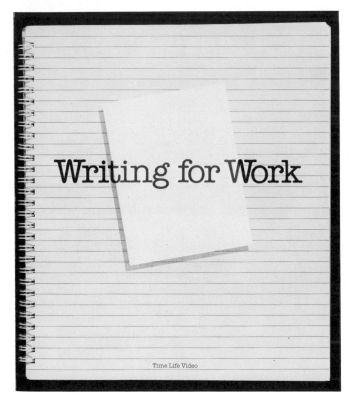

1048
Art Director: **Barbara Knowles**
Designers: **Betsy and Giulio Maestro**
Artist: **Giulio Maestro**
Writer: **Betsy Maestro**
Client: **Harcourt Brace Jovanovich, Publishers**
Editor: **Barbara Lucas**
Publisher: **Harcourt Brace Jovanovich, Publishers**

1049
Art Director: **Bruce Withers**
Designer: **Laura Torrisi Goldsmith**
Artist: **Gerry Gersten**
Writers: **Geraldine Richelson, Richard M. Kahn**
Client: **Amy S. Meltzer/Time Life Video**
Publisher: **Time Life Inc.**
Agency: **Bruce Withers Graphic Design Inc.**

1050
Art Director: **Jurek Wajdowicz**
Designer: **Jurek Wajdowicz**
Artists: **A. Dudzinski, J. Morgan, J. Wajdowicz**
Writer: **Edward M. Gottschall**
Client: **Prentice-Hall, Inc.**
Editors: **John Duhring, Sonia Meyer**
Publisher: **Prentice-Hall, Inc.**
Production Co.: **Emerson, Wajdowicz Studios, Inc.**
Agency: **Emerson, Wajdowicz Studios, Inc.**

1051
Art Director: **Ken Parkhurst**
Designer: **Julie Riefler**
Client: **Los Angeles County Museum of Art**
Agency: **Bright & Associates**

1052
Art Director: **Dorothy Fall**
Designer: **Dorothy Fall**
Artist: **Dorothy Fall**
Writer: **James R. Marks**
Client: **Insurance Information Institute**
Editor: **John D. Craigie**
Publisher: **Insurance Information Institute**
Director: **James R. Marks**
Printer: **Colortone Press**

1053
Art Director: **Kenneth Gruskin**
Designer: **Kenneth Gruskin**
Artists: **Various**
Photographers: **Various**
Writers: **Various**
Client: **The Cornellian, Inc.**
Editor: **Marlene Gaeta Wagner**
Publisher: **The 1981 Cornellian**

1054
Art Director: **Carole Palmer**
Designer: **Carole Palmer**
Editor: **Donald Canty**
Publisher: **Michael Hanley**

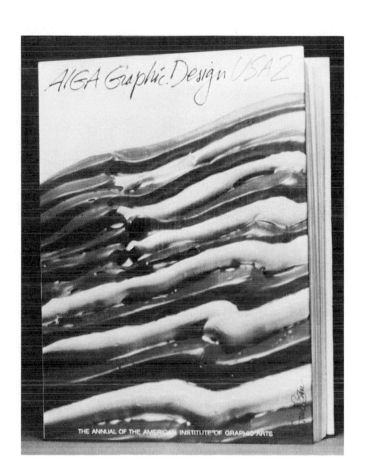

1055   SILVER AWARD
Art Directors: **Saul Bass, Art Goodman**
Designer: **Saul Bass**
Photographer: **George Arakaki**
Artists: **Saul Bass, Art Goodman**
Client: **AIGA**
Publisher: **Watson-Guptill Publications**
Agency: **Saul Bass/Herb Yager & Associates**

1056 DISTINCTIVE MERIT
Art Director: **R.D. Scudellari**
Designer: **R.D. Scudellari**
Artist: **Rockwell Kent**
Client: **Alfred A. Knopf**
Editor: **Bobbi Bristol**
Publisher: **Alfred A. Knopf**
Director: **Robert Gottlieb**
Producer: **Ellen McNeilly**
Agency: **Corporate Design Dept.**

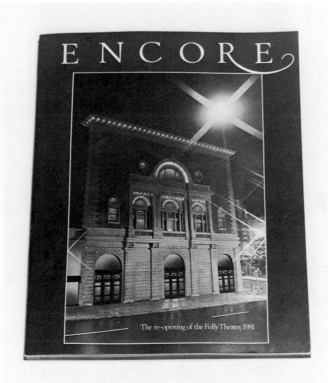

1057
Art Director: **Gary Mallen**
Designer: **Garry Mallen**
Photographer: **Mike Laurance**
Writer: **Patricia Glenn**
Client: **Folly Theater**
Editor: **Patricia Glenn**
Publisher: **Folly Theater**

1058
Art Director: **Toshiaki Ide**
Designer: **Seymour Chwast**
Artist: **Seymour Chwast**
Client: **New York City Department of Cultural Affairs**

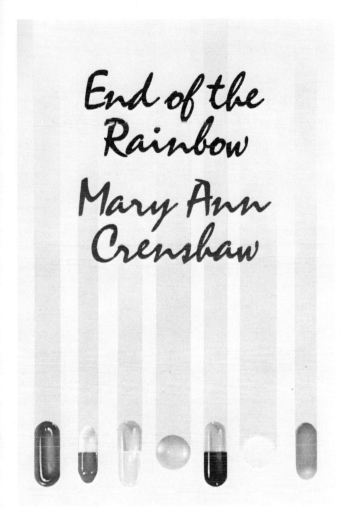

1059
Art Director: **Jackie Merri Meyer**
Designer: **Jackie Merri Meyer**
Artist: **Jose Cruz**
Editor: **George Walsh**
Publisher: **Macmillan Publishing Company, Inc.**

1060
Art Director: **Frank Kozelek**
Designer: **Tony Greco**
Photographer: **Herman Estévez**
Writer: **Thomas Keneally**
Client: **Berkley Publishing**
Publisher: **Rena Wolner**

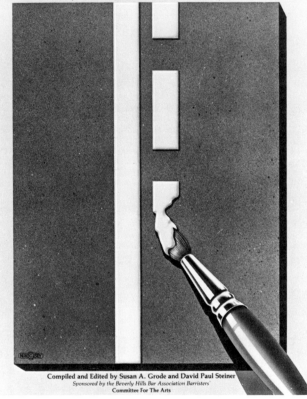

1062
Art Director: **Bob Reed**
Designer: **Wendell Minor**
Artist: **Wendell Minor**
Writer: **Douglas C. Jones**
Client: **Holt, Rinehart, Winston**
Editor: **Don Hutter**
Publisher: **Holt, Rinehart, Winston**

1061
Art Director: **Jackie Merri Meyer**
Designer: **Jackie Merri Meyer**
Artist: **Manny Leite**
Editor: **Charles Levine**
Publisher: **Macmillan Publishing Company, Inc.**

1063
Art Director: **Tom Nikosey**
Designer: **Tom Nikosey**
Artist: **Tom Nikosey**
Writers: **Susan Grode, David Steiner**
Client: **Beverly Hills Bar Association**
Editor: **Susan Grode**
Publisher: **Committee for the Arts**

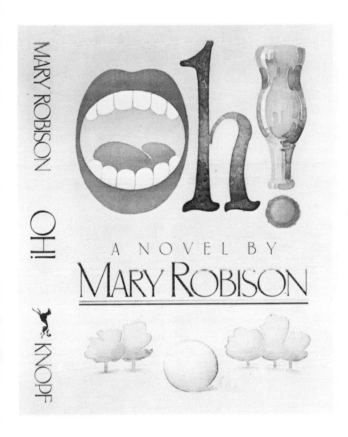

1065
Art Director: **Francis Morgan**
Designer: **Francis Morgan**
Photographer: **Bill Keller**
Client: **University of Arizona Press**
Publisher: **University of Arizona Press**

1064
Art Director: **Lidia Ferrara**
Designer: **John Alcorn**
Artist: **John Alcorn**
Client: **Alfred A. Knopf, Inc.**
Editor: **Gordon Lish**
Publisher: **Alfred A. Knopf, Inc.**
Agency: **Alfred A. Knopf, Inc.**

1066
Art Director: **Susan English**
Designers: **Susan English, Jerry Hunter**
Photographer: **Adams Studio, Inc.**
Artist: **Gloria Marconi**
Writer: **Kathryn Tidyman**
Client: **Man-Made Fiber Producers Association, Inc.**
Agency: **Graham Associates, Inc.**

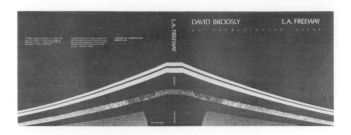

1068
Art Director: **Steve Renick**
Designer: **Steve Renick**
Editor: **Jack Miles**
Publisher: **University of California Press**

1069
Art Directors: **David S. Shapiro, Tom Poth**
Designers: **David S. Shapiro, Tom Poth, Mike Hicks**
Photographer: **Rick Patrick**
Artists: **David S. Shapiro, Molly Smith**
Writer: **Texas Monthly Press**
Client: **Texas Monthly Press**
Editor: **Anne Dingus**
Publisher: **Texas Monthly Press**
Production Co.: **Cathy Berend/Texas Monthly Press**
Agency: **HIXO Inc., Austin**

1070
Art Director: **Frank Kozelek**
Designer: **Tony Greco**
Artist: **Frank Johnson**
Writer: **Garson Kanin**
Client: **Berkley Publishing**
Publisher: **Rena Wolner**

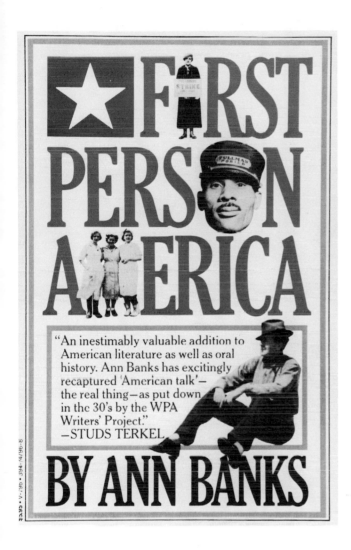

1071
Art Director: **Judith Loeser**
Designer: **Paul Gamarello**
Editor: **Anne Freedgood**
Publisher: **Random House**

1072
Art Director: **Frank Metz**
Designer: **Louise Fili**
Photographer: **Unknown**
Letterer: **Louise Fili**
Writer: **A.J. Langguth**
Client: **Simon & Schuster**
Editor: **Alice Mayhew**
Publisher: **Simon & Schuster**
Production Co.: **Simon & Schuster**

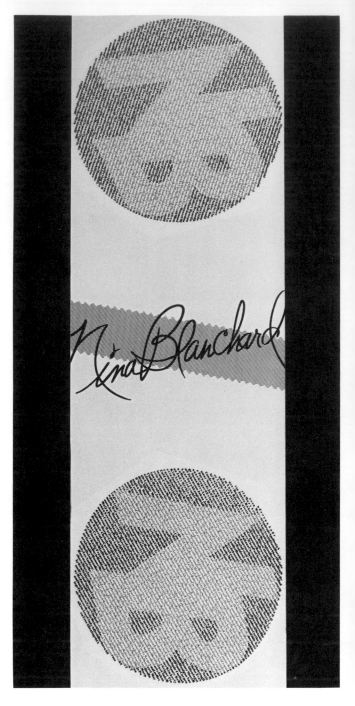

1073
Art Director: **Rubin Pfeffer**
Designer: **Paul Gamarello**
Editor: **Helen Wolff**
Publisher: **Harcourt Brace Jovanovich**

1074
Art Director: **Andrew Janson**
Designer: **Andrew Janson**
Artist: **John Van Hamersveld**
Client: **Nina Blanchard Model Agency**
Editors: **Andrew Janson, James Kellahin**
Publisher: **James Kellahin, Inc.**
Creative Director: **James Kellahin**
Production Co.: **James Kellahin, Inc.**
Agency: **Andrew Janson & Associates**

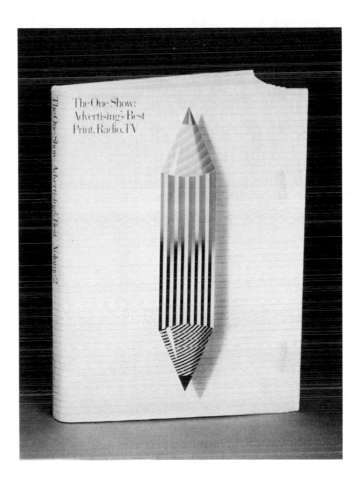

1075
Art Director: **Barry L.S. Mirenburg**
Designer: **Barry L.S. Mirenburg**
Artist: **Barry L.S. Mirenburg**
Publisher: **Quick Fox/Music Sales Corporation**

1076
Art Director: **Seymour Chwast**
Designers: **Seymour Chwast, Richard Mantel**
Artist: **(Cover) Richard Mantel**
Client: **American Showcase**
Agency: **Push Pin Studios**

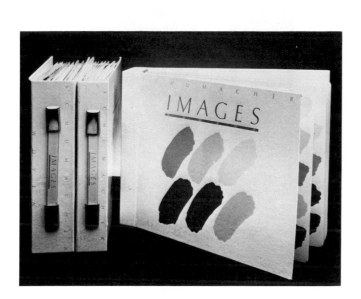

1082
Art Directors: **Raymond Waites, Cheryl Lewin**
Designer: **Cheryl Lewin**
Photographer: **Bruce Wolf**
Client: **Schumacher, Inc.**
Agency: **Gear**

1083
Art Director: **Lynn Hollyn**
Designer: **Mary Mietzelfeld**
Artist: **Mary Mietzelfeld**
Writer: **Natsume Soseki**
Client: **Perigee Books**
Editor: **Sam Mitnick**
Publisher: **Perigee Books**

1084
Art Director: **Albert Squillace**
Designer: **Albert Squillace**
Photographer: **Albert Squillace**
Writer: **Inez Krech**
Client: **Crown Publishers, Inc.**
Editor: **Pam Thomas**
Publisher: **Ruth Birnkrant**

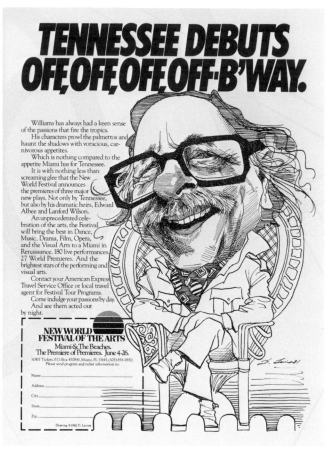

1085   DISTINCTIVE MERIT
Art Director: **John C. Jay**
Designer: **Charles Banuchi**
Artist: **Antonio Lopez**
Client: **Bloomingdale's**
Creative Director: **John C. Jay**
Agency: **Bloomingdale's Adv. Dept.**

1086
Art Director: **David Thall**
Designer: **David Thall**
Artist: **David Levine**
Writer: **Jerry Brown**
Client: **New World Festival of the Arts**
Agency: **BS & Partners (Miami)**

I WANT YOU

1088
Art Directors: **Jeff Stahler, Alan E. Cober**
Designer: **Alan E. Cober**
Artist: **Alan E. Cober**
Writer: **Alan E. Cober**
Client: **The Columbus Society of Communicating Arts**

1087
Art Director: **Marilyn Hoffner**
Designer: **Marilyn Hoffner**
Artist: **Gerald Gersten**
Client: **Cooper Union Annual Fund**

1089
Art Director: **Vincent E. Catteruccia**
Designer: **Gregg Klees**
Artist: **Gregg Klees**
Writer: **Lennox Samuels**
Client: **The Milwaukee Sentinel**
Editor: **Robert H. Wills**

Depression — 'Downer' Without Drugs

"Depression is a natural disaster. It breaks up marriages, costs jobs, hampers the capacity to mother."

The Signs Of Depression

Security-Conscious Hollywood Becomes 'Fear City'

Terrified celebrities are arming themselves, getting fierce dogs and living in prison-like environments

1091
Art Director: **R.J. Shay**
Designer: **R.J. Shay**
Artist: **R.J. Shay**
Writer: **Jane See White**
Client: **Associated Press**
Editor: **Pulitzer Publishing Co.**

1090
Art Director: **Warren Weilbacher**
Designer: **Gary Viskupic**
Artist: **Gary Viskupic**
Writer: **Michael D. Mosettig**
Client: **Newsday "Books"**
Editor: **Nina King**
Publisher: **Newsday Inc.**

1092
Art Director: **R.J. Shay**
Designer: **R.J. Shay**
Artist: **R.J. Shay**
Writer: **John Collins**
Client: **International Features**
Editor: **Pulitzer Publishing Co.**

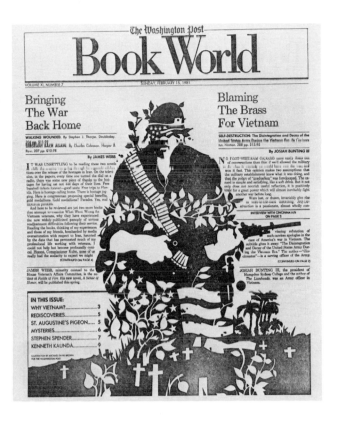

1093
Art Director: **Francis Tanabe**
Designer: **Michael David Brown**
Artist: **Michael David Brown**
Client: **Washington Post**

1094
Art Director: **William Prindle**
Designers: **William Prindle, Michael David Brown**
Artist: **Michael David Brown**
Client: **Student National Educational Assn.**

1095
Art Director: **Miriam Smith**
Designer: **Lee Hill**
Artist: **Gary Viskupic**
Writer: **Cristina Robb**
Client: **Newsday**
Editor: **Stan Green**
Publisher: **Newsday**

1096
Art Director: **Jerelle Kraus**
Designer: **Jerelle Kraus**
Artist: **Anita Siegel**
Writer: **Harry Rositzke**
Client: **The New York Times**
Editor: **Charlotte Curtis**
Publisher: **The New York Times**
Production Co.: **The New York Times**

1097
Art Directors: **Bill Caldwell, Becky Eason**
Designer: **Bill Caldwell**
Photographer: **Virginia Lithograph**
Artist: **Ken Krafchek**
Writers: **Bill Caldwell, Becky Eason**
Client: **Washington Art Directors Club**
Editor: **Becky Eason**
Publisher: **Washington Art Directors Club**
Director: **Bill Caldwell**

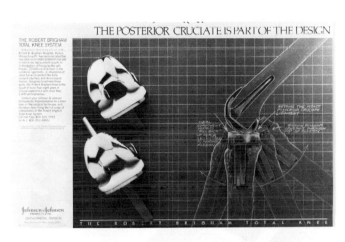

1098
Art Director: **Miriam Smith**
Artist: **Ned Levine**
Writers: **Daniel Goleman, Jonathan Freedman**
Client: **Newsday**

1099
Art Director: **R.J. Shay**
Designer: **R.J. Shay**
Artist: **R.J. Shay**
Writer: **Joel Spiegelman**
Client: **High Fidelity Magazine**
Publisher: **Pulitzer Publishing Co.**

1100
Art Directors: **Rocco Volpe, William C. Beauchamp**
Designer: **Rocco Volpe**
Photographer: **Michael Furman**
Artist: **William C. Beauchamp**
Client: **Johnson and Johnson, Orthopaedic Division**
Agency: **Simms and McIvor, Incorporated**

1101
Art Director: **Don Boswell**
Designer: **Jerre Sicuro**
Illustrator: **Ed Lindlof**
Writer: **Pal Byers**
Client: **Kocide Chemical Corporation**
Agency: **Don Boswell Incorporated**

1106
Art Director: **Tom Yurcich**
Designer: **Tom Yurcich**
Artist: **Tom Yurcich**
Writer: **Tom Yurcich**
Client: **Stroh Brewery-White Horse Distillery**

1107
Art Director: **Dave Boss**
Designer: **Andy Zito**
Artist: **Andy Zito**
Client: **National Football League Properties, Inc.**

PANTHERFOOT   **ES KOMMT**

1109
Art Director: **Errol R. Beauchamp**
Designer: **Vicki J. Gullickson**
Artist: **Vicki J. Gullickson**
Writer: **Errol R. Beauchamp**
Client: **Bag Advertising, Inc.**
Agency: **Bag Advertising, Inc.**

1108
Art Director: **Terry Watson**
Artist: **Doug Johnson**
Client: **Upjohn**
Agency: **Gilmore Advertising**

1110
Art Director: **Warren Hanson**
Designers: **Warren Hanson, Joan Clothier**
Photographer: **Rick Dublin**
Artist: **Warren Hanson**
Writer: **Warren Hanson**
Client: **Webster Lumber Company**

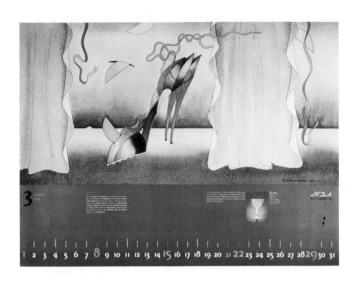

1111
Art Director: **Shinichiro Tora**
Artist: **Barbara Nessim**
Client: **Hotel Barman Association**
Agency: **Dai Nippon Printing Co. Creative Design Center**

1112
Art Directors: **Doug Johnson, Anne Leigh**
Designer: **Anne Leigh**
Artist: **Doug Johnson**
Client: **Doug Johnson**
Agency: **Performing Dogs**

1113
Art Director: **Carlos A. Huerta**
Designer: **David Nakashita**
Artist: **David Nakashita**
Writer: **Alan Barzman**
Client: **Barzman & Company**
Agency: **Huerta Design Associates**

1114
Designer: **Gary W. Priester**
Artist: **Mary E. Carter**
Writer: **Mary E. Carter**
Client: **Mary E. Carter**
Producer: **Joncea Stemnock**

1115
Art Director: **Dagmar Frinta**
Designer: **Dagmar Frinta**
Photographer: **Dagmar Frinta**
Artist: **Dagmar Frinta**
Client: **Dagmar Frinta**
Agency: **The Dagmar Frinta Agency**

1116
Art Director: **Liane Fried**
Designer: **Liane Fried**
Artist: **Liane Fried**
Agency: **"Word of Mouth"**

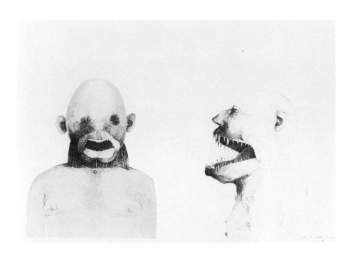

1117
Art Director: **Alan E. Cober**
Designer: **Jan Nyman**
Artist: **Alan E. Cober**
Agency: **Arbcam/Lenskog — Sweden**

1118
Creative Director: **Charles V. Blake**
Art Directors: **Elaine Zeitsoff, Vasken Kalayjian**
Designer: **Steve Gansl**
Writer: **Hal Alterman**
Client: **NBC Marketing**
Production Co.: **Crafton Printers**

1119
Art Director: **Gary Kelley**
Designer: **Gary Kelley**
Artist: **Gary Kelley**
Writers: **Various**
Client: **Theatre UNI/UNI Lyric Theatre**
Editor: **D. Terry Williams**
Publisher: **University of Northern Iowa**
Agency: **Hellman Associates, Inc.**

1120
Art Directors: **Anne Norton, George Grodzicki**
Designer: **Doug Johnson**
Artist: **Doug Johnson**
Client: **Burlington Industries**

1121
Art Directors: **Chris Nylander, Don Weller**
Designer: **Don Weller**
Artist: **Don Weller**
Writer: **Chris Nylander**
Client: **Spokane Falls Community College**
Publisher: **Spokane Falls Community College**
Agency: **The Weller Institute for the Cure of Design, Inc.**

1129
Art Director: **Toshiaki Ide**
Designer: **Seymour Chwast**
Artist: **Seymour Chwast**
Client: **New York City Department of Cultural Affairs**

1130
Art Director: **Bil Sontag**
Designer: **Bill Sontag**
Photographer: **Corson Hirshfeld**
Artist: **Bill Sontag**
Writer: **Kirby Sullivan**
Client: **Murray Ohio Manufacturing Company**
Agency: **Sive Associates, Inc.**

1131
Art Directors: **John Risinger, Michael E. Frakes**
Designer: **Michael E. Frakes**
Artist: **Michael E. Frakes**
Writer: **Ellen Trelmer**
Client: **Iowa Public Broadcasting Network**

1132
Art Directors: **John Risinger, Michael E. Frakes**
Designer: **Michael E. Frakes**
Artist: **Michael E. Frakes**
Client: **Iowa Public Broadcasting Network**

1133
Art Director: **Steve Rutland**
Designer: **Steve Rutland**
Artist: **John Robinette**
Writers: **Ward Archer Jr., David McGuire**
Publisher: **Memphis Publishing Company**
Agency: **Ward Archer & Associates**

1134
Art Directors: **Barbara Nessim, Mare Earley**
Designer: **Barbara Nessim**
Artist: **Barbara Nessim**
Writers: **Barbara Nessim, Mare Earley**
Client: **Scarlett Letters**
Agency: **Barbara Nessim Graphics**

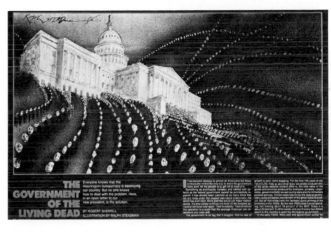

1135   DISTINCTIVE MERIT
Art Director: **Tom Staebler**
Designer: **Bob Post**
Artist: **Vincent Topazio**

1137
Art Director: **Joe Brooks**
Designer: **Claire Victor**
Artist: **Ralph Steadman**
Writer: **Robert Sherrill**
Client: **Penthouse International**
Editor: **Peter Bloch**
Publisher: **Bob Guccione**

1136   DISTINCTIVE MERIT
Art Director: **Frank M. Devino**
Designer: **Margaret Richichi**
Artist: **Charles Pfahl**
Writer: **Robert Silverberg**
Client: **Omni Magazine**
Editor: **Ellen Datlow**
Publisher: **Bob Guccione**

1138
Art Director: **Tom Staebler**
Artist: **Milton Glaser**

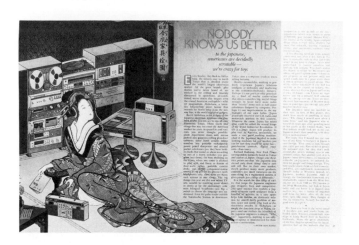

Lily of the Nile
Agapanthus orientalis

The agapanthus is a herbaceous perennial with strap-like, arching leaves growing in large clumps. The leafless flower stalk terminates in a globe of up to 100 blue or white (cultivar 'Alba') bell-shaped flowers. The large, fleshy roots may be divided every five years or so to keep the plant in bounds. Agapanthus make excellent container plants that can be moved indoors in cold winter climes. Partial sun and moist, loamy, well-draining soils are preferred. The plants usually grow to a height of 2 to 4 feet, though dwarf varieties are less than 2 feet tall. Established plants will tolerate some drought but often develop large, tan-colored spots when they need more water. —Dennis Beck, Ornamental Horticulture Department, California Polytechnic State University

Illustration by Pat Wong

13

SEPTEMBER 1981

1139
Art Director: **Tom Staebler**
Designer: **Len Willis**
Artist: **Kinuko Y. Craft**

1140
Art Director: **M.J. Cody**
Designer: **M.J. Cody**
Artist: **Bill Prochnow**
Editor: **Constance J. Sidles**
Publisher: **Barbara Cady**
Producer: **Flowers &**

1141
Art Director: **M.J. Cody**
Artist: **Pat Wong**
Editor: **Constance J. Sidles**
Publisher: **Barbara Cady**
Producer: **Flowers &**

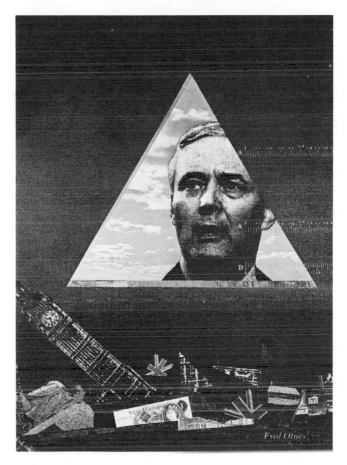

1143
Art Director: **Frank M. Devino**
Designer: **Elizabeth Woodson**
Artist: **H.R. Giger**
Client: **Omni Publications Int'l. Ltd.**
Publisher: **Bob Guccione**

1142
Art Directors: **Ron Meyerson, Bob Engle**
Artist: **Richard Newton**
Editor: **Lester Bernstein**
Publisher: **Charles J. Kennedy**

1144
Art Director: **Louise Kollenbaum**
Designer: **Dian-Aziza Ooka**
Artist: **Fred Otnes**
Writer: **Christopher Hitchens**
Client: **Mother Jones Magazine**
Publisher: **Foundation for National Progress**

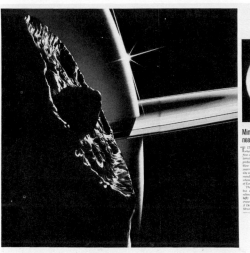

1145
Art Director: **Thomas Darnsteadt**
Design Director: **John Newcomb**
Designer: **Kathleen Cuddihy**
Photographer: **Stephen Munz**
Artist: **Janice Conklin**
Writers: **Seth L. Haber, M.D., Marcia C. Inhorn**
Client: **MEDICAL LABORATORY OBSERVER Magazine**
Editor: **Robert Fitzgibbon**
Publisher: **H. Mason Fackert**
Production Co.: **Medical Economics Co., Inc.**

1146
Art Director: **Mary Zisk**
Design Director: **Frank Rothmann**
Designers: **Mary Zisk, Nancy Oatts**
Artist: **Eraldo Carugati**
Editor: **Scott DeGarmo**
Publisher: **Science Digest/Hearst Corp.**

1147
Art Directors: **Craig Bernhardt, Janice Fudyma**
Designer: **Janice Fudyma**
Artist: **Kimmerle Milnazik**
Client: **W.R. Grace & Co.**
Editor: **Joyce Cole**
Publisher: **W.R. Grace & Co.**
Agency: **Bernhardt/Fudyma Design Group**

1148
Art Director: **Jan Adkins**
Artist: **William H. Bond**
Editor: **Wilbur E. Garrett**
Publisher: **National Geographic Society**

THE
LIMITS
OF
EXCELLENCE

Can you throw a 140 mile-per-hour fastball?
Can you kick an 80-yard field goal?
Can anyone here outjump Bob Beamon? Well, why not.

By David Owen

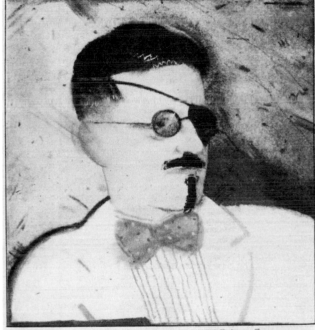

AND YES I SAID YES...

For James Joyce fans, June 16 is a mythic literary holiday called Bloomsday. To celebrate, John Crelan has put together another evening of music, poetry, and dramatic readings culled from and elaborating on Joyce's works. The spirit of Joyce — his lyricism, his bitter bite, his public and private lives — will be evoked in a variety of modes including part of the long stream-of-consciousness soliloquy from *Ulysses* as well as letters from Nora Joyce to her husband. There will be a composition by Mark Harvey derived from *Portrait of the Artist* and songs by Pulitzer Prize-winning composer Donald Martino from *Pomes Penyeach*. Tenor Karl Dan Sorenson, and many others, will be on the program.

You can buy tickets at Jordan Hall before the performance, which starts at 8 p.m.

BLOOMSDAY, JUNE 16
JORDAN HALL
30 GAINESBOROUGH STREET
BOSTON 02115

1149
Art Director: **Vincent Winter**
Designer: **Vincent Winter**
Artist: **Brad Holland**
Writer: **David Owen**
Client: **Inside Sports**
Editor: **John A. Walsh**
Publisher: **E. Daniel Capell**

1150
Art Director: **Ronn Campisi**
Designer: **Catherine Aldrich**
Artist: **Vivienne Flesher**
Editor: **Al Larkin**
Publisher: **The Boston Globe**

AERIE   BY MICHAEL CRAWFORD

1151
Art Director: **Mary Zisk**
Design Director: **Frank Rothmann**
Designer: **Mary Zisk**
Photographer: **Len De Lessio**
Sculptor: **Judith Jampel**
Client: **Science Digest**
Editor: **Scott DeGarmo**
Publisher: **Science Digest/Hearst Corp.**

1152
Art Directors: **Richard Creighton, Dorothy Fall**
Designer: **Dorothy Fall**
Artist: **Michael David Brown**
Client: **District of Columbia Bar Assn.**

1153
Art Director: **Judy Garlan**
Artist: **Michael Crawford**
Client: **The Atlantic Monthly Co.**
Editor: **William Whitworth**
Publisher: **The Atlantic Monthly Co.**

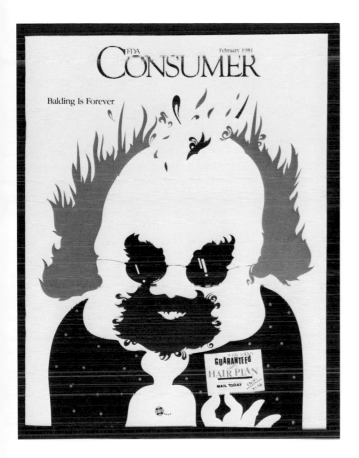

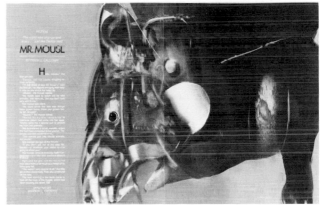

1155
Art Director: **Nancy Butkus**
Designer: **Nancy Duckworth**
Artist: **G. Allen Garns**
Writer: **Michael Fessier, Jr.**
Client: **New West Magazine**
Editor: **William Broyles, Jr.**
Publisher: **John Marin**

1154
Art Director: **Jesse Nichols**
Designer: **Michael David Brown**
Artist: **Michael David Brown**
Client: **Food & Drug Administration**

1156
Art Director: **Frank M. Devino**
Designer: **Margaret Richichi**
Artist: **Marshall Arisman**
Client: **Omni Publications Int'l. Ltd.**
Publisher: **Bob Guccione**

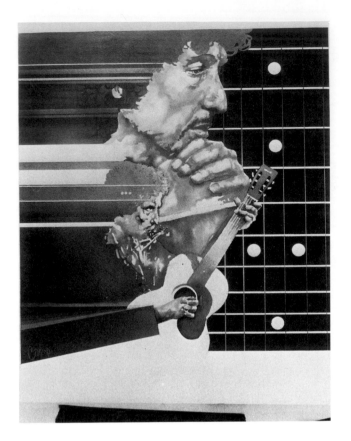

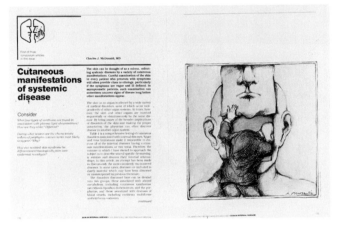

1157
Art Director: **Vernon H. Carne**
Designer: **Vernon H. Carne**
Artist: **Vernon H. Carne**
Client: **The Atlanta Constitution**
Editor: **Lisa Velders**
Publisher: **Atlanta Newspapers**

1159
Art Director: **Vincent Winter**
Designer: **Vincent Winter**
Artist: **Jim Franklin**
Writer: **Gary Cartwright**
Client: **Inside Sports**
Editor: **John A. Walsh**
Publisher: **E. Daniel Capell**

1158
Art Director: **Susan Reinhardt**
Designer: **Susan Reinhardt**
Artist: **Blair Drawson**
Writer: **R.V. Denenberg**
Client: **The Dial**
Editor: **Don Erickson**
Publisher: **Public Broadcasting Communications, Inc.**

1160
Art Director: **Tina Adamek**
Designer: **Geoffrey Moss**
Artist: **Geoffrey Moss**
Editor: **Beth Grendahl**
Publisher: **McGraw-Hill, Inc.**

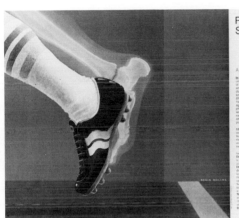

1161
Art Director: **Tina Adamek**
Designer: **Steve Blom**
Artist: **Robin Moline**
Editor: **Francis Caldwell**
Publisher: **McGraw-Hill, Inc.**

1163
Creative Director: **Charles V. Blake**
Art Directors: **Elaine Zeitsoff, Vasken Kalayjian**
Designer: **Steve Gansl**
Artist: **Ray Barber**
Writer: **Steve Jaffe**
Client: **NBC Marketing**
Production Co.: **Jurist Co., Inc.**

1162
Art Director: **Tina Adamek**
Designer: **Tina Adamek**
Artist: **David Gambale**
Editor: **Beth Grendahl**
Publisher: **McGraw-Hill, Inc.**

1164
Art Director: **Barry Vetere**
Designer: **Barry Vetere**
Artist: **Charlie White**
Client: **Dunkin' Donuts**
Agency: **Ally & Gargano, Inc.**

Not just another faceless cigarette

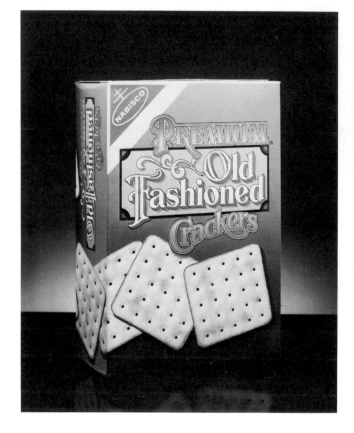

1165
Art Director: **Reinhold Schwenk**
Designers: **Reinhold Schwenk, David Garner**
Client: **Lorillard**
Agency: **Jordan, Case & McGrath**

1166
Art Director: **Frank Nichola**
Designer: **Józef Sumichrast**
Artist: **Józef Sumichrast**
Client: **Leo Burnett Co.**

1167
Art Directors: **John Lister, Helen Rettger, Karen Kaplan**
Artists: **Gerard Huerta, Roger Huyssen**
Client: **Lister Butler**

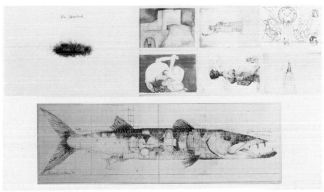

1168
Art Directors: **Acy R. Lehman, Dick Smith**
Designers: **Acy R. Lehman, Dick Smith**
Artist: **Dennis Luzak**
Client: **RCA "SelectaVision" VideoDiscs**

1169   GOLD AWARD
Art Director: **Gordon Fisher**
Designers: **Gordon Fisher, Alan E. Cober**
Artist: **Alan E. Cober**
Writers: **Gordon Fisher, Sue Smith**
Client: **Neenah Paper**
Agency: **Creative Dimensions**

1171
Art Director: **Dugald Stermer**
Designer: **Dugald Stermer**
Artist: **Dugald Stermer**
Writer: **Dugald Stermer**
Publisher: **Lancaster-Miller**

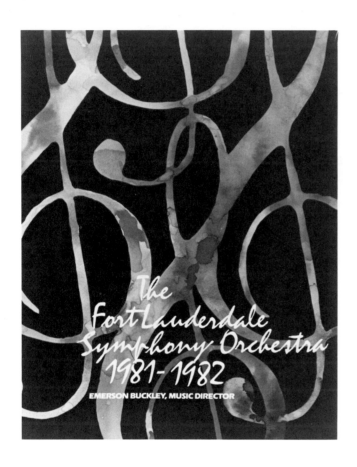

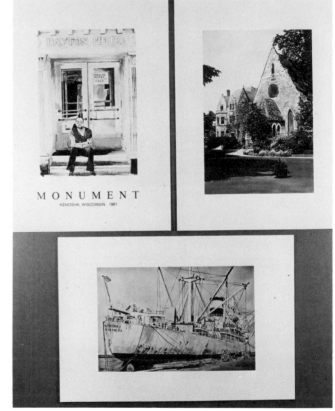

1172
Executive Art Director: **Bernard T. Anastasia**
Designer: **Bernard T. Anastasia**
Artist: **Jose Lopez**
Client: **The Fort Lauderdale Symphony Orchestra**
Executive Editor: **Michael P. Savas**
Publisher: **G.M. Feldman & Co.**
Agency: **G.M. Feldman & Co.**

1173
Art Director: **Brad Bennett**
Designer: **Brad Bennett**
Artist: **Brad Bennett**
Client: **Brad Bennett Studio**

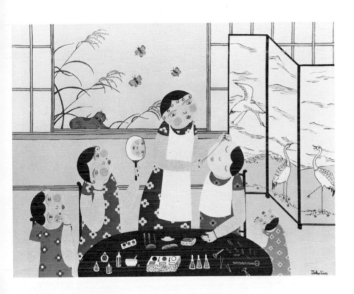

1174
Artist: **John Lim**
Writer: **John Lim**
Publisher: **Tundra**

1176
Art Director: **Nancy Butkus**
Designer: **Nancy Butkus**
Artist: **Dugald Stermer**
Writer: **Dexter Kelly**
Client: **New West Magazine**
Editor: **William Broyles, Jr.**
Publisher: **John Marin**

1175
Art Director: **Mary Zisk**
Design Director: **Frank Rothmann**
Designer: **Mary Zisk**
Artist: **Alan E. Cober**
Client: **Science Digest**
Editor: **Scott DeGarmo**
Publisher: **Science Digest/Hearst Corp.**

1177
Art Director: **Tom Staebler**
Designer: **Kerig Pope**
Artist: **Brad Holland**

1178
Art Director: **Judy Garlan**
Designer: **Judy Garlan**
Artist: **David Levine**
Client: **The Atlantic Monthly Co.**
Editor: **William Whitworth**
Publisher: **The Atlantic Monthly Co.**

1180
Art Director: **Michael Gass**
Designer: **Michael Gass**
Artist: **Michael Gass**
Client: **ABC-TV "Good Morning America"**

1179
Art Director: **Frank M. Devino**
Designer: **Margaret Richichi**
Artist: **Friedrich Hechelmann**
Client: **Omni Publications Int'l. Ltd.**
Publisher: **Bob Guccione**

1181
Art Director: **Piet Halberstadt**
Artist: **Piet Halberstadt**
Client: **WOR-TV News / News at Noon**
Director: **Neil Borrell**
Producer: **Steve Osborne**

1183
Art Directors: **Beverly Littlewood, Gary E. Teixeira**
Designer: **Gary E. Teixeira**
Artist: **Gary E. Teixeira**
Client: **WNBC-TV News 4 New York**

1182
Art Director: **Michael Gass**
Designer: **Michael Gass**
Artist: **Michael Gass**
Client: **ABC-TV "Good Morning America"**

1184
Art Director: **Maria LoConte**
Designer: **Maria LoConte**
Photographer: **Ed Malitsky**
Client: **WNAC-TV, Boston**
Agency: **WNAC TV/Art Department**

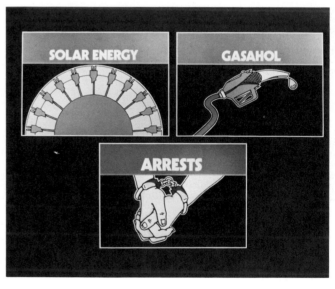

1185
Art Director: **Ernesto Mendoza**
Designer: **Ernesto Mendoza**
Artist: **Ernesto Mendoza**
Client: **WCBS-TV, New York**
Agency: **WCBS-TV**

1186
Art Director: **Michael Gass**
Designer: **Michael Gass**
Artist: **Michael Gass**
Client: **ABC-TV "Good Morning America"**

1187
Art Director: **Susan Ferber**
Artist: **Susan Ferber**
Client: **KTVI Channel Two, St. Louis**
Agency: **KTVI Channel Two**

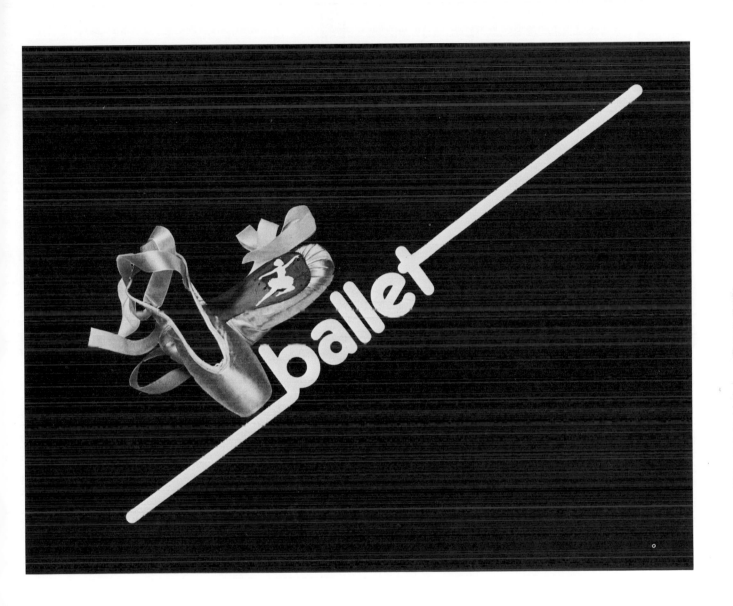

1188
Art Directors: **Steven Manowitz, Ben Blank**
Designer: **Steven Manowitz**
Client: **WABC News, New York**

PHOTOGRAPHY

1189
Art Director: **Fred Devito**
Photographer: **Erica Lennard**
Client: **Bloomingdale's**
Creative Director: **John C. Jay**
Agency: **Bloomingdale's Adv. Dept.**

1190
Art Director: **Dick Henderson**
Photographer: **Phillip Vullo**
Writer: **Jim Cole**
Client: **Wilkins Industries, Inc.**
Agency: **Cole Henderson Drake, Inc.**

1191
Art Director: **Carole Palmer**
Photographer: **Steve Rosenthal**
Editor: **Donald Canty**
Publisher: **Michael Hanley**

1190A
Art Director: **Bob Camuso**
Photographer: **Chuck Kuhn/Chuck Kuhn Photography**
Writer: **John Brown**
Client: **Wendy Amdal/Madison Park Salon**
Agency: **John Brown & Partners**

1192
Art Director: **George Hartman**
Designer: **Howard Sperber**
Photographer: **Jerry N. Uelsmann**
Client: **Glamour Magazine**
Publisher: **Condé Nast Publications Inc.**

1193
Art Director: **Ira Madris**
Designer: **Ira Madris**
Photographer: **Gary A. Perweiler**
Writer: **Bruce Nelson**
Client: **Lufthansa**
Agency: **McCann-Erickson, Inc.**

1196
Art Director: **Barbara Schubeck**
Designer: **Barbara Schubeck**
Photographer: **Phil Marco**
Writer: **Rav Freidel**
Client: **Sony**
Agency: **Ammirati & Puris**

1195
Art Director: **Edward Seymore**
Designer: **Edward Seymore**
Photographer: **Harry Pesin**
Writer: **Harry Pesin**
Client: **Waterford Crystal**
Agency: **Pesin, Sydney & Bernard**

1197
Art Director: **David Deutsch**
Photographer: **George Ratkai**
Writer: **John Clarkson**
Client: **Oneida Silversmiths**
Agency: **David Deutsch Associates, Inc.**

1198
Art Director: **Laura Vergano**
Designer: **Laura Vergano**
Photographers: **Charles Gold — "Vegetables" &**
"Mussels", Phil Marco — "Coffee"
Writers: **Lynn Stiles, Anne Conlon**
Client: **Hilton International**
Agency: **Lord, Geller, Federico, Einstein Inc.**

1200
Art Director: **Woodrow Lowe**
Photographer: **Chuck Kuhn/Chuck Kuhn Photography**
Writer: **Peter Angelos**
Client: **Liberty Orchard**
Production Co: **duMas Production Services**
Agency: **The Solkover Group**

1199
Art Director: **Roger Hines**
Photographer: **Eric Meola**
Writer: **Cappy Capossela**
Client: **Almay Cosmetics**
Agency: **Geer DuBois Inc.**

1202
Art Director: **Frank White**
Designer: **Debbie Wetmore**
Photographer: **Frank White**
Client: **Artifacts**

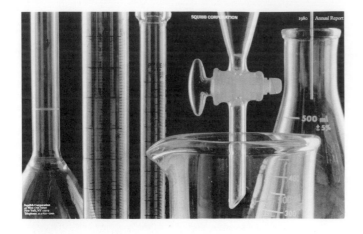

1203
Art Director: **Bruce Blackburn**
Designers: **Bruce Blackburn, G. Bruce Johnson**
Photographer: **Eric Meola**
Artists: **Petrea McDonald, Juliet Schen,**
Phil Goldberg
Client: **Squibb Inc.**
Publisher: **Squibb Inc.**
Agency: **Danne & Blackburn Inc.**

1204
Art Director: **Dick Hesser**
Designer: **Don Nagle**
Photographer: **Tom Weigand**
Writer: **Dan Fura**
Client: **Carpenter Technology Corp.**
Agency: **Beaumont, Heller & Sperling, Inc.**

1205
Art Director: **Tyler Smith**
Designer: **Tyler Smith**
Photographer: **John Goodman**
Writers: **Ray Welch, Geoff Currier**
Client: **Louis**
Agency: **Welch, Currier, Smith**

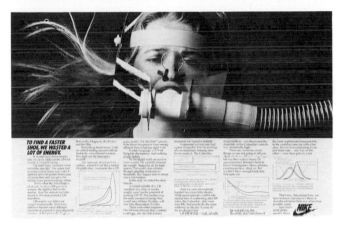

1207
Art Director: **Diana Graham**
Photographer: **Stephen Wilkes**
Client: **Fischer Brothers Investment Builders**
Agency: **Gips & Balkind**

1206
Art Director: **Richard Mallette**
Designer: **Richard Mallette**
Photographer: **Arthur Meyerson**
Writer: **Kathy Johnston**
Client: **Houston Homebuilders Assn.**
Agency: **K. Johnston Advertising**

1208
Art Director: **David Kennedy**
Photographer: **Chuck Kuhn/Chuck Kuhn Photography**
Writer: **Dan Wieden**
Clients: **Blue Ribbon Sports, Nike**
Agency: **William Cain, Inc.**

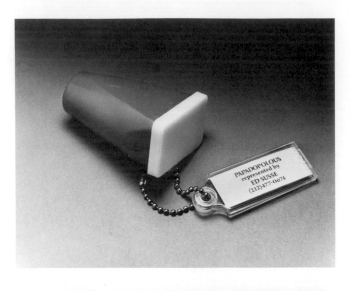

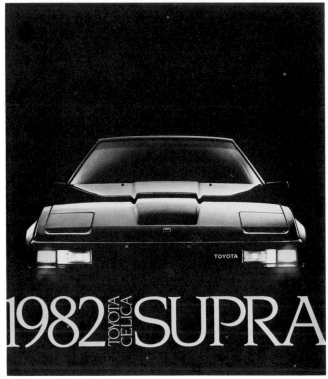

1209
Art Director: **Matt Lester**
Designer: **Matt Lester**
Photographer: **Jeff Perkell, Stock**
Writer: **Helaine Weinberg**
Client: **ACCO**
Agency: **Ketchum Advertising, New York**

1211
Art Directors: **Peter Papadopolous, Ed Susse**
Photographer: **Peter Papadopolous**
Client: **Self Promo**

1210
Art Director: **John Savage**
Photographer: **Michael S. Weinberg**
Client: **McGraw-Edison: Bussmann**

1212
Art Director: **Jim Doyle**
Designer: **Jim Doyle**
Photographer: **Mickey McGuire/Boulevard Photographic Inc.**
Artist: **Konrad Kahl**
Writer: **Jim Lodge**
Client: **Toyota Motor Sales, U.S.A., Inc.**
Publisher: **Anderson Litho Co. Los Angeles, CA**
Creative Director: **Sean K. Fitzpatrick**
Agency: **Dancer Fitzgerald Sample, Inc., S. Calif.**

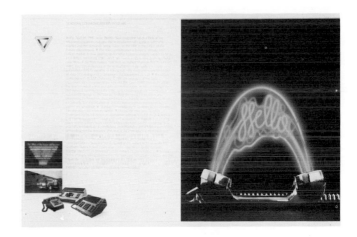

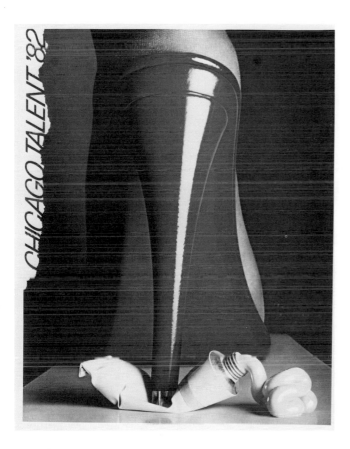

1215
Art Director: **Brian Sewart**
Designer: **Brian Stewart**
Photographer: **Steve Neidorf**
Artist: **Prism Studios**
Writer: **Richard Cohen**
Client: **Norstan Inc.**
Agency: **Stewart & Stewart**

1214
Art Director: **Jeff Barnes**
Designer: **Jeff Barnes**
Photographer: **Dennis Manarchy**
Client: **Chicago Talent, Inc.**
Publisher: **Chicago Talent, Inc.**
Director: **Paul Casper**
Agency: **Alexander Communications**

1216
Art Directors: **Tohru Nakamura, Kiyoshi Kanai**
Designer: **Kiyoshi Kanai**
Photographer: **Tohru Nakamura**
Client: **Tohru Nakamura Studio**

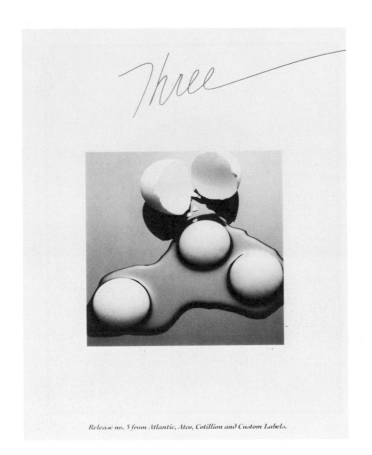

Release no. 3 from Atlantic, Atco, Cotillion and Custom Labels.

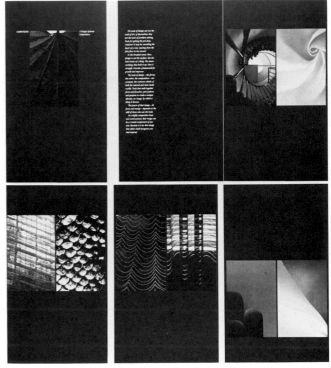

1217
Art Director: **Bob Defrin**
Designer: **Bob Defrin**
Photographer: **Allen Levine**
Client: **Atlantic Records**

1219
Designer: **Chris Hill**
Photographer: **Gary Braasch**
Client: **Compendium, Inc., Houston**
Agency: **Loucks Atelier**

1221   DISTINCTIVE MERIT
Picture Editor: **Steve Ettlinger**
Art Director: **John Tom Cohoe**
Photographer: **Bruno Barbey, Magnum**
Writer: **Frank Gibney**
Client: **GEO Magazine**
Editor: **David Maxey**
Publisher: **Knapp Communications Corp.**

1220
Art Director: **Philip Bauer**
Designer: **Philip Bauer**
Photographer: **Tony Sollecito**
Writer: **Philip Bauer**
Client: **Imahara & Keep Advertising**
Publisher: **House of Printing**
Production Co.: **Focus 4**
Agency: **Imahara & Keep Advertising**

1222   DISTINCTIVE MERIT
Picture Editor: **Steve Ettlinger**
Art Director: **Greg Leeds**
Photographer: **Reinhard Kuenkel**
Writer: **Harold Hayes**
Client: **GEO Magazine**
Editor: **David Maxey**
Publisher: **Knapp Communications Corp.**

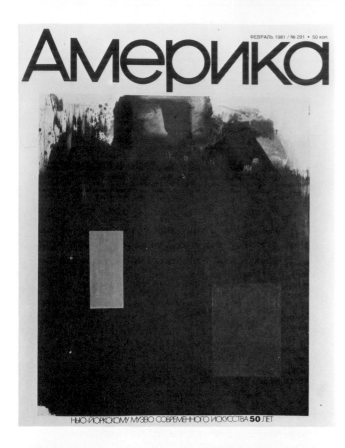

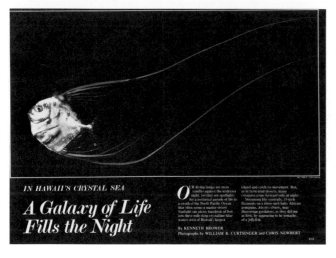

1223
Photographer: **Bob Gomel**
Client: **America Illustrated**
Publisher: **International Communication Agency**

1224
Art Director: **Howard E. Paine**
Designer: **Constance H. Phelps**
Photographer: **William R. Curtsinger**
Editor: **Wilbur E. Garrett**
Publisher: **National Geographic Society**

1225
Picture Editor: **Steve Ettlinger**
Art Director: **John Tom Cohoe**
Photographer: **Thomas Hoepker**
Writer: **Hisako Matsubara**
Client: **GEO Magazine**
Editor: **David Maxey**
Publisher: **Knapp Communications Corp.**

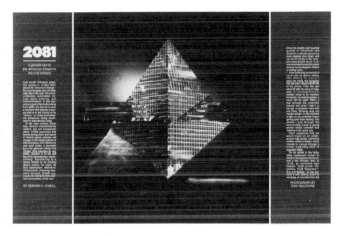

1226
Art Director: **Don Owens**
Designer: **Don Owens**
Photographer: **Arthur Meyerson**
Client: **Houston City Magazine**
Publisher: **Houston City Magazine**

1227
Art Director: **Frank M. Devino**
Designer: **Margaret Richichi**
Photographer: **Tony Guccione**
Client: **Omni Publications Int'l. Ltd.**
Publisher: **Bob Guccione**

1228
Art Director: **Suez B. Kehl**
Designer: **Suez B. Kehl**
Photographer: **Paul Chesley**
Picture Editor: **John Agnone**
Writer: **Michael Robbins**
Client: **National Geographic Society**
Editor: **Ron Fisher**
Publisher: **National Geographic Society**
Director: **Donald J. Crump**

1229
Picture Editor: **Elisabeth Biondi**
Art Director: **Greg Leeds**
Photographer: **Michael K. Nichols**
Writer: **Shiva Nalpaul**
Client: **GEO Magazine**
Editor: **David Maxey**
Publisher: **Knapp Communications Corp.**

1230
Picture Editor: **Steve Ettlinger**
Art Director: **John Tom Cohoe**
Photographer: **Jose Azel**
Writer: **James Stolz**
Client: **GEO Magazine**
Editor: **David Maxey**
Publisher: **Knapp Communications Corp.**

1232
Picture Editor: **Elisabeth Biondi**
Art Director: **John Tom Cohoe**
Photographer: **Peter Menzel**
Writer: **Marc Reisner**
Client: **GEO Magazine**
Editor: **David Maxey**
Publisher: **Knapp Communications Corp.**

1231
Picture Editor: **Elisabeth Biondi**
Art Director: **Greg Leeds**
Photographer: **Michael O'Brien**
Writer: **Frank Trippett**
Client: **GEO Magazine**
Editor: **David Maxey**
Publisher: **Knapp Communications Corp.**

1234
Art Director: **Louise Kollenbaum**
Designer: **Dian-Aziza Ooka**
Photographer: **Susan Meiselas/Magnum Photos**
Writer: **Margaret Randall**
Client: **Mother Jones Magazine**
Editor: **Deirdre English**
Publisher: **Foundation for National Progress**

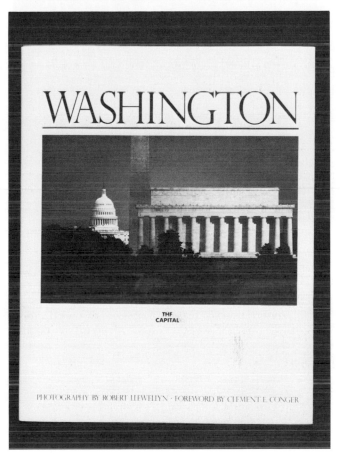

1236
Art Dirtector: **Wayne Roth**
Designer: **Corporate Annual Reports, Inc.**
Photographer: **Gary Gladstone**
Writer: **Courtenay Wyche Belnhorn**
Client: **Rexham Corporation**
Agency: **Corpcom Services Inc.**

1237
Art Director: **Debbie Lawrence**
Photographer: **Mark Heayn**
Creative Director: **Mike Koelker**
Writer: **Mike Koelker**
Client: **Levi Strauss & Co.**
Agency: **Foote Cone & Belding/Honig**

1238   SILVER AWARD
Art Director: **Les Meyers**
Designer: **Steven C. Wilson**
Photographers: **Steven C. Wilson, Karen C. Hayden**
Artist: **Calligrapher Tim Girvin**
Writer: **Steven C. Wilson**
Client: **Conoco/National Audubon Society**
Editor: **Steven C. Wilson**
Publisher: **Entheos**

1239   SILVER AWARD
Art Director: **John Grant**
Designer: **John Grant**
Photographer: **Robert Llewellyn**
Client: **Thomasson-Grant, Inc.**
Publisher: **Thomasson-Grant, Inc.**

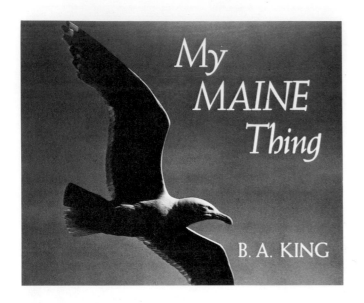

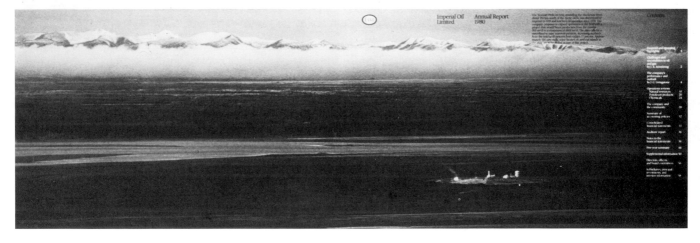

1240
Art Director: **Guy Russell**
Designer: **Guy Russell**
Photographer: **B.A. King**
Artist: **B.A. King**
Writer: **B.A. King**
Client: **Black Ice Publishers**
Editor: **Guy Russell**
Publisher: **Guy Russell Graphics**

1242
Art Director: **Robert Burns**
Designer: **Scott Taylor**
Photographer: **Peter Christopher**
Writers: **Jim Hynes, Jim Knight**
Client: **Imperial Oil Limited**
Agency: **Burns, Cooper, Hynes Limited**

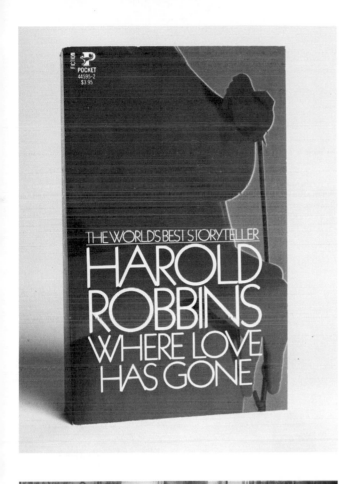

1243
Art Director: **Milton Charles**
Designer: **Milton Charles**
Photographer: **Bill Charles**
Writer: **Harold Robbins**
Client: **Pocket Books**
Editor: **Marty Asher**
Publisher: **Pocket Books**

1245   GOLD AWARD
Art Director: **Robin McDonald**
Designer: **Robin McDonald**
Photographer: **Herbert Migdoll**
Writer: **Judith Jedlicka**
Client: **Horizon Magazine**
Editor: **David Fryxell**
Publisher: **Gray Boone**

1244
Art Director: **Alex Gotfryd**
Designer: **Michael Flanagan**
Photographer: **Deborah Turbeville**
Writer: **Louis Auchincloss**
Editor: **Jacqueline Onassis**
Publisher: **Doubleday & Co., Inc.**

1246   SILVER AWARD
Art Director: **Bob Ciano**
Designer: **Carla Barr**
Photographer: **Patrick Lichfield**
Writer: **Harriet Heyman**
Editor: **Philip Kunhardt**

1247   SILVER AWARD
Art Director: **Thomas Ridinger**
Designer: **Thomas Ridinger**
Photographer: **Reinhart Wolf**
Writer: **Le Corbusier**
Editor: **Jim Hughes**
Article Editor: **Laurance Wieder**
Publisher: **Ziff-Davis Publishing Company**

1249
Art Director: **Frank M. Devino**
Designer: **Elizabeth Woodson**
Photographer: **Malcolm Kirk**
Client: **Omni Publications Int'l., Ltd.**
Publisher: **Bob Guccione**

1248   SILVER AWARD
Art Director: **Brenda Suler**
Designer: **Brenda Suler**
Photographer: **Jerome Ducrot**
Writer: **Arthur Goldsmith**
Client: **Photography Annual**
Editor: **Jim Hughes**
Publisher: **Ziff-Davis Publishing Co.**

1250
Art Director: **Will Hopkins**
Designer: **Louis F. Cruz**
Photographer: **Kenda North**
Writer: **Nancy Stevens**
Client: **CBS Publications**
Editor: **Sean Callahan**
Publisher: **Gary Fisher**

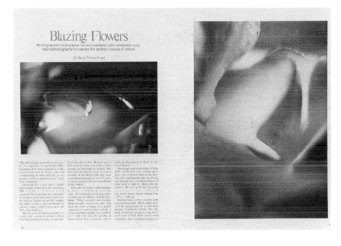

1252
Art Director: **Joe Brooks**
Designer: **Claire Victor**
Photographer: **Pete Turner**
Writer: **Ed Emmerling**
Client: **Penthouse International**
Editor: **Ed Emmerling**
Publisher: **Bob Guccione**

1253
Art Director: **Gordon Bowman**
Designer: **William Wondriska**
Photographer: **Jay Maisel**
Writer: **M. Kraegel**
Client: **United Technologies Corp.**
Agency: **United Technologies/In House**

1254
Art Director: **Constance H. Phelps**
Photographer: **Jay Maisel**
Writer: **John Putman**
Client: **National Geographic Society**
Editor: **Taylor Gregg**
Publisher: **National Geographic Society**

1255
Art Director: **Shinichiro Tora**
Designer: **Shinichiro Tora**
Photographer: **John Lindstrom**
Writer: **Nancy Timmes Engel**
Client: **Popular Photography**
Editor: **Nancy Timmes Engel**
Publisher: **Ziff-Davis Publishing Co.**

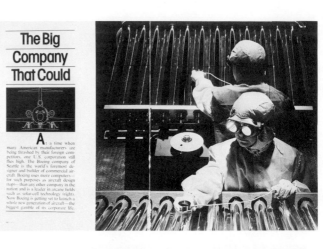

1257
Art Director: **Nancy Butkus**
Designer: **Nancy Duckworth**
Photographer: **Mikkel Aaland**
Writer: **Jon Carroll**
Client: **New West Magazine**
Editor: **William Broyles, Jr.**
Publisher: **John Marin**

1258
Art Director: **Shinichiro Tora**
Designer: **Shinichiro Tora**
Photographer: **Ralph Gibson**
Writer: **Arthur Goldsmith**
Client: **Popular Photography**
Editor: **Arthur Goldsmith**
Publisher: **Ziff-Davis Publishing Co.**

1259
Picture Editor: **Elisabeth Biondi**
Art Director: **John Tom Cohoe**
Photographer: **Harald Sund**
Writer: **Kenneth Labich**
Client: **GEO Magazine**
Editor: **David Maxey**
Publisher: **Knapp Communications Corp.**

1260
Picture Editor: **Elisabeth Biondi**
Art Director: **Greg Leeds**
Photographer: **Michael O'Brien**
Writer: **Frank Trippett**
Client: **GEO Magazine**
Editor: **David Maxey**
Publisher: **Knapp Communications Corp.**

Remembrance of Fins Past

Elongated, extravagant, eclectic? Of course. That's why the cars of the Fifties were heaven on wheels.

BY CHARLES LOCKWOOD

PHOTOGRAPHS · CURTICE TAYLOR

1261
Art Director: **Alfred Zelcer**
Designer: **Marcia Wright**
Photographer: **Curtice Taylor**
Writer: **Charles Lockwood**
Client: **Trans World Airlines**
Editor: **David Martin**
Publisher: **Larry S. Toulouse**
Director: **Brian J. Kennedy**
Production Co.: **The Webb Company**

1262
Picture Editor: **Elisabeth Biondi**
Art Director: **Greg Leeds**
Photographer: **Rebecca Colette**
Writer: **Tony Astrachan**
Client: **GEO Magazine**
Editor: **David Maxey**
Publisher: **Knapp Communications Corp.**

1263
Art Director: **Thomas Ridinger**
Designer: **Thomas Ridinger**
Photographer: **Scott MacLeay**
Writer: **Stephen DeGange**
Editor: **Jim Hughes**
Publisher: **Ziff-Davis Pubishing Company**

1264
Art Director: **Thomas Ridinger**
Designer: **Thomas Ridinger**
Photographer: **Denny Moers**
Writer: **Denny Moers (as interviewed by Steve Pollock)**
Editor: **Jim Hughes**
Publisher: **Ziff-Davis Publishing Company**

1265
Art Director: **Jim Darilek**
Designer: **Jim Darilek**
Photographer: **Geoff Winningham**
Client: **Texas Monthly**
Editor: **Greg Curtis**
Publisher: **Mediatex Communications Corp.**

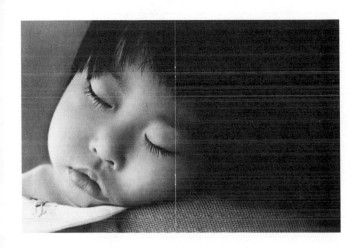

1266
Art Director: **Walter Herdig**
Photographer: **Jay Maisel**
Writer: **Allan Porter**
Client: **Graphis Press Corp., Zurich, Switzerland**
Publisher: **Graphis Press Corp.**

1268
Art Director: **Shinichiro Tora**
Designer: **Shinichiro Tora**
Photographer: **Michael O'Brien**
Writer: **John Durniak**
Client: **Popular Photography**
Editor: **Ken Poli**
Publisher: **Ziff-Davis Publishing Co.**

1267
Art Director: **Brenda Suler**
Designer: **Brenda Suler**
Photographer: **Jesse Fernandez**
Writer: **Larry Frascella**
Client: **Photography Annual**
Editor: **Jim Hughes**
Publisher: **Ziff-Davis Publishing Co.**

1269
Art Director: **Thomas Ridinger**
Designer: **Thomas Ridinger**
Photographer: **Ruffin Cooper**
Writer: **Geoffrey C. Ward**
Editor: **Jim Hughes**
Article Editor: **Laurance Wieder**
Publisher: **Ziff-Davis Publishing Company**

TELEVISION

1270
Art Director: **Dennis Hodgson**
Writer: **Carol Ogden**
Client: **McCulloch Corp.**
Editor: **James Hanley Films**
Agency Producer: **Vicki Blucher**
Director: **Bob Eggers**
Producer: **Amanda Carmel/Eggers Films**
Agency: **Benton & Bowles, Inc.**

1271
Art Director: **Bob Gage**
Photographer: **Ernesto Caparros**
Writer: **Jack Dillon**
Client: **Polaroid Corporation**
Editor: **Pelco**
Director: **Bob Gage**
Production Co.: **Director's Studio Inc./**
Rose Presley, Eugene Mazzola
Agency: **Doyle Dane Bernbach**
Agency/Producers: **Doyle Dane Bernbach/**
Joseph Scibetta, Jane Liepshutz

MCCULLOCH
10-second
BARNEY: You've got power.
Sharp teeth.
Even chain brake.
Next to a guy like me, you've got everything.
ANNCR: See the feature-loaded McCulloch 310 at your
McCulloch dealer.

NO REASON
10-second
JIM: You don't need a reason to have enough Polaroid
Time-Zero Supercolor film.
MARI: Why not wait for a reason?
JIM: Then you won't have the film.

1272
Art Director: **Bob Gage**
Photographer: **Ernesto Caparros**
Writer: **Jack Dillon**
Client: **Polaroid Corporation**
Editor: **Pelco**
Director: **Bob Gage**
Production Co.: **Director's Studio Inc./**
Rose Presley, Eugene Mazzola
Agency/Producers: **Doyle Dane Bernbaoh/**
Joseph Scibetta, Jane Liepshutz

1273
Art Director: **Bob Gage**
Photographer: **Ernesto Caparros**
Writer: **Jack Dillon**
Client: **Polaroid Corporation**
Editor: **Pelco**
Director: **Bob Gage**
Production Co.: **Director's Studio Inc./**
Rose Presley, Eugene Mazzola
Agency/Producers: **Doyle Dane Bernbach/**
Joseph Scibetta, Jane Liepshutz

THEY SENT ME TWO
10-second
MARI: This is Polaroid's new Sun Camera, with a piece of the sun in it.
JIM: How did you get one.
MARI: Didn't you get one . . . that's funny they sent me two.
JIM: Then one is mine.

GRADUATION DAY
10-second
JIM: Here comes graduation and you don't have Polaroid's new Time-Zero Supercolor!
MARI: It's very important!
JIM: What kind of parents are you!
MARI: Yeah!

1290
Art Director: **Bob Gage**
Photographer: **Ernesto Caparros**
Writer: **Jack Dillon**
Client: **Polaroid Corporation**
Editor: **Pelco**
Director: **Bob Gage**
Production Co.: **Director's Studio Inc./**
Rose Presley, Eugene Mazzola
Agency/Producers: **Doyle Dane Bernbach/**
Joseph Scibetta, Jane Liepshutz

MADE IN HEAVEN
10-second
JIM: Polaroid's Time-Zero OneStep comes with Time-Zero
Supercolor because they're made for each other.
MARI: Made in Heaven!
JIM: Massachusetts.

1291
Art Director: **Bob Gage**
Photographer: **Ernesto Caparros**
Writer: **Jack Dillon**
Client: **Polaroid Corporation**
Editor: **Pelco**
Director: **Bob Gage**
Production Co.: **Director's Studio Inc./**
Rose Presley, Eugene Mazzola
Agency/Producers: **Doyle Dane Bernbach/**
Joseph Scibetta, Jane Liepshutz

NOT US
10-second
JIM: What comes in a Made-For-Each-Other-Pack?
MARI: Us?
JIM: Polaroid's Time-Zero OneStep and Time-Zero
Supercolor film.
MARI: Not us.

1292
Art Director: **Bob Gage**
Photographer: **Ernesto Caparros**
Writer: **Jack Dillon**
Client: **Polaroid Corporation**
Editor: **Pelco**
Director: **Bob Gage**
Production Co: **Director's Studio Inc./**
Rose Presley
Agency/Producer: **Doyle Dane Bernbach/**
Joseph Scibetta

1293
Art Directors: **Ted Shaine, Jay Taub**
Writers: **Jay Taub, Ted Shaine**
Client: **Chemical Bank (Brian McGirl)**
Editor: **Ed Shea/Jeff Dell Editorial**
Director: **Steve Horn**
Producer: **Linda Horn**
Agency: **Della Femina, Travisano &**
Partners, Inc.

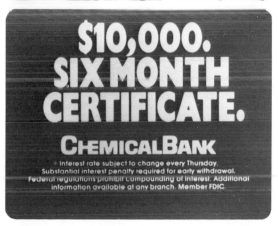

CHRISTMAS STOCKING FOZZIE
10-second
KERMIT: Put some Polaroid film in someone's Christmas stocking.
FOZZIE: . . . And watch 'em try and walk!
KERMIT: Polaroid's not laughing, Fozzie.
GANG: (SINGING) Polaroid means fun.

SHIRT
10-second
MAN: I recently invested a chunk of money on a sure thing.
Know what happened?
ANNCR: Right now, Chemical Bank guarantees a _____%
interest rate on $10,000.
SUPER:
$10,000
Six Month
Certificate
Chemical Bank
The Chemistry's just right for savers at Chemical.
*Substantial interest penalty required for early withdrawal.
Federal regulations prohibit compounding of interest.
Additional information available at any branch.
Member FDIC.

1294
Art Director: **Bob Gage**
Photographer: **Ernesto Caparros**
Writer: **Jack Dillon**
Client: **Polaroid Corporation**
Editor: **Pelco**
Director: **Bob Gage**
Production Co.: **Director's Studio Inc./**
Rose Presley, Eugene Mazzola
Agency/Producers: **Doyle Dane Bernbach/**
Joseph Scibetta, Jane Liepshutz

1295
Art Director: **Bob Gage**
Photographer: **Ernesto Caparros**
Writer: **Jack Dillon**
Client: **Polaroid Corporation**
Editor: **Pelco**
Director: **Bob Gage**
Production Co.: **Director's Studio Inc./**
Rose Presley, Eugene Mazzola
Agency/Producers: **Doyle Dane Bernbach/**
Joseph Scibetta, Jane Liepshutz

BIRTHDAY
10-second
JIM: You'd better have enough Time-Zero Supercolor film for
that big Birthday party.
MARI: Cake's more important!
JIM: Not to us!

JUST LIKE US
10-second
JIM: You get Polaroid's OneStep and Time-Zero Supercolor
together because they're made for each other.
MARI: Just like us?
JIM: How'd you get out of the box.

1296
Art Director: **Mike Withers**
Writer: **Hy Abady**
Client: **Aamco Transmissions, Inc.**
Editors: **Peggy DeLay, Morty Ashkinos**
Director: **Joe Sedelmaier**
Production Co: **Sedelmaier Films, Inc./**
Frank DiSalvo (Agency)
Agency: **Calet, Hirsch, Kurnit & Spector, Inc.**

1297
Art Director: **Bob Gage**
Photographer: **Ernesto Caparros**
Writer: **Jack Dillon**
Client: **Polaroid Corporation**
Editor: **Pelco**
Director: **Bob Gage**
Production Co: **Director's Studio Inc./**
Rose Presley, Eugene Mazzola
Agency/Producers: **Doyle Dane Bernbach/**
Joseph Scibetta, Jane Liepshutz

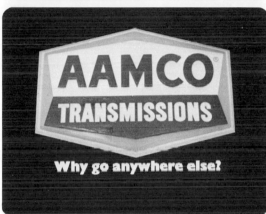

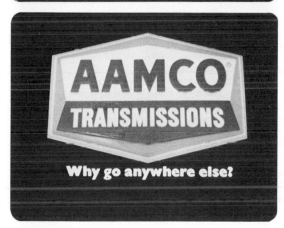

NIGHTMARE
10-second
ANNCR (VO): Don't have nightmares about who's fixing your
transmission.
Bring your car to the transmission specialist.
AAMCO: (BEEP-BEEP) Why go anywhere else?

NO HOLIDAY
10-second
JIM: Make sure you get enough Polaroid Time-Zero
Supercolor film for the holiday weekend.
MARI: There's no holiday this weekend!
JIM: Shhhh!

1298
Art Director: **Michael Tesch**
Writer: **Patrick Kelly**
Client: **Federal Express**
Editor: **Peggy DeLay/Sedelmaier**
Director: **Joe Sedelmaier**
Production Co: **Maureen Kearns/A&G,
Ann Ryan/Sedelmaier**
Agency: **Ally & Gargano, Inc.**

1299
Art Director: **George Euringer**
Writer: **Helayne Spivak**
Client: **Kayser-Roth**
Editors: **Peggy DeLay/Sedelmaier, Morty
Ashkinos/Take Five**
Director: **Joe Sedelmaier**
Producers: **Jerry Haynes/A&G, MaryAnn
Blossom/Sedelmaier**
Agency: **Ally & Gargano, Inc.**

FAST PACED WORLD
10-second
SPLEEN (OC): Congratulationsonyourdealin Denver, David.
I'mputtingyoudowntodealwithDon.
Donisitadeal? Dowehaveadeal? Ihaveacallcomingthrough.
ANNCR (VO): In this fast paced world aren't you glad
there's one company that can keep up with it all?
Dick,What'sthedealwiththedeal? Arewedealing?

TENNIS
(MUSIC THROUGHOUT)
Don't you think it's time to change your socks?
To Interwoven.

1300
Art Director: **Michael Tesch**
Writer: **Patrick Kelly**
Client: **Federal Express**
Editor: **Peggy DeLay/Sedelmaier**
Director: **Joe Sedelmaier**
Producers: **Maureen Kearns/A&G,**
Ann Ryan/Sedelmaier
Agency: **Ally & Gargano, Inc.**

1301
Art Director: **George Euringer**
Writer: **Tom Messner**
Client: **MCI**
Editors: **Peggy DeLay/Sedelmaier,**
Morty Ashkinos/Take Five
Director: **Joe Sedelmaier**
Producers: **Maureen Kearns/A&G,**
Joseph Sedelmaier
Agency: **Ally & Cargano, Inc.**

PICK UP THE PHONE
ANNCR (VO): Federal Express is so easy to use. All you have
to do is pick up the phone.
(SFX: RRRRRRRRIIIIIIIIPPPPPPPPPPPPPP!!)
(SFX: WATER)

WARM & FRIENDLY
ANNCR (VO): Are your long distance bills
(SFX) More than $25.00 a month?
(MUSIC UNDER) Call MCI. You aren't talking too much.
Just paying too much.

1302
Art Director: **George Euringer**
Writer: **Helayne Spivak**
Client: **Kayser-Roth**
Editors: **Peggy DeLay/Sedelmaier,
Morty Ashkinos/Take Five**
Director: **Joe Sedelmaier**
Producers: **Jerry Haynes/A&G,
MaryAnn Blossom/Sedelmaier**
Agency: **Ally & Gargano, Inc.**

1303
Art Director: **Michael Tesch**
Writer: **Patrick Kelly**
Client: **Federal Express**
Editor: **Peggy DeLay/Sedelmaier**
Director: **Joe Sedelmaier**
Producers: **Maureen Kearns/A&G,
Ann Ryan/Sedelmaier**
Agency: **Ally & Gargano, Inc.**

RESTAURANT
(MUSIC THROUGHOUT)
Don't you think it's time to change your socks?
To Interwoven.

PICK UP
ANNCR (VO): The nice thing about Federal Express is
(SFX: HORN) We'll come to your office and pick up
the package.
You don't have to take it anywhere.
(SFX: HORN)

1304
Art Director: **Allan Beaver**
Writer: **Larry Plapler**
Client: **Kronenbourg USA**
Editors: **Ed Shea, Jeff Dell**
Director: **Michael Ulick**
Production Co: **Michael Ulick Production**
Agency: **Levine, Huntley, Schmidt, Plapler & Beaver, Inc.**

1305
Art Director: **George Euringer**
Writer: **Helayne Spivak**
Client: **Kayser-Roth**
Editors: **Peggy DeLay/Sedelmaier, Morty Ashkinos/Take Five**
Director: **Joe Sedelmaier**
Producers: **Jerry Haynes/A&G, MaryAnn Blossom/Sedelmaier**
Agency: **Ally & Gargano, Inc.**

A MAN & A WOMAN
10-second
MAN: We Europeans like Heineken. But Kronenbourg that's love.
VO: Kronenbourg. Europe's #1 bottle of beer.

BOARDROOM
10-second
(MUSIC THROUGHOUT)
Don't you think it's time to change your socks?
To Interwoven.

1306
Art Director: **Michael Tesch**
Writer: **Patrick Kelly**
Client: **Federal Express**
Editor: **Peggy DeLay/Sedelmaier Films**
Director: **Joe Sedelmaier**
Producers: **Maureen Kearns/A&G,
Ann Ryan/Sedelmaier**
Agency: **Ally & Gargano, Inc.**

1308
Art Director: **Dick Bell**
Writer: **Fred Bergendorff**
Client: **KNX Newsradio**
Creative Director: **Fred Bergendorff**
Director: **Ed Winkle**
Production Co.: **Vik-Winkle Productions**
Agency: **Bell-Jesnes Advertising**

BURIED
10-second
(SFX UNDER)
ANNCR (VO): The post office handles over 300 million
pieces of mail a day.
And you're going to put your important business letter
in that pile.
(SFX OUT)
Federal Express has an alternative.

RAIDERS
10-second
John Matuszak for the World Champion Raiders . . . Join me
for a nice, friendly game of football . . . ("CRUNCH" SOUND
EFFECT AS HE EATS THE MIKE).
. . . on KNX Newsradio Ten Seventy.
(EATING) Good station too!

1309
Art Director: Nick Rice
Writer: Terry Bremer
Client: University of Mn. Gophers
Director: Steve Griak
Producers: Nick Rice, Terry Bremer,
Wilson-Griak, Em Com
Agency: Chuck Ruhr Advertising, Inc.

1310
Art Director: Mark Moffett
Photographers: Cailor-Resnick
Writer: Frank Fleizach
Client: The Hertz Corporation
Editor: Perpetual Motion Pictures
Director: Gary Grossman
Production Co.: Gary Grossman, Hal
Hoffer/Perpetual Motion Pictures
Agency: Scali, McCabe, Sloves, Inc.

DAVID AND GOLIATH
10-second
(EARTH SHAKING GRUMBLE)
Celebrate one hundred years of Gopher football as we
take on the giants of the Big Ten.
Be a Gopher fan. Again.
(SOUND OF FOOTBALL SOARING THROUGH THE AIR AND
HITTING GOLIATH IN THE NOSE.)

UNDER-RENTED
10-second
VO: If you compare the rates . . . of all the major truck rental
companies, you'll discover . . .
Hertz will not be . . . under-rented.

1311
Art Director: **Pat Burnham**
Writer: **Phil Hanft**
Client: **Northwestern Bell**
Director: **Walter Goins**
Production Co.: **L.E.O. Productions**
Agency: **Bozell & Jacobs, Inc./Mpls.**

1312
Art Director: **Preuit Holland**
Writer: **Tony Burke**
Client: **North Carolina National Bank**
Director: **Larry Gardner**
Production Co.: **Preuit Holland/Audiofonics**
Agency: **McKinney Silver & Rockett**

TOO BUSY? DON'T WORRY!
10-second
MUSIC: SPEEDED UP DECK THE HALLS.
ANNCR (VO): Say, ah . . . Too busy to make all your
Christmas calls on Christmas Day?
Well, don't worry.
You can get a special 50% discount on direct dial calls
within Iowa . . .
. . . the day after.

MONEY MARKET CERTIFICATE
10-second
YOUNG WOMAN: Even as I speak, my money is earning
interest like this through NCNB's new short term, low
minimum certificates.
What's your money doing? (LAUGHS)

1313
Art Director: **Earl Cavanah**
Writer: **Larry Cadman**
Client: **Playboy Enterprises**
Editor: **Follow-Ciro**
Director: **Tim Newman**
Producers: **Karen Spector (SMS)/**
Jenkins Covington Newman
Agency: **Scali, McCabe, Sloves, Inc.**

1314   GOLD AWARD
Art Director: **Michael Tesch**
Writer: **Patrick Kelly**
Client: **Federal Express**
Editor: **Peggy DeLay/Sedelmaier Films**
Director: **Joe Sedelmaier**
Producers: **Maureen Kearns/A&G,**
Ann Ryan/Sedelmaier
Agency: **Ally & Gargano, Inc.**

U.S. NEWS
WALL STREET JOURNAL
BOARDROOM
10-second
MAN: I'm a reader of U.S. News and World Report.
There's no trivia, no jokes . . . no fun.
That's why I also read Playboy.
SUPER: 17 million men round out their lives with Playboy.

PICK UP THE PHONE
PICK UP
FAST PACED
ANNCR (VO): Federal Express is so easy to use, all you have
to do is pick up the phone.
(SFX: RRRRRRRRIIIIIIIPPPPPPPPPPPPPPIII)
(SFX: WATER)

1315   GOLD AWARD
Art Director: **George Euringer**
Writer: **Helayne Spivak**
Client: **Kayser-Roth**
Editors: **Peggy DeLay/Sedelmaier,**
Morty Ashkinos/Take Five
Director: **Joe Sedelmaier**
Producers: **Jerry Haynes/A&G,**
MaryAnn Blossom/Sedelmaier Films
Agency: **Ally & Gargano, Inc.**

1316
Art Director: **Bob Gage**
Writer: **Jack Dillon**
Client: **Jim Andrews/Polaroid Corporation**
Director: **Bob Gage**
Production Co.: **Director's Studio Inc.**
Agency/Producer: **Doyle Dane Bernbach/**
Jim McConnell

RESTAURANT—BOARDROOM—TENNIS
(MUSIC THROUGHOUT)
Don't you think it's time to change your socks?
To Interwoven.

AND WEDDING—WE WHO—DON'T WHAT IT UP
10-second
KERMIT: Polaroid instant pictures are fun for birthdays, parties
and holidays.
PIGGY: And Weddings.
KERMIT: What?
PIGGY: Well they are.
GANG: (SINGING) Polaroid means fun.

1317
Art Director: **Barbara Simon**
Writer: **Chris Rowean**
Client: **Zayre Corporation**
Editor: **Mike Charles Editorial**
Production Co.: **Sid Myers/Myers & Griner,**
Cuesta
Agency: **Ingalls Associates**

1318
Art Director: **Peggy Cox**
Writer: **Robert Power**
Client: **Dallas Power & Light**
Director: **Jim Rowley**
Production Co.: **Southwest Producers Services**
Agency: **Arnold Harwell McClain**
& Assoc., Inc.

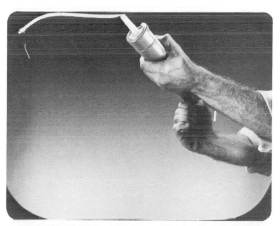

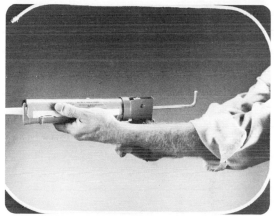

DRACULA — SCROOGE — WHISTLER'S MOTHER
10-second
SFX: TV sounds of old western shoot-out
ANNCR (VO): Friday night (tonite) . . . why lie around doing
the same old thing . . .
(SFX: TV SWITCHES OFF AND RACE CAR REVVES AND TAKES
OFF.)
ANNCR: Come have the thrill of your life at the Zayre Nite
Lite Sale.
From seven till eleven* . . .
Friday night (tonite) at Zayre.
*eight until midnight
seven until midnight

CAULKING — WEATHERSTRIP — MAINTENANCE
10-second
ANNCR (VO): Caulking around windows and doors can
save energy and money.
Anyone can do it.
Contact your electric company for a free booklet that
shows how.
(THREE COMPANY LOGOS)

1319
Art Director: **John C. LePrevost**
Designer: **John C. LePrevost**
Client: **CBS Entertainment**
Editor: **Lynne Lussier**
Animation Production Co.: **The Jay Teitzell Company**
Animation Producer: **Lewis Hall**

1320
Art Director: **Charley Rice**
Writer: **Pete Faulkner**
Client: **Stroh Brewery**
Editor: **Milt Loonan (Prime Cut)**
Director: **N. Lee Lacy**
Production Co.: **N. Lee Lacy Productions**
Agency: **Doyle Dane Bernbach**

QUESTION 1 — QUESTION 2 — QUESTION 3

MUSIC — SFX

JET SPRINT
30-second
BUSINESSMAN: Hey, Gale, how's the trip?
GALE SAYERS: Great . . . OH NO!
(SFX: WHINE OF JET BEGINNING TAKEOFF)
SAYERS: Wait! Wait! My Stroh's!
1ST BAGGAGEMAN: Hey! Look at that guy!
SAYERS: Wait! Wait!
(SFX: JET ENGINES CUT OFF)
2ND BAGGAGEMAN: Wow! He caught that jet!
(SFX: SCREECH OF BAGGAGEMEN'S CART STOPPING NEXT TO SAYERS)
1ST BAGGAGEMAN: It's Gale Sayers!
(SFX: SIZZLING SOUNDS OF SAYER'S SMOKING SHOES)
2ND BAGGAGEMAN: Boy, Mr. Sayers, you were really flyin'!
PLEASED SAYERS: Had to. Nobody's takin' off with my Stroh's!
(SFX: FADE UP STROH'S THEME)

1321
Art Director: **Charles Abrams**
Writer: **Perri Feuer**
Client: **Procter & Gamble/Gain**
Editor: **Joe Laliker/Pelco**
Director: **Joe DeVoto**
Production Co: **Hy Weiner/Joel Productions**
Agency/Producer: **Doyle Dane Bernbach/
Bob Samuel**

1322
Art Director: **Charley Rice**
Writer: **Camille Larghi**
Client: **Ore-Ida**
Editor: **Pelco**
Director: **Herb Stott**
Production Co: **Spungbuggy Productions**
Agency: **Doyle Dane Bernbach**

LIGHTS OUT
30-second
WIFE: Have a cold?
HUSBAND: No . . . Pillow's not clean.
WIFE: (TO HERSELF) Now he's sniffing pillows.
WIFE: It's clean.
HUSBAND: Smell it.
WIFE: (DOUBTFULLY) I think it's clean.
HUSBAND: It's a dark print. How can you tell?
ANNCR: You can . . . with clean smelling Gain.
Gain gets out dirt, . . .
like garden dirt, . . .
that you can see,
and even smelly dirt
you can't see.
WIFE: See how nice and clean your pillow is?
HUSBAND: Who needs to see?

RICH LITTLE
30-second
LITTLE AS JOHN WAYNE: These are Ore-Ida brand Tater Tots.
And there's lots of different ways you can eat them, pilgrim.
DISSOLVE TO LITTLE AS JIMMY DURANTE: These lightly
seasoned potato nuggets go great wit meatballs.
DISSOLVE TO LITTLE AS PAUL LYNDE: They're wonderful in
casseroles.
DISSOLVE TO LITTLE AS BORIS KARLOFF: They even go with
anti-pasto.
(SFX: WOLF HOWL.)
DISSOLVE TO LITTLE AS HUMPHREY BOGART: Sweetheart,
now that's different and awfully good.
CAMERA PULLS BACK, SEE LITTLE AS BOGART AND LITTLE AS
KARLOFF TOGETHER.
BOTH VOICES: Ore-Ida Tater Tots are all-righta.
(SFX: THUNDER.)

1323
Art Director: **Roy Grace**
Designer: **Roy Grace**
Writer: **Tom Yobbagy**
Client: **IBM Office Products Division**
Editor: **Stone-Cutters/Dick Stone**
Director: **Henry Sandbank**
Producer: **Rosemary Barre**
Agency: **Doyle Dane Bernbach**

1324
Art Director: **Charley Rice**
Writer: **Camille Larghi**
Client: **Ore-Ida**
Editor: **Pelco**
Director: **N. Lee Lacy**
Production Co: **N. Lee Lacy Productions**
Agency: **Doyle Dane Bernbach**

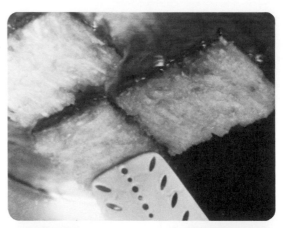

BOXES
30-second
MAN: IBM has a big surprise for you: Our Executive Copier.
LADY: It has excellent copy quality.
FINANCIAL MAN: It's extremely reliable, and comes with IBM service.
GIRL: It's easy to use.
ANNCR (VO): And it's very . . .
. . . very . . .
. . . very . . . small.
The IBM Executive Copier.

MUHAMMAD ALI
30-second
COOK: When you cook for a real man . . .
ALI: (OFF CAMERA) I'm hungry!
(SFX: DOOR SLAM.)
COOK: like I do, meals just can't be skimpy.
ALI: (OFF CAMERA) I could eat a bear!
COOK: (VO HASH BROWNS FRYING) One way I make them heartier is with Ore-Ida Hash Browns . . .
ALI: (OFF CAMERA) Hash Browns! I need Hash Browns!
COOK: . . . the crispy golden brown patties or the chunky tasty Southern Style.
ALI: (OFF CAMERA) Where are my Hash Browns?
COOK: (VO HASH BROWNS MEAL) Why this kind of meal just knocks him out.
ALI: (ON CAMERA) Hash Browns! All-righta! Hash Bro . . . !

1325
Art Director: **Lester Feldman**
Writer: **Mike Mangano**
Client: **GTE**
Director: **Pat Pitelli**
Production Co.: **Pitelli Productions**
Agency: **Doyle Dane Bernbach**

1326
Art Director: **Lester Feldman**
Writer: **Mike Mangano**
Client: **GTE**
Director: **Joe DeVeto**
Production Co.: **Joel Productions**
Agency: **Doyle Dane Bernbach**

LETTER
30-second
ANNCR: According to a recent survey, the average cost of
sending a business letter is . . .
$1.83 for the executive's time . . .
$1.98 for secretarial time . . .
$1.72 for overhead,
. . . and 54¢ for mailing costs
. . . A total of . . .
six dollars and seven cents.
. . . Just for sending one letter.
This message is brought to you by your telephone company.

CLOCK
30-second
VO: If you can restrain your family from calling long
distance till after 5PM, you can save yourself a lot of money

1328
Art Director: **Jack Piccolo**
Designer: **Jack Piccolo**
Writer: **Ted Bell**
Client: **Hershey Corporate**
Editor: **Larry Plastrik/Cinemetric**
Director: **Jack Piccolo**
Production Co: **Ulick Productions**
Agency: **Doyle Dane Bernbach**

1329
Art Director: **Joe Sedelmaier**
Writer: **Tom McElligott**
Client: **Mr. Coffee**
Editor: **Peggy DeLay**
Director: **Joe Sedelmaier**
Production Co: **Sedelmaier Film Productions, Inc.**
Agency: **Marketing Communications Inc.**

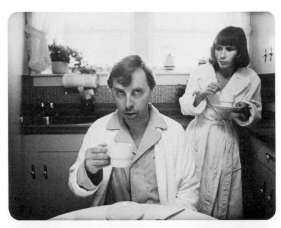

GHOST STORY
30-second
(MUSIC UNDER THROUGHOUT)
GHOST: Who so glum, chum?
COWBOY: I lost all my Trick or Treat candy.
GHOST: Take some of mine.
COWBOY: Wow!
Hershey bars . . . Mr. Goodbar . . .
Kit Kats . . . Rolos . . .
Whatchamacallits . . . Reese's . . .
all my favorites . . . Let's go get some more.
GHOST: Sure, lemme go ask my Mom.
VO: Nobody says boo to Hershey's.

YESTERDAY'S COFFEE
30-second
(NATURAL SFX THROUGHOUT)
ANNCR (VO): Does it sometimes seem like today's coffee tastes like yesterday's?
PERSON: When you gonna make some fresh coffee?
PERSON: That is fresh.
ANNCR (VO): Maybe the problem isn't your coffee brand, but your coffee filter.
PERSON: I threw out the old coffee.
PERSON: Old? I just made it.
ANNCR (VO): There's one coffee filter that gives you pure, fresh coffee flavor. No oils. No sediments. No bitterness. Mr. Coffee coffee filters . . .
If you're going to own America's perfect coffee maker, shouldn't you be using America's perfect coffee filters?

1330
Art Director: **Charley Rice**
Writer: **Camille Larghi**
Client: **Ore-Ida**
Editor: **Pelco**
Director: **Ron Finley**
Production Co.: **Ron Rinley Films**
Agency: **Doyle Dane Bernbach**

1331   SILVER AWARD
Art Director: **Paul Jervis**
Writer: **Larry Vine**
Client: **Ovaltine Products, Inc.**
Editor: **Morty Ashkinos**
Producers: **Robert Warner, Jody Mellen**
Director: **Tony Menninger**
Production Co.: **Abel Associates**
Music Production Co.: **Ciani/Musica Inc.**
Agency: **Smith/Greenland Inc.**

SUPERMAN
30-second
LOIS LANE: (IN PENTHOUSE KITCHEN) I'm cooking for the
world's most exciting man.
So what I make has to be terrific.
That's why I depend on Ore-Ida French Fries.
'Cause I know every batch will taste great.
(CU OF FRIES)
(SFX: FLYING SOUND STARTS TO GROW) When I make
Ore-Ida fries, why he just flies home.
(SFX: THOOMP.) Oh, that's him now!
ANIMATED SUPERMAN: (ON TERRACE, SKYLINE BEHIND HIM)
Smells good!
LOIS: Ore-Ida French Fries.
SUPERMAN: All-right! Lois, you're su . . . perb.
LOIS: (STARRY-EYED) Oooooh.

CHOCOLATE SHAPES
30-second
(MUSIC UP AND UNDER)
ANNCR (VO): The taste of chocolate.
There's nothing in the world like it.
Maybe that's why there are so many ways to enjoy it. But
one of the best ways is when is comes fortified with seven
essential vitamins and minerals.
And that's when it comes this way.
Ovaltine.
Add Ovaltine flavoring to milk and you turn an . . .
. . . ordinary glass of milk . . .
. . . into an extraordinary treat.
So, if you're looking for a chocolate taste that's nutritious
and delicious . . .
. . . look no further.

1332   GOLD AWARD
Art Director: **Joe Sedelmaier**
Writer: **Jeff Gorman**
Client: **Independent Life Insurance**
Editor: **Peggy DeLay**
Director: **Joe Sedelmaier**
Production Co: **Sedelmaier Film Productions Inc.**
Agency: **Cecil West**

1333
Art Director: **Lester Feldman**
Writer: **Mike Mangano**
Client: **Airwick**
Director: **Joe DeVoto**
Production Co: **Joel Productions**
Agency: **Doyle Dane Bernbach**

FAMILY
30-second
ANNCR (VO): You've both worked hard to establish a good way of life for the family.
But what if one of you was no longer in the picture?
Luckily, you have Total Way of Life coverage from Independent Life.
For the kid's all-important education. And Independent Life's Couple Coverage.
So you can continue to life the good life.
When an agent from Independent Life calls, talk to him about Total Way of Life.

PUSH-UPS
30-second
MAN: Take it from me . . .
MAN: . . . nothing holds odors like a carpet.
MAN: And my wife says no rug and room deodorizer gets them out better than what she just bought — Carpet Fresh.
MAN (VO): She says that it gets right to the source of odors caused by . . .
MAN (VO): . . . dogs, cigars, whatever.
MAN: I'm convinced — nothing ever made this room and rug smell better than Carpet Fresh. Take it from me.
MAN: An expert.
VO: Airwick's Carpet Fresh. America's number one rug and room deodorizer.

1334
Art Director: **John Eding**
Writer: **Iva Silver**
Client: **Bristol Myers**
Editor: **Dick Stone**
Director: **Henry Sandbank**
Agency: **Doyle Dane Bernbach**

1335
Art Director: **Marcia Christ**
Writer: **Jimmy Cohen**
Client: **Joanne Black/American Express**
Editor: **Ray Chung**
Director: **Neil Tardio**
Production Co.: **Annie Friedman/Lovinger,
Tardio, Melsky**
Agency: **Ogilvy & Mather**

HIGH NOON
30-second
VO: The hotter things are the better the Lady likes them.
That's why the Lady uses Tickle.
Tickle anti-perspirant in four fabulous fragrances.
Tickle.

PHONE BOOTH
30-second
(SFX: RAIN, THUNDER)
HUSBAND: There is . . . there's a phone booth honey.
WIFE: You find the numbers of the travelers cheques. I'll call
American Express.
HUSBAND: Ok.
WIFE: Oh, what a way to start a vacation.
HUSBAND: Wait a minute!
Wait a minute!
WIFE: What?
HUSBAND: They didn't give me American Express.
WIFE: What do you mean they didn't give you American
Express? Didn't you ask . . .
(SFX: RAIN)
MALDEN: If you want American Express Travelers Cheques

1340   DISTINCTIVE MERIT
Art Director: **Peter Hirsch**
Writer: **Ken Majka**
Client: **Toshiba America, Inc.**
Editor: **John Starace**
Director: **Dick Stone**
Production Co.: **Stone/Clark**
Productions/Frank DiSalvo: (Agency)
Agency: **Calet, Hirsch, Kurnit & Spector, Inc.**

1341
Art Director: **Paul Jervis**
Writer: **Larry Vine**
Client: **Russ Togs, Inc.**
Editor: **Morty Ashkinos**
Prducers: **Robert Warner, Jody Mellen**
Director: **William Helburn**
Production Co.: **Helburn Productions**
Music Production Co.: **Ciani/Musica, Inc.**
Agency: **Smith/Greenland Inc.**

RABBITS
30-second
ANNCR (VO): (MUSIC UNDER) Few things reproduce as fast as the Toshiba 7511.
Your first copy appears in just five seconds.
It continues to create 25 perfect duplicates a minute.
Minute after minute.
Month after month.
And is available with automatic feeding, sorting and reduction capability.
The Toshiba 7500 series copiers.
They can be a very productive addition to your office.
(LIVE LOCAL ANNCR)

WINDOW DRESSING
30-second
(MUSIC UP AND UNDER)
ANNCR (VO): Women's fashions have never been harder to pin down.
Just when you get used to one thing . . .
. . . it's another thing.
Instead of letting it drive you crazy, take a look at Russ.
. . . classically designed and reasonably priced.
Fashions that will be in style today as well as tomorrow.
After all isn't there enough things to drive you crazy without fashions being one of them.
Russ. The smart way to dress.

1342
Art Director: **Anthony Angotti**
Writer: **Tom Thomas**
Client: **Xerox Corporation**
Director: **Lear Levin**
Agency: **Needham, Harper & Steers, Inc.**

1343
Art Director: **Anthony Angotti**
Writer: **Tom Thomas**
Client: **Xerox Corporation**
Director: **Bill Stettner**
Agency: **Needham, Harper & Steers, Inc.**

THE 9-TO-5 JOB
30-second
ANNCR (VO): Whatever became of the 9-to-5 job?
With so many people working late.
Why isn't more work getting done? At Xerox, our business is
helping people get work done—not by working longer, but
better.
With advanced machines that perform office jobs faster
and better, saving businesses millions of dollars in wasted
time and effort.
To help you keep up with all those other people who have
9-to-5 jobs.

2995 AND DOWN
30-second
1ST VOICE: You can get this Xerox desktop copier for just . . .
how much?
2ND VOICE: It lists for $2995, but . . .
1ST VOICE: Just $2995 for the quality and reliability you'd
expect . . .
2ND VOICE: Could be a couple of hundred less with
trade-in.
1ST VOICE: Just $2795 for . . .
2ND VOICE: Many trade-ins run around five hundred.
1ST VOICE: Just $2495 . . .
2ND VOICE: Trade-ins go as high as $1000 or more.
1ST VOICE: Just $1995 . . .
2ND VOICE: They also help you finance it—at low interest
rates

1344
Art Director: **John Sullivan**
Writer: **Cara Hetson**
Client: **Ciba Geigy**
Editor: **Startmark**
Director: **Bob Newcombe**
Production Co.: **Jefferson Productions**
Agency: **Dancer Fitzgerald Sample, Inc.**

1345
Art Director: **Tom Kostro**
Writer: **John Schmidt**
Client: **King-Seeley Thermos Co.**
Editor: **Morty Ashkinos**
Director: **Michael Ulick**
Production Co.: **Michael Ulick**
Productions/Mindy Gerber: (Agency)
Agency: **Calet, Hirsch, Kurnit & Spector, Inc.**

DINERS
30-second
SPIDER: More wine, my good roach?
ANT: She's spraying!
ROACH: Big deal, Ant. So we'll leave for a few days.
ANT: Not this time!! She's using Spectracide Professional Home Pest Control.
SPIDER & ROACH: Professional?
ANNCR: Right. Spectracide works as well as a pro 'cause it's the same long lasting formula.
That's why Spectracide kills virtually all indoor bugs the professional way.
BUGS: Professional!
ANT: I knew we shouldn't've stayed for dessert!
ANNCR: Spectracide. Every spray kills the professional way.

WITH ONE HAND
30-second
(SFX: NATURAL PRESENCE)
VO: When you have your hands full, even simple things can become difficult.
Like pouring a cup of coffee.
So Thermos invented the Flip 'N' Pour Stopper.
It's easy to open, easy to pour . . . and easy to close.
The new Flip 'N' Pour. What could be easier than that?
The Flip 'N' Pour.
Only from Thermos.

1346
Art Director: **F. Paul Pracilio**
Writer: **Robert Neuman**
Client: **Smith Barney Harris Upham**
Editor: **Dennis Hayes**
Director: **Norm Griner**
Production Co: **Griner Cuesta & Associates**
Agency: **Ogilvy & Mather**

1347
Art Director: **Mike Withers**
Writer: **Hy Abady**
Client: **Getty Refining**
Editor: **Morty Ashkinos**
Director: **Michael Ulick**
Production Co: **Ulick Productions/Frank DiSalvo: (Agency)**
Agency: **Calet, Hirsch, Kurnit & Spector, Inc.**

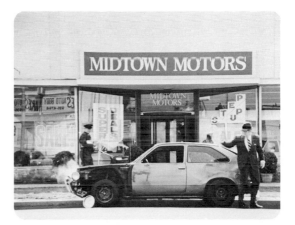

NURSERY
30-second
ANNCR (VO): John Houseman for the investment firm of
Smith Barney.
JOHN HOUSEMAN: Being born with a silver spoon in one's
mouth is not enough.
How quickly it can tarnish in today's Topsy Turvy economy.
When it comes to growth and the preservation of capital,
many prudent investors look to Smith Barney.
Smith Barney.
(SFX: BABY) They make money the old fashioned way, they
earn it.

MIKE'S PAINT & BODY
30-second
ANNCR (VO): If you've shopped for a new car lately, . . . you
may be a little surprised at what you have to spend.
So you might decide to take better care . . . of your present
car to make sure it lasts.
That's why you should use a quality gasoline and motor oil.
Like Getty.
Getty helps your car run smoothly mile after mile.
At Getty, we want you to get the most out of your car.

1348
Art Director: **John Safrit**
Writer: **Jerry Stankus**
Client: **Gino's**
Editor: **Follow Ciro, Ciro De Nettis**
Production Co.: **Frank Cunningham/Johnston Films**
Agency: **Lewis & Gilman, Inc.**

1349
Art Director: **Bill Yamada**
Writer: **Peter Bregman**
Client: **Volkswagen Corp. of America**
Editor: **Joe Laliker/Pelco**
Director: **Henry Trettin**
Production Co.: **Bob Samuels/N. Lee Lacy**
Agency: **Doyle Dane Bernbach**

TOLD YOU SO
30-second
(MUSIC: A MARCH. ESTABLISH, THEN UNDER)
ANNCR (VO): Gino's . . . 1957.
MAN: You don't have any roast beef sandwiches?
WOMAN: Told you so!
MAN: Who asked you!
ANNCR (VO): . . . 1965 . . .
MAN: You don't have roast beef?
WOMAN: Told you so!
MAN: It's okay!
ANNCR (VO): . . . 1976 . . .
MAN: Still no roast beef?
WOMAN: I told you so!
MAN: I didn't ask you!
ANNCR (VO): But now comes Gino's 1981. And yes, we have

HOLY RABBIT
30-second
VO: Reverend! You drive a Volkswagen Rabbit?
REV: Yes, my son. It's a mixed blessing.
VO: It is?
REV: Yes. It's not only economical, which is good for the parish; but I must confess with C.I.S. fuel injection and front-wheel drive, it's sinfully fun.
. . . And, it's the only one in it's fold to have all that.
VO: Wow, I guess you take it out often!
REV: Religiously!!!

1350
Art Director: **Thom Higgins**
Designer: **Tina Raver**
Writer: **Jeffrey Klarik**
Client: **Royal Crown Cola Co.**
Editor: **Dennis Hayes**
Director: **Bruce Dowad**
Production Co.: **Sarah Jenks, John Diaz/Rabko**
Agency: **Ogilvy & Mather**

1351   SILVER AWARD
Art Directors: **Gene Federico, Seymon Ostilly**
Writer: **Marty Everds**
Client: **Vassarette**
Editor: **Sol Landa**
Director: **Neil Tardio**
Production Co.: **Lovinger, Tardio, Melsky Inc.**
Agency: **Lord, Geller, Federico, Einstein, Inc.**
Agency Producer: **Robert L. Dein**

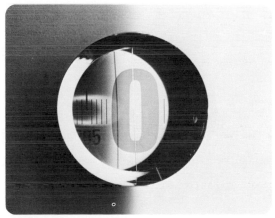 

FENCE
30-second
ANNCR (VO): What's so exciting about RC 100 Cola?
GUY: Nothing!
SONG: RC 100's got nothing —
nothing . . . nothing
no sugar and no caffeine, nothing but taste . . .
RC 100's got nothing
GIRL: It's like nothing I've ever seen!
ANNCR (VO): If you haven't tasted caffeine-free RC 100 . . .
GIRL: You ain't tasted nothing yet!
SONG: RC 100's got nothing . . .
It's got . . . nothing but taste!
GIRL: Thanks for nothing!

CUSTOMS
30-second
CUSTOMS LADY: Did you buy anything in Paris?
PASSENGER: No, this was a business trip.
CUSTOMS LADY: Don't tell me these didn't come from Paris!
PASSENGER: No, they're Vassarette. I bought them here. I wouldn't dream of buying French lingerie when I can get pretty things like this from Vassarette.
CUSTOMS LADY: Pretty? They're beautiful! Vassarette, hm?
PASSENGER: Vassarette.
CUSTOMS LADY: Welcome home.
PASSENGER: Thanks.
CUSTOMS LADY: (TURNING TO LITTLE MAN) Business or pleasure?
MAN: Er . . . Vassarette . . . I mean pleasure . . . er . . . business . . .

1352   GOLD AWARD
Art Director: **Phil Snyder**
Designer: **Kurt Lundel**
Writer: **Jack Reynolds**
Client: **E.F. Hutton**
Editor: **Bob Lynch/Editors Hideaway**
Agency Producer: **Jane Haeberly**
Director: **Tibor Hirsch**
Production Co: **THT Productions**
Agency: **Benton & Bowles, Inc.**

1353
Art Director: **Bob Gage**
Photographer: **Ernesto Caparros**
Writer: **Jack Dillon**
Client: **Polaroid Corporation**
Editor: **Pelco**
Director: **Bob Gage**
Production Co: **Director's Studio Inc./
Rose Presley**
Agency/Producer: **Doyle Dane Bernbach/
Joseph Scibetta**

ALPHABET/FP
30-second
TEACHER: Alright, children, who's going to be the first one to
recite the alphabet? How 'bout you Ann?
ANN: A . . . b . . . c . . . d . . .
. . . e . . . f . . . e . . . f . . . E.F. Hutton!
ANNCR (VO): When E.F. Hutton talks, people listen.

DEAD PARTY
30-second
KERMIT: (RUSHING IN) Quick, where's my OneStep?
PIGGY: Why? What's happening?
KERMIT: Nothing. This party's dead.
PIGGY: I hear laughing.
KERMIT: They're laughing at the hors d'oeuvres.
PIGGY: Oh . . .
KERMIT: I got it.
PIGGY: (SADLY) And I worked so hard.
KERMIT: Smile, everybody!
STATLER: Why, is the party over?
KERMIT: (WHOOSH!) No, it just started.
FOZZIE: Hey, everybody looks happy.
WALDORF: I thought camera's didn't lie.
KERMIT: A Polaroid OneStep brings a dead party to life in

1354
Art Director: **Bob Gage**
Photographers: **Ernesto Caparros**
Writer: **Jack Dillon**
Client: **Polaroid Corporation**
Editor: **Pelco**
Director: **Bob Gage**
Production Co: **Director's Studio Inc./Rose
Presley, Eugene Mazzola**
Agency/Producers: **Doyle Dane Bernbach/
Joseph Scibetta, Jane Liepshutz**

1355
Art Director: **Tony Oestreicher**
Writer: **Tony Oestreicher**
Client: **Ernie Speranza**
Editor: **Follow Ciro, Ciro De Nettis**
Director: **Bob Bean**
Producer: **Mike Salzer**
Agency: **S&B/Donna Vento**

CLEVER IDEA
30-second
MARI: The clever idea of the film cartridge is just drop it in
and shoot. But this is just what comes out of the camera.
And you have to shoot and develop the whole thing to see
one picture. Isn't that clever?
Not with Polaroid's Time-Zero OneStep. It's the world's fastest
developing color. You won't believe so much color so
fast — and you don't shoot the whole pack to see one
picture. That's why the OneStep's America's most popular
camera.
So, which would you rather pass around at a party?
GIRL: Take some more!
MARI: See!

WHAT SIZE?
30-second
SALESMAN: (SYNC) Help you?
CUSTOMER: I'm into running, tennis and basketball, soccer,
baseball, racquetball, hurdling, and I need shoes. I want to
look at Adidas, Brooks, Tiger, Puma, Nike, Converse, K-Swiss,
Saucony, Tretorn, New Balance, Diadora, Mitre, Superga
and Pony.
SALESMAN: What size?
ANNCR: Foot Locker. America's most complete athletic
footwear store.

1356
Art Director: **Jack Piccolo**
Writer: **Ted Bell**
Editor: **Howie Lazarus/Take Five**
Director: **Denny Harris**
Agency: **Doyle Dane Bernbach**

1357
Art Director: **Frank DeVito**
Writer: **George Miller**
Client: **William Schermerhorn**
Editor: **Steve Bodner/Follow Ciro**
Director: **Melvin Sokosky**
Production Co.: **Sunlight Pictures Corp.**
Agency: **Young & Rubicam**

SHOW AND TELL
30-second
TEACHER: Next, "How to make chocolate milk . . . without making a mess" (LAUGH) by Marvin.
GIRL: Messy Marvin's more like it.
MARVIN: For delicious chocolate milk and no mess . . .
One, I always use thick, rich Hershey's Syrup.
Two, stir well.
and three,
it's always delicious. So remember,
TEACHER: Oh, Marvin.
VO: Good old-fashioned Hershey's Syrup in the no-mess bottle. It's delicious.

WHISTLING
30-second
DAVID: (WHISTLING) I'm a Pepper, He's a Pepper, She's a Pepper . . .
DAVID: (WHISTLING) He's a Pepper
MICKEY: (WHISTLING) Uh, uh.
MICKEY: (WHISTLING) Whew!! I'm a Pepper.
ALL: (WHISTLING) Wouldn't you like to be a Pepper too?
ALL: (WHISTLING) Be a Pepper, Drink Dr Pepper
Be a Pepper, Drink Dr Pepper

1358
Art Director: **Roy Grace**
Designer: **Roy Grace**
Writer: **Ted Bell**
Client: **Chanel Inc.**
Editor: **Stone-Cutters/Dick Stone**
Director: **Henry Sandbank**
Producer: **Lee Weiss**
Agency: **Doyle Dane Bernbach**

1359
Art Director: **Paul Jervis**
Writer: **Larry Vine**
Client: **Wellington Importers, Inc.**
Editor: **Frank Cioffredi**
Producer: **Jody Mellen**
Director: **Michael Ulick**
Production Co: **Ulick Productions**
Agency: **Smith Greenland, Inc.**

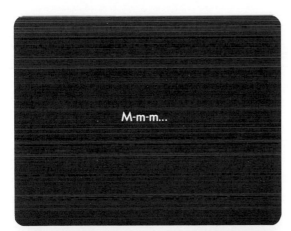

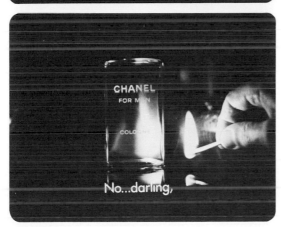

MATCH
30-second
WOMAN: (SNIFFS) M-m-m-m . . .
qu'est-ce tu portes?
MAN: Chanel Pour Homme.
WOMAN: Ah . . . c'est nouveau?
MAN: Non . . .
C'est comme moi. Classique.
Elégant, raffiné . . .
tu sais . . . subtil.
WOMAN: (GIGGLES) Subtil?
Ha!
Je peux essayer?
MAN: Non . . . ma chère, c'est pour les hommes.
Regarde!
Vite!

COMING HOME
30-second
SON (OC): Mom!
MOM (OC): Larry!
SON (OC): I'm at the airport. I'll be home soon.
MOM (OC): I'll cook something special.
SON (VO): Great!
SON (OC): I'm bringing Barbella.
MOM (OC): Barbella. You never mentioned a girl named
Barbella.
OPERATOR (VO): Please deposit 5¢ . . .
. . . For the next five minutes.
SON (OC): Can't talk now Mom.
MOM & FATHER (OC): Barbella.
ANNCR (VO): There may still . . .
. . . Who don't know Barbella.

1360
Art Director: **Joe DeMare**
Designer: **Joe DeMare**
Writer: **Nicole Cranberg**
Client: **GTE Phone Mart**
Editor: **Len Mandelbaum**
Agency Producer: **Tom Dakin**
Director: **Tibor Hirsch**
Production Co.: **Bob Mander/THT Productions**
Agency: **Doyle Dane Bernbach**

1361
Art Director: **Lester Feldman**
Writer: **Mike Mangano**
Client: **GTE**
Director: **Pat Pitelli**
Production Co.: **Pitelli Productions**
Agency: **Doyle Dane Bernbach**

SANTA'S WORKSHOP, INC.
30-second
(DISSOLVE THROUGH DOOR INTO BOARDROOM. WE HEAR
ELF CHATTER.)
SANTA: Gentle elves, we've been in business almost 2,000
years now. And our product line is getting a little stale.
(SANTA HOLDS UP TIE AND SOCK)
ELF: Right, S.C.
SANTA: The public wants something new and fresh . . .
something that'll have everyone talking.
(ELVES PRODUCE ALL KINDS OF GTE PHONES)
ELVES: Just what we thought, S.C.
ELF: These'll have 'em talking!
SANTA: A telephone for Christmas . . . has a nice ring to it.
Make me twelve million!
ELF: (HOLDS UP GTE SHOPPING BAG) Sure! We can pick

HALLWAY
30-second
VO: Remember the good old days?
MOTHER: Somebody . . . get that!
VO: When most homes had just one telephone.
FATHER: Get that!
GIRL: I'll get it!
BOY: I'll get it!
VO: Well, GTE presents the good new days.
Now, for very little money a day you can have an extension
phone . . .
in any room that's necessary.
And even in some rooms that aren't so necessary.

1362
Art Director: **Ed Martel**
Writer: **John Eickmeyer**
Client: **Haggar**
Director: **Victor Haboush**
Producer: **Michael Jollvette**
Agency: **Tracy-Locke Advertising**

1363
Art Director: **Michelle Troiani**
Writer: **Nancy Jordan**
Client: **Kraft/Parkay**
Editor: **Szabo-Tohtz**
Director: **Vern Gillum**
Production Co.: **Vern Gillum & Friends**
Agency: **Needham, Harper & Steers**

WASHABLE SUIT TAKE 2
30-second
LEADING MAN: Victoria, darling, my heart . . .
DIRECTOR: Stop camera! Wash the suit!
LEADING LADY: Wash the suit?!
VO: It's the Haggar Washable Suit in VISA fabrics. Made a new way to be machine washed and dried.
DIRECTOR: Action.
LEADING MAN: Victoria, my . . .
DIRECTOR: Cut, cut, cut! I don't believe it!
VO: The Haggar Washable Suit is guaranteed to keep its great looks and fit for its normal life, or your money back. The Haggar Washable Suit. Guaranteed wash, after wash, after wash.

OPERA
30-second
OPERA SINGER: Mi mi mi mi mi
PARKAY: Butter. Butter.
OPERA SINGER: You, you Parkay Margarine.
PARKAY: Butter
OPERA SINGER: Parkay.
PARKAY: Butter.
OPERA SINGER: Parkay.
PARKAY: Butter.
OPERA SINGER: Parkay.
PARKAY: Butter.
OPERA SINGER: Let me taste . . . so light, so creamy. Butter!
PARKAY: Parkaaaay!
ANNCR (VO): Parkay Margarine from Kraft. The flavor says . . .

1364
Art Director: **Roy Grace**
Designer: **Roy Grace**
Writer: **Diane Rothschild**
Client: **Miles Laboratories, Inc.**
Editor: **Stone-Cutters/Dick Stone**
Director: **Tibor Hirsch**
Producer: **Rosemary Barre**
Agency: **Doyle Dane Bernbach**

1365
Art Director: **Anthony Angotti**
Writer: **Tom Thomas**
Client: **Xerox Corporation**
Director: **Gomes-Loew/Dick Loew**
Agency: **Needham, Harper & Steers, Inc.**

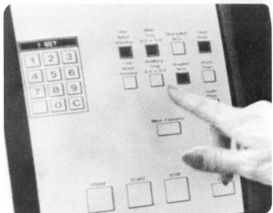

PEOPLE III
30-second
ANNCR (VO): You know who uses S.O.S.?
Practically everybody and why not?
Nothing cleans burnt-on . . .
stuck on . . .
splattered-on messes . . .
faster or easier . . .
than a super grease cutting S.O.S. soap pad.
It's no coincidence that Americans use more than 2 million
S.O.S. pads everyday.
We deserve every dirty pan we get.

MOZART
30-second
(SFX: MOZART MUSIC)
ANNCR (VO): It's been said that when Mozart is performed
before an audience of chickens . . .
an interesting thing happens . . .
. . . productivity increases.
That's fine for hen houses.
Now, what can be done for offices.
Xerox can help. With advanced machines that perform
office jobs faster and better, saving businesses millions of
dollars in wasted time and effort.
As for hen houses . . .
. . . they're doing fine without our help.

1366
Art Director: **Herb Jager**
Designer: **Michele Krause**
Writer: **Jeffrey Klarik**
Client: **Royal Crown Cola Co.**
Director: **Phil Marco**
Production Co.: **Phil Marco Productions**
Agency: **Ogilvy & Mather**

1367
Art Director: **Rock Obenchain**
Writer: **Jim Glynn**
Client: **Mountain Bell Yellow Pages**
Editor: **Jerry Kleppel**
Agency Producer: **Ed Rizzo**
Director: **Jonathan Yarbrough**
Production Co.: **Summerhouse Films**
Agency: **Tracy-Locke, Denver**

TASTE TEST — STRAWS
30-second
ANNCR (VO): Recently, right here in this city, America's 3
favorite diet colas were tested in a blind taste test.
Diet Pepsi . . .
(SFX: GULPING NOISE)
ANNCR (VO): didn't win!
Tab . . .
(SFX: GULPING NOISE)
ANNCR (VO): didn't win!
Diet Rite Cola . . .
(SFX: SLURPING NOISE)
ANNCR (VO): did win!
In fact, nobody beat the taste of delicious Diet Rite Cola.
Taste the one that won. Delicious Diet Rite Cola.
It's got what it takes to beat the best.

ALWAYS AROUND TO HELP
30-second
(MUSIC: WHIMSICAL TROUGHOUT)
ANNCR (VO): The good old Yellow Pages.
It's always around to help.
But the way it helps most is the way it's used most.
The way 8 out of 10 people use it when they're ready to buy.
An average of 3 times every week.
To find your company.
MAN (OC): Hello, Pest Control?
ANNCR (VO): What better reason for you to advertise boldly.
The Bell System Yellow Pages.
It gets used.
So it gets results.

1368
Art Director: **Joe Sedelmaier**
Writer: **Jeff Gorman**
Client: **Independent Life Insurance**
Editor: **Peggy DeLay**
Director: **Joe Sedelmaier**
Production Co.: **Sedelmaier Film
Productions, Inc.**
Agency: **Cecil West**

1369
Art Director: **Mike Lawlor**
Designer: **Mike Lawlor**
Photographer: **Mike VanHawton**
Writer: **Marvin Honig**
Client: **American Greeting**
Director: **Allan Dennis**
Producer: **Jill Gordon**
Agency: **Doyle Dane Bernbach**

COUPLE
30-second
ANNCR (VO): You've both worked hard to establish a
wonder way of life.
But if one of you were no longer in the picture?
Luckily, you have Total Way of Life Coverage from
Independent Life. it protects your total lifestyle.
So that you can go on living in the manner to which you've
grown accustomed.
When an agent from Independent Life calls, talk to him
about Total Way of Life.

JULIUS
30-second
MAN: Well?
WOMAN: Not enough warmth.
MAN: Not enough what?
Not enough what?
(MUSIC UNDER)
VO: It's a problem as old as birthdays. Finding just the right
card.
So American Greetings creates the unique. Like Ziggy, and
Strawberry Shortcake, and our beautiful Soft Touch cards.
VO: American Greetings
The right card for that special person.

1370
Art Director: **John Eding**
Writer: **Jane Talcott**
Client: **Volkswagen of America, Inc.**
Editor: **Dick Stone**
Director: **Henry Sandbank**
Agency: **Doyle Dane Bernbach**

1371
Art Director: **Paul Jervis**
Designer: **Paul Jervis**
Writer: **Rick Meyer**
Client: **Kraft, Inc.**
Director: **Dick Loew**
Production Co.: **Gomes-Loew**
Agency: **Manoff Geers Gross**

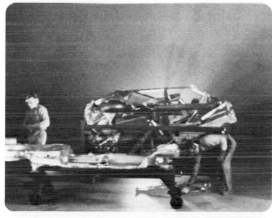

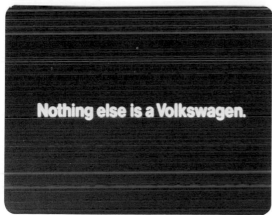

THIS RABBIT DIED
30-second
VO: At Volkswagen, we pull Rabbits off our American assembly line, at random, and give them this little test . . .
. . . We test every weld to make absolutely sure the metal breaks before the weld does. There's no law in any book that says we have to do this, but we let some Rabbits die so that yours will live longer.

MOM
30-second
SAM: Thicker, richer.
AVO: When it came to making great sour cream only one person was as demanding as Sam Breakstone.
SAM: Mother!
MOM: Sam.
MOM: It's not thick enough Sam.
SAM: Hmmmm.
MOM: It needs more cream Sam.
SAM: Grrrr.
AVO: But if Sam and his mother hadn't been so demanding . . .
MOM: I've done it again.
AVO: Breakstone's Sour Cream wouldn't be so good.
MOM: What a cute little doggie.

1372
Art Director: **Michael Uris**
Writer: **Diane Rothschild**
Client: **Volkswagen of America**
Editor: **Ray Chung**
Director: **Howard Zieff**
Production Co.: **Independent Artists, Inc.**
Agency: **Doyle Dane Bernbach**

1373
Art Director: **Lou Musachio**
Designer: **Kurt Lindel**
Client: **Schlitz Brewing Company — Schlitz Malt Liquor**
Editors: **Prime Cut/Rick Wysocki**
Director: **Jean Marie Perier**
Production Co.: **Independent Artists**
Agency: **Benton & Bowles**

CHICKEN
30-second
(MUSIC THROUGHOUT AND UNDER)
INT: Hey, that chicken is a Rabbit.
MAN: Wrong. This chicken is a Rabbit diesel.
INT: AH, a Volkswagen Rabbit diesel. The best mileage car in America.
MAN: YUP, We get about 600 buckets to the gallon with this Rabbit. It's saving us a fortune.
INT: GEE, that means you can pass the savings along to your customers.
MAN: No it doesn't.

DU-WOPS
30-second
THE PLATTERS: I could hold you all night. Any day of the year. The way that you taste. I love you, my beer.
KOOL & THE GANG: Bull!
ONE OF THE PLATTERS: Bull?
KOOL & THE GANG: Why don't you get into the groove. One sip'll make it clear. The bull's got more taste than beer.
PLATTERS: Bye bye beer . . . yeah.
MAN & WOMAN: Hello bull.
ALL: The Schlitz Malt Liquor Bull is tops so . . . Don't say beer say bull.
KOOL & THE GANG: Say bull.
ALL: Say Schlitz Malt Liquor Bull.

1374
Art Director: **Dave Lowenbein**
Designer: **Peter Kuntz**
Writer: **Carey Fox**
Client: **Getty Refining & Marketing Co.**
Editor: **John Starace**
Director: **Dick Clark**
Production Co.: **Clark/Stone Productions/Ron Weber: (Agency)**
Agency: **Calet, Hirsch, Kurnit & Spector, Inc.**

1375
Art Director: **Ervin Jue**
Writer: **Nicole Cranberg**
Client: **GTE**
Editor: **Pelco**
Director: **Mark Story**
Production Co.: **Jim Callan/Pfieffer/Story**
Agency: **Doyle Dane Bernbach**

SPUTTERS
30-second
Does your car sound like it needs a tune-up? Listen . . . what you hear may be nothing more than cold starts, knocks and run ons.
Before you got a costly tune-up try a Getty fill-up. With Getty Premium Unleaded. It can help absorb the knocks and pings and keep your car running soundly between tune-ups.
(SFX: HEALTHY ENGINE RUNNING)
Try Getty Premium Unleaded.
It can help you get the most out of your car.

YOU'RE ALL GRANDPARENTS
30-second
(OPEN ON HOSPITAL ROOM, WOMAN IN BED, HUSBAND ON PHONE)
HUSBAND: Guess what? You're all grandparents!
ANNCR (VO): With a GTE conference call, you can talk to all four grandparents at once. Even if one set lives in Cleveland . . .
(CUT TO ONE SET OF GRANDPARENTS, SHARING PHONE)
GRANDMA #1: (TO GRANDPA) He has my nose . . . and your eyes . . .
ANNCR (VO): . . . and the other set lives in Chicago.
(CUT TO OTHER SET OF GRANDPARENTS ON PHONE)
GRANDMA #2: (TO GRANDPA) He has your hair. (GRANDPA LAUGHS)
(CUT BACK TO HOSPITAL)

1376

Art Director: **Dom Marino**
Designer: **Dom Marino**
Writer: **Joe Nunziata**
Client: **Volkswagen of America**
Editor: **The Editors**
Producer: **Mark Sitley**
Director: **Joe DeVoto**
Production Co.: **Joel Productions**
Agency: **Doyle Dane Bernbach**

1377   DISTINCTIVE MERIT

Art Director: **Roy Grace**
Designer: **Roy Grace**
Writer: **Deanna Cohen**
Client: **American Tourister Inc.**
Editor: **Stone-Cutters/Dick Stone**
Director: **Steve Horn**
Producer: **Susan Calhoun**
Agency: **Doyle Dane Bernbach**

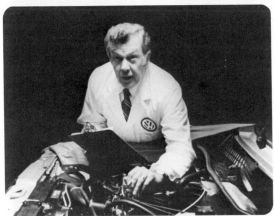

SERVICE
30-second
MECHANIC: Getting things fixed — it's one of the greatest aggravations in life. But Volkswagen is doing something about it. Not only do you get a trained Volkswagen Technician . . .
QUALITY INSPECTOR: . . . you get a Quality Inspector to be sure it was done right the first time, and then . . .
ACCOUNT EXECUTIVE: . . . you get a call a few days later, to check if you're happy with our service. You see, we want to make Volkswagen Service as good as we make Volkswagens. After all . . .
ALL THREE IN UNISON: . . . three heads are better than one.

HOTEL
30-second
ANNCR (VO): We at American Tourister know that waiting for every suitcase is the unexpected.
That's why we reinforce our beautiful American Tourister lightweights with a steel frame, rugged rubber wheels, and tough protective corners.
To us at American Tourister . . .
It's not just how good it looks . . .
It's how long it looks good.

1378
Art Director: **Roy Grace**
Designer: **Roy Grace**
Writer: **Diane Rothschild**
Client: **Miles Laboratories, Inc.**
Editor: **Stone-Cutters/Dick Stone**
Director: **Tibor Hirsch**
Producer: **Rosemary Barre**
Agency: **Doyle Dane Bernbach**

1379
Art Director: **Lester Feldman**
Writer: **Mike Mangano**
Client: **GTE**
Director: **Pat Pitelli**
Production Co.: **Pitelli Production**
Agency: **Doyle Dane Bernbach**

NEW YORK LADIES I
30-second
S.O.S. LADY: Grace, is that you?
BRILLO LADY: No, it's Miss America. I'm here doing dishes between appearances.
S.O.S. LADY: (LAUGHS) Still with the jokes. Listen, did you get S.O.S.?
BRILLO LADY: No.
S.O.S. LADY: No!? But I told you it's better than Brillo.
BRILLO LADY: I know.
S.O.S. LADY: The soap lasts longer.
BRILLO LADY: I know.
S.O.S. LADY: And it cuts grease quicker than Brillo.
BRILLO LADY: I know.
S.O.S. LADY: So, Grace, S.O.S. could get you out of the kitchen faster.

INSTALLATION
30-second
VO: Remember the good old days?
. . . When the telephone system wasn't figured out till after the building was built.
Well, GTE Presents the good new days.
Today, we have people who actually help you plan your phone system . . .
before and during the building's construction. And our specialists work with you . . . as part of the team
. . . almost.

1380
Art Director: **Bob Gage**
Photographer: **Ernesto Caparros**
Writer: **Jack Dillon**
Client: **Polaroid**
Editor: **Pelco**
Director: **Bob Gage**
Production Co.: **Directors Studio Inc./
Rose Presley, Eugene Mazzola**
Agency/Producers: **Doyle Dane Bernbach/
Joseph Scibetta, Jane Liepshutz**

1381
Art Director: **Peter Hirsch**
Writer: **Ken Majka**
Client: **Corning Glass Works**
Editor: **Coast Productions/Reese Overacker**
Director: **Ray Rivas**
Production Co.: **Coast Productions/
Ron Weber (Agency)**
Agency: **Calet, Hirsch, Kurnit & Spector, Inc.**

HORSES AND BRIDGE
30-second
JIM: Guess what I've got in here?
MARI: What?
JIM: A piece of the sun.
MARI: No wonder I can't get a tan.
JIM: It's Polaroid's new Sun Camera. A new system that can turn bad light into good pictures. Go on, take my picture.
MARI: (WHOOSH!) You know you'll be dark.
JIM: Nope. You've never been so sure of an instant picture.
MARI: Great. But doesn't this cost a lot?
JIM: No, but wasting film in bad light does. Besides, you never buy flash or extra batteries.
MARI: That sun looks the same. Where'd they take the piece from?
JIM: The other side.

HECTIC WORLD
30-second
(SFX: MUSIC UNDER)
GRANDAD: Today, just because people live together . . . doesn't mean they eat together. So these Corning Ware Little Dishes come in handy. They hold just enough of one. And you can put them in the oven or the microwave. Make yourself a meal in a hurry.
GIRL: Bye, Grandpa.
GRANDAD: And I run with a fast crowd.
ANNCR (VO): Corning Ware Little Dishes. For the way you eat today.

1382
Art Director: **Dom Marino**
Designer: **Dom Marino**
Writer: **Deanna Cohen**
Client: **O.M. Scott & Son**
Editor: **Pelco**
Director: **Bob Giraldi**
Producer: **Stuart Raffel**
Agency: **Doyle Dane Bernbach**

1383
Art Director: **Joe Sedelmaier**
Writer: **Tom McElligott**
Client: **Mr. Coffee**
Editor: **Peggy DeLay**
Director: **Joe Sedelmaier**
Production Co.: **Sedelmaier Film Productions Inc.**
Agency: **Marketing Communications Inc.**

HUNGRY LAWN
30-second
(MUSIC THROUGHOUT)
ANNCR (VO): It's our duty to tell you that your lawn is hungry. Even if you fed it earlier this spring, that won't get it through the summer . . .
sure, you give it water, but that won't keep it from losing its color.
Your lawn needs . . .
A helping of Turfbuilder Fertilizer from Scotts.
It's loaded with nourishing ingredients that will help keep your lawn lusciously green and full this summer.
MAN: Dinner . . . is served!
ANNCR (VO): Turfbuilder and water . . .
a good solid meal for a good green lawn.

REMEMBER
30-second
(NATURAL SFX THROUGHOUT)
ANNCR (VO): Remember your first cup of coffee?
Did it ever get any better . . .
. . . or did you just get used to it?
Mr. Coffee thinks its about time
you tasted coffee the way it was meant
to be . . .
Mr. Coffee. America's perfect coffee maker.
With a patent to prove it.

1384
Art Director: **Charles Piccirillo**
Writer: **Michael Mangano**
Client: **Gagliardi Bros.**
Editor: **Pelco**
Director: **Allan Brooks**
Producer: **Allan Brooks**
Agency: **Doyle Dane Bernbach**

1385
Art Director: **Barnet Silver**
Writer: **Jim Walsh**
Client: **Volkswagen of America, Inc.**
Director: **Henry Trettin**
Producer: **Jill Gordon**
Agency: **Doyle Dane Bernbach**

DELEGATES
30-second
RUSSIAN: Stoyetta . . . (What is it?)
ANNCR (VO): Put ten people around a table and very often
you have ten different tastes to satisfy. Well, now there's
something . . .
we think they'll all like a steak sandwich made with
Steak-Umm sandwich steaks.
Lean, 100% beef Steak-Umm cooks in just 60 seconds.
And its taste is so universally delicious.
it just could be the thing . . .
to bring everyone . . .
together.
RUSSIAN: Comrade . . . pass the red onions.

FAST LOOK
30-second
ANNCR (VO): Take a fast look at Volkswagen's 1982
Scirocco.
As you can see, it's been totally redesigned.
Take a closer look . . .
. . . and you'll see a lower, aerodynamically sleeker front
end, curved glass areas and a functional rear spoiler for
better handling and performance. All of which makes the
'82 Scirocco one good-looking German sports car. The only
problem is . . .
. . . getting a good look at one.

1386
Art Director: **Bob Gage**
Photographer: **Ernesto Caparros**
Writer: **Jack Dillon**
Client: **Polaroid**
Editor: **Pelco**
Director: **Bob Gage**
Production Co: **Directors Studio Inc./**
Rose Presley, Eugene Mazzola
Agency/Producers: **Doyle Dane Bernbach/**
Jane Liepshutz, Joseph Scibetta

1387
Art Director: **Thom Higgins**
Designer: **Tina Raver**
Writer: **Jeffrey Klarik**
Client: **Royal Crown Cola Co.**
Editor: **Dennis Hayes**
Director: **Bruce Dowad**
Producers: **Sarah Jenks, John Diaz/Rabko**
Agency: **Ogilvy & Mather**

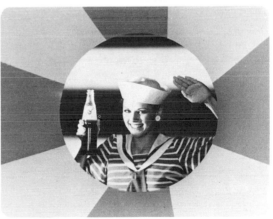

CHRISTMAS SNOOP
30-second
JIM: Ah, the Mother Lode. Let's see
. . . ah a necktie . . .
. . . nobody knows.
Sinbad . . . Sinbad's a cat, he got a mouse.
Jim's golf balls.
What do we have here . . .
Ah, Polaroid's new Sun Camera . . .
Now this is a Christmas gift.
Oh Boy.
MARI: (SHE GIGGLES)
SINGERS: You've never been so sure

INNERTUBE
30-second
ANNCR (VO):What's so exciting about RC 100 Cola?
GIRL: Nothing!
SONG: RC 100's got nothing —
nothing . . . nothing
no sugar and no caffeine, nothing but taste . . .
RC 100's got nothing
GIRL: It's nothing I've ever seen!
ANNCR (VO): If you haven't tasted caffeine-free RC 100 . . .
GIRL: You ain't tasted nothing yet!
SONG: RC 100's got nothing . . .
It's got . . . nothing but taste!
GIRL: Thanks for nothing!

1400
Art Director: **Tony Romeo**
Writer: **Patty Volk Blitzer**
Client: **Hershey/Mr. Goodbar**
Director: **Norm Griner**
Production Co.: **Myers & Griner Cuesta**

1401
Art Director: **Sam Cordero**
Artist: **Sam Cordero**
Writer: **Maureen Moore**
Client: **Continental Illinois National Bank**
Editor: **Bob Blanford**
Director: **Richard Shirley**
Production Co.: **Carol Lang/Richard Shirley
Productions, Inc.**
Agency: **Tatham-Laird & Kudner**

GOODBAR MARCHES ON
30-second
WOMAN: Mr. Goodbar, please.
ANNCR (VO): Lots of things have changed since 1925. But
not the goodness of peanuts and chocolate.
WOMAN: Oooh!
ANNCR: Even in the bad times . . .
MAN: Can you spare a Mr. Goodbar?
ANNCR (VO): Even in the good times . . .
MAN: Keep the change.
ANNCR (VO): There was always time . . .
GUY: Another Mr. G.
ANNCR (VO): For crunchy peanuts and creamy chocolate.
And billions of Mr. Goodbars later one thing's still true: Good
peanuts, and good chocolate, make a very good bar.
WOMAN: Shouldn't that be Ms. Goodbar?

A LITTLE DINNER MUSIC
30-second
ANNCR: Continental Bank proudly presents . . . a little dinner
music . . . and a classic offer.
Get substantial savings on Weber's classic barbecue kettles.
This virtuoso - only $39.95.
Or this light classical version just $14.95.
Deposit $500 in any new or existing Continental savings
account. And get summer off on the right note . . .
With a Weber barbeque kettle.
From Continental. The Smart Money Bank.

Art Director: **Joe Sedelmaier**
Writer: **Tom McElligott**
Client: **Mr. Coffee**
Editor: **Peggy DeLay**
Directorl: **Joe Sedelmaier**
Production Co.: **Sedelmaier Film Productions Inc.**
Agency: **Marketing Communications, Inc.**

Art Directors: **John Clapps, Rick Paynter**
Writer: **Leland Rosemond**
Client: **First National State Bank**
Editor: **Sandpiper**
Director: **R.O. Blechman**
Producers: **Dan Kohn, Cathleen Bauer**
Agency: **Bozell & Jacobs N.J.**

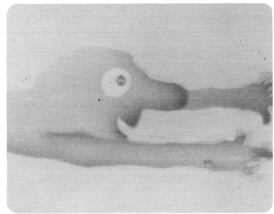

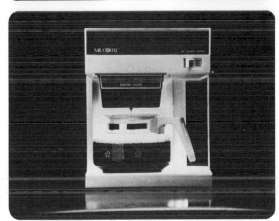

DANGEROUS
30-second
(NATURAL SFX THROUGHOUT)
ANNCR (VO): There was a time in America when making a
bad cup of coffee could be very dangerous.
Unfortunately, things aren't so simple anymore . . . but there is
a way Americans can avoid bad coffee.
Mr. Coffee . . . the only coffee maker that precisely controls
coffee brewing time and temperature, for perfect coffee
every time.
Mr. Coffee . . . America's perfect coffee maker. With a
patent to prove it.

TV SET
30-second
VO: Out-of-state banks aim a lot of advertising at people in
New Jersey. Offering them services like international
banking. Cash management.
And a full range of savings, checking and investment
programs.
But First National State Bank is right here.
The largest statewide banking organization in New Jersey's
history. Meeting the needs of people and business in the
Garden State since 1812.
So wake up to First National State.
The bank whose first concern is New Jersey.
First National State.

1404
Art Director: **Richard Kimmel**
Designers: **Bob Peluce, Bob Kurtz**
Writer: **James Kochevar**
Client: **Eureka Co.**
Director: **Bob Kurtz**
Production Co.: **Kurtz and Friends**
Agency: **Young & Rubicam, Chicago**

1405
Art Director: **John Dolby**
Writer: **David Bender**
Editor: **Szabo-Tohtz, Chicago**
Client: **International Harvester**
Director: **Hil Covington**
Producer: **Jenkins Covington**
Agency: **BBDM Advertising, Inc.**

GOOD BYE DIRT REV.
30-second
WOMAN (VO): I know you're down there, dirt. I know you're hiding in my carpet. I can't see you. Laughing at me.
Ruining the fibers. But you're there.
Know what I got today?
A Eureka E.S.P. self propelled vacuum cleaner.
Heh, heh, heh, heh, Bye!
ANNCR (VO): A clean looking carpet can hold more than its own weight in hidden dirt. But a Eureka E.S.P. self propelled upright vacuum gets out hidden dirt with a touch of your fingers.
WOMAN (VO): You little stinkers.
ANNCR (VO): Eureka gets the dirt you can't see.

DECISION
30-second
You know at first we considered buying one of those bargain lawn and garden tractors.
"We?"
But alot of the older Cub Cadets are selling for more now then they did new—these things are reliable.
He's big on reliability.
Three things seem to get more valuable as they get older.
My house, my Cub Cadet and my wife. It's nice to know somethings going to be around to get the job done.
International Harvester
ANNCR (VO): Cub Cadet from International Harvester

1406
Art Director: **Jack Mariucci**
Designer: **Jack Mariucci**
Client: **Weight Watchers**
Editor: **Ciro DeNettis**
Directors: **Steve Horn, Mathew Brady**
Production Co.: **Steve Horn Inc.**
Agency: **Doyle Dane Bernbach**

1407
Art Director: **Bob Gage**
Photographer: **Ernesto Caparros**
Writer: **Jack Dillon**
Client: **Polaroid**
Editor: **Pelco**
Director: **Bob Gage**
Production Co.: **Director's Studio Inc./
Rose Presley**
Agency: **Doyle Dane Bernbach/
Joseph Scibetta**

CARROT TOP
30-second
VO: Getting a little bored with your diet!
Got carrots coming out of your ears?
Well here's some food for thought:
Weight Watchers announces spicier pizza, chunkier chicken,
saucier lasagna, food so sinful . . .
you can't be bored off any diet! Weight Watchers 19 New
Frozen Meals.
SUPER: 19 NEW MEALS
Try it.
(SFX: RUMBLE . . . RUMBLE)
(SFX: BANG)
You'll diet.

MERRY CHRISTMAS FOZZIE
30-second
KERMIT: Merry Christmas, Fozzie!
FOZZIE: Oh boy! what is it?
STATLER: It's a bird house.
PIGGY: (SWEETLY) It's a OneStep, Fozzie.
KERMIT: Just point it and press the button.
WALDORF: That's got to be over his head.
FOZZIE: Point it at what?
PIGGY: At us!
FOZZIE: Now what?
WALDORF: It is over his head.
GANG: Press the button!
FOZZIE: (WHOOSH!) Hey, this is easy.
PIGGY: I'm beautiful. Take more.
KERMIT: (TO US) You see OneStep pictures, when you see

1408
Art Directors: **Mike Faulkner, Dennis Hodgson**
Writer: **Marilyn Miller**
Client: **McCulloch Corp.**
Editor: **James Hanley Films**
Agency Producer: **Vicki Blucher**
Director: **Bob Eggers**
Production Co.: **Amanda Carmel/**
Eggers Films
Agency: **Benton & Bowles, Inc.**

1409   DISTINCTIVE MERIT
Art Director: **Bob Gage**
Photographer: **Ernesto Caparros**
Writer: **Jack Dillon**
Client: **Polaroid**
Editor: **Pelco**
Director: **Bob Gage**
Production Co.: **Director's Studio Inc./**
Eugene Mazzola, Rose Presley
Agency/Producers: **Doyle Dane Bernbach/**
Joe Scibetta, Jane Liepshutz

ELECTRIC CHAIN SAW/NATIONAL VERSION
30-second
SUPER: McCulloch Corporation© 1981®
BARNEY: Hey, you're gonna need help!
BILLY: Yeah, electric saws get tired easy.
MAN: Not the new McCulloch.
BILLY & BARNEY: An electric McCulloch!!
MAN: Yup. It's warrantied for 2 years, twice as long as other
electrics.
SUPER: 2 year limited personal use warranty. Return to
authorized dealer for repair.
BARNEY: Oh, Yeah?
BILLY: Bet it can't outlast the two of us.
BARNEY: Sure eats quiet.
BILLY: It's sharpening itself.
BARNEY: Hey, that's cheating.

SILENT SPRING
30-second
JIM: Hi! Who's your friend?
Hey, what if I take your picture?
Well, do you want to smile? You don't
Well you're pretty anyway.
You see how fast the color comes in?
That's Polaroids new Time-Zero, the world's fastest
developing color film.
JIM: You come back anytime, we'll have another big day
just like this!

1410
Art Director: **Mike Withers**
Writer: **Hy Abady**
Client: **Aamco Transmissions, Inc.**
Editors: **Peggy DeLay, Morty Ashkinos**
Director: **Joe Sedelmaier**
Production Co: **Sedelmaier Films, Inc./**
Frank DiSalvo (Agency)
Agency: **Calet, Hirsch, Kurnit & Spector, Inc.**

1411
Art Director: **F. Paul Pracilio**
Writer: **Robert Neuman**
Client: **Smith Barney Harris Upham**
Editor: **Dennis Hayes Film Editing**
Director: **Steve Horn**
Producer: **Linda Heuston Horn**
Agency: **Ogilvy & Mather**

HORRORS
30-second
ANNCR (VO): If your transmission ever breaks down . . .
you'll probably imagine all sorts of horrors.
SVCE MGR (ECHOED): Fix your transmission? Fine. We have
a 15-year waiting list.
BACKGROUND VO (ECHOED): Don't worry. Our mechanics
are experts.
MGR (ECHOED): That'll be 22,000 dollars.
MECHANIC (ECHOED): Twenty-two . . . two . . . two.
ANNCR (VO): Don't let your fears run wild. Call the
transmission specialist that's . . .
fast, reliable, with over 900 locations coast to coast.
MAN: AAMCO?
ANNCR (VO): AAMCO. (BEEP-BEEP)
Why go anywhere else?

ITZHAK PERLMAN
30 second
PERLMAN: (HE PLAYS SOME RAGTIME)
Do you know me?
I've taken ragtime to Vienna.
(HE PLAYS A LITTLE BEETHOVEN)
And Beethoven to Kalamazoo. And wherever I travel, I use
the American Express Card.
For the same reason I use a Stradivarius.
ANNCR: To apply for a Card,
look for this display wherever the Card is welcomed.
ANNCR: The American Express Card. (FLOURISH ON THE
VIOLIN) Don't leave home without it.

1412
Art Director: **Ron Travisano**
Photographer: **Allen Greene**
Writer: **Sheila Moore**
Client: **AAA/Robert Morrow**
Editor: **Ed Shea/Jeff Dell Editorial**
Director: **Joe DeVoto**
Production Co: **Hy Weiner/Joel Productions**
Agency: **Della Femina, Travisano & Partners, Inc.**

1413
Art Director: **Charles Piccirillo**
Writer: **Michael Mangano**
Client: **Gagliardi Bros.**
Editor: **Pelco**
Director: **Allan Brooks**
Producer: **Allan Brooks**
Agency: **Doyle Dane Bernbach**

SNOWSTORM
30-second
VO: Sooner or later, just about everybody gets stuck. And if you belong to the wrong auto club, you're not only stuck . . . you're alone.
ATTENDANT: Uh, my tow truck's got a flat.
(SFX: RECEIVER LIFT, HAWAIIAN MUSIC.)
RECORD: The Hawaiian Tourist Bureau reminds you that it's warm and wonderful in Waikiki . . . .
VO: With AAA, you're never alone. Unlike other auto clubs, AAA gives you one number to call in any major city . . . and we find a garage for you . . . at any hour.
RECORD: Hi, we're closed now, but we'll help you in the morning. . . .
AAA. We'll never leave you all alone.

WORKING WOMEN
30-second
ANNCR (VO): According to the latest figures . . .
over 50% of the women in this country . . .
work outside the home.
However, their families want a hot delicious meal just the same,
Well, fortunately now there's Steak-Umm sandwich steaks.
Steak-Umm cooks in just 60 seconds.
and it's 100% lean beef with no additives whatsoever . . .
LITTLE BOY: Great Mom!
MOTHER: (DENTIST) Don't forget to brush your teeth.
VO: Steak-Umm all beef sandwich steaks.

1414
Art Director: **Milt Marcus**
Writer: **Ken Musto**
Client: **AMTRAK, The Nat'l RR Passenger Corp.**
Director: **Lear Levin**
Producer: **Leslie McNeil**
Agency: **Needham, Harper & Steers, Inc.**

1416
Art Director: **Tony DeGregorio**
Designer: **Tony DeGregorio**
Photographer: **Rick Levine**
Writer: **Phil Peppis**
Client: **Sony Corporation of America**
Director: **Rick Levine**
Production Co: **Levine-Pytka**
Agency: **McCann-Erickson, Inc.**

ANTELOPES
30-second
MUSIC: (AFRICAN RHYTHM)
ANNCR (VO): What you're looking at isn't the plains of
Africa or the outback of Australia.
ANNCR (VO): This is America. As seen form the window of
an Amtrak train.
SINGERS: "Something about a train that's magic . . ."
ANNCR (VO): If you want to see America as you've never
seen it before . . .
ANNCR (VO): . . . See it at see level
SINGERS: "America's getting into training . . ."
SINGERS: . . . Training the
SINGERS: Amtrak way!

MAN ON ROOF
30-second
(MUSIC UNDER THROUGHOUT)
PHIL: "Help! Hey! Over here!"
PHIL (OC): "Hey, hey, hey, here, here."
PHIL: "Yeah, yeah."
PHIL: "Just come around here. Yeah."
SHERIFF: "Hiya, Phil. Looks like we got here just in time."
PHIL: "Am I glad to see you."
SHERIFF: "Hop on in here."
PHIL: "Okay,"
(SFX: DOG BARKING)
(SFX: DOG BARKING, BIRD CHIRPING)
SHERIFF (OC): "Woah! Hey!"
SHERIFF: "Wait a minute. We don't have room for your TV."
PHIL: "Uh, well, uh, I guess I'll just have to wait for the next

1417
Art Director: **Michael McLaughlin**
Creative Director: **Gary Gray**
Writer: **Stephen Creet**
Client: **Lowney Inc.**
Editor: **Andrew Walsh**
Director: **George Pastik**
Producer: **Roger Harris**
Agency: **Vickers & Benson Ltd.**

1418
Art Director: **Hy Varon**
Designer: **Hy Varon**
Photographer: **James Szalapski**
Artist: **R.O. Blechman**
Writer: **Jack Silverman**
Client: **IBM General Systems Division**
Editor: **Sandpiper Editorial**
Director: **R.O. Blechman**
Production Co.: **Lois Goldberg/The Ink Tank**
Agency: **Leber Katz Partners**

BUNKHOUSE
30-second
(GUITAR)
VOICE STARTS: (SINGING)
I'm longing tonight
Once again to roam
In a beautiful valley
I could always call home.
There's a girl I adore
And I'm longing to see
In a beautiful
Yoho valley.
VO: Eatmore. A good chew and peanuts too.
SINGING: My little Yoho lady-o.
ady-o, ady-o, ady-o, ady-o, ady-o
(SOUND: SCRATCH . . . .)

SHACKLES
30-second
VO: To all independent business people who are losing their
independence to the shackles of business drudgery, IBM
offers freedom.
MAN: Freedom!
VO: Introducing the small business system that's all business,
yet starts at under $10,000. Datamaster from IBM. A data
processor that can be a word processor, too.
Visit IBM and judge Datamaster for yourself.
A little IBM can mean a lot of freedom.
SUPER: A little IBM can mean a lot of freedom. IBM
System/23 Datamaster.
SUPER: IBM (LOGO) 1-800-241-2003

1419
Art Director: **Tom Denhart**
Writer: **Larry Kopald**
Client: **Joanne Black/American Express**
Editor: **Ray Chung**
Director: **Neil Tardio**
Production Co.: **Lovinger, Tardio, Melsky**
Agency: **Ogilvy & Mather**

1420
Art Director: **Dianne Fiumara**
Writer: **Ron Burkhardt**
Client: **The Minolta Corporation**
Director: **Joe Sedelmaier**
Producer: **Bonnie Singer**

AIRPORT (PLANE)
30-second
HUSBAND: I gotta get to a phone. Honey, take the kids and get on the plane.
WIFE: No, we'll stay here.
HUSBAND: We're gonna make this vacation.
WIFE: Come on . . .
AIRPORT ANNCR: Flight 14 now boarding through gate 5 . . .
OPERATOR: American Express Refund Center.
HUSBAND: We lost our travelers cheques . . .
WIFE: Don't run.
HUSBAND: They were gone.
OPERATOR: Where did you purchase your checks?
CHILD: Where is Dad?
HUSBAND: That's it? A full refund? Thanks.
MALDEN: The majority of people who call American Express

OVERWORKED
30-second
MAN: "Is it workin'?"
VO: When you overwork a small copier . . .
WOMAN: "Is it workin'?"
VO: and make it do the job of a big copier . . .
ANOTHER MAN: "Is it workin'?"
VO: it can break down.
(SFX: MACHINE GRINDS AND SPUTTERS.)
OLD WOMAN: "It's not workin!"
VO: That's why your next copier should be the Minolta EP 520. It makes crisp, clear copies on any kind of paper, and works harder than an ordinary small copier. Because it was designed to do a bigger job. The Minolta EP 520.
OLD WOMAN: "It's workin!"

1421
Art Director: **John Eding**
Writer: **Nicole Cranberg**
Client: **Hershey**
Editor: **Dick Stone**
Director: **Joe Pytka**
Production Co.: **Levine-Pytka**
Agency: **Doyle Dane Bernbach**

1422
Art Director: **Lars Anderson**
Writer: **Rodney Underwood**
Client: **Burmah-Castrol, Inc.**
Editor: **Randy Ilowite**
Director: **Henry Sandbank**
Production Co.: **Dane Johnson**
(SMS)/Sandbank Films, Inc.
Agency: **Scali, McCabe, Sloves, Inc.**

SWEDISH SENSATION
30-second
(OPEN ON LUSH SWEDISH SETTING. SVEN IS RUNNING
THROUGH MEADOW.)
SVEN: Inga!
ANNCR (VO): (MELODRAMATIC) Just released from Sweden
. . . it's Skor. (SKOR IS SUPERED IN 3-D) Starring a sensuous
Swedish chocolate . . .
(CUT TO INGA MUNCHING SKOR) . . . and crunchy butter
toffee.
(SVEN CRUNCHES INTO BAR IN FRONT OF WATERFALL)
(VARIOUS SHOTS OF SVEN AND INGA IN SWEDISH
COUNTRYSIDE)
Never seen before in America, Skor is destined to be the
most talked-about candy bar of our time. No wonder the
critics raved.

DRUM
30-second
(SFX: UNDER)
ANNCR (VO): In case you haven't noticed cars and their
engines have been getting smaller. And smaller engines
have to rev higher and work harder. That's why there's
Castrol Motor Oil. Tests show even at high revs, Castrol
doesn't suffer a significant loss of viscosity. And that's
important. Because if you make things too hard on your
engine,
(SFX: SPUTTER SPUTTER)
ANNCR (VO): your engine could make things hard on you.
Castrol, engineered for smaller cars.

1423
Art Director: **Clarice Bonzer**
Writer: **Randall B. Krueger**
Client: **Columbia Savings & Loan**
Editor: **Michael Swerdloff**
Agency Producer: **Robynjill Harwood**
Director: **Bruce Nadel**
Production Co.: **Nadel**
Agency: **Tracy-Locke, Denver**

1424
Art Director: **Bob Tore**
Writer: **Tom Mabley**
Client: **IBM Corporation**
Editor: **Alan Rozek**
Director: **Jeff Lovinger**
Agency Producer: **Robert Dein**
Production Co.: **Lovinger, Tardio, Melsky Inc.**
Agency: **Lord, Geller, Federico, Einstein Inc.**

CONCERTO FOR PREMIUMS AND ORCHESTRA
30-second
ANNCR (VO): Columbia Savings presents a new
arrangement of French style kitchenware from LeClair . . .
Moulinex . . .
and Corning.
Free or at great savings with qualifying deposits. Only from
Columbia.
So come in and see how you and our investment instruments
can make beautiful music together.
(SFX: COLUMBIA SAVINGS THEME MUSIC ARRANGED FOR
PREMIUMS AND ORCHESTRA.)

FLOWER
30-second
VO: IBM put a lot of what it knows about computers into the
new IBM Personal Computer.
Not to make it complicated,
but to make it simple.
So it's easy to understand,
and easy to use.
IBM made its person computer
to help a person be more productive,
to help a person be more creative . . .
and those are good reasons
for a person to feel good.
The IBM Personal Computer.
Now at selected stores across the country.

1425
Art Directors: **Milt Marcus/Ken Amaral**
Writers: **Ken Musto, Stephen Fenton**
Client: **AMTRAK, The Nat'l. RR Passenger Corp.**
Director: **Tibor Hirsch**
Agency: **Needham, Harper & Steers, Inc.**

1426
Art Director: **Bill Bartley**
Writer: **Michael Wagman**
Client: **Winchell's**
Editor: **Jacques Dury**
Director: **Elbert Budin**
Producer: **Len Levy**
Agency: **Foote, Cone & Belding/Honig**

BEAUTIFUL, BEAUTIFUL
30-second
Amtrak versus the car.
VO: Taking Amtrak on business is just . . .
. . . like taking the car. And then again it isn't.
MAN: (SARCASTICALLY) Beautiful. Beautiful.
CONDUCTOR: Your ticket, sir?
POLICEMAN: Ticket, sir.
MAN: (SARCASTICALLY): Beautiful. Beautiful.
AMTRAK ATTENDANT: Fill'er up?!
GAS STATION ATTENDANT: Fill'er up?
MAN: (SARCASTICALLY): Beautiful. Beautiful.
ANNCR (VO): Next trip, don't drive yourself crazy.
Take Amtrak
CONDUCTOR: Enjoy your trip, sir?
MAN: Beautiful, Beautiful!

HANDS-30
30-second
HAND: Hi there, here's an offer from Winchell's (INTO BOX: Uh, bring out the glass). You can get a flaired antique-style glass like this for just 49 cents when you buy anything at Winchell's (INTO BOX: Put out a donut for the folks to see.) You can buy one glass—or start a collection. (INTO BOX: Fill the glass so the people can see how nice it looks.) Get a flaired glass for just 49 cents apiece, when you buy anything at Winchell's. Excuse me folks. (INTO BOX: That was my donut.)

1427
Art Director: **Alan Chalfin**
Designer: **Alan Chalfin**
Producer: **Tanya English**
Writer: **Dick Tarlow**
Client: **Ben Scrimizzi/Purolator Courier**
Editor: **Plasterick**
Director: **Richard Greenberg**
Production Co.: **R. Greenberg Assoc.**
Agency: **Kurtz & Tarlow**

1428
Art Director: **Bob Gage**
Photographer: **Ernesto Caparros**
Writer: **Jack Dillon**
Client: **Polaroid**
Editor: **Pelco**
Director: **Bob Gage**
Production Co.: **Directors Studio Inc./**
Rose Presley, Eugene Mazzola
Agency: **Doyle Dane Bernbach/**
Joseph Scibetta, Jane Liepshutz

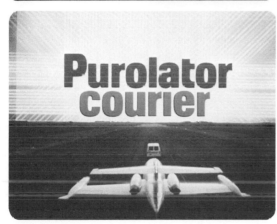

GIANT SHADOW
30-second
MUSIC-SFX

BLACK TIME-ZERO
30-second
JIM: This is Polaroid's new Time-Zero OneStep.
MARI: Pretty. Why is it Black?
JIM: So you'll know it's the Time-Zero OneStep.
And here's the world's fastest developing color. You see it in seconds now. Not minutes
MARI: Look at the color!
But why a Time-Zero OneStep?
JIM: It comes with a pack of Time-Zero Supercolor film. In this Made-For-Each-Other-Pack.
MARI: Certainly made for each other.
JIM: Just like coffee and cream.
MARI: Rolls and Royce.
JIM: Or me and you.
MARI: Try ham and cheese.

1429
Art Director: **Tod Seisser**
Photographer: **Bob Bailin**
Writer: **Jay Taub**
Client: **Chemical Bank/Susan Fisher**
Editor: **Morty Ashkinos**
Director: **Geoffrey Mayo**
Production Co.: **Alan Kolter/Giraldi Productions**
Agency: **Della Femina, Travisano & Partners, Inc.**

1430
Art Director: **Paul Rubinstein**
Writer: **Larry Kopald**
Client: **Brian Kennedy/TWA**
Agency: **Ogilvy & Mather**

$20 CASH PROMOTION
30-second
VO: At Chemical Bank, we've spent years developing programs to help our customers.
But now we need your help.
Our branches have been plagued with an overabundance of twenty dollar bills.
Twenties that, without you, will have nowhere to go.
If you'd like to take one home, simply invest in one of Chemical's six-month Super Saver Certificates, and we'll give you a twenty on the spot.
Please, won't you help?
SUPER: Get $20 at Chemical.
MANDATORY SUPERS:
—Member FDIC.
—Additional information available at any branch.

AMERICA THE BEAUTIFUL
30-second
(MUSIC UNDER)
CHORUS SINGS: Oh beautiful
for spacious skies . . .
ANNCR (VO): Announcing a beautiful way to see America.
TWA's new Anywhere Fare.
Fly anywhere in the U.S. for $149.00 or less.
$149.00 anywhere we fly.
Kids go for just $49.00.
TWA's new Anywhere Fare.
Now everyone can see what
makes America beautiful.
CHORUS SINGS: You're gonna like us,
TWA . . . You're gonna like us . . .

1431
Art Director: **Mark Shap**
Writer: **John Gruen**
Client: **American Express Co.**
Editor: **Morty Ashkinos**
Director: **Steve Horn**
Production Co.: **Sue Chiafullo/Steve Horn, Inc.**
Agency: **Ogilvy & Mather**

1432
Art Director: **Pat Chiono**
Writer: **Rodney Underwood**
Client: **GAF Corporation**
Editor: **Editors Gas**
Director: **Michael Butler**
Production Co.: **Richard Berke (SMS)/Kira Films**
Agency: **Scali, McCabe, Sloves, Inc.**

THE FIRST TIME
30-second
MARVIN HAMLISH (VO): In 1974, my friends and I had some music just waiting for Broadway. . . .
PRODUCER (OC): No stars . . . no sets . . . just a chorus line?
HAMLISH (OC): Yeah, it's got a great finish. . . .
(SINGS) "One Singular Sensation."
(SFX: CLINK)
HAMLISH (NARRATIVE): That was the first time I needed the American Express Card. Since then, it's paid for a lot of meals . . . hotel rooms. . . .
(MUSIC UP)
even tickets to a hit show.
Sure helps to play the right card.
ANNCR (VO): The American Express Card.
Apply for yours.

ELEPHANTS
30-second
(SFX: MUSIC UNDER)
ANNCR (VO): We just put down a beautiful GAF Vinyl Floor in the home of a very large discriminating family. And while they may be a little rougher on a floor than some families and perhaps more careless than others, it's no problem. Because only GAF Floors have the tough SVS no wax surface that's a cinch to keep looking clean and beautiful, even if your family doesn't have extra help with the housekeeping.
(SFX: ELEPHANT TRUMPETING)

1433

Art Director: **Earl Cavanah**
Writer: **Larry Cadman**
Client: **Volvo of America Corporation**
Editor: **Dennis Hayes**
Director: **Henry Sandbank**
Production Co.: **Dane Johnson (SMS)/
Sandbank Films Co. Inc.**
Agency: **Scali, McCabe, Sloves, Inc.**

1434

Art Director: **Vince Salmieri**
Writer: **Robert M. Oksner**
Client: **Fisher-Price Toys**
Director: **Dick Loew**
Production Co.: **Gomes-Loew**
Agency: **Waring & LaRosa, Inc.**

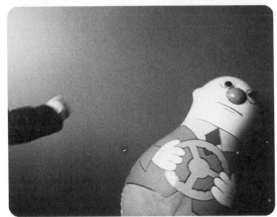

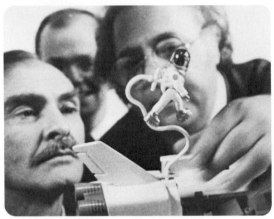

BOZO
30-second
ANNCR (VO): America's long-suffering car buyer.
First they hit you with planned obsolescence.
Then they sold you a gas guzzler.
Then the gas crisis hit.
Now they lure you with small cars . . .
then sock you with the price.
If you're feeling punchy,
. . . consider a Volvo.
It's roomy . . . well-built . . .
and it's an excellent value for the money.
The choice is simple.
Look at a Volvo.
Or continue to be treated like a bozo.

ALPHA PROBE REV. II
30-second
1ST MAN: It's finished.
2ND MAN: Let's show Jim.
1ST MAN: The Alpha Probe!
2ND MAN: The Recon sled here.
1ST MAN: The electronic sound system. Blast off . . .
(SFX: BLAST OFF SOUND)
Communications . . .
(SFX: COMMUNICATION SOUND . . .)
And red alert . . .
(SFX: RED ALERT SOUND . . .)
HANS: Two astro-pilots here . . .
und here.
Life support cable for space walking und docking.
ED: Looks great. Now for the crucial test.

1435
Art Director: **Jim Perretti**
Writer: **Larry Cadman**
Client: **Volvo of America Corporation**
Editor: **Steve Schreiber/Editor's Gas**
Director: **Rick Levine**
Production Co: **Richard Berke (SMS),**
Levine/Pytka & Assocs.
Agency: **Scali, McCabe, Sloves, Inc.**

1436
Art Director: **Earl Cavanah**
Writer: **Larry Cadman**
Client: **Volvo of America Corporation**
Editor: **Dennis Hayes**
Sound Design: **Dane Johnson,**
Thomas Clack
Director: **Henry Sandbank**
Production Co: **Dane Johnson (SMS)/**
Sandbank Films Co., Inc.
Agency: **Scali, McCabe, Sloves, Inc.**

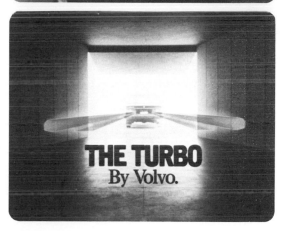

COUNTRY CLUB
30-second
PA: Attention please will the owner of . . .
the blue Mercedes, license number (STATIC) please come . . .
to the parking lot. Your car has been in a minor accident.
VO: If you're looking for a European luxury sedan . . .
that offers the amenities a person of means expects . . .
but you don't . . .
want to follow . . .
the crowd,
consider a Volvo.
It's not outrageously priced.
And it's not for people who are . . .
looking for status.
Volvo's a car for people who already have it.

BLACK TURBO
30-second
(MUSIC)
VO: If you have fond memories of those muscle cars of the past, . . . cars that were virtually legislated off the highways, take heart.
There's a new car that automotive writers have called . . .
"a blast". . .
"spectacular". . .
Stepping on the gas, they say, is like cutting in an afterburner.
It's a car that can blast a V-8 right off the road. The car?
The Turbo . . .
by Volvo.
It'll blow the past right out of your mind.

1437
Art Director: **Roy Grace**
Designer: **Roy Grace**
Writer: **John Noble**
Client: **Mobil Oil Corporation**
Editor: **Stone-Cutters/Dick Stone**
Director: **William Helburn**
Producer: **Susan Calhoun**
Agency: **Doyle Dane Bernbach**

1438
Art Director: **Steve Brodwolf**
Writer: **Jeff Sherman**
Client: **Lanier Business Products**
Editor: **Rick Ledyard**
Director: **George Gomes/Gomes-Loew**
Producer: **Sharon Pittman**
Agency: **Foote, Cone & Belding**

CANS—PEAS VERSION
30-second
(DRAMATIC MUSIC UNDER)
ANNCR (VO): Here come all the leading oils that save gas.
And a brand new one . . .
Mobil Super.
And here comes something even more amazing:
All the leading oils that save gas and can go 25,000 miles
between oil changes.
Mobil 1.
Now from Mobil:
Two oils that save you gas.
And what could be more amazing than that?

WHEREWOLF
30-second
GIRL: Our boss, Mr. Wolf. We used to call him the Where
Wolf.
WOLF: Where's my budget report?
Where's those letters?
Where's the flow charts?
GIRL: Then we got Lanier's new Typemaster. To master the
work of up to 3 ordinary typewriters.
WOLF: Must be a monster! Where am I gonna put it?
GIRL: Typemaster gives you No Problem typing in the space
of a regular typewriter. Now Mr. Wolf's like a pussy cat.
WOLF: (SHOUTING) Where you been all my life?!
GIRL: Almost.
ANNCR: The new Typemaster . . . from Lanier. We make your
good people even better.

1439   SILVER AWARD
Art Director: **Bob Gage**
Photographer: **Ernesto Caparros**
Writer: **Jack Dillon**
Client: **Polaroid**
Editor: **Pelco**
Director: **Bob Gage**
Production Co.: **Director Studio Inc./**
Eugene Mazzola, Rose Presley,
Agency: **Doyle Dane Bernbach/**
Joe Scibetta, Jane Liepshutz

1440
Art Director: **Rock Obenchain**
Writer: **Jim Glynn**
Client: **Mountain Bell Yellow Pages**
Editor: **Jerry Kleppel**
Agency Producer: **Ed Rizzo**
Director: **Jonathan Yarbrough**
Production Co.: **Summerhouse Films**
Agency: **Tracy-Locke, Denver**

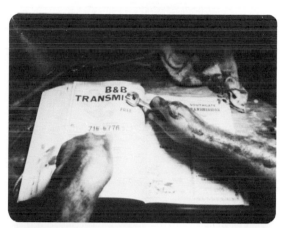

ALL ABOUT EVE
30-second
GIRL: Oh, did you take those?
JIM: You like them?
GIRL: You're awfully good.
JIM: Oh, well this is Polaroid's new time-zero . . .
. . . Do you want me to take your picture?
GIRL: Oh, could you?
JIM: That's what the camera's for!
GIRL: This is fun, it's so fast.
JIM: The world's fastest developing color.
GIRL: May I keep this?
JIM: Then we won't have one of you.
GIRL: You could take another.
JIM: O.K. just kind of look over your shoulder. Ah, there,
that's it!
(NERVOUSLY) Hi!

EVER WONDER
30-second
(MUSIC UNDER)
ANNCR (VO): Ever wonder why your good old Yellow Pages
always looks old before its time?
(SFX: CAR ENGINE MISFIRING)
ANNCR (VO): Turning to a business or service you need.
(SFX: GROWLING DOG)
ANNCR (VO): An average of 3 times every week.
(SFX: BUZZING FLY)
ANNCR (VO): And every time you do
(SFX: THE CRACK OF BREAKING PLASTER)
ANNCR (VO): You prove why it's the most effective
advertising tool your company can buy.
(SFX: WIND)
ANNCR (VO): The Bell System Yellow Pages. It gets used. So
it gets results.

1441

Art Director: **Stan Block**
Photographer: **Jerry Cotts**
Writer: **Jay Taub**
Client: **Chemical Bank/Susan Fisher**
Editor: **Morty Ashkinos**
Director: **Jerry Cotts**
Producer: **Joan Babchak/Jeffrey Metzner Production**
Agency: **Della Femina, Travisano & Partners, Inc.**

1442

Art Director: **Ron Travisano**
Photographer: **Dan Quinn**
Writer: **Jerry Della Femina**
Client: **American Isuzu Motors Inc/Jack Reilly**
Editor: **Barry Moross**
Director: **Bob Giraldi**
Producer: **Barbara Michaelson/ Giraldi Production**
Agency: **Della Femina, Travisano & Partners, Inc.**

BULL
30-second
ANNCR: Money market funds seem like a solid investment. But, they're not FDIC insured. In a bull market their interest rates can drop and taxes could eat up to 50% of what you've earned. In short, they're not as solid as Chemical's Tax Shelter C.D. It's FDIC insured, pays high interest, and could yield up to $2,000 (Dollars.) Tax Free. Chemical Bank. We've got the bull by the horns.

BACKWARD NAME—GESUNDHEIT
30-second
VO: Introducing the advanced car, with the backward name.
CUSTOMER: This is a great looking car — what do you call it?"
SALESMAN: Isuzu!
CUSTOMER: Gesundheit.
WIFE: It goes from 0 to 50 . . .
HUSBAND: Faster than any other diesel in its class . . . I don't care if they call it Irving.
VO: Introducing the '81 Isuzu Diesel.* It gets incredible mileage . . . and is priced from under $6700** When you make a car this good, it doesn't matter what you call it.
CUSTOMER: Wait 'til the neighbors hear we own an '81 Isuzu.
SALESMAN: Gesundheit!

1443
Art Director: **Neal Werner**
Designer: **Neal Werner**
Writer: **Sharon Hewitt**
Client: **The American Fur Industry**
Editor: **Dominic Cervone/Editing Concepts**
Director: **Gordon Munro**
Producers: **Herb Miller, Judith Mayer**
Agency: **Leber Katz Partners**

1444
Art Director: **Hal Tench**
Designer: **Hal Tench**
Writer: **Bill Westbrook**
Client: **Bank of Virginia**
Director: **Joe Adler**
Production Co.: **AFI**
Agency: **The Martin Agency**

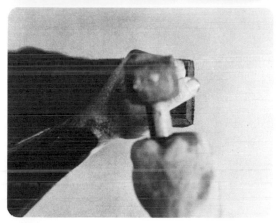

GLAMOUR
30-second
Sink into something a little more sumptuous.
Furrrrrr.
And let it betray a beauty, reveal a rarity all its own.
You won't even have to lift a finger.
For once you invest in the sheer luxury of fur . . . you can only
be expected to enjoy yourself.

DRAGNET
30-second
1ST OFFICER: My partner and I were working the night shift
out of bunko when we saw the suspect trying to get into a
savings and loan.
CUSTOMER: I just need money out of my new checking
account. It's supposed to be convenient.
2ND OFFICER: Just the facts, mister.
1ST OFFICER: Don't you know there's a 24-hour Ginny
machine at Bank of Virginia?
CUSTOMER: But, I want interest on my checking too.
2ND OFFICER: They pay 5-1/4%.
CUSTOMER: Oh.
1ST OFFICER: You better open an Interest/Checking account
at Bank of Virginia soon, mister.
CUSTOMER: I can go?

1445
Art Directors: **Ted Shaine, Jay Taub**
Writers: **Jay Taub, Ted Shaine**
Client: **Chemical Bank/Peggy Casper**
Editor: **Morty Ashkinos**
Director: **Bob Giraldi**
Production Co.: **Barbara Michaelson/ Giraldi Productions**
Agency: **Della Femina, Travisa & Partners, Inc.**

1446
Art Directors: **Anthony Angotti, Neil Leinwohl**
Writers: **Tom Thomas, Ed Butler**
Client: **Xerox Corporation**
Director: **Henry Sandbank**
Agency: **Needham, Harper & Steers. Inc.**

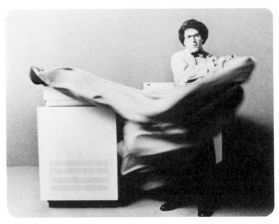

RICH MAN
30-second
(SINGING) If I was a rich man, ya, ba, ba, ba, ba, ba. . . .
Ya, ba, ba, ba, ba, ba, ba, bum, All day lond I'd . . . .
Bitty, bitty, bum If I were a wealthy man . . . .
I wouldn't have to work hard
(UNDER) deedle, deedle, deeedle, bum, bumm, bum.
(FULL) ANNCR: This message is brought to you from
Chemical Bank, who's Savings Programs can make you a
little richer.
(UNDER) All day long I'd bitty, bitty, bum . . . .
If I were a wealthy man.
ANNCR: The Chemistry's just right for savers at Chemical.

PUSH THE BUTTON
30-second
MAN (OC): You're about to see an incredible machine. This
is the 8200 copier from Xerox.
It feeds originals automatically. It gives you XL-10 quality
copies. On both sides of the paper. It reduces, it collates . . .
it even staples. Now, to operate a machine that does as
much as the 8200, you'll have to acquire some very special
skills.
You'll have to learn how to do this.

1447
Art Director: **Dave Miller**
Photographer: **George Greenough**
Client: **General Cinema**
Editor: **David Szabo**
Director: **Dan Nichols**
Producer: **Bob Jackson**
Agency: **Foote, Cone & Belding**

1448
Art Director: **Bob Curry**
Writer: **Peter Nichols**
Client: **New England Ford Dealers**
Production Co.: **Ray Reeves/Coast Productions**
Agency: **Hill, Holliday, Connors, Cosmopulos**

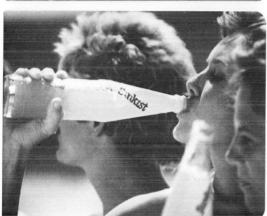

BIG WAVE
30-second
(MUSIC ANTICIPATORY, VOICES DOUBLED)
Gotta keep those Sunkist
vibrations happenin with you
(MUSIC CLIMB)
Good Good Good Vibrations
Sunkist Orange Soda taste sensations
Bubbly orange jubilation
Sunkist is giving out good vibrations
Good Good Good Vibrations

NO WAY JOSE
30-second
(SFX: SHOP AMBIANCE)
JAPANESE BUSINESSMAN: We can't prep these cars fast
enough, they're selling like hot cakes . . . Holy Toledo, it's got
front wheel drive, rack 'n pinion steering and lots of room. A
Toyota? Datsun?
No way, Jose, it's a Ford. The new Escort. And you better
believe Escort gets great gas mileage. You know what else
makes this Ford Escort great? It's made right here in good
old U.S. of A!
JINGLE: We're in your corner . . . New England . . . . Ford . . .
Dealers . . .

1449
Art Directors: **John Clapps, Rick Paynter**
Writer: **Tony Lamont**
Client: **N.J. Bell**
Editor: **EUE**
Director: **Ted Devlet**
Producers: **Dan Kohn, Cathleen Bauer**
Agency: **Bozell & Jacobs, N.J.**

1450
Art Director: **Reinhold Schwenk**
Designers: **Veronica Soul, Reinhold Schwenk**
Artist: **Paul Davis**
Writer: **Bill McCullam**
Client: **New York Shakespeare Festival**
Editor: **Jeff Schon**
Producer: **Peter Cohen**
Production Co.: **Seven Hills Productions**
Agency: **Jordan, Case & McGrath**

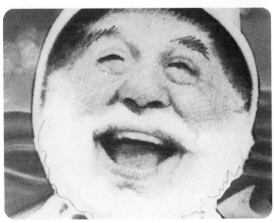

ATLANTIC CITY
30-second
ANNCR: Are you sitting in front of the TV again?
Isn't that where you were last night?
And with so much exciting entertainment so close. Pick up the phone. Go ahead. Dial 976-0711. The Atlantic City Report.
Find out where the big stars are playing, what's happening on the beach and in the hotels. All for only a dime anywhere in New Jersey. Now I don't want to see you sitting there tomorrow night.

PIRATES
30-second
ANNCR (VO): Joseph Papp presents Gilbert and Sullivan's The Pirates of Penzance. The Broadway smash musical that asks: Can a young apprentice pirate grow up to marry the beautiful daughter of a major-general? "If you only go to the theater once this year," said Newsweek, "This is the show!" Call for your seats . . . and get carried away by Pirates!

1451
Art Director: **Ron Travisano**
Photographer: **Allen Greene**
Writer: **Sheila Moore**
Client: **AAA/Robert Morrow**
Editor: **Ed Shea, Jeff Dell Editorial**
Director: **Joe DeVoto**
Production Co.: **Hy Weiner, Joel Productions**
Agency: **Della Femina, Travisano &
Partners, Inc.**

1452
Art Director: **Hector Robledo**
Writer: **Ted Littleford**
Client: **Newsweek**
Director: **Richard Greenberg**
Production Co.: **R. Greenberg Associates/
Michael Pollock (Producer)**
Agency: **Foote, Cone & Belding**

RAINSTORM
30-second
VO: Sooner or later, just about everybody gets stuck. And if you belong to the wrong auto club . . .
. . . You're not only stuck, you're alone.
WOMAN: $35 for a tow? . . . Will you take a personal check?
VOICE ON PHONE: Ha ha ha ha ha ha ha . . .
(HYSTERICAL LAUGHTER)
WOMAN: I've got a credit card . . . see!
VOICE ON PHONE: We don't take that one.
VO: With AAA, you're never alone. In any major city just call us and we'll find a garage for you . . . at any hour.
VO: AAA. We'll never leave you all alone.

NEWS
30-second
(MUSIC UNDER, THROUGHOUT. MAP OF POLAND FILLS SCREEN)
ANNCR (VO): December 1st, Warsaw. Our competition got its news about strike leader Walesa from reporters.
(MAP CRACKS OPEN TO SOLARIZED IMAGE OF WALESA. FOCUSES INTO CU)
ANNCR (VO): At Newsweek, we got ours from Walesa in an exclusive interview.
(CUT TO PHOTO OF JIMMY THE WEASEL)
ANNCR (VO): Our competition saw him as just another hood.
(IMAGE CRACKS OPEN TO CU)
ANNCR (VO): We saw him as the greatest Mafia squealer in history.

1453   DISTINCTIVE MERIT
Art Director: **Ron Becker**
Writer: **Harold Karp**
Client: **Breakstone's**
Editor: **Dennis Hayes**
Director: **Dick Loew**
Producer: **Jean Muchmore**
Agency: **Geers Gross**

1454
Art Director: **Jan Koblitz**
Writer: **Harvey Cohen**
Client: **American Telephone & Telegraph—Long Lines Department**
Editor: **Howard Lazarus - Take Five**
Director: **Steve Horn**
Agency Producer: **Gaston Braun**
Producer: **Linda Horn/Steve Horn Inc.**
Agency: **NW Ayer Incorporated**

LOW FAT
30-second
COP: Eating up all the profits Sam?
AVO: Where did Sam Breakstone get the idea for a delicious cottage cheese . . .
that's lower in fat and calories?
KID: Gee Ma, he's fat.
SAM: Darling boy. Go play with the dog.
AVO: Sam was so . . .
demanding . . .
SAM: Make it with less fat, but make it with great taste!
AVO: his low fat cottage cheese has less fat and calories than his regular cottage cheese—but still . . . has a delicious taste.
SAM: I'm not fat, I have big bones.

FATHER/DAUGHTER
30-second
LYRICS: He's my Dad, my dear old Dad, the only mom I've ever had
It wasn't easy on his own
So he held my hand till I had grown
My dear old Dad,
I love him so . . .
DAD: I sure hope you're taking good care of my grandchildren.
GIRL: Don't worry, I had a very good teacher.
MUSIC & SINGING: Reach out, reach out and touch someone.

1455
Art Director: **Larry Leblang**
Writer: **Mike Sloan**
Client: **Florida Department of Commerce, Division of Tourism**
Editor: **Bobby Smallheiser**
Director: **Burt Steinhauser**
Production Co: **Burt Steinhauser Productions**
Agency: **Mike Sloan, Inc. Advertising**

1456
Art Director: **Ron Becker**
Writer: **Rick Meyer**
Client: **Ludens**
Editor: **First Edition**
Director: **Joe DeVoto**
Producer: **Jean Muchmore**
Agency: **Geers Gross**

WINTER
30-second
(SFX: FLORIDA MUSIC UNDER THROUGHOUT.)
MAN: I need it bad.
BOY: Mom, I need it bad.
CHORUS: You need the sunshine
And the palm trees
Of Florida . . . Florida.
When you need it bad,
We've got it good.
When you need it bad
Come to Florida . . .
ESKIMO: I need it bad.

THE SOFT MINT
30-second
FIRST MAN: I just broke into the mint.
SECOND MAN: Was it hard?
FIRST MAN: No, it was soft.
SECOND MAN: You mean it was a piece of cake?
FIRST MAN: No, it was a piece of candy.
ANNCR (VO): When you've got a Mellomint you've got it soft.
WOMAN: My ex-husband said he was going to leave me a mint and I'd have it soft for the rest of my life.
ANNCR (VO): Soft, refreshing peppermint surrounded by rich, dark chocolate.
FATHER: Son, getting a mint today isn't hard. It's soft. The hard part is keeping it.
Look, you just lost your first mint.
ANNCR (VO): Mellomint. The soft mint.

1457
Art Director: **Harvey Gabor**
Writer: **Alice Henry**
Client: **Chesebrough Ponds**
Editor: **Dennis Hayes Editorial**
Director: **Steve Horn**
Producer: **Sue Chiafullo, Steve Horn Inc.**
Agency: **Ogilvy & Mather**

1458
Art Director: **Gary D. Johns**
Agency Producer: **Lynne Kluger**
Writer: **Jim Weller**
Client: **Ale - 8 - of America**
Editor: **Stuart Wax**
Director: **Tony Scott**
Producer: **Howard Bailin / Sunlight Pictures**
Agency: **Della Femina, Travisano & Partners**

HOW TO CLEAN AN EAR
30-second
MAN: Everybody's always telling you how to clean things . . .
your hair . . . . your nails . . . . your sink.
Anybody ever tell you how to clean an ear?
Well, I'm gonna tell you.
First, find an ear.
Now. Grasp a nice soft Q-Tips Swab, firmly.
Stroke gently—Careful! Only on the outside!
Ahhh, soft.
Oh! And remember: Never put anything inside your ear . . .
except your elbow.

SQUIRREL
30-second
MUSIC & LYRICS: "Well, you can give it to your girl.
Or share it with a squirrel.
But it by the case.
And pour it in your face.
Ale-8. The Soft drink of tomorrow.
Ale-8. A new kind of taste.
Ale-8. They got it full of flavor.
Cause new Ale-8 is from another place.
New Ale-8 is here."

1459
Art Director: **Michael Tesch**
Writer: **Patrick Kelly**
Client: **Federal Express**
Editor: **Peggy DeLay/Sedelmaier**
Director: **Joe Sedelmaier**
Producers: **Maureen Kearns/A&G, Ann Ryan/Sedelmaier**
Agency: **Ally & Gargano, Inc.**

1460
Art Director: **Lou Colletti**
Writer: **Lee Garfinkel**
Client: **Lesney Products & Co.**
Editor: **The Editors**
Director: **Dominic Rossetti**
Production Co.: **Rossetti Films**
Agency: **Levine, Huntley, Schmidt, Plapler & Beaver, Inc.**

FAST PACED WORLD
30-seconds
MR. SPLEEN (OC): OkayEunice,travelplans,Ineedtobein
NewYorkonMonday,LAonTuesday,NewYorkon
Wednesday,LAonThursday,andNewYorkonFriday.
Gotit? Soyouwanttoworkhere,
wellwhatmakesyouthinkyoudeserveajobhere?
GUY. Wellsirlthinkonmyfeel,
I'mgoodwithfiguresandIhaveasharpmind.
SPLEEN: Excellent,canyoustartMonday?
OC: And Inconclusion,Jim,Bill,BobandTed,businessis
businesssolet'sgettowork. Thankyoufortakingthismeeting.
OC: Peteryoudidabang-upjob,
I'mputtingyouinchargeofPittsburgh.
PETER (OC): Pittsburgh'sperfect.
SPLEEN: Iknowit'sperfect,Peter,that'swhyIpickedPittsburgh.

SALESMAN
30-second
CACTUS BILL: You want a car that's built to last. This cream
puff just came off the assembly line. (TAPS CAR WHEEL
FALLS OFF)
FAST FREDDIE: You'll get a lot of mileage out of this baby as
long as you don't play with it.
MATCHBOX SALESMAN: (CONFIDENT) At Matchbox, we
don't give you fast talk or fancy gimmicks. Because our cars
are the best you can buy. (CUT TO PRODUCT SHOT) Like this
'57 Chevy, every Matchbox car is built to last and has a very
reasonable price. So when you're buying something as
important as a car, buy it from someone you can trust.
Matchbox.
SUPER: Matchbox

1465

Art Directors: **Rich Martel, Al Merrin**
Writers: **Al Merrin, Ted Sann**
Client: **Vic Alcott**
Editor: **Chris Horn**
Director: **Neil Tardio**
Production Co.: **Jeff Fishgrund/Lovinger,
Tardio, Melsky**
Agency: **BBDO**

NUMBERS
30-second
DAD: What's for dinner, 238?
MOM: No, 355.
DAD: 4's?
MOM: No, fresh 3's . . .
KID: 3's again!
MOM: . . . and a 125 for dessert!
AVO: GE presents Cooking By Numbers. Simply punch in a
pre-programmed recipe code or let special GE electronic
sensors take over and control the cooking until it's done.
Either way, it makes microwave cooking as easy as
. . . 1, 2, 4.
DAD: Billy eat your 3's . . . or no . . .
MOM: . . . 125.
DAD: Right!
SINGERS: GE. We Bring Good Things To Life.

1466

Art Director: **Barry Vetere**
Animator: **Jack Zander**
Writer: **Ron Berger**
Client: **Dunkin' Donuts**
Editors: **Morty Ashkinos/Take Five,
Ron Silver/Zanders**
Directors: **Tim Newman, Jack Zander**
Producers: **Maureen Kearns/A&G, Gary
Buonanno/Jenkins Covington Newman,
Jack Cohen/Zanders**
Agency: **Ally & Gargano, Inc.**

JUST FOR KIDS
30-second
(MUSIC AND SFX THROUGHOUT)
GUY 1: Hey, How ya doin'?
GUY 2: Here comes the jelly!
(LITTLE MEN GIGGLE)
FATHER (OC): Hmmm . . .
GUY 1: Here you go. Put that in the coconut.
GUY 2: Whoops!
GUY 3: Whoa!
GUY 1: Shh! Quiet!!!
FATHER (OC): Hmm . . .?!?
GUY 1: That was close. Watch out!!!
GUY 3: Get it!!!
GUY 4: There it goes!!!
ANNCR (VO): Munchkin Donut hole treats from Dunkin' Donuts.
They're made just for kids.

1467
Art Director: **Michael Tesch**
Writer: **Patrick Kelly**
Client: **Federal Express**
Editor: **Peggy DeLay/Sedelmaier**
Director: **Joe Sedelmaier**
Producers: **Maureen Kearns/A&G,**
Ann Ryan/Sedelmaier
Agency: **Ally & Gargano, Inc.**

1468
Art Director: **Michael Tesch**
Writer: **Patrick Kelly**
Client: **Federal Express**
Editor: **Peggy DeLay/Sedelmaier**
Director: **Joe Sedelmaier**
Producers: **Maureen Kearns/A&G,**
Ann Ryan/Sedelmaier
Agency: **Ally & Gargano, Inc.**

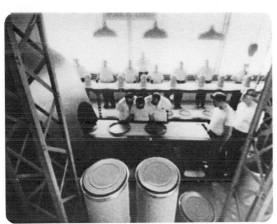

WHERE'S KRADDOCK?
30-second
(MUSIC UNDER THROUGHOUT)
(SFX: WHISTLE UNDER)
BOSS (OC): Kraddock, Kraddock, Kraddock, Kraddock . . .
Keener, have you seen Kraddock?
KEENER (OC): Not me, maybe Krenshaw.
BOSS (OC): Krenshaw, have you seen Kraddock?
KRENSHAW (OC): Not me, maybe Keener.
BOSS (OC): Are you sure you haven't seen Kraddock?
KEENER (OC): I'm sure, maybe Krenshaw isn't sure.
BOSS (OC): OK look
If either of you guys see Kraddock, tell him the parts I told
him to send to Kalamazoo yesterday
did not get there. And I tell you,
when we get our hands on Kraddock . . .
are you sure you haven't seen Kraddock?

POST OFFICE STEPS
30-second
(SFX OF WIND UNDER)
ANNCR (VO): The United States
Postal Service handles 300 million pieces of mail a day.
Well, that's their job.
But that doesn't mean you have to put your important
business letter into that pile.
(SFX: WIND)
Now you have an alternative. Introducing
the Federal Express overnight letter.
It costs only 9.50 when you drop it off,
and it gets delivered practically anyplace in the country
overnight.
Absolutely,
Positively.
(SFX: WIND)

1469　GOLD AWARD

Art Director: **Michael Tesch**
Writer: **Patrick Kelly**
Client: **Federal Express**
Editors: **Peggy DeLay/Sedelmaier Films**
Director: **Joe Sedelmaier**
Producers: **Maureen Kearns/A&G,
Ann Ryan/Sedelmaier**
Agency: **Ally & Gargano, Inc.**

1470　DISTINCTIVE MERIT

Art Director: **George Euringer**
Writer: **Helayne Spivak**
Client: **Kayser-Roth**
Editors: **Peggy DeLay/Sedelmaier Films,
Morty Ashkinos/Take Five**
Director: **Joe Sedelmaier**
Producers: **Jerry Haynes/A&G, Mary Ann
Blossom, Sedelmaier Films**
Agency: **Ally & Gargano, Inc.**

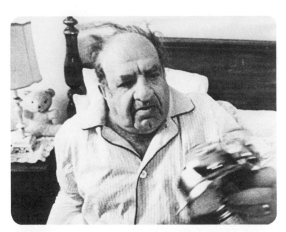

YOU CAN'T COUNT ON ANYTHING
30-second
(MUSIC THROUGHOUT)
(SFX: BIRDS CHIRPING)
(SFX: RATTLE OF ALARM CLOCK)
(SFX: ENGINE)
(SFX: FLAT TIRE)
ANNCR (VO): You can't count on anything these days . . .
(SFX: FOOTSTEPS)
(SFX: TYPING)
MAN (OC): Did you type the letter I told you to type?
SECRETARY (OC): No.
ANNCR (VO): With possibly one exception:
Federal Express.
When it absolutely, positively has to be there overnight.

REMINDER
30-second
(MUSIC THROUGHOUT)
ANNCR (VO): Just a reminder from Interwoven
that the only times that you should ever have to think about your socks are
when you put them on, when you take them off, and when you buy them.
So next time, think of the No. 1 sock in department and other fine stores.

1471
Art Director: **Joe Sedelmaier**
Writer: **Jeff Gorman**
Client: **Independent Life Insurance Company**
Editor: **Peggy DeLay**
Director: **Joe Sedelmaier**
Production Co: **Sedelmaier Films**
Agency: **Cecil West & Associates**

1472
Art Director: **Chris Blum**
Designer: **Chris Blum**
Photographer: **Laszlo Kovacs**
Artist: **Brian Eatwell**
Writer: **Mike Koelker**
Client: **Levi Strauss & Co.**
Editor: **Rick Ross**
Director: **Robert Abel**
Producer: **Robert Abel/Robert Abel & Associates**
Agency: **Foote, Cone & Belding/Honig**

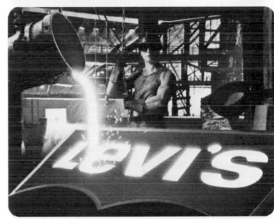

NO INSURANCE
30-second
(MUSIC: ORGAN)
1ST MAN: No insurance.
WIFE: Bernard always said food came first.
2ND MAN: No insurance.
WIFE: Bernard always said shelter came first.
3RD MAN: No insurance.
WIFE: Bernard always said clothing came first.
ANNCR (VO): It's strange. Life insurance is never one of life's necessities when you're alive.
WIFE: But, Bernard, you never said you'd go first.
ANNCR: When your Independent Life agent calls, talk to him about Total Way of Life coverage. It's a necessity.

WORKING MAN
30-second
(SFX: THROUGHOUT THE COMMERCIAL) INDUSTRIAL
ANNCR: He's the working man,
Forging dreams with fire,
Building,
(MUSIC UP)
ANNCR: Moving mountains,
Always reaching higher.
He's the wheels that move a nation,
The stitching in the seams,
He holds it all together,
He wears Levi's jeans.
'Cause he knows . . . we still build the Levi's jeans,
(MUSIC OUT)
ANNCR: that helped build America.

1473
Art Director: **Michael Tesch**
Writer: **Patrick Kelly**
Client: **Saab-Scania**
Editor: **Morty Ashkinos/Take Five**
Director: **Mike Cuesta**
Agency/Producer: **Janine Marjollet/A&G**
Agency: **Ally & Gargano, Inc.**

1474
Art Director: **Dennis D'Amico**
Writer: **Ron Berger**
Client: **Timberland**
Editor: **Jerry Bender**
Director: **Henry Sandbank**
Producers: **Beth Forman/A&G, Richard Cohen/Sandbank**
Agency: **Ally & Gargano, Inc.**

BEAUTIFUL CAR
30-second
(SFX AND MUSIC THROUGHOUT)
ANNCR (VO): Some people think Saabs are not the most beautiful cars in the world.
(SFX: ENGINE ROAR)
But what do you call a car that can go like this?
Stop like this?
Corner like this?
Climb like this?
Save gas like this?
And survive something like this?
Some say Saabs aren't beautiful but if this isn't beautiful, what is?
(SILENT)

GETTING SOAKED
30-second
ANNCR (VO): Here's what you could be getting into when you buy a pair of work boots.
This is a $45 boot after 3 hours in water.
(SFX)
This, a $60 boot.
This, an $80 boot.
While this is a Timberland work boot.
Timberland, waterproof, insulated boots start at about $60.
So if you're spending $45 or more
and not getting work boots as good as Timberlands,
your feet aren't the only thing getting soaked.

1475
Art Director: **George Euringer**
Writer: **Patrick Kelly**
Client: **Keller-Geister**
Editor: **Peggy DeLay/Sedelmaier Prod.**
Director: **Joe Sedelmaier**
Producers: **Jerry Haynes/A&G, Ann Ryan/Sedelmaier**
Agency: **Ally & Gargano, Inc.**

14/6
Art Directors: **Rich Martel, Al Merrin**
Writer: **Al Merrin**
Client: **Vic Alcott**
Editor: **Steve Schreiber/Editor's Gas**
Director: **Matthew Brady**
Production Co.: **Nancy Ianicelli/Matthew Brady Prod.**
Agency: **BBDO**

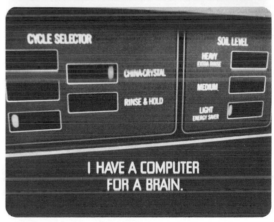

ALEXIS CHATEAU
30-second
ALEXIS: Keller-Geister. The delicious imported white wine that accompanies any food.
The perfect companion for fillet of sole,
or if you so desire, boiled Okra.
WOMAN: Alexis!
ALEXIS: For that matter, the perfect compliment for bricks and mortar.
As an after dinner encore,
Keller-Geister is beyond repute.
1ST MAN: Mein bevorzugter wein.
(Translation: My favorite wine.)
ALEXIS: Bravo, Emil!
2ND MAN: C'est delicieux avec un bon gout.
(Translation: It's delicious, with good taste.)

BEEP
30-second
(SFX: BEEP, BEEP, BEEP THROUGHOUT)
SUPER: Hello.
Allow me to introduce my remarkable self.
I am the new GE 2500 dishwasher.
I have a computer for a brain.
I can put 25 cleaning cycles at your fingertips.
I can clean your pots
. . . pamper your china
. . . help you save energy
. . . and tell you when your dishes will be clean.
AVO: The GE 2500. It can do almost everything . . . but talk.
SINGERS: GE . . . We Bring Good Things to Life.
(SFX: BEEP, BEEP.)

1477
Art Director: **Michael Tesch**
Writer: **Patrick Kelly**
Client: **Federal Express**
Editor: **Peggy DeLay/Sedelmaier**
Director: **Joe Sedelmaier**
Producers: **Maureen Kearns/A&G,
Ann Ryan/Sedelmaier**
Agency: **Ally & Gargano, Inc.**

1478
Art Director: **George Euringer**
Writer: **Tom Messner**
Client: **MCI**
Editors: **Peggy DeLay/Sedelmaier,
Morty Ashkinos/Take Five**
Director: **Joe Sedelmaier**
Producers: **Maureen Kearns/A&G, Joseph
Sedelmaier**
Agency: **Ally & Gargano, Inc.**

NEVER HEAR THE END OF IT
30-second
(SFX: APPLAUSE)
MR. BUNDLE: . . . and in conclusion,
I'd just like to say you've all
done an excellent job, except for croller . . .
MAN 1: Cruller.
MR. BUNDLE: Croller? Cruller . . .
Cruller,
(SFX CROWD)
Who I told to send a package to L.A.
MAN 1: And it never got there.
MAN 2: Never got there?
MR. BUNDLE (OC): And it never got there.
ANNCR (VO): Next time, send it Federal Express, or you may
never hear the end of it.

MAILMAN
30-second
(MUSIC UNDER LAUGHTER)
ANNCR (VO): Bell Telephone's done a wonderful job
helping people stay close.
You've seen those "Reach out and touch someone"
commericals.
We at MCI, thought you'd like to see something they
never show you:
What goes on when the bill arrives.
(SFX)
If your long distance bills are $25.00 or more,
call MCI and start saving 30, 40, even 50% on long
distance.

14/9
Art Director: **Ron Anderson**
Designer: **Ron Anderson**
Writer: **Tom McElligot**
Client: **Poppin' Fresh Pie Restaurants**
Director: **Joe Sedelmaier**
Production Co.: **Sedelmaier Film Productions, Inc.**
Agency: **Bozell & Jacobs, Inc./Mpls.**

1480
Art Director: **William Taubin**
Designer: **William Taubin**
Writer: **Edward Smith**
Client: **Porsche/Audi**
Editor: **Joe Lallker/Pelco**
Director: **Werner Hlinka**
Production Co.: **Sheldon Levy, Tibor Hirsch Inc.**
Agency: **Doyle Dane Bernbach**

MAN/TACO SALAD
30-second
(MUSIC UP AND UNDER)
FAT MAN: Hey, I'll bet you didn't know Poppin Fresh put out a taco salad like this . . . huh? huh?
Look . . . look at the fresh crisp lettuce and tomatoes an cheese and beef and tortilla chips.
You know you oughta taste this. It's perfect for the diet.
Go ahead Amigo try it . . . go ahead . . .
Mean time I'll just get started on this French silk pie.

MUSEUM
30-second
In Bavaria for centuries they've produced masterpieces . . .
Is this yet another . . . The new Audi Coupe.
A work of art in automotive design . . .
With an aerodynamic body.
Five cylinder engine.
Front wheel drive,
five speed transmission,
Audi brings new ideas . . . from the old world . . .
Audi . . . the art of engineering.

1481
Art Director: **Ron Anderson**
Designer: **Ron Anderson**
Writer: **Tom McElligot**
Client: **Poppin' Fresh Pie Restaurants**
Director: **Joe Sedelmaier**
Production Co: **Sedemaier Film Productions, Inc.**
Agency: **Bozell & Jacobs, Inc./Mpls.**

1482
Art Director: **Ron Anderson**
Designer: **Ron Anderson**
Writer: **Tom McElligot**
Client: **Minnesota Public Radio**
Director: **Walter Goins**
Production Co: **L.E.O. Productions**
Agency: **Bozell & Jacobs, Inc./Minneapolis**

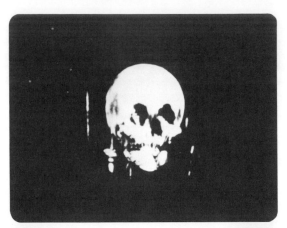

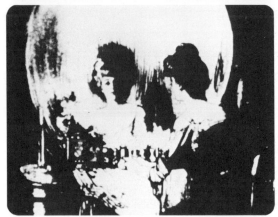

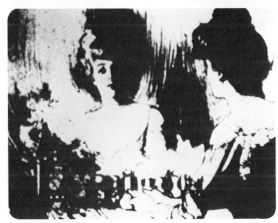

ITALIAN MAN/LASAGNA
30-second
UNCLE WILLIAM: Well William, I'm more than glad we could
have this hearty lunch together today.
WILLIAM: Thank you very much Uncle William.
UNCLE: William, I'll bet you a nickel you didn't know that
Poppin' Fresh had Lasagna Pie.
WILLIAM: No. I didn't Uncle William.
UNCLE: Most people don't. This is excellent Lasagna. Doesn't
that look good, William?
WILLIAM: It certainly does Uncle William.
UNCLE: And it's good for you too. Why don't we begin.
(MUSIC TRACK UNDER . . . . . .)
And I'll just get a head start on this lemon meringue pie.
(MUSIC TRACK OUT . . .)

THINGS AREN'T WHAT THEY SEEM
30-second
ANNCR (VO): This is a sign of danger. But the danger here
has to do with ideas. How it often takes more than just a
headline to express an idea. How too little information can
even obscure the truth. That's why thoughtful people tune in
Morning Edition, weekdays on KSJN Radio 1330 AM. Morning
Edition doesn't give its stories time limits. It gives them time to
be understood.
Because things are not always what they first appear to be.

1483
Art Director: **Roy Tuck**
Writer: **Bill Appelman**
Client: **Merrill Lynch**
Director: **Dick Miller**
Producer: **Scott Kulok**
Agency: **Young & Rubicam**

1484
Art Director: **John Lucci**
Set Designer: **Ken Davles**
Photographer: **Mel Sokolsky**
Writer: **Jud Alper**
Client: **Dr Pepper**
Editor: **Steve Bodner**
Agency Producer: **Mootsy Elliot**
Director: **Mel Sokolsky**
Production Co.: **Sunlight**
Agency: **Young & Rubicam**

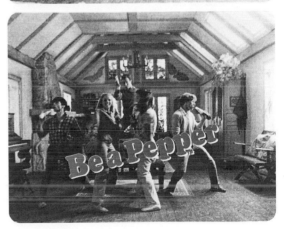

HAYSTACK
30-second
ANNCR (VO): Looking for the right fields to invest in, and the right investments in these fields, can be frustrating. That's why Merrill Lynch does the groundwork with research. To seek out the best investments, Merrill Lynch brought together the best researchers. And it is turning up the unseen or over-looked . . . that makes us what we are.
MERRILL LYNCH, A BREED APART.

REVOLVING ROOM
30-second
(MUSIC UNDER)
PATTY: (SINGING) To be a Pepper, original like a Pepper all you gotta do is taste.
SINGERS: Be a Pepper . . . to know the pleasure of a flavor you will treasure . . . All you gotta do is taste. Be a Pepper. The flavor's got a feeling, original and appealing, and all you gotta do is . . . taste. To be a Pepper, open up a Dr Pepper, and all you gotta do is taste.
Be a Pepper, yeah.

1485
Art Directors: **Gene Trentacoste,**
Betty Freedman
Writers: **Jack Aaker, Betty Freedman**
Director: **Gene Harrison**
Producers: **Maura Dausey (Grey), Dove Films**
Agency: **Grey Advertising, Inc.**

1486
Art Director: **Paul Rubinstein**
Writer: **Larry Kopald**
Client: **Eileen McKenna/TWA**
Editor: **Lenny Friedman**
Director: **Linda Mevorach**
Production Co: **Art Califano/Eyepatch**
Productions
Agency: **Ogilvy & Mather**

ASHLEY WHIPPET MULTI CATCH
30-second
(MUSIC: VO—BEETHOVEN'S 5TH PIANO CONCERTO)
ANNCR (VO): Presenting world champion catcher—Ashley
Whippet, age 10. He's a Cycle dog. He follows the Cycle
Feeding Program.
(MUSIC)
ANNCR (VO): Cycle Dog Foods can help your dog . . . be in
peak condition for life.

ROLL-OUT
30-second
(MUSIC UNDER)
ANNCR (VO): Right before your eyes, TWA is creating a
brand new way for business flyers to fly coast-to-coast. It's a
separate business class with bigger, wider seats than in
coach. But less seats, so you're less crowded. It's TWA's new
Ambassador Class to California. With enough room . . . for
anybody.
CHAMBERLAIN: Even if you're seven foot one.
JABBAR: Or taller.
CHAMBERLAIN: Taller?
JABBAR: A little.
SINGERS: You're going to like us . . . TWA . . .

1487
Art Director: **Roger Mosconi**
Designer: **Roger Mosconi**
Writers: **Roger Mosconi, Jean-Claude Kaufmann**
Client: **Coca Cola/Tab**
Editors: **Dennis Hayes Editorial/Frank Cioffredi**
Director: **Hobby Morrison**
Producer: **Debra Srettin**
Agency: **McCann Erickson Inc. New York**

1488
Art Director: **Carol Frederick**
Photographer: **Michael Boddiker**
Music: **John Tartaglia**
Writer: **Gabe Massimi**
Client: **Allegheny International**
Editor: **Rob Kirsner/Filmcore**
Director: **Mike Cuesta/Myers & Griner Cuesta**
Producer: **Patricia A. Turnbull**
Agency: **Burton-Campbell, Inc.**

 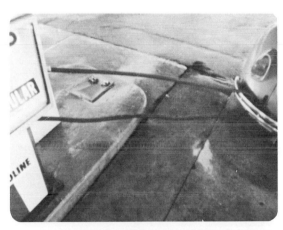

GIRL ON THE BEACH
30-second
(MUSIC STARTS AND CONTINUES THROUGHOUT)
SINGERS: TAB . . .
TAB Cola, what a beautiful drink.
TAB . . .
TAB Cola for beautiful people.
TAB . . .
TAB Cola, you're beautiful to me. Real Cola taste, just one calorie.
TAB . . .
TAB Cola, what a beautiful drink.
TAB . . .
TAB Cola, for beautiful people.
TAB . . .
TAB Cola, it's beautiful to be.

ALLEGHENY INTERNATIONAL
30-second
ANNCR (VO): A true story from Allegheny International
Disaster about to happen . . .
ATTENDANT (VO): Watch it, look out.
OWNER: Hey lady . . .
ANNCR (VO): but lives and property were saved . . .
ANNCR (VO): by an automatic fire suppression system . . .
made by Allegheny International.
We also make special fire systems . . . to protect ships,
planes, oil rigs, and even computers.
GROUP OR ONE: That's incredible!
At Allegheny International, we have special skills for special
needs.

1489
Art Director: **Roger Flint**
Designer: **Warren Wildes, Jr.**
Writer: **Jim Glynn**
Client: **Public Service of Colorado**
Editors: **Roger Flint, Hal Cohen**
Director: **Roger Flint**
Production Co.: **Flint Productions, Inc.**
Agency: **Tracy Locke**

1490
Art Director: **Dick Pantano**
Writers: **Jay Hill, Jack Wallwork**
Client: **Wang Laboratories, Inc.**
Production Co.: **Jennie and Company**
Agency: **Hill, Holliday, Connors, Cosmopulos**

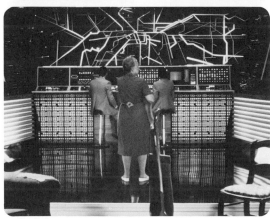

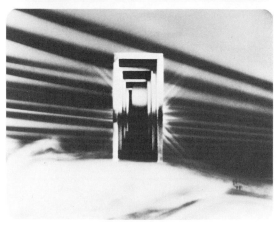

CONTROL CENTER — V-8
30-second
ANNCR: "Ever wonder whats behind the simple act of
plugging in a plug? The world of Public Service Company
and new ideas like our master control center, keeping
power reliable by monitoring every inch of our system,
spotting trouble in an instant and by designing it ourselves
saving eight million dollars so you don't have to give your
power a second thought. Because we do. We're putting all
our energy to work for you."

DOORS TO THE FUTURE
30-second
VO: For over 25 years, the most powerful tool of the 20th
century was kept in the back room. Until Wang opened
the door to office automation.
Wang put the computer at everyone's fingertips . . . by
simplifying data processing . . . revolutionizing word
processing . . . and combining them on one system.
And the future looks even brighter . . . Because at Wang,
we never stop opening doors.

1491
Art Director: **Joe Minnella**
Writer: **Anna Kabot**
Client: **Faygo Beverages**
Editor: **Bill Riss**
Director: **Bill Alton**
Production Co.: **John Saag/E.U.E.**
Agency: **W.B. Doner and Company**
Advertising

1492
Art Director: **John Constable**
Photographer: **James Middleton**
Artist: **Bajus-Jones**
Writers: **Steve Laughlin, Dennis Frankenberry**
Client: **Oshkosh B'Gosh**
Directors: **Mike Jones, Bajus-Jones**
Producer: **John Constable**
Agency: **Frankenberry, Laughlin &
Constable, Inc.**

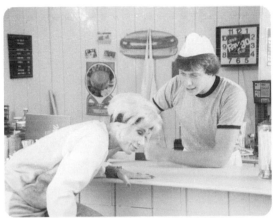

JOGGER
30-second
JOAN: (HEAVY BREATHING)
COUNTER MAN: Well, Joan, how far today?
JOAN: Two blocks.
COUNTER MAN: Twice as far as yesterday.
(LAUGHS)
JOAN: Cute. Give me a Diet Faygo Orange.
COUNTER MAN: Ya know, maybe you should run a little
slower.
JOAN: I'm already so slow I got a ticket for loitering. My
mascara runs faster than I do. (SIPS) Thanks, isn't this
regular Faygo?
COUNTER MAN: No, it's diet.
JOAN: Oh, it's delicious, and delicious is-s-s-S-S DIET
FAYGO!

BACK-TO-SCHOOL
30-second
SINGERS: Goin' back-to-school . . .
. . . Oshkosh B'Gosh . . .
Goin' back-to-school . . .
. . . Oshkosh B'Gosh . . .
. . . Oshkosh B'Gosh . . .
ANNCR (VO): When you're wearin' Oshkosh B'Gosh, you're
wearin' the Genuine Article . . .
. . . heh, heh . . .
. . . Since 18 hundred and ninety five.
SINGERS: Oshkosh B'Gosh kosh B'Gosh.

1493
Art Director: **B.A. Albert**
Agency Producer: **Nancy Esserman**
Writer: **Bob Richardson**
Client: **Telecredit, Inc.**
Editor: **Richie Nuchow**
Director: **Alex Fernbach**
Production Co: **Diane Miller/Sunlight Pictures**
Agency: **Cargill, Wilson & Acree Inc.**

1494
Art Director: **B.A. Albert**
Agent Producer: **Nancy Esserman**
Writer: **Mike Gaffney**
Client: **Georgia Power**
Editor: **Larry Krantz**
Director: **Jimmy Collins**
Production Co: **Susan Haislip/Jayan Films**
Agency: **Cargill, Wilson & Acree Inc.**

HONEST FACE/SHOPPING SPREE
30-second
(MUSICAL INTRO.)
(MUSICAL INTRO.)
(MUSICAL INTRO.)
(MUSICAL INTRO.)
MUSICAL VO: Honest Face . . .
. . . Honest Face.
Use it almost any place.
Use it for . . .
. . . a shopping bash.
Use a check. You don't need cash.
Honest Face, Honest Face.
For this . . .
. . . for that.
Anything or . . .

GOOD CENTS APTS./CLOUDS
30-second
VO: From the very first day you move in, you can save . . .
. . . energy and money in a Good Cents apartment or condominium
And that's why a day seeking out an apartment or condominium . . .
. . . with a Good Cents sign . . .
. . . is a day well spent.

1495
Art Director: **Jim Cameron**
Writer: **Jim Anderson**
Client: **Chesapeake & Potomac Co.**
Editor: **Bill Bruder**
Director: **Jeff Lovinger**
Production Co.: **Lovinger, Tardio, Melsky**
Agency: **Ketchum Advertising, Pittsburgh**

1496
Art Director: **Clyde Hogg**
Writer: **Linda Morse**
Client: **Tindol Services, Inc.**
Director: **Linda Morse**
Production Co.: **B/H Productions**
Agency: **Bowes/Hanlon Advertising, Inc.**

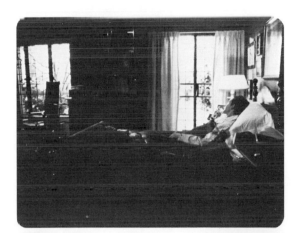

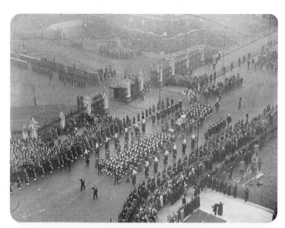

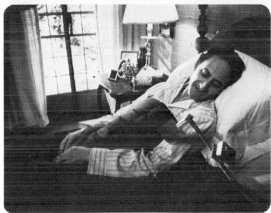

SPECIAL PHONES
30-second
VO: A lot of people take the telephone for granted. But
suppose you couldn't move your legs to walk to the phone . . .
. . . Couldn't move your hand to dial the phone . . .
Couldn't call the Fire Department . . .
Or talk to friends . . .
That's why we've designed special phones for special
people . . .
Phones that can open a new world . . .
Phones that are like . . .
(HE BLOWS ON CARD . . . DIAL TONE IS HEARD)
VO: . . . a breath of fresh air.
OPERATOR: Operator . . . may I help you?
VO: For more information, look under Disabled Services in
the Consumer Guide of your White Pages.

FUNERAL
30-second
(SFX: DISTANT ORGAN MUSIC AND HUSHED CROWD
WHISPERS.)
ANNCR: The only real difference between having some big
company kill your termites and Tindol kill your termites . . . is
how expensive the funeral's going to be.
So, this termite season, call the Tindols. Because you can't
buy a deader termite, only a more expensive way to kill it.

1497
Art Director: **Mike Ward**
Writers: **Roy Youngmark, John DeCerchio**
Client: **Canadian Tire**
Editor: **Andrew Brown**
Director: **Marty Lieberman**
Production Co.: **Linda Wolfe/Trio Films**
Agency: **W.B. Doner & Company Advertising**

1498
Art Director: **Curtis Loftis**
Writer: **Gabe Massimi**
Client: **The High Museum of Art**
Directors: **Jamie Cook, Curtis Loftis**
Production Co.: **Chuck Clemens/ Cook Clemens Prod.**
Agency: **Burton-Campbell, Inc.**

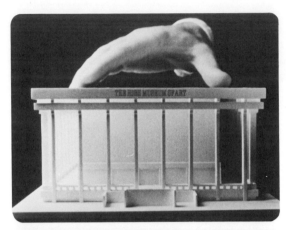

NOT VERY PRETTY
30-second
VO: What's going on inside your car's engine . . . isn't very pretty.
Corrosion can destroy modern engines which contain many alloys, including aluminum.
Ordinary anti-freeze can do little to stop it.
But new Perma-3 from Canadian Tire isn't ordinary. Perma 3's powerful corrosion inhibitors . . .
can help save your car's engine.
Perma 3 Anti-freeze from Canadian Tire. Helps stop corrosion . . . before corrosion stops you.

MODEL
30-second
ANNCR (VO): Most people think Atlanta's High Museum of art is that big building on Peachtree Street.
But take away . . . the Atlanta College of Art, Symphony Hall, The Alliance Theater, auditorium, lounges, and offices . . .
What's left is the High Museum . . . so small only one out of every five works of art can be displayed.
Help build a museum big enough for Atlanta . . . to replace that little building on Peachtree Street.

1499
Art Director: **Curtis Loftis**
Writer: **Gabe Massimi**
Client: **The High Museum of Art**
Director: **Jerry Wilson**
Production Co: **George
Booker/Booker-Wilson, Prod.**
Agency: **Burton-Campbell, Inc.**

1500
Art Directors: **Ron Howell, Larry Reinschmiedt**
Writer: **Paul Decker**
Client: **Soloflex, Inc.**
Producer: **Sherry Krizner**
Editor: **Greg Laube**
Director: **Santiago Suarez**
Production Co: **Ampersand Productions, Inc.**
Agency: **Chickering/Howell**

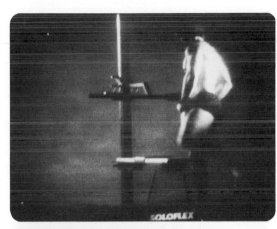

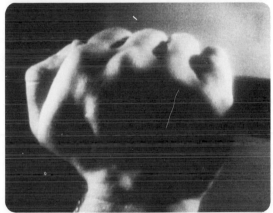

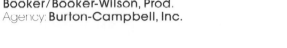

GUARD
30-second
ANNCR (VO): Atlanta's High Museum has over four thousand
works of art.
But only one out of five sees the light of day . . .
the rest are in storage. There just isn't enough room to show
them. The museum is too small . . . too small for most
traveling exhibits . . . like King Tut or Picasso . . . too small for
a great city like Atlanta.
Help build a new High Museum . . . help bring Atlanta's art
treasures out of the dark.

INCREDIBLE MACHINE
30-second
ANNCR: Presenting Soloflex . . .
The incredible machine that can help develop the body
you want . . . right in your own home.
ANNCR: SOLOFLEX . . .
ANNCR: For a free brochure, call this number.

1501
Art Directors: **Tom Kelly, Carol MacIntosh**
Writer: **Dave Newman**
Client: **Omark Industries, Consumer Products Group**
Editors: **Mike McNamara, Walt Dimmick**
Director: **Mike NcNamara**
Production Co.: **International Media Systems**
Agency: **Borders, Perrin and Norrander, Inc.**

1502
Art Directors: **Steven Rosenhaus, Roger Flint**
Designers: **Jim Dultz, Alex Hajdu**
Writer: **David Leddick**
Client: **Timex**
Editors: **Roger Flint, Hal Cohen**
Director: **Roger Flint**
Production Co.: **Flint Productions, Inc.**
Agency: **Grey Advertising, Inc.**

WOOD GRENADE
30-second
(OPEN ON KID STANDING AMONG SEVERAL LOGS READY
TO BE SPLIT; AX IS STUCK IN ONE LOG; HE'S GOT A WOOD
GRENADE IN HIS HAND.)
Splittin' firewood is tough . . . even for a guy like me.
(HE HOLDS UP GRENADE)
But this makes it almost easy.
The OREGON Wood Grenade.
(HE LOOKS AT IT IN HIS HAND)
Cute name.
(HE PLOPS IT ONTO A LOG IN FRONT OF HIM; ON THAT
ACTION, CUT TO PRODUCT DEMONSTRATION — CLOSEUPS)
The conical shape makes the Wood Grenade drive right
into a log . . . (POUND, POUND) . . . and breaks it to pieces
. . . fast.

NIGHTSKIES
30-second
ANNCR: "From the depths of space, from the edge of the
earth, Timex takes quartz to make a watch beyond time as
we know it. The new Timex. The new Timex Quartz. A watch
so accurate you may have to reset it only once this year.
Thin, sleek and more beautiful than any watch you've
owned before. Have the Timex of your life. The new,
affordable Timex Quartz."

1503
Art Directors: **Bob Egusa, Dennis Kuhr**
Cinematographer: **Norm Toback**
Writer: **Gary Wexler**
Client: **Straw Hat Pizza**
Editor: **Gary Freund**
Director: **Norm Toback**
Producer: **Michael Porte**
Production Co: **Associates & Toback**
Agency: **McCann-Erickson, Inc.**

1504
Art Director: **Dick Rucker**
Writer: **Jim Nicoll**
Client: **Chevrolet Motor Division**
Editor: **Harvey Schlags**
Director of Broadcast: **Dennis Plansker**
Director: **Dick Rucker**
Agency: **Campbell-Ewald Co.**

HAT SALESMAN, REV. 1
30-second
CONWAY: You sell hats, don't ya?
COUNTER BOY: Oh, yes sir. We do.
CONWAY: Oh good, so do I. I'd like to show you some
samples. I got beanies, berets. I have a fez with an electric
tassel.
COUNTER BOY: No. We sell hot hats.
CONWAY: I'm strictly legit.
COUNTER BOY: Oh, no sir. Hot Hat Sandwiches. Ham and
Cheese, Meatballs, and more. Each wrapped in pizza
dough and baked to a golden brown.
CONWAY: Now, is that formal wear?
COUNTER BOY: Oh, no sir. You don't wear them, you
eat them.
CONWAY: Oh, well, give me one with a pastrami in six and

SINGLEPERSON
30-second
(MUSIC: UP THROUGHOUT)
VO: Why is our Citation X-11 such a hero with
performance-minded Americans?
Let's ask SINGLEPERSON
SINGLE PERSON: Citation X-11. SUPER CAR — the handling is
impressive, yet I've got 40 cubic feet of space here for all
my toys.
More amazing, it carries five adults comfortably.
VO: Then your Citation X-11 will fit right in when you're
married and have kids?
SINGLE PERSON: I'm going to pretend   you never said
that.
SINGERS: CHEVY MAKES GOOD THINGS HAPPEN

1505

Art Director: **Kerry Colonna**
Designer: **Kerry Colonna**
Photographer: **Michael Lawler**
Computer Camerman: **Tony Venezia**
Artist: **David Blum**
Writer: **Hal Silverman**
Client: **Volkswagen of America, Inc.**
Editor: **Marcia Dripchak**
Director, Technical: **R.T. Taylor, Clint Colver**
Producer: **Tim Bloch/Midocean Motion Pictures**
Agency: **Doyle Dane Bernbach**

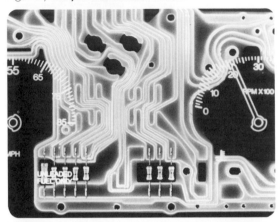

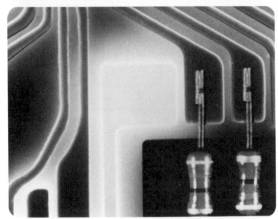

UPSHIFT
30-second
How do you know exactly when to shift gears to get top gas
mileage?
Until now only an engineer could tell you that.
But now there's a car that can tell you.
How does it tell you?
By making this little dashboard light go on. Shift up each
time you see it and you save up to seven percent on gas.
Where can you find that kind of science fiction technology?
Only in an '82 Volkswagen in case you hadn't guessed.

1506

Art Director: **Chris Armstrong**
Writer: **Geoff Moore**
Client: **General Foods/Lean Strips**
Editor: **David Lee**
Director: **Elbert Budin**
Producer: **Michael Delgato/
Ampersand Produc.**
Agency: **Ogilvy & Mather, Inc.**

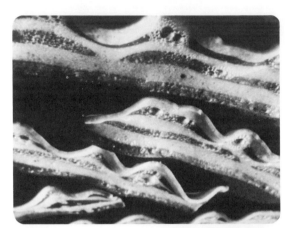

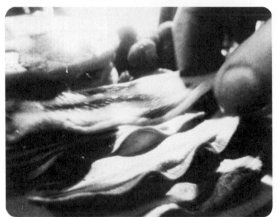

REJOICE
30-second
(MUSIC UNDER: "ODE TO JOY")
It has . . .
no cholesterol, only 25 calories a strip, and it's not bacon. It's
Lean Strips.
The delicious alternative to bacon. Lean Strips sizzle and
smell and taste like bacon.
Yet they're made with soy beans, egg whites, and wheat . . .
so they have no cholesterol and only 25 calories a strip,
So . . .
If you are a bacon lover . . .
Rejoice!
(MUSIC UP AND OUT)

1507
Art Directors: **Bill Murphy, Chuck Beisch**
Writers: **Chris Rowean, Mark Lawrence**
Client: **Preview Subscription Television**
Editor: **Viz Wiz—Boston/VideoCom—Dedham**
Director: **Harry Hamburg**
Producer: **N. Lee Lacy**
Agency: **Ingalls Associates**

1508
Art Director: **Vera Carbo**
Writer: **Alan Johnson**
Client: **Tastykake**
Editor: **Peter Stassi/Start mark**
Director: **Santiago Suarez/Ampersand**
Producer: **Michael DelGado/Ampersand**
Agency: **Weightman, Inc.**

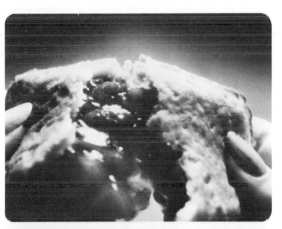

PRICE
30-second
ORSON WELLES: If you want to see a good movie, well you can go spend four dollars, eat overpriced popcorn and sit next to a stranger . . . or . . . for the price of a candy bar you may view exactly the same film at home . . . and see over 50 fine films every month. Uncut. Each for the price of a candy bar? That's ridiculous! No, that's Preview. Call now. It's the best show in town.
SINGERS: P-R-E-V-I-E-W

TASTYKAKE
30-second
"Nobody bakes a cake as tasty as a Tastykake"

1509
Art Director: **Karen Stivers**
Writer: **Bert Huebener**
Client: **The New Chrysler Corporation/Dodge**
Editor: **Suzanne Pancrazi**
Director: **John Stephens**
Production Co.: **Hisk**
Agency: **K&E/Lee Zimmerman**

1510
Art Director: **Dave Bradley**
Writers: **Jim Longstaff, Jim Stein**
Client: **Ray-O-Vac**
Editor: **Chris Kern**
Director: **Howard Morris**
Production Co.: **Coast Productions, Hollywood**
Agency: **Campbell-Mithun, Inc.**

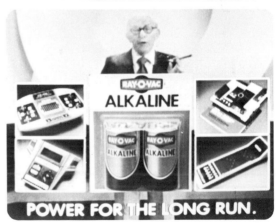

DODGE CHARGER 2.2
30-second
ANNCR: If you want a machine that really moves you, the
'81 Cobra, Datsun 280ZX, Porsche 924 and Trans Am are the
ones to beat. And here's a machine that does.
Dodge Charger 2.2.
Charger leaves them all behind . . . in mileage and
acceleration.
0 to 50 in 6.6 seconds.
Dodge Charger 2.2
Under $7300
America's Driving Machine.
Get $300 to $1000 cash on select new Dodge cars and
trucks.
See participating dealers for complete details.

GEORGE BURNS
30-second
VOA: George Burns.
GEORGE: That's my name, too.
VOA: George, what's the secret of long life?
GEORGE: Ray-O-Vac Alkaline batteries.
VOA: Ray-O-Vac Alkaline batteries?
GEORGE: They'll play the Minute Waltz 4000 times . . . or . . .
TAPE: (GEORGE SINGS) You're the flower of my heart, Sweet
Alkaline.
GEORGE: (TO GIRL) Pretty . . . you too . . . too tall.
VOA: But the secret of long life can't be a battery!
GEORGE: (OPENING COAT TO REVEAL BATTERIES). Are you
kidding? (POINTS TO 1 BATTERY) This one's for dancing.
VOA: Ray-O-Vac Alkalines really are the secret of long life.
2ND VOA: Ray-O-Vac Alkaline.
GEORGE: Power for the long run.

1511
Art Director: **Warren Margulies**
Photographer: **Dejan Georgevich**
Writer/Creative Director: **Buddy Radisch**
Client: **MasterCard International**
Editor: **Tony Marino**
Director: **Sol Goodnoff**
Producer: **W. Hamilton/Lee Rothberg Prods.**
Agency: **William Esty Company**

1512
Art Director: **Mel Abert**
Designer: **Mel Abert**
Writer: **Linda Chandler Frohman**
Client: **Brentwood Savings &
Loan Association**
Editor: **Stuart Waks**
Director: **Reid Miles**
Productions Co.: **Reid Miles, Inc.**
Agency: **Abert, Newhoff & Burr, Inc.**

LIGHT TALK
30-second
SPOKESMAN: Now, you can shop with money in your
checking account and never write the check.
MasterCard II
It looks almost like the MasterCard card.
It's accepted like the credit card around the world
and goes through the imprinter the same way, but what you
spend is paid from your personal checking account. No bills,
no interest. That's it.
It looks like a credit card, but MasterCard II works like a
check. Carry both
You'll want the II too.
CHORUS SINGS: "We can do it all!"

BRENTWOOD SAVINGS
30-second
(MUSIC: MOOD MUSIC SCORED UNDER)
GEORGE BURNS: So long, sweetheart. That was my bank
teller, Louise. I just told her that I was withdrawing from the
bank. She was so upset, she refused to validate my parking.
What can a man do? Brentwood is offering me a service
called the "Interest Checking Account." So now I can do
both my checking and saving at Brentwood. That's
convenient. And Brentwood will also pay me interest on my
checking account. Louise, you paid me compliments . . .
but, sweetheart, now Brentwood is paying me interest.

1513
Art Director: **Ron McCroby**
Writer/Producer: **Ron McCroby**
Client: **Kenner Products**
Producer: **Kent Wakeford, Los Angeles**
Agency: **Sive Associates**

1514
Art Director: **Harvey Baron**
Writer: **Francine Wilvers**
Client: **Warner Communications/Atari**
Editor: **Morty Ashkinos**
Director: **Michael Ulick**
Production Co.: **Michael Ulick Productions**
Agency: **Doyle Dane Bernbach**

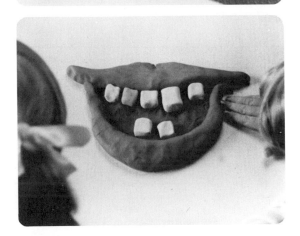

PLAY-DOH 4-PACK
30-second
MOM: "When you give your child a 4-pack of Play-Doh in regular or bright day-glo colors . . .
you give fun that lasts as long as their imagination!"
KIDS VOCAL: "Play-Doh is . . .
squishing and squashing . . .
a little tiny mouse.
Play-Doh is . . . shaping and rolling . . .
a great big house.
Trees and frogs, monsters and logs.
A fierce alligator . . .
a volcano crater . . .
a wide, wide smile.
You can make it with . . .
Play-Doh!"
PLAY-DOH BOY: "From Kenner."

MARTIAN FAMILY
30-second
MARTIAN WOMAN (VO): Dear Atari Anonymous, ever since my husband Luno returned from Earth with Asteroids, the new Atari home video game, he and the rest of the family do nothing but play Asteroids.
Luno says Asteroids is good practice for his interplanetary flights.
WOMAN (ON CAMERA): Biddy biddy. Biddy biddy.
WOMAN (VO): Tell me, Dear Atari Anonymous, with everybody hooked on Asteroids, what on earth is a poor Martian mother to do?
ANNCR (VO): New Atari Asteroids, now available for your home.

1515
Art Director: **Bill Yamada**
Writer: **Joe Nunziata**
Client: **G.T.E.**
Editor: **Joe Laliker/Pelco**
Director: **Ron Finley**
Producer: **Jim Callan/Ron Finley Films**
Agency: **Doyle Dane Bernbach**

1516
Art Director: **Bob Dion**
Writer: **Bob Chandler**
Client: **Skipper's**
Director: **John Urie**
Production Co.: **Videography**
Agency: **Chiat/Day**

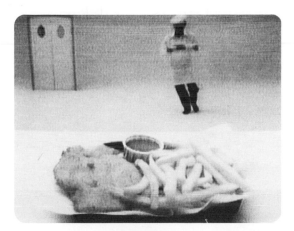

FLIPPED-OUT HIP CHICK
30-second
(MUSIC UNDER)
ANNCR (VO): People all over are flipping over the new GTE
Flip-Phone.
Some flip over
(GIRL FLIPS)
its sleek style.
Others flip over the way it redials
(MAN FLIPS)
. . . at the touch of a button.
While some flip because it's so light.
(WOMAN FLIPS)
But everybody flips over the new Flip-Phone, because the
Flip-Phone flips.

HARD CHOICES W/BEER
30-second
(MUSIC IN AND UNDER: FAST PACED)
VO: The Seafood Choice Meal at Skipper's . . .
VO: . . . you get a tasty cod fillet and fries . . .
(MUSIC CARRIES.)
VO: . . . coleslaw and chowder.
VO: Then you'll have to make up your mind.
VO: Will you also have tender fried clams . . .
(MUSIC CARRIES.)
VO: . . . or succulent scallops
VO: . . . or delicious Gulf shrimp?
VO: Then will it be a large soft drink . . .
VO: . . . or a beer?
VO: Well, make up your mind. For only $3.99. At Skipper's.
Where you get good seafood without getting soaked.

1517
Art Director: **Celia Johnson**
Writers: **Harvey Herman, Chas. Rosner**
Client: **MTA**
Editor: **Harvey Eckhart**
Director: **Harvey Herman**
Production Co.: **Len Lipson/Lipson Film**
Agency: **Herman & Rosner Enterprises, Inc.**

1518
Art Director: **John Armistead**
Designer: **John Armistead**
Writer: **Linda Chandler Frohman**
Client: **Universal Studios Tour**
Editor: **Rick Ross**
Directors: **Stu Berg, Rick Ross**
Producer: **Robert Abel**
Agency: **Abert, Newhoff & Burr, Inc.**

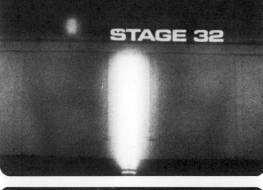

MTA CHAIN SNATCHING
30-second
MAN'S VOICE: (SOFT, SOOTHING.) What are you wearing? A gold or silver chain? You think it looks attractive right? So do other people. People who steal things.
"It's chain-snatching season. Last year the Transit Police made 800 Chain-Snatching arrests, but they can't be everywhere all the time. So when you're out on the buses and subways, tuck in your chains. Don't flash your bracelets, turn your rings so the stones don't show.
"If you want to keep it please, don't flaunt it".
"We're working to make things safer. You can help".

NEW SOUND STAGE
30-second
VO: Universal Studios proudly invites you to discover how some of the most spectacular moments in film history were created, and you might take part of the magic. The Special Effects Stage is now open to the public.

1519
Art Director: **Arnold Levine**
Designer: **Patricia Kiesling**
Writers: **Mark Levitt, Ted Nugent**
Client: **CBS Records**
Editor: **John Carter**
Director: **Arnold Levine**
Production Co: **Yvonne May & Robbie Tucker,
CBS Records**

1520
Art Director: **John Constable**
Writers: **Steve Laughlin, Dennis Frankenberry**
Client: **WITI, TV6**
Director: **Viv Mainwaring/
The Black Swan, Inc.**
Producer: **Steve Laughlin/
The Black Swan, Inc.**
Agency: **Frankenberry, Laughlin &
Constable, Inc.**

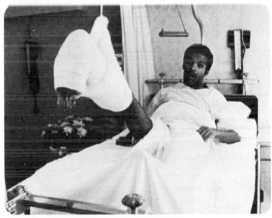

TED NUGENT
30-second
MUSIC — SFX

RIGHT & WRONG
30-second
(MUSIC: COMEDIC TRACK UP & UNDER)
(SFX: BROKEN GLASS.)
VO: With all the things that go wrong in life, isn't it nice to
know there's someone who makes things right? Tom Hooper
and Contact 6. Only on TV6 News. At six and ten.

1525
Art Director: **Nick Rice**
Writer: **Terry Bremer**
Client: **University of Minnesota Gophers**
Director: **Steve Griak**
Production Co.: **Em Com/Wison-Griak,
Nick Rice, Terry Bremer**
Agency: **Chuck Ruhr Advertising, Inc.**

1526
Art Director: **Ron McCroby**
Writer: **Ron McCroby**
Client: **Kenner Products**
Production Co.: **Chambers & Associates,
Los Angeles**
Agency: **Sive Associates, Inc.**

DAVID AND GOLIATH
30-second
DAVID: (WHISTLING MINNESOTA FIGHT SONG.)
(EARTH SHAKING GRUMBLE.)
(SOUND OF FOOTBALL SOARING THROUGH THE AIR AND
HITTING GOLIATH IN THE NOSE.)
Celebrate one hundred years of Gopher football as we
take on the giants of the Big Ten. Be a Gopher fan. Again.

KRAZY CLONE LABORATORY
30-second
SPOOKY ANNCR: "It's Kenner's Krazy Clone Laboratory. Just
add water and mix!
Stir the mix . . . until it's right!
Stick in your finger . . .
what a sight!
Wait a few minutes, then pour the mix into the mold . . .
to make a finger . . .
that looks like your own!
Hand, fingers and toes, one by one . . .
Krazy Clone Laboratory's . . .
lots of fun!
Ha! Ha! Ha!
Krazy Clone Laboratory!
From Kenner."

1527
Art Director: **Richard Williams**
Writer: **Dave Allemeier**
Client: **Anheuser-Busch, Inc.—Natural Light**
Director: **Brian Gibson**
Producers: **Craig MacGowan, N. Lee Lacy**
Agency: **D'Arcy-MacManus & Masius,
St. Louis**

1528
Art Director: **Harvey Baron**
Writer: **Francine Wilvers**
Client: **Warner Communications, Atari**
Director: **Michael Ulick**
Production Co: **Michael Ulick Productions**
Agency: **Doyle Dane Bernbach**

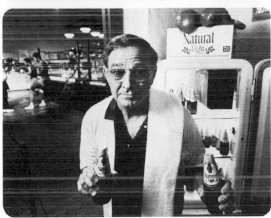

ANGELO DUNDEE
30-second
NORM (VO): Hey, look who's drinkin' Natural Light!
ANGELO: Sure, you never saw Angelo Dundee with a loser,
did ya?
NORM (VO): I bet I know why a rough and fumble guy goes
for Natural.
ANGELO: You been fightin' without a mouthpiece?
NORM (VO): You like it for all those rich natural ingredients.
ANGELO: Yeah, 'cause Natural Light packs taste. Every
mouthful is a left, a right, a left. Then, it goes down easy. For
me, the taste of Natural knocks the other lights . . . out!
(SFX: BELL)
NORM (VO): Alright!
ANNCR (VO): Natural Light from Anheuser-Busch. Taste is
why you'll switch.
ANGELO: Wanna go another round?

EMPTY SCREEN
30-second
BOY: As an intelligent consumer, I wanted to compare Atari
Asteroids with other companies Asteroids. But other
companies don't make Asteroids.
I wanted to compare Atari Missile Command with other
companies Missile Command. But other companies don't
make that, either.
Finally, I wanted to compare the new Atari Warlords.
Unfortunately, other companies don't make it.
When it comes to the video games the world wants most,
nobody compares to Atari.

1529
Art Director: **Burton Blum**
Writer: **Bill Murtha**
Client: **Ford Dealers of New Jersey**
Director: **Fred Levenson**
Producer: **Mary Ellen Pirozzoli**
Agencies: **Rosenfeld, Sirowitz & Lawson, Inc.
& Gallagher Group, Inc.**

1530
Art Director: **Celester Santee**
Creative Director: **Ken Duskin**
Writer: **Alan Mond**
Client: **The New Chrysler
Corporation—Plymouth**
Editor: **Morty Perlstein**
Director: **Melvin Sokolsky**
Production Co.: **Sunlight Pictures**
Agency Prod.: **K&E—Burns Patterson**

The American way to get your moneysworth.

YOUR WORLD/RALLY
30-second
BOSS (VO): Will ya bring down Smitty's EXP?
ANNCR (VO): the only thing that compares to
owning a new FORD EXP is driving one.
Behind the wheel you'll experience
its world class technology . . .
first-hand.
Its ready response to the wheel . . .
its surefooted stance . . .
the sheer excitement of a personal sport coupe.
Experience EXP right here . . . in your world.
ATTENDANT: Smitty . . . you're lookin' good!
(SFX: ELECTRONIC SFX.)
ANNCR: Your Ford Dealer's got what it takes
for your world.

VEGETABLE STAND: '81 PRICE VERS.
30-second
(SFX UNDER: OUTDOOR, HIGHWAY PRESENCE)
JOHN HOUSEMAN (OC): A time comes when you must
watch your money carefully. So quality and value are a
necessity. Can you find them in an American car?
Absolutely. In Plymouth, yes, Plymouth. The new Horizon
Miser; built with advanced technology and front-wheel-drive
for the best gasoline economy of any American car. Five
passenger Horizon Miser.
And not a penny more than '81.
It's the American way to get your moneysworth.

1531
Art Director: **John Armistead**
Designer: **John Armistead**
Writer: **Linda Chandler Frohman**
Client: **Brentwood Savings & Loan
Association**
Editor: **Stuart Waks**
Director: **Reid Miles**
Production Co.: **Reid Miles, Inc.**
Agency: **Abert, Newhoff & Burr, Inc.**

1532
Art Director: **Gary Goldsmith**
Writer: **Christine Osborne**
Client: **Polaroid Corporation**
Editor: **Pelco**
Director: **Mark Storey**
Production Co.: **Pfeiffer, Storey, Inc.**
Agency/Producer: **Doyle Dane Bernbach,
Joseph Scibetta**

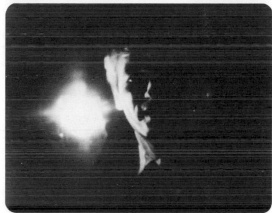

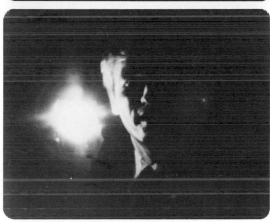

NEW KEOGH/IRA
30-second
CONSCIENCE: George, wake up, it's your conscience.
GEORGE BURNS: I go out with younger women. How else
can I meet their mothers?
CONSCIENCE: No George, I'm talking about your retirement.
Listen, at Brentwood everybody can now put up to two
thousand dollars into an I.R.A. account. And if you're
self-employed, up to fifteen thousand into a Keogh plan.
They're tax-deferred, George.
BURNS: But who's retiring?
CONSCIENCE: George, one day you won't be a sex symbol
anymore.
BURNS: So I'll wear makeup.
VO: Brentwood Savings. It's a nice place to visit your money.

HOW WOULD THEY KNOW
30-second
This is Polaroid's wafer-thin Polapulse battery.
It powers a unique new automotive warning signal:
Polaroid's Safety Flasher.
So compact and lightweight, you can wear it for protection
when you run, ride your bike, or walk your dog. With the
Safety Flasher, you're visible at night over a mile away.
Without it, how would anyone know you're there?
The Safety Flasher. New from the Polaroid Battery Division.

1533
Art Director: **Fern H. Cohen**
Designer: **Fern H. Cohen**
Writer: **Anne Cifu**
Client: **Laser Beams**
Editor: **Jeff Cahn Editorial**
Director: **Klaus Lucka**
Producer: **Robert Goldblatt**
Agency: **AC&R Advertising, Inc.**

1535
Art Director: **Joe Shelesky**
Designer: **Joe Shelesky**
Client: **Bill Booth**
Producer: **Tex East/Coane Productions**
Agency: **Wunderman, Ricotta & Kline**

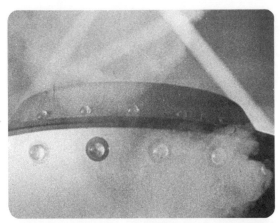

LASER BEAMS
30-second
We saw the future
and it wore Laser Beams.
Laser Beams sweatsuiting
in laser light colors.
His . . . hers . . . yours.
Laser Beams sweatsuiting!
Interconnect . . .
Inter-cut . . .
Interchange . . .
Inter-play.
We saw the future and it wore Laser Beams.

THE GREAT OUTDOORS-ALL PAPERS
30-second
(MUSIC UNDER)
ANNCR (VO): Two things we have plenty of here in Maine.
The great outdoors and time. Time to do things right.
One man took our love of the outdoors and our habit of
careful work and turned it into a worldwide business. His
name was L.L. Bean.
He gave the world outdoor products that he knew were
right because he used them himself.
Clothing tough enough for the wilderness yet sporty enough
for a day in town.
And as for service, he'd send you a missing button
20 years later.
Well, the world's a lot faster since L.L. Bean began, but here
in Maine,

1536
Art Director: **Preuit Holland**
Writer: **Steve Bassett**
Client: **Carolina Power & Light Company**
Producer: **Preuit Holland/Digital Effects**
Agency: **McKinney Silver & Rockett**

1537
Art Director: **Matt Basile**
Writers: **Ken Musto, Klaus Gensheimer**
Client: **Gulf**
Director: **D. Devries**
Producers: **Manny Perez, Ian Shand**
Agency: **Young & Rubicam**

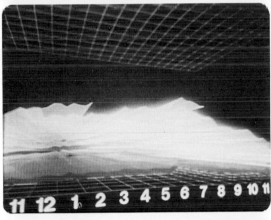

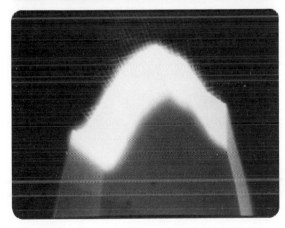

PIKE'S PEAK
30-second
VO: Pike's Peak, the time of day the Pike family uses the most electricity. Add Brown's Peak, Johnson's Peak, and over half a million others, all happening at the same time, and that's CP&L's Peak.
(PAUSE)
And the bigger our peak gets, the more expensive electricity will get. Use less during peak periods. Beat the peak—before it beats us.
SUPER: BEAT THE PEAK.
Carolina Power & Light

GRAVEYARD
30-second
WOMAN: Didn't have to happen, Harold.
HAROLD: I know.
WOMAN: Should've taken better care.
HAROLD: I know.
ANNCR (VO): Thousands of cars meet their fate before their time. That's why there's Gulfpride Motor Oil, an oil so tough, it was tested over a million miles without a single engine failure.
HAROLD: Next time I'll take better care.
MAN: Protect your engine with Gulfpride, the tough oil. It could save you a lot of grief.

1538
Art Director: **Anestos Trichonis**
Photographer: **Adrian Lyon**
Writer: **David Leddick**
Client: **Revlon**
Producer: **John Greene/Grey, Jennienco Co.**
Agency: **Grey Advertising, Inc.**

1539
Art Director: **Doug Bartow**
Writer: **Janis Gott**
Client: **Bloomingdales**
Producer: **Bruce Allen, Grey, Harrison Productions**
Agency: **Grey Advertising, Inc.**

WATERMELON I
30-second
ANNCR (VO): Now there's . . .
(MUSIC UNDER)
. . . Lipcolor that you can't . . .
eat off!
It's new . . .
. . . from Natural Wonder.
This could be your first lipstick
. . . with eat-and-drink proof color!
Natural Wonder has
A unique double-color formula . . .
. . . so it stays on . . .
. . . while you munch . . .
. . . brunch or lunch.
But is it kissproof?

PARTY WHISPER SOFT SATIN
30-second
ERIN: That award-winning playwrite finds some of his best
material at Bloomingdale's Talk of the Town White Sale.
Discover the true meaning of sensuality in the Ultra Satin
ensemble of Whispersoft.
No-iron satin sheets with contrast piping. In ultra-rich shades.
And to top off your most memorable evenings? Warm,
luxurious color-coordinated comforters. All very exciting. And
all at White Sale Savings.
At the Talk of the Town White Sale at Bloomingdale's
It's like no other store in the world.

1540
Art Director: **Frank DeVito**
Writer: **George Miller**
Client: **William Schermerhorn**
Editor: **Steve Bodner/Follow Ciro**
Director: **Melvin Sokolsky**
Production Co.: **Sunlight Pictures Corp.**
Agency: **Young & Rubicam**

1541
Art Director: **Joe Sedelmaier**
Writer: **Tom McElligott**
Client: **Mr. Coffee**
Editor: **Peggy DeLay**
Director: **Joe Sedelmaier**
Production Co.: **Sedelmaier Film Productions Inc.**
Agency: **Marketing Communications Inc.**

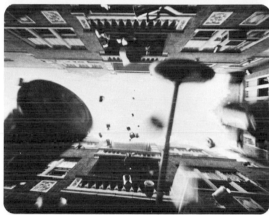

WHISTLING
60-second
DAVID: (WHISTLING) I drink Dr Pepper and I'm proud
I used to be alone in a crowd
But now you look around these days
There seems to be a Dr Pepper craze
. . . I'm a Pepper, he's a
pepper, she's a pepper . . .
DAVID: (WHISTLING) He's a Pepper
MICKEY: (WHISTLING) Uh uh.
MICKEY: (WHISTLING) Whew! I'm a Pepper
ALL: (WHISTLING) Wouldn't you like to be a Pepper too?
ALL: (WHISTLING) Be a Pepper, Drink Dr Pepper
Be a Pepper, Drink Dr Pepper.

ANGRY
60-second
(NATURAL SFX THROUGHOUT)
(MUSIC UNDER)
ANNCR (VO): All across America, people are getting fed up with bad coffee.
Fortunately, they have an alternative: Mr. Coffee. Only Mr. Coffee precisely controls coffee brewing time and temperature for perfect coffee every time. Mr Coffee . . . America's perfect coffee maker with a patent to prove it.

1542
Art Director: **Jim Perretti**
Writer: **Larry Cadman**
Client: **Volvo of America Corporation**
Editor: **Steve Schreiber/Editor's Gas**
Director: **Rick Levine**
Producer: **Richard Berke (SMS)/Levine Pytka
& Association**
Agency: **Scali, McCabe, Sloves, Inc.**

1543
Art Director: **Boyd Jacobson**
Designer: **Boyd Jacobson**
Photographer: **Haskell Wexler**
Writer: **John van der Zee**
Client: **Wells Fargo Bank**
Director: **Boyd Jacobson**
Producer: **Jim Allen (McCann)/Wexler-Hall
Productions**
Agency: **McCann-Erickson, Inc.**

COUNTRY CLUB
60-second
PA: Attention please will the owner of . . . the blue
Mercedes, license number (STATIC) please come to the
parking lot. Your car has been in a minor accident.
VO: If you're looking for a well-built European luxury sedan
. . . that offers the amenities a person of means expects . . .
but you don't . . .
want to follow . . .
the crowd,
consider a Volvo.
It's not outrageously priced.
And it's not for people who are running around . . .
looking for status.
WOMAN: Your drink Mr. Baily?
VO: Volvo's a car for people who already have it.

CHRISTMAS
60-second
MUSIC — SFX

1544
Art Director: **Bob Gage**
Photographer: **Ernesto Caparros**
Writer: **Jack Dillon**
Client: **Polaroid Corporation**
Editor: **Pelco**
Director: **Bob Gage**
Production Co.: **Director's Studio Inc.,/
Rose Presley, Eugene Mazzola,
Joseph Scibetta, Jane Liepshutz**
Agency: **Doyle Dane Bernbach**

1545
Art Director: **Sam Scali**
Writer: **Geoffrey Frost**
Client: **Sperry Corporation**
Editor: **Howard Lazarus**
Production Cos.: **Bob Giraldi Productions/
C.P.C. Assocs., Inc. (Special Effects)**
Director: **Bob Giraldi**
Producer: **Richard Berke (SMS)**
Agency: **Scali, McCabe, Sloves, Inc.**

JIM'S BIG NIGHT
60-second
JIM: Come on, we're late.
MARI: It's just a party!
JIM: Polaroid's giving in my honor.
MARI: You don't know that.
JIM: Why else would they ask us?
MESS: (HANDS OVER PACKAGE) Polaroid wanted you to get this before the party.
JIM: Who's this party for, do you know?
MESS: I don't know, some old guy.
MARI: Alright, I'm Beautiful
What's that?
JIM: Oh, probably some award they're giving me . . . No it's their new Time-Zero OneStep.
MARI: Did they engrave it?

HISTORY II
60-second
ANNCR (VO): Bruised by his new bicycle's bone-rattling ride,
a ten year-old complains.
And his father listens.
Looking for a way to cushion the bumps, John Dunlop
invents the inflatable tire.
For twenty-seven years . . .
automobiles had been reserved for the rich.
But a young American engineer . . .
hears what the world really wants —
a car anyone can afford —
and changes the shape of a century.
At Sperry, history has convinced us
that listening inspires new inventions, ignites new thoughts,
uncovers whole new worlds of fresh ideas.

1546
Art Director: **Anthony Angotti**
Writer: **Tom Thomas**
Client: **Xerox Corporation**
Director: **Dick Loew**
Agency: **Needham, Harper & Steers, Inc.**

1547   SILVER AWARD
Art Director: **Bob Tore**
Writer: **Tom Mabley**
Client: **IBM Corporation**
Editor: **Alan Rozek**
Director: **Jeff Lovinger**
Production Co: **Lovinger, Tardio, Melsky Inc.**
Agency: **Lord, Geller, Federico, Einstein Inc.**
Agency Producer: **Robert Dein**

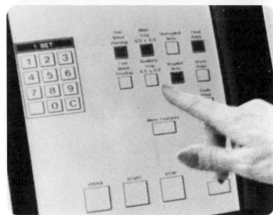

MOZART
60-second
(SFX: MOZART MUSIC)
ANNCR (VO): It's been said that when Mozart is performed
before an audience of chickens . . . an interesting thing
happens . . .
. . . productivity increases.
That's fine for hen houses.
Now, what can be done for offices.
Xerox can help. With advanced machines that copy, sort
and even reduce as fast as two pages a second.
Machines that let you process information faster than
humanly possible.
That print out computer information must faster than ordinary
computer printers.
Even a special Ethernet cable that lets office machines work

HOUSE
60-second
VO: The very first computers
seemed as big as houses
and so mysterious,
that for most of us
the computer was behind a closed door.
But IBM was thinking how to
make the computer more useful,
and as one good idea lead to another
it began getting smaller . . . faster . . .
. . . less expensive . . . and easier to use.
Today, a new IBM computer has reached
a personal scale.
A person can afford it.
A person can put it anywhere,

1548
Art Director: **Jeff Young**
Writers: **Mark Schneider, John Gruen**
Client: **General Foods Corporation**
Editor: **Steve Schreiber**
Director: **Rick Levine**
Production Co.: **Skip Allocco, Levine-Pytka & Assoc.**
Agency: **Ogilvy & Mather**

1549
Art Director: **Bob Gage**
Photographer: **Ernesto Caparros**
Writer: **Jack Dillon**
Client: **Polaroid Corporation**
Editor: **Pelco**
Director: **Bob Gage**
Production Co.: **Director's Studio, Inc./ Rose Presley, Eugene Mazzola**
Agency Producers: **Doyle Dane Bernbach, Joseph Scibetta, Jane Liepshutz**

CARIN'
60-second
(MUSIC UNDER)
Tis the season, people caring.
Helping others, time for sharing.
WOMAN: Coffee Mrs. Jones?
SONG: Everyone is warming up
with the taste of Maxwell House.
People that you've come to count on,
friendships that are true.
Spend some time with friends and
loved ones . . .
Maxwell House and you.
Get that "Good to the Last Drop"
Feeling . . . with Maxwell House.
Only Maxwell House.

SILHOUETTE
60-second
JIM: Now you don't worry where the sun is when you take a picture.
MARI: As long as it's on what you're shooting
JIM: No more. Now the sun can be behind you, in front of you or not even out.
MARI: The sun's gotta be somewhere.
JIM: Got it right in here. There's a piece of the sun in Polaroid's new Sun Camera
MARI: Not the real sun?
JIM: Don't quibble. It's a new system with the fastest color print film made. 600 speed. Now you can turn bad light into good pictures. Here I'll shoot you with the sun behind you.
MARI: You'll get a silhouette.
JIM: (WHOOSH!) Not any more.

1550
Art Director: **Barry Littmann**
Photographer: **Jim Dickson**
Writer: **Matt de Garmo**
Client: **United States Air Force**
Editor: **Frameworks**
Director: **Bernie Haber**
Production Co.: **Gil Rosoff/**
Horizon Studios
Agency: **D'Arcy, MacManus & Masius**

1551 DISTINGUISHED MERIT
Art Director: **Lynn Crosswaite**
Writer: **Bob Scarpelli**
Client: **McDonald's Corporation**
Editor: **Tim McGuire, Cutters**
Director: **Dan Nichols**
Production Co.: **Michael/Daniel Productions**
Agency: **Needham, Harper & Steers**

ON THE JOB (WHISTLING)
60-second
(WHISTLING: "THE AIR FORCE SONG")
(WHISTLING SEGUES INTO AN ORCHESTRATION OF "THE AIR FORCE SONG")
(MUSIC CONTINUES UNDER VOICE-OVER)
"There's a spirit in the air. Find out how you can be a part of it.
Air Force.
A Great Way of Life."
(ORCHESTRATION OF THE "AIR FORCE SONG" NOW SEGUES BACK TO ONE MAN WHISTLING.)

BEST FRIENDS—BREAK
60-second
DENISE (VO): Chrissie's my very best friend in the whole world. We're exactly alike. We both have trouble with math.
CHRISSIE (OC): What's the square root of 164?
DENISE (VO): We both love horses. And we both hate our hair.
GIRLS (OC): Yuck!!
DENISE (VO): We even liked the same guy. Then we found out he likes Marcia Wilk.
GIRLS (OC): Marcia Wilk?!
SINGERS: No two are closer than you
She shares in all that you do
A best friend's someone to care
Someone who'll always be there
Everything is more fun

1552
Art Director: **Jeff Young**
Writers: **Mark Schneider, John Gruen**
Client: **General Foods Corporation**
Editor: **Steve Schreiber**
Director: **Bill Hudson**
Production Co.: **Ed Kleban/Bill Hudson Films**
Agency: **Ogilvy & Mather**

1553
Art Director: **Neil Leinwohl**
Writer: **David Cantor**
Client: **Ad Council**
Director: **Lear Levin**
Agency: **Needham, Harper & Steers**

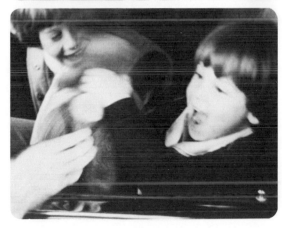

A REAL TROOPER
60-second
(SFX: BUGLE)
SONG: Mornings seem to start out better,
KIDS: Camping!
SONG: You seem to go much better,
MOM: Coffee?
DAD: Yeah.
SONG: When you start your day together.
You and Maxwell House.
DAD: Alright, now go get the bags, Okay?
SONG: Flavor that you've come to count on.
DAD: Coffee ready?
SONG: Taste that's always true.
OLDER CHILD: You don't take bunnies . . . .
SONG: What a perfect combination. Maxwell House and you.

VERNON PARISH
60-second
In Vernon Parish, Louisiana, volunteers are modifying
disabled people's homes to make them more accessible.
In fact, all across America, disabled and non-disabled
people are participating in similar community programs.
This is the International Year of Disabled Persons. Is this the
year you get involved?
Call the office of your Mayor or County Commissioner for
more information.

1554
Art Director: **Neil Leinwohl**
Writer: **David Cantor**
Client: **Ad Council**
Director: **Lear Levin**
Agency: **Needham, Harper & Steers, Inc.**

1555   SILVER AWARD
Art Director: **Herm Siegel**
Writer: **Stafford Ordahl, Jr.**
Client: **St. Regis Paper Company**
Editor: **First Edition**
Director: **Fred Levinson**
Production Co.: **Fred Levinson Productions**
Agency: **Cunningham & Walsh Inc.**

COMPOSITE
60-second
ANNCR (VO): At Mama Grisanti's restaurant in Louisville,
Kentucky, blind people don't have to ask what's on the
menu.
They can read it themselves . . . in Braille.
The Braille menus are there because a group of local
people thought it would be a good idea.
They got together and made it happen.
In fact, all across America, people are participating in
similar community programs.
In Vernon Parish, Louisiana, volunteers are modifying
disabled people's homes to make them more accessible.
And in Champagne, Illinois disabled children are able to
share a playground because a group of volunteers got
involved.

BOXER
60-second
BOXING ANNCR: Ladies and gentelmen,
in this corner
the former heavyweight champion of the world
Smokin'
Joe
Frazier!
And in this corner St. Regis with a
paper bag, made with
their shipping sack paper.
REFEREE: Paper bag?!
BOXING ANNCR.: Can he punch his way out of it?
BOXING ANNCR (VO): Watch!
ST. REGIS ANNCR (VO): How can Kraft paper stand up
to this kind of punishment?

1556
Art Director: **Bob Gage**
Photographer: **Ernesto Caparros**
Writer: **Jack Dillon**
Client: **Polaroid**
Editor: **Pelco**
Director: **Bob Gage**
Producers: **Rose Presley, Eugene
Mazzola/Directors Studio Inc.**
Agency Producers: **Doyle Dane
Bernbach/Joseph Scibetta, Jane Liepshutz**

1557
Art Director: **Charley Rice**
Writer: **Pete Faulkner**
Client: **Stroh Brewery**
Editor: **Milt Loonan/Prime Cut**
Director: **Ron Finley Films**
Production Co.: **Ron Finley Films**
Agency: **Doyle Dane Bernbach**

A PIECE OF THE SUN
60-second
JIM: When we take pictures, most of us drag somebody out into the sun . . .
MARI: Where we squint and look awful.
JIM: The best pictures are unposed. And they're usually not in the sun. So we waste a shot.
. . . But now you don't have to worry where the sun is.
MARI: What's that?
JIM: A piece of the sun.
MARI: I didn't know we're that tall.
JIM: Here. Hold this.
MARI: OOh! Tinkerbell!
JIM: This is Polaroid's new Sun Camera, a whole new system with the fastest color print film made 600 speed. But it needs one more thing to turn bad light into good pictures.

BIG LIFT OFF
60-second
(SFX: CARGO THROWN OUT OF PLANE)
CAPTAIN: Guys, she's still too heavy.
UPSET TRADER: What are we gonna do?
CAPTAIN: Well, I hate to say it, but we gotta unload the you-know-what.
ANNOYED BUSINESSMAN: Leave the Stroh's!
ANGRY SOLDIERS: Negative!!
CAPTAIN: O.K., but then some of you have to stay behind.
UPSET WOMAN: Well, you're certainly not leaving me behind!
INSPIRED CO-PILOT: (YELLS) I got it! Captain, I got it!
(SFX: ENGINES REVVING FOR TAKEOFF)
PLEASED CAPTAIN: Joe, I gotta hand it to ya!
(SFX: TAKEOFF OF SKELETAL PLANE)

1558
Art Director: **Don Ross**
Writer: **Jim Johnston**
Client: **Marathon Oil**
Director: **Jim Johnston**
Producer: **Noel Campbell**
Agency: **Marathon Oil**

1559
Art Director: **Hy Varon**
Designer: **Hy Varon**
Artist: **R.O. Blechman**
Writer: **Martin Kaufman**
Client: **IBM General Systems Division**
Editor: **Sandpiper Editorial**
Creative Directors: **David Curtis, R.O. Blechman**
Producer: **Lois Goldberg/The Ink Tank**
Agency: **Leber Katz Partners**

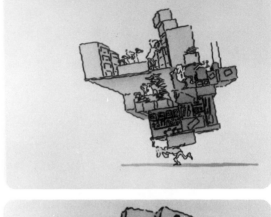

A little IBM can mean a lot of freedom.

MARATHON OIL
60-second
SUPER (VO): Marathon, Greece 490 B.C.
ANNCR: The first Marathon
26 miles . . . 385 yards . . .
it took incredible endurance . . .
it took incredible spirit . . .
spirit that pushed on and on . . .
farther and farther . . .
far beyond the point where others would have stopped.
It's the spirit to do more than is expected . . .
to go farther than you have to . . . the spirit to excel.
We at Marathon Oil remember that spirit.
It's the spirit that constantly pushes our company further to
pursue excellance in everything that carries our name
Marathon Oil . . . the spirit to excel . . . to go farther
Marathon . . . the long distance gasoline.

FREEDOM
60-second
ANNCR (VO): Do you sometimes feel like you're carrying
your whole business on your back?
SECRETARY: Harvey's Hardware, please hold. Harvey, these
accounts payable are piling up.
HARVEY: I'm working on it.
ANNCR (VO): Are you a businessman or a beast of burden?
WORKER: What about the inventory?
HARVEY: I'm working on it!
ANNCR (VO): Are you running your business, or is your
business running you?
WORKERS: Harvey, how about the payroll?
ANNCR (VO): Wouldn't you like to get it all off your back?
HARVEY: With what, a forklift?
ANNCR (VO): No, with a small business computer from IBM.
HARVEY: IBM makes small computers?

1560
Art Director: **Agi Clark**
Designer: **Frank Gentile**
Writer: **Bryon Barclay**
Client: **Bahamas Ministry of Tourism**
Editor: **Dick Langenbach/Splice Is Nice**
Director: **Andy Jenkins**
Producer: **Frank Moccio/Jenkins, Covington, Newman, Inc.**
Agency: **N W Ayer Incorporated**
Agency Producer: **Maury Penn**

1561   GOLD AWARD
Art Director: **Michael Tesch**
Writer: **Patrick Kelly**
Client: **Federal Express**
Editor: **Peggy DeLay/Sedelmaier Films**
Director: **Joe Sedelmaier**
Producers: **Maureen Kearns/A&G, Ann Ryan, Sedelmaier**
Agency: **Ally & Gargano, Inc.**

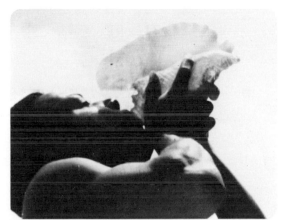

THINGS TO DO
60-second
(MUSIC UP)
SINGERS: Oooh Bahamas . . .
(MUSIC)
SINGERS: Welcome to your Bahamas . . .
(MUSIC)
SINGERS: Oooh . . .
Bahamas . . .
Crystal clear the water
Sun she smooth your skin
(MUSIC)
SINGERS: Oooh Bahamas
(MUSIC)
VO: In the Bahamas you never run out of things to do . . .
until you want to.
SINGERS: Oooh Bahamas . . .

FAST PACED WORLD
60-second
MR. SPLEEN (OC): Okay, Eunice, travel plans. I need to be in New York on Wednesday, LA on Thursday, New York on Friday. Got it?
EUNICE (VO): Got it.
MR. SPLEEN (OC): So you want to work here, well what makes you think you deserve a job here?
GUY: Well sir, I think on my feet, I'm good with figures and I have a sharp mind.
SPLEEN: Congratulations, welcome aboard.
(SFX)
OC: Wonderful, wonderful, wonderful And in conclusion Jim, Bill, Bob, Paul, Don, Frank, and Ted. Business is business es and sd we all know in order to get something done you've got to do something. In order to do something you've got to get to work so let's all get to work.
Thank you for attending this meeting. (SFX)

1562
Art Directors: **Phil Dusenberry, Ted Sann**
Writers: **Phil Dusenberry, Ted Sann**
Clients: **Len Vickers, Bart Snider**
Editors: **Steve Schreiber, Howie Weisbrot**
Director: **Bob Giraldi**
Producer: **Jeff Fishgrund, Bob Giraldi Prod.**
Agency: **BBDO**

1563
Art Directors: **Phil Dusenberry, Ted Sann**
Writer: **Phil Dusenberry, Ted Sann**
Clients: **Bart Snider, Len Vickers**
Editor: **Steve Schreiber**
Director: **Bob Giraldi**
Producer: **Jeff Fishgrund/Bob Giraldi Prod.**
Agency: **BBDO**

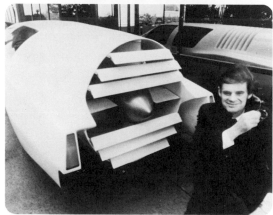

BASEBALL
60-second
(MUSIC)
AVO: On a summer's evening in 1924, in Lynn,
Massachussetts, perhaps the most significant game in the
long history of baseball was played.
It wasn't the pitching that was so extraordinary, nor the
hitting. And the fielding, well it was less than exemplary.
No, what made this game truly historic was the time of day.
(SFX: NIGHTFALL)
For it was on this night that this small group of GE engineers
ushered in the era of night baseball. Baseball under the
lights.
And while the names of "Yugo" Fee and Tommy Perkins
and Hank Innes will never be recorded in the Hall of Fame,
It was this earnest band of GE pioneers that made possible
for us all the many brilliant nights to come.

INNOVATORS
60-second
(MUSIC)
ANNCR (VO): To all you students of innovation,
to you inspired to try what's
never been tried before,
To all those consumed with an
insatiable curiosity,
a penchant for ingenuity,
To you who seek and search
And blaze new trails,
Who try and fail and try again;
To all you children of imagination,
You sons and daughters and mothers
of invention,
Dreamers and doers, thinkers and
Tinkerers all, we at General

1564
Art Director: **Tom Peck**
Writer: **Geraldine Newman**
Client: **Eastman Kodak**
Director: **Dick Miller**
Producer: **Scott Kulok**
Agency: **Young & Rubicam**

1565   SILVER AWARD
Art Director: **John Lucci**
Set Designer: **Ken Davies**
Photographer: **Mel Sokolsky**
Writer: **Jud Alper**
Client: **Dr Pepper**
Editor: **Steve Bodner**
Agency Producer: **Mootsy Elliot**
Director: **Mel Sokolsky**
Production Co.: **Sunlight**
Agency: **Young & Rubicam**

HOMECOMING II
60-seconds
(MUSIC UNDER)
WOMAN SINGS: I'll be seeing you in all the old familiar
places, that this heart of mine embraces all year through.
ANNCR (VO): Christmas. When everyone comes home.
WOMAN SINGS: I'll be seeing you, your smiling face this
holiday.
ANNCR (VO): Share every glorious instant, in glorious instant
pictures by Kodak.
WOMAN SINGS: Share love and joy the special way.
ANNCR (VO): This Christmas bring home the gift of a smile,
the gift of love and the gift that lets you share them.
The Kodak Colorburst Instant Camera.
WOMAN SINGS: When we share these special times, I'll be
seeing you.
ANNCR (VO): Give the gift of instant joy.

REVOLVING ROOM
60-second
(MUSIC)
BOY: Hey Patty, what do you have to do to be a Pepper?
PATTY: It's easy.
PATTY: (SINGING) To be a Pepper, original like a Pepper all
you gotta do is taste.
SINGERS: Be a Pepper to know the pleasure of a flavor you
will treasure. All you gotta do is taste. Be a Pepper. The
flavor's got a feeling, original and appealing, and all you
gotta do is taste. To be a Pepper, open up a Dr Pepper,
and all you gotta do is taste. Be a Pepper, drink Dr Pepper.
Be a Pepper, yeah. The more you pour it, the more you will
adore it. And all you gotta do is taste. To be a Pepper.
Open up a Dr Pepper. And all you gotta do is taste. Be a
Pepper, drink Dr Pepper, yeah.

1566
Art Director: **Boleslaw Czernysz**
Writer: **Sue Read**
Client: **Jamaica Tourist Board**
Director: **Jeff Lovinger**
Producer: **Scott Kulok**
Agency: **Young & Rubicam**

1567
Art Director: **Mark Norrander**
Writer: **Bill Borders**
Client: **KINK FM Radio**
Director: **Chuck East**
Production Co.: **The Charles East Co., Inc.**
Agency: **Borders, Perrin & Norrander, Inc.**

COME BACK TO GENTILITY
60-second
(MUSIC UNDER)
WOMAN SINGS: Come back to Jamaica:
MAN: Come back to gentility
WOMAN SINGS: What's old is what's new.
WOMAN: Come back to our beauty.
WOMAN SINGS: We want you to join us.
MAN: Come back to our people.
WOMAN SINGS: We made it for you.
WOMAN: Come back to hospitality.
WOMAN SINGS: SO make it Jamaica.
WOMAN: Come back to our bounty.
WOMAN SINGS: Make it your own.
WOMAN: Come back to tranquility.
WOMAN SINGS: Make it Jamaica.

GORILLA
60-second
VO: What happens when a normally docile primate is subjected to the harsh repetitive music of most rock stations? Watch.
(CUT OF HARD ROCK)
(SECOND CUT OF HARD ROCK)
(THIRD CUT OF HARD ROCK)
(REPEAT SECOND CUT AGAIN)
(REPEAT FIRST CUT)
Not very pretty is it. Now, observe while the same subject is exposed to the softer, more varied sounds of K-I-N-K.
(CUT #1 OF "MELLOW ROCK")
(CONTINUE CUT #1)
(CUT #2 OF "MELLOW ROCK")
(CUT #3 OF FUSION OR?)

1568
Art Director: **Rick Marchesano**
Artist: **Steven Oakes**
Writer: **Dennis Coffey**
Client: **PBS**
Production Co.: **Broadcast Arts**
Agency: **Goldberg/Marchesano and Associates, Inc.**

1569
Art Director: **Bob Kuperman**
Writer: **Robert Saxon**
Client: **Fisher Corporation**
Director: **Melvin Sokolsky**
Production Co.: **Sunlight Pictures Corp.**
Agency: **BBDO/West**
Producer: **Jordan Kalfus**

 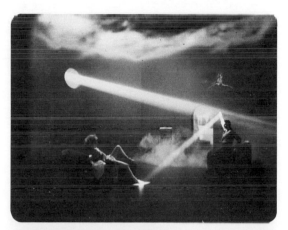

FESTIVAL METAMORPHOSIS
60-second
(CROWD NOISE AND RUSTLING)
VO: Expect the unexpected during Festival Nights on Public TV.
(CROWD QUIETS)
VO: . . .Unexpected superstars!
VOICE OF PAUL SIMON: (SINGING) ". . . Still crazy after all these years."
(FADE OUT)
(CROWD APPLAUSE)
VO: . . . Voices to thrill any house.
VOICE OF BEVERLY SILLS SINGING: ". . ."
(CROWD NOISE: "Bravo, bravo!")
VO: . . . unexpected laughs.
ALLEN'S VOICE: (DELIVERING FUNNY LINE) "Give me three

SEXY
60-second
(MUSIC—ROD STEWART SONG, (DO YOU THINK I'M SEXY?)
She sits alone, waiting for suggestions
He's so nervous, avoiding all the questions.
His lips are dry; her heart is gently pounding.
Don't you just know exactly what they're thinking?
ANNCR (VO): Recording by Rod Stewart.
Authentic reproduction by the Fisher 8500.
A perfectly matched component system.
With Fisher's programmable direct-drive turntable, quartz digital tuner, direct drive cassette deck, graphic equalizer, Fisher 900 series speakers, plus 100 watts of power per channel.
The Fisher System 8500.
(MUSIC—UP)

1570
Art Directors: **John Broutin, Sam Minnella**
Designer: **Peter Richardson**
Cameraman: **Peter McDonald**
Agency Producers: **Manny Perez, Dave Haldeman**
Writer: **Bob Paklaian, Josh Carlisle**
Client: **Lincoln Mercury Division**
Editor: **Jerry Bender**
Director: **Nick Lewin**
Production Co.: **Jennie & Company**
Agency: **Young & Rubicam**

1571
Art Director: **Israel Liebowitz**
Writer: **Janet Carlson**
Client: **Merle Norman Cosmetics**
Editor: **Ace & Edie, Inc.**
Director: **Israel Liebowitz**
Production Co.: **Robert Elias, Inc.**
Agency: **Carlson, Liebowitz, & Olshever, Inc.**

CONTINENTAL ARCH
60-second
ANNCR: The approach . . . clearly new.
The discovery . . . unexpected.
A new Continental.
The trimmest Continental ever fashioned.
Yet, one of the finest-riding Continentals ever built.
The 1982 Continental.
The most unconventional Continental in 40 years.

1.5 MILLION WOMEN
60-second
ANNCR (VO): Last year, the Merle Norman Studios taught one million five hundred thousand women they were more beautiful than they thought they were. Come to Merle Norman for your free makeover today.
Now, it's your turn.

1572
Art Director: **Rich Seidelman**
Writer: **Christie McMahon**
Client: **McDonald's Corporation**
Editor: **Yamus-Optimus**
Director: **Denny Harris**
Production Co: **Rob Lieberman/Harmony Pictures**
Agency: **Needham, Harper & Steers, Inc.**

1573
Art Director: **Jim Nawrocki**
Writer: **Josephine Cummings**
Client: **McDonald's Corporation**
Editor: **Szabo-Tohtz**
Director: **Rob Lieberman**
Production Co: **Harmony Pictures**
Agency: **Needham, Harper & Steers, Inc.**

CAN'T STOP
60-second
(MUSIC INTRO)
SINGERS: Sometimes you can't slow down
You're movin'
Can't stop that feeling inside
You're dancin'
It keeps you spinnin' around
Keep goin'
You gotta go for the ride
Yeah just look at you go
You're rollin
Look at you doin' the town
You're shinin'
Big Mac
And a coke on the go

DADDY'S GIRL
60-second
MALE SOLO: Where did all the day go
GIRL SOLO: I'm so sleepy, goodnight
MALE SOLO: Miss her more than she knows
Sometimes you can't seem to find . . .
GIRL SOLO: Do you have to go dad?
MALE SOLO: . . . A minute of time
There's so much to be said.
GIRL SOLO: I've got homework to do
MALE SOLO: How can it be so tough
GIRL SOLO: Have to go to my class.
DAD SOLO: A little times all you need
You never see her enough
GROUP: Get together, get away
GIRL: Yes, I'll have a cheeseburger fries . . .

1574
Art Director: **Susan Emerson**
Writer: **Jim Glover**
Client: **McDonald's Corporation**
Editor: **Cutters**
Director: **Lear Levin**
Producer: **Lear Levin**
Agency: **Needham, Harper & Steers, Inc.**

1575
Art Director: **Lee Gleason**
Writers: **David Lamb, David Klehr**
Client: **Anheuser-Busch/Budweiser Light**
Editor: **Optimus**
Director: **Joe Pytka**
Producer: **Levine/Pytka**
Agency: **Needham, Harper & Steers, Inc.**

FIRST LIGHT
60-second
SINGER: Nobody
rises up in the city
quite the way we do
Up with the dawn
Hot Coffee's on
Another day is headed toward you
Early showers
Those bloomin' flowers
Say it's morning
Won't you stroll on in
with our Egg McMuffin
We do it
Nobody can do it
Like only . . . .
McDonald's can.

FOOTBALL
60-second
(MUSIC)
ATHLETE: I wasn't drafted till the seventh round.
They don't even know my name.
SINGERS: Bring out your best
ANNCR: The best never comes easy. That's why there's
nothing else like it.
Budweiser Light.
SINGERS: Bring out your best
Budweiser Light
Bring out your best
Budweiser Light
Bring out your best
ANNCR: The best.
(SFX: WHISTLE)
ATHLETE: Kroeter, huh.

1576
Art Director: **Joe Herrick**
Writer: **Bill Evans**
Client: **The Evening Sun (Baltimore)**
Editor: **Bobby Smalheiser/First Edition, N.Y.**
Soundtrack: **Suzanne Ciani**
Director: **Jerry Levin**
Producer: **Makin' Movies**
Agency: **Richardson, Myers & Donofrio**

1577
Art Director: **Barry Vetere**
Writer: **Tom Messner**
Client: **Time, Inc.**
Editor: **Jerry Kleppel**
Director: **Jean Marie Perrier**
Producers: **Maureen Kearns/A&G/
Susan Kirson/The Film Consortium**
Agency: **Ally & Gargano, Inc.**

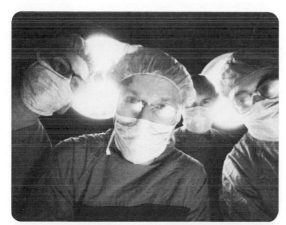

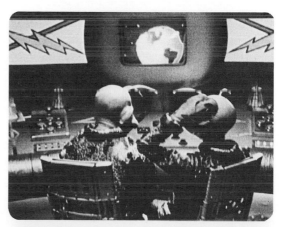

GRAY MATTER
60-second
(SFX: RHYTHMIC POP, POP, POP OF HEART MONITOR.)
VO: The gray convolutions of the brain sparkle beneath the powerful operating theater spotlights. The microscopic landscape heaves and subsides in rhythm to the heart monitor.
(SFX: TYPING SOUND MIXED TO BLEND WITH HEART MONITOR IN SAME RHYTHM.)
VO: The probing tweezers are gentle, firm, deliberate, probing slower than the hands of the clock.
(SFX: TYPING)
VO: The aneurism finally appears at the end of the tunnel, throbbing, visibly thin, swelling out from the once strong arterial wall, a tire about to blow out, a time bomb the size of a pea.
(SFX: TYPING)

TIME IN SPACE
120-second
(MUSIC UNDER)
(MUSIC)
ANNCR (VO): If you had to find out everything you could about what's happening in the world, where would you look?
Think about that for a moment.
(SFX AND DRUMS)
(SFX)
What's the one source likely to tell you almost everything worth knowing about?
If you say Time Magazine, you'll get few arguments.
More people rely on Time than any other single news source in the universe.
A lively report about the nation and the world.
For insight into people, science, religion

1578
Art Director: **Barry Vetere**
Writers: **Tom Messner, Bob Fisler, Amil Gargano**
Client: **Time, Inc.**
Editor: **Mike Biondi/E.U.E.**
Director: **Jean Marie Perrier**
Producers: **Janine Marjollet/A&G,
Chuck Sloan/The Film Consortium**
Agency: **Ally & Gargano, Inc.**

1579
Art Directors: **Tony Carillo, Marilyn Susser**
Writer: **Roger Feuerman**
Client: **Time Magazine**
Director: **Jeff Lovinger**
Producer: **Will Wright**
Agency: **Young & Rubicam**

TIME IN A BOTTLE
120-second
(MUSIC UNDER)
ANNCR (VO):If in all the world, you could have only one
source of news and information, what would it be?
Think about that for a second. Only one source of news and
information.
What would it be?
(MUSIC)
(MUSIC)
If you say TIME Magazine, you're not alone.
More than 29,000,000 people all over the world turn to
TIME's lively pages each week to catch up on what's news
everywhere in every field.
With writing so fresh and pictures so colorful, you enjoy every
minute and start looking forward to the next issue . . .

TIME FLIES
60-second
MAN: When you read TIME . . . you know more than what's
happening, you understand why.
SONG: TIME flies . . . and you are there.
TIME cries . . . and lets you share.
TIME reaches highs . . . beyond compare.
Yes TIME brings you closer to living.
TIMES soars . . . and you feel near.
TIMES roars . . . and makes it clear.
TIME opens doors . . . to new ideas.
Yes TIME just never stops giving.
ANNCR: Each week your complex world keeps changing,
and each week TIME Magazine helps you make sense out
of it all. So read TIME and understand.
SONG: Throughout your world . . . throughout your land . . .

1580
Art Director: **Gerald Andelin**
Writer: **Hal Riney**
Client: **Blitz Weinhard Brewing Co.**
Editor: **Jacques Dury**
Director: **Joe Pytka**
Producer: **Lark Navez/Levine Pytka & Assocs.**
Agency: **Ogilvy & Mather, San Francisco**

1581
Art Director: **Joel Machak**
Writer: **Aaron Buchman**
Client: **Commonwealth Edison**
Editor: **Tony Izzo**
Director: **Joe Pytka**
Producer: **Meg Mathews, Levine Pytka
& Assocs.**
Agency: **Leo Burnett — Chicago**

COLORADO
60-second
ANNCR: These days, in Arizona and Colorado, people are beginning to ask for a very special beer.
MAN #1: "Henry's"
MAN #2: "Make that two."
MAN #3: "Three"
ANNCR: A beer that, until recently, has been available only on the west coast. Henry Weinhard's Private Reserve.
MAN #1: "Henry's for the house."
ANNCR: A beer brewed only in Oregon — in limited quantities —
WORKER #1: "Thanks"
ANNCR: — in the old fashioned, traditional way.
MAN #3: "Tastes mighty good —"
WORKER #2: "It must get pretty hot out on the range."

WEE SMALL HOURS
60-second
ANNCR (VO): In the wee small hours, the world is asleep. And a sleeping world doesn't use much electricity. The generators making it don't have to breathe hard. So it's cheaper to provide. When the world wakes up, though, the demand goes way up. Way up.
And all our people, all our generators, have to go all out. We even have to add generators that guzzle expensive oil. So electricity costs a lot more to make. And that means everybody has to pay more for it.
Now, if we could all use a little less during the day, wait till nine or ten p.m. to run our dishwashers or our clothes dryers, easy things like that . . . it can keep the cost of electricity from . . . getting away from us. and help us get some control over tomorrow.

1582
Art Director: **Joe Sedelmaier**
Writer: **Tom McElligott**
Client: **Mr. Coffee**
Editor: **Peggy DeLay**
Director: **Joe Sedelmaier**
Production Co.: **Sedelmaier Film
Productions Inc.**
Agency: **Marketing Communications Inc.**

1583   Distinctive Merit
Art Director: **Rich Kimmel**
Designer: **Robert Peluce**
Agency Producer: **Lee Lanardi**
Artist: **Robert Peluce**
Writer: **Jim Kochevar**
Client: **Eureka Vacuum Cleaners**
Editor: **Mike Tomack**
Production Company Producer: **Loraine Roberts**
Director: **Bob Kurtz**
Production Co.: **Kurtz & Friends**
Agency: **Young & Rubicam, Chicago**

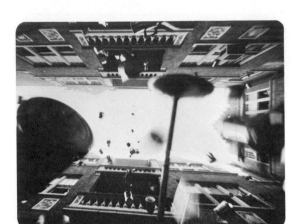

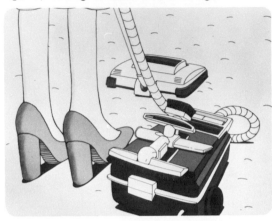

**ANGRY
YESTERDAY'S COFFEE,
DANGEROUS**
30-second
(NATURAL SFX THROUGHOUT)
(MUSIC UNDER)
ANNCR (VO): All across America, people are getting fed up
with bad coffee.
Fortunately, they have an alternative: Mr. Coffee. Only Mr.
Coffee precisely controls coffee brewing time and
temperature for perfect coffee every time.
Mr. Coffee . . . America's perfect coffee maker with a patent
to prove it.

**POWER TEAM CURTAIN'S
LURKING
GOODBYE DIRT**
30-second
WOMAN: Yoohoo, dirt, hiding all over my house. Look
what I got.
A new Eureka Power Team Vacuum cleaner.
There's a powerful motor in the cannister.
So if you're in my drapes, it's curtains. And life won't be so
easy in the chair.
There's even a motor driven beater in this carpet cleaner.
Let's me get down to the nitty gritty.
VO: A house can hold a lot of hidden dirt, but a Eureka
Power Team Vacuum Cleaner with two motors . . . gets the
dirt you can't see.

1584
Art Director: **Bob Gage**
Photographer: **Ernesto Caparros**
Writer: **Jack Dillon**
Client: **Polaroid Corporation**
Editor: **Pelco**
Director: **Bob Gage**
Production Co.: **Director's Studio Inc./**
Rose Presley, Eugene Mazzola
Agency Producers: **Doyle Dane Bernbach/**
Joseph Scibetta, Jane Liepshutz

1585
Art Director: **Bob Gage**
Photographer: **Ernesto Caparros**
Writer: **Jack Dillon**
Client: **Polaroid Corporation**
Editor: **Pelco**
Director: **Bob Gage**
Production Co.: **Director's Studio Inc/**
Rose Presley
Agency Producer: **Doyle Dane Bernbach/**
Joseph Scibetta

PIECE OF THE SUN
CANOE
HORSES & BRIDGE
30-second
JIM: This is Polaroid's new Sun Camera—a new system with the fastest color print film made (PICKS UP PACK.) 600 speed. But it needs one more thing to turn bad light into good pictures.
MARI: What's that?
JIM: A piece of the sun.
MARI: Daddy longlegs.
JIM: There . . . a piece of the sun does it.
MARI: Turns bad light into a good picture.
JIM: (WHOOSH!) Sure, you use this on every shot.
See, you've never been so sure of an instant picture.
MARI: Lovely, now you just reach up.
JIM: Well, don't waste it.

DEAD PARTY
RENTED CAKE
MERRY XMAS FOZZIE
30-second
KERMIT: (RUSHING IN) Quick, where's my OneStep?
PIGGY: Why? What's happening?
KERMIT: Nothing. this party's dead.
PIGGY: I hear laughing.
KERMIT: They're laughing at the hors d'oeuvres.
PIGGY: Oh . . .
KERMIT: I got it.
PIGGY: (SADLY) And I worked so hard.
KERMIT: Smile, everybody!
STATLER: Why, is the party over?
KERMIT: (WHOOSH!) No, it just started.
FOZZIE: Hey, everybody looks happy.
WALDORF: I thought camera's didn't lie.

1586

Art Director: **Mike Withers**
Writer: **Hy Abady**
Client: **Aamco Transmissions, Inc.**
Editors: **Peggy DeLay, Morty Ashkinos**
Director: **Joe Sedelmaier**
Production Co: **Sedelmaier Films, Inc./**
Frank DiSalvo:Agency
Agency: **Calet, Hirsch, Kurnit & Spector, Inc.**

1587

Art Director: **Ron Travisano**
Photographer: **Dan Quinn**
Writer: **Jerry Della Femina**
Client: **American Isuzu Motors Inc., Jack Reilly**
Editor: **Barry Moross**
Director: **Bob Giraldi**
Production Co: **Barbara Michaelson/**
Giraldi Productions
Agency: **Della Femina, Travisano &**
Partners, Inc.

BREAKDOWN
HORRORS,
TURNAROUND
30-second
ANNCR (VO): Ever notice how things break down right after the warranty expires?
Most warranties only last a short time.
But if you ever have a transmission problem, you can get a warranty that lasts as long as you own your car.
It's AAMCO's car-ownership warranty.
You get free annual checkups, and you never have to pay for transmission repair again.
Wouldn't it be nice if every warranty was this way?
AAMCO: (BEEP-BEEP) Why go anywhere else?

FAST STARTING DIESEL
QUIET DIESEL
ACCELERATE
30-second
ANNCR (VO): You knew that the diesel getting over 40 miles to the gallon would be the hot car in the 80's. What you didn't know was how it would start . . . when the temperature was in the 20's. In Japan, Isuzu motors has worked for decades to develop a diesel that would start quickly. And now we have a diesel that's ready to start in just three-and-a-half-seconds even in 0°. The Price? (1) From under $6700. (2)
The Isuzu diesel is coming to California.
Starting Immediately.
(1) PRICE SUHER: Priced from $6699. Manufacturer's suggested retail price P.O.E. excluding tax, license,

1588
Art Director: **Bob Gage**
Photographer: **Ernesto Caparros**
Writer: **Jack Dillon**
Client: **Polaroid Corporation**
Editor: **Pelco**
Director: **Bob Gage**
Production Co: **Director's Studio, Inc./**
Rose Presley, Eugene Mazzola
Agency Producer: **Doyle Dane Bernbach,**
Joseph Scibetta, Jane Liepshutz

1589
Art Director: **Lester Feldman**
Writer: **Mike Mangano**
Client: **GTE**
Director: **Pat Pitelli**
Production Co: **Pitelli Productions**
Agency: **Doyle Dane Bernbach**

O.K. I'M BEAUTIFUL
CLEVER IDEA
MADE FOR EACH OTHER
30-second
MARI: O.K. I'm beautiful.
JIM: I want proof of this!
MARI: No you don't we're late already.
JIM: Don't worry, this is the world's fastest developing color.
You see it in seconds now, not minutes.
MARI: Well there's your proof.
But go on. Get it all out of your system.
JIM: The Time-Zero OneStep and Time-Zero Supercolor film
are made for each other. That's why they both come
together in Polaroid's new Made-For-Each-Other-Pack.
MARI: Feel better now?
JIM: O.K. Let's go.

HALLWAY
NEW YORK TO CAL.
INSTALLATION
30-second
VO: Remember the good old days?
MOTHER: Somebody . . . get that!
VO: When most homes had just one telephone.
FATHER: Get that!
GIRL: I'll get it!
BOY: I'll get it!
VO: Well, GTE presents the good new days.
Now, for very little money a day you can have an extension
phone . . .
in any room that's necessary.
And even in some rooms that aren't so necessary.

1590

Art Director: **Mark Shap**
Writers: **John Gruen, Harvey Gabor**
Editor: **The Editors**
Directors: **Michael Ulick, Ed Kleban,
Dominick Rossetti**
Producers: **Emma Lou Santos, Ed Kleban,
Sue Chiafullo**
Agency: **Ogilvy & Mather**

1591

Art Director: **Ron Travisano**
Photographer: **Allen Greene**
Writer: **Sheila Moore**
Client: **American Automobile Association,
R. Morrow**
Editor: **Ed Shea, Jeff Dell Editorial**
Director: **Joe DeVoto**
Production Co: **Hy Weiner/Joel Productions**
Agency: **Della Femina, Travisano &
Partners, Inc.**

**NAMATH — MISTAKEN IDENTITY
RINGSIDE
LUIGI'S RESTAURANT**
30-second
(SFX: BER)
WOMAN: It's you!
MAN: Me?
WOMAN: Joe Namath!
MAN: Oh, hey you've got . . .
MAN 2: Hey, I . . . uh, you've got . . .
WOMAN: Oh, I just knew he comes here.
MAN 1: Hey, you've got . . .
MAN 2: You've got to join us for a beer. (SIGH)
(MUSIC UNDER)
MEN SING: Ah ha, sittin' pretty . . . all together in Schaefer
City.
MAN 2: How are you doin' Joe?

**SNOWSTORM
RAINSTORM
TRAFFIC JAM**
30-second
VO: Sooner or later, just about everybody gets stuck. And if
you belong to the wrong auto club, you're not only stuck . . .
you're alone.
ATTENDANT: Uh, my tow truck's got a flat.
(SFX: RECEIVER LIFT, HAWAIIAN MUSIC.)
RECORD: The Hawaiian Tourist Bureau reminds you that it's
warm and wonderful in Waikiki . . .
VO: With AAA, you're never alone. Unlike other auto clubs,
AAA gives you one number to call in any major city . . . and
we find a garage for you . . . at any hour.
RECORD: Hi, we're closed now, but we'll help you in the
morning . . .
AAA. We'll never leave you all alone.

1592
Art Director: **Dom Marino**
Designer: **Dom Marino**
Writers: **Walt Hampton, Deanna Cohen**
Client: **O.M. Scott & Sons**
Editor: **Pelco**
Directors: **Michael Ulick, Bob Giraldi, John Gati**
Producers: **Sheldon Levy/Stuart Raffel**
Agency: **Doyle Dane Bernbach**

1593   DISTINCTIVE MERIT
Art Directors: **Earl Cavanah, Jim Perretti**
Writer: **Larry Cadman**
Client: **Volvo of America Corporation**
Editor: **Steve Schreiber, Editor's Gas, Dennis Hayes**
Production Co.: **Sandbank Films Co., Inc., Levine/Pytka & Assocs.**
Directors: **Henry Sandbank, Rick Levine**
Producer: **Dane Johnson (SMS), Richard Berke (SMS)**
Agency: **Scali, McCabe, Sloves, Inc.**

Same lawn
26 days later

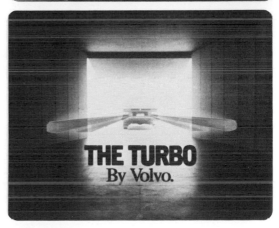

THE TURBO
By Volvo.

WHAT DANDELION
HUNGRY LAWN
VEGETABLE SYMPHONY
30-second
MAN: Gentlemen, it's curtains.
I told you dandelions not to come back again.
But you didn't listen, did you?
No more Mr. Nice Guy!
ANNCR (VO): Turf Builder Plus 2 Weed and Feed from Scotts gets rid of dandelions, root and all.
And 40 other weeds, while it helps thicken your lawn with Turf Builder fertilizer.
MAN: See, I told you I meant business.
WIFE: Ralph are you out there talking to those dandelions again?
MAN: What dandelions? Do you see any dandelions?
ANNCR (VO): You'll have a better lawn with Scotts.

BLACK TURBO
BOZO
COUNTRY CLUB
30-second
VO: It you have fond memories of those muscle cars of the past, ... cars that were virtually legislated off the highways, take heart.
There's a new car that automotive writers have called ...
"a blast" ...
"spectacular" ...
Stepping on the gas, they say, is like cutting in an afterburner.
It's a car that can blast a V-8 right off the road.
The car?
The Turbo ...
by Volvo.
It'll blow the past right out of your mind.

1594
Art Director: **Michael Tesch**
Writer: **Patrick Kelly**
Client: **Federal Express**
Editor: **Peggy DeLay-Sedelmaier**
Director: **Joe Sedelmaier**
Producers: **Maureen Kearns/AG&G,
Ann Ryan/Sedelmaier**
Agency: **Ally & Gargano, Inc.**

1595
Art Director: **William Taubin**
Designer: **William Taubin**
Writer: **Edward Smith**
Client: **Porsche/Audi**
Editor: **Joe Laliker/Pelco**
Director: **Werner Hlinka**
Producers: **Shelden Levy, Phil Bodwell,
Tibor Hirsch, Inc.**
Agency: **Doyle Dane Bernbach**

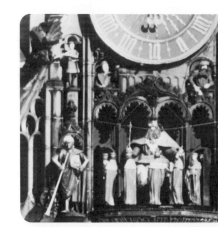

**YOU CAN'T COUNT ON ANYTHING
KRADDOCK
FAST PACED**
30-second
(MUSIC THROUGHTOUT) (SFX: BIRDS CHIRPING)
(SFX: RATTLE OF ALARM CLOCK)
(SFX: ENGINE)
(SFX: FLAT TIRE)
(SFX: DOG BARKING)
ANNCR (VO): You can't count on anything these days . . .
(SFX: FOOTSTEPS)
(SFX: TYPING)
MAN (OC): Did you type the letter I told you to type?
SECRETARY (OC): No.
ANNCR (VO): With possibly one exception:
Federal Express.
When it absolutely, positively has to be there overnight.

**GLOCKENSPIEL
MUSEUM REV
1931**
30-second
You'd never suspect . . .
from the storybook land of Bavaria . . .
come very innovative cars . . .
The Audi 5000 Turbo
with great power.
The Audi 4000 5 Plus 5
with great performance.
The Audi Diesel with extraordinary fuel economy.
Audi beings new ideas from the old world
to the New World.
Audi . . . the art of engineering.

1596
Art Director: **Tom Peck**
Writer: **Geraldine Newman**
Client: **Eastman Kodak**
Director: **Mel Sokolsky**
Producer: **Erin Ragan**
Agency: **Young & Rubicam**

1597
Art Director: **Jean Govoni**
Writer: **Cliff Freeman**
Client: **General Mills**
Editor: **Start-Mark**
Production companies: **Lovinger-Tardio-Melsky, The Ink Tank, Johnston Films**
Producer: **Janet Pangborn**
Agency: **Dancer-Fitzgerald-Sample, Inc.**

NEW CITIZEN
MATERNITY
FISHING
30-second
SUNG: Kodak . . . brings . . . the . . . instant . . . to life.
PAPA: I'm an American citizen.
VO: If Papa could only see his face.
Introducing the Kodak Colorbrust 350 . . .
SON: Closer!
VO: . . . the only instant camera with a built-in close-up lens.
SON: Closer!
VO: And the sharp, rich, vivid color . . . of 100 years of Kodak experience.
PAPA: I look like an American.
VO: New Kodak Colorbrust 350.
SUNG: Kodak brings the instant . . .
PAPA: (KISSING SOUND)

JUDD HIRSCH
DICK TRACY
ISABEL SANFORD
30-second
ANNCR (VO): The yogurt of France is called Yoplait. To some Americans just saying it's the yogurt of France means nothing till they first taste Yoplait. Then they'll believe it's creamy, smooth all natural yogurt with real fruit. It's just amazing what happens when a real American gets his first taste of French culture.
JUDD HIRSCH: Yoplait est delicieux. Et les fruits sont naturels. C'est si cremeux, si doux. Yoplait est incroyable! Naturellement les Americans aiment Yoplait.
ANNCR: Yoplait Yogurt. Get a little taste of French culture.

1599
Art Director: **David Henry**
Writer: **Nicholas Wakefield**
Client: **WSBK-TV, Boston**
Producer: **Nicholas Wakefield**

1600
Art Director: **Gayl Ware**
Creative Director: **Chuck Carlberg**
Writers: **Dick Sinreich, Leon Jaworski,
Alex Haley, Kristy McNichol**
Client: **Houston Chronicle**
Editor: **Bobby Smalheiser/First Editions**
Director: **Henry Sandbank**
Producer: **John Kamen/Sandbank Films**
Agency: **Rives Smith Baldwin & Carlberg,
Y&R, Houston**

DEER HUNTER 1
DEER HUNTER 2
DEER HUNTER 3
MUSIC — SFX

JAWORSKI
HALEY
MCNICHOL
30-second
ANNCR: The Houston Chronicle asked Leon Jaworski to talk
about newspapers.
JAWORSKI: Television and radio whet my appetite for news.
Then I turn to a newspaper for the full stories. Because
newspapers don't have to squeeze a whole day's news into
seconds. I could give you many more reasons why I read a
newspaper. But on television, there just isn't time.
ANNCR: A lot of powerful people read a newspaper. In
Houston, they read the Chronicle.

1601

Agency Producer: **Michael Collins**
Writer: **Terry O'Malley**
Client: **Planters (Division of Lowney Inc.)**
Editor: **Ron Vester**
Director: **Ian Leech**
Producer: **Nell Frair**
Agency: **Vickers & Benson Ltd.**

1602

Art Director: **Ron Spataro**
Producers: **Bob Miller, Ron Spataro — B&J**
Prod'n Co: **The Haboush Company**
Cinematographer: **Victor Haboush**
Writer: **Bob Miller**
Client: **RepublicBank Houston**
Editor: **Al Derise**
Director: **Victor Haboush**
Agency: **Bozell & Jacobs of Houston**

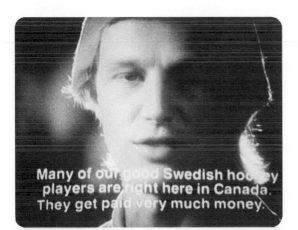

SWEDE
RUSSIAN
CZECH
30-second
YOUNG SWEDE: (IN SWEDISH) Many of our good Swedish hockey players are right here in Canada. They get paid very much money. When they asked me to come I said I would only stay a little while and I would play for peanuts. Planter's Peanuts. Because they are very crunchy. Very tasty. And best of all, very fresh. (SOUND OF VACUUM PACK). It's nice here but now that we have our Planter's, I think it best we go back home before the long Swedish winter nights set in.

LEE GRANT NAME CHANGE
DANNY THOMAS NAME CHANGE
RED BUTTONS NAME CHANGE
30-second
LEE GRANT: When you're a kid, and everyone on the block is named Jane or Sally and you're Lyova, you want to change your name. Especially if you're star-struck, and you have a crush on Cary Grant. So, I changed my name from Lyova Rosenthal to Lee Grant. It helped make me a star. And if it can do it for me, it can do it for Houston National Bank.
ANNCR (VO): We're making a new name for ourselves. RepublicBank Houston.

1603

Art Directors: **Tom Kelly, Carol MacIntosh**
Writer: **Dave Newman**
Client: **Omark Industries, Consumer
Products Group**
Editors: **Mike McNamara, Walt Dimmick**
Director: **Mike McNamara**
Production Co: **International Media Systems**
Agency: **Borders, Perrin & Norrander, Inc.**

1604

Art Director: **John R. Chepelsky**
Photographer: **National Geographic Society**
Writer: **Mabon Childs**
Client: **Gulf Oil Corporation**
Editor: **Bobby Smalheiser**
Producers: **John Chepelsky, Mabon Childs**
Agency: **Ketchum Advertising, Pittsburgh**

**LIFT 'N CUT
WOOD GRENADE
ROUGHNECK**
30-second
(OPEN ON MEDIUM WIDE SHOT OF KID NEXT TO A BIG LOG)
Liftin' and cuttin' a log this size can take a lot out of a man.
(CUT TO CLOSER SHOT OF KID WITH A LIFT 'N CUT)
But not since I started using this—the OREGON Lift 'N Cut.
(HE HOLDS IT UP)
(DISSOLVE TO DEMONSTRATION OF THE PRODUCT BY AN
UNSEEN DEMONSTRATOR—CLOSEUPS)
The Lift 'N Cut clamps onto a log: then uses leverage to lift it
off the ground.
(CHAIN SAW STARTS CUTTING LOG)
And it keeps my Dad's chain saw out of the dirt.
(DISSOLVE TO KID WITH LIFT 'N CUT NOW CLAMPED IN THE

**ETOSHA
GORILLA
NATIONAL PARKS**
30-second
VO: They're coming. The new National Geographic
Specials. Filmmakers, underwritten by a grant from Gulf Oil,
have been around the world.
And now they're back.
The season premiere shows you an Africa you've never seen
before. Africa the way the animals see it.
Watch Etosha, Place of Dry Water, a new National
Geographic Special, this week on Public Television.
Brought to you by Gulf Oil Corporation.

1605
Art Director: **Harvey Baron**
Writer: **Francine Wilvers**
Client: **Warner Communications, Atari**
Directors: **Dick Loew, Michael Ulick**
Production Co: **Gomes-Loew/Michael Ulick**
Agency: **Doyle Dane Bernbach**

1606
Art Director: **James Rocco**
Photographer: **Fred Hoffman**
Writer: **Joe DePascale**
Client: **Audrey Nizen**
Editor: **Bob DeRise**
Director: **Jay Gold**
Producer: **Irene Siegel**
Agency: **GSN Advertising, Inc.**

**MARTIAN FAMILY
NATION
BORIS**
30-second
MARTIAN WOMAN (VO): Dear Atari Anonymous,
ever since my husband Luno returned from Earth with Asteroids,
the new Atari home video game,
he and the rest of the family do nothing but play Asteroids.
Luno says Asteroids is good practice
for his interplanetary flights.
WOMAN (ON CAMERA): Biddy biddy. Biddy biddy
WOMAN (VO): Tell me, Dear Atari Anonymous,
with everybody hooked on Asteroids, what on earth is a
poor Martian mother to do?
ANNCR (VO): New Atari Asteroids, now available for your
home.

**SASSON FASHIONS GALORE
JUNIOR FASHIONS
WOMEN'S WEAR**
30-second
VO: Sasson Shirts . . .
Catch 'em Before They Take Off.
Sasson Skirts . . .
They're Hot Off The Runway.
Sasson Leather and Suede . . .
The Season's Most Sensual Departure.

1607
Art Directors: **Fred Seibert, Marcy Brafman**
Writers: **Jay Dorfman, Marcy Brafman,
Richard Schenkman**
Client: **MTV: Music Television**
Editors: **John Tierney, Mike Ehrman,
John Custodio**
Producers: **Marcy Brafman,
Richard Schenkman**
Logo Design: **Manhattan Design**
Creative Director: **Fred Seibert**

1608
Art Directors: **Fred Seibert, Marcy Brafman**
Writers: **Jay Dorfman, Marcy Brafman,
Richard Schenkman**
Client: **MTV: Music Television**
Editors: **John Tierney, Robert Artell**
Producers: **Marcy Brafman,
Richard Schenkman**
Logo Design: **Manhattan Design**
Creative Director: **Fred Seibert**

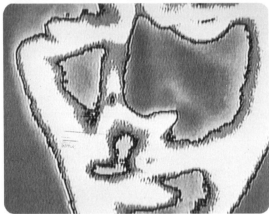

**BIKE CRASHING
FLYING
MARATHON DANCERS**
30-second
ANNCR: Before MTV, people had to work hard to entertain
themselves
After MTV, it's as simple as turning on your television.
The first stereo music TV channel
MTV: Music Television.

**SILENT ROCK N ROLL
HALF THE PICTURE
STEREO TEST #41**
30-second
ANNCR: Before sound was introduced to moving pictures,
people had to rely on their imaginations.
Now, MTV: Music Television, takes you beyond your
imagination with the introduction of stereo to the medium of
television.
MUSIC: Rough Boys, Don't Walk Away" [The Who]
MUSIC: "Tattooed Love" [The Pretenders]
MUSIC: "Heart of Glass" [Blondie]
ANNCR: The first stereo video music channel, MTV: Music
Television.

1609
Art Director: **Jeff Young**
Writers: **Mark Schneider, John Gruen**
Client: **General Foods Corporation**
Editor: **Steve Schreiber**
Directors: **Bill Hudson, Rick Levine**
Producers: **Ed Kleban/Bill Hudson Films, Skip Allocco/Levine/Pytka**
Agency: **Ogilvy & Mather**

1610
Art Directors: **Susan Emerson, Bernic Nosbaum**
Writers: **Jim Glover, Jennifer Fields**
Client: **McDonald's Corporation**
Editor: **Cutters**
Directors: **Lear Levin, Andy Jenkins**
Producers: **Lear Levin, Jenkins/Covington**
Agency: **Needham, Harper & Steers, Inc.**

**A REAL TROOPER
CROSSING GUARD
CHRISTMAS GARIN**
60 second
(SFX: BUGLE)
SONG: Mornings seem to start out better,
KIDS: Camping!
SONG: You seem to go much better,
MOM: Coffee?
DAD: Yeah.
SONG: When you start your day together.
You and Maxwell House.
DAD: Alright, now go get the bags, Okay?
SONG: Flavor that you've come to count on.
DAD: Coffee ready?
SONG: Taste that's always true.

**FIRST LIGHT
RAINY DAY WEEKEND
MORNING SONG**
60-second
SINGER: Nobody
rises up in the city
quite the way we do
Up with the dawn
Hot coffee's on
Another day is headed toward you
Early showers
Those bloomin' flowers
Say it's morning
Won't you stroll on in
With our Egg McMuffin
We do it

1615
Art Directors: **Ron Travisano, Ron DeVito**
Writers **Ron Travisano, Ron DeVito, Neal Rogin**
Client: **The Hunger Project**
Director: **Nick Samardge**
Producer: **Nick Samardge**
Agency: **Della Femina, Travisano & Partners, Inc.**

1616
Photographer: **Woody Omens**
Writer: **James Gartner**
Client: **The Church of Jesus Christ of Latter-day Saints**
Editor: **Roger Roth**
Director: **Stu Hagmann**
Agency Producer: **James Gartner**
Agency: **Bonneville Prod.**

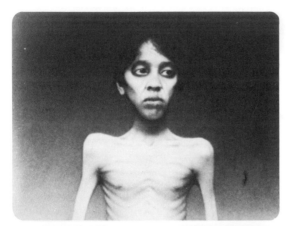

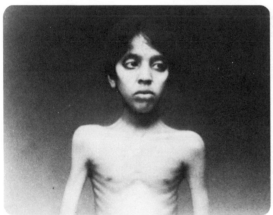

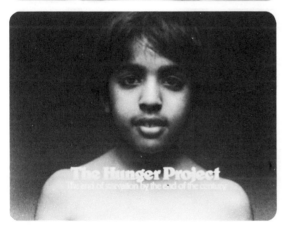

THE HUNGER PROJECT
30-second
VO: The time has come on our planet for hunger and starvation to end. Not just merely dealt with, not just handled more effectively . . . but to be ended. Finally, once and for all, forever. Starvation will end on this planet by the end of this century. It's an idea whose time has come. The hunger project. The end of starvation by the end of the century.

JULIE THROUGH THE GLASS
2-minute
(MUSIC IN)
LYRICS: Julie through the glass
Just born a day ago . . .
Who knows where you've been
And where you're gonna go . . .
Julie through the glass
Lookin' up at me . . .
You've just got to be
The sweetest thing I've ever seen.
We want you to learn
To love the world.
To know it well
And play a part . . .
And we'll help you to

1617
Art Director: **Ken Barre**
Writer: **Bob Veder**
Client: **Consumer Product Safety Commission**
Editors: **Joe Sedelmaier, Jeff Dell**
Producer: **Maura Dausey (Grey)/Sedelmaier Films**
Agency: **Grey Advertising, Inc.**

1618
Art Director: **Ken Barre**
Writer: **Bob Veder**
Client: **Consumer Product Safety Commission**
Editors: **Joe Sedelmaier, Jeff Dell**
Producer: **Maura Dausey (Grey)/Sedelmaier Films**
Agency: **Grey Advertising, Inc.**

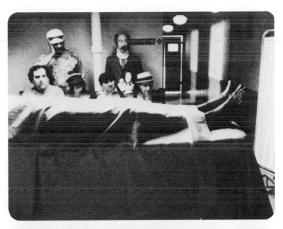

KITCHEN
60-second
MAN: You know (SFX: COFFEE CUT SET DOWN) I keep seeing these product recall notices. Look, I don't have time tor that sort ot thing. (SFX: PUSH DOWN TOASTER, FRIG DOOR OPENING). One notice says my toaster has a bad (SFX: FRIG DOOR CLOSING) connectlon. (SFX: TOAST POPPING OUT). And another one says my hot water heater might be faulty. Later Carl. And there are all kinds of recall notices on my kid's toys, (SFX: FRIG DOOR OPEN) my lawnmower, all telling me these products could (SFX: SHOCK SHOCK) be hazardous to my health. Later Carl. Look if I had to worry . . . (FADE TO ANNCR. COPY). Every year a lot of people pay attention to recall notices and get injured or killed.
So take recall notices seriously. And write the Consumer

EMERGENCY ROOM
30-second
ANNCR (VO): Every year thousands of people aren't careful with the products they use and hurt or kill themselves. So choose your products carefully. Use and maintain them properly.
And write the Consumer Product Safety Commission (SFX: DOLLY WHEELS SQUEAKING) for free and vital information on product safety. Wrlte Safety, WashIngton, 20207

1619
Art Director: **Ken Barre**
Writer: **Bob Veder**
Client: **Consumer Product Safety Commission**
Editors: **Joe Sedelmaier, Jeff Dell**
Producer: **Maura Dausey (Grey)/Sedelmaier Films**
Agency: **Grey Advertising, Inc.**

1620   SILVER AWARD
Art Director: **Ken Barre**
Writer: **Bob Veder**
Client: **Consumer Product Safety Commission**
Editors: **Joe Sedelmaier, Jeff Dell**
Producer: **Maura Dausey (Grey)/Sedelmaier Films**
Agency: **Grey Advertising, Inc.**

BANDAGES
60-second
MAN: You know, I just don't understand why people worry about hurting themselves with the simple little things they use around the house every day. This here's nothin.
ANNCR: Last year a lot of people were hurt or killed because they didn't take safety seriously.
MAN: My wife's got this step ladder. We kinda like to stand on top of it.
ANNCR: So for your sake and your family's sake, take product safety seriously.
MAN: But how careful can you be; I don't know, maybe a little careful. But, of course, every now and then there's a couple of other things that happen, every now and then.
ANNCR: Choose your products carefully. Use and maintain them properly. And write the Consumer Product Safety

BANDAGES, KITCHEN, QUESTION-ANSWER
30-second
VOICE: Did you see this recall notice for a toy?
MAN: uhh, yes.
VOICE: Your kid still (SFX: Sniff Sniff) have the toy?
MAN: uh, I think so.
VOICE: What about this product recall notice?
MAN: The one with the faulty wiring?
uh, excuse me, uhh.
ANNCR: Take recall notices seriously. And write the Consumer Product Safety Commission for free vital information on recalls. But hurry before its too late.
Write recalls, Washington, D.C. 20207

1621
Creative Director: **Charles V. Blake**
Art Directors: **E. Zeitsoff, Paul Fuentes**
Designers: **Paul Fuentes, Monica McCabe**
Artist: **Jim Lebbad**
Client: **NBC Television**
Director: **Lewis Cohen**
Production Co.: **IF Studios**

1622
Creative Director: **Charles V. Blake**
Designers: **Paul Fuentes, Stewart Stoltz**
Artist: **Stanislaw Zagorski**
Client: **NBC Television**
Director: **Bob Kurtz**
Producer: **Kurtz & Friends**

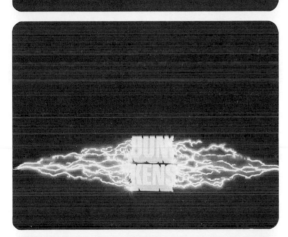

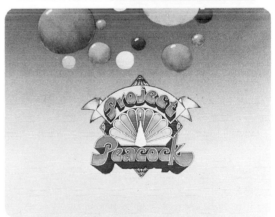

YOUNG FRANKENSTEIN
MUSIC — SFX

PROJECT PEACOCK
MUSIC — SFX

1623
Creative Director: **Charles V. Blake**
Art Directors: **Elaine Zeitsoff, Paul Fuentes**
Designers: **Paul Fuentes, Bill Feigenbaum**
Client: **NBC Enterprises**
Director: **Stanley Beck**
Production Co: **Edstan Studios**

1624
Art Directors: **George McGinnis, Lee Bawers**
Designer: **Chris Buchinski**
Photographer: **John Lowler**
Writer: **Tom Pedulla**
Client: **WABC-TV**
Editor: **Film Core LA**
Directors: **Lee Bawers, George McGinnis**
Production Co: **Image Factory Inc./
George McGinnis**
Agency: **Image Network Inc.**

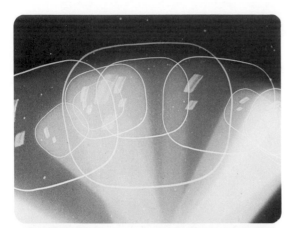

NBC HOME VIDEO
MUSIC — SFX

EYEWITNESS LA
MUSIC — SFX

1625
Art Director: **Bob Pook**
Designer: **Joan Newman**
Photographer: **Patti Perret**
Client: **NBC — Saturday Night Live**

1626
Art Director: **Bob Pook**
Designer: **Edie Baskin**
Photographer: **Edie Baskin**

SATURDAY NIGHT LIVE — DOUMANIAN
MUSIC — SFX

SATURDAY NIGHT LIVE — HALLOWEEN
MUSIC — SFX

1627
Art Director: **John C. LePrevost**
Designers: **John C. LePrevost, Jim Deesing**
Writer: **Mark Klastorin**
Client: **CBS Entertainment**
Animation Production Company: **The Jay Teitzell Company**
Animation Producer: **Lewis Hall**

1628
Art Director: **Bruce Woodside**
Designer: **Paul Coker, Jr.**
Animators: **Pam Cooke, Tom Hush, Mike Sanger, Margaret Parkes**
Writer: **Stan Phillips, Bruce Woodside**
Client: **Southern California Edison Company**
Director: **Bruce Woodside**
Producer: **Stan Phillips, Stan Phillips & Associates, Inc.**

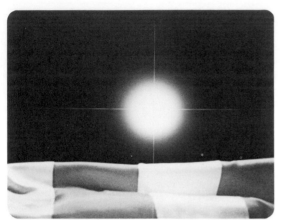

REACH FOR THE STARS
MUSIC — SFX

CURRENT EVENTS
7-1/2 minutes
CURRENT EVENTS is an animated film on electrical energy conservation, consisting of brief, humorous vignettes depicting the uses (and abuses) of electricity. In order to make the message accessible to audiences of all ages and cultures, no dialogue or narration is used. The comic predicaments are accompanied only by sound effects and original music.

1629
Art Director: **Arnold Levine**
Designer: **Mark Larsen**
Writer: **Arnold Levine, Jim Steinman**
Client: **CBS Records**
Editor: **John Carter**
Director: **Arnold Levine**
Producers: **Robbie Tucker, Ken Schreiber/
CBS Records**

1630
Art Director: **Arnold Levine**
Designer: **Michael Richman**
Writers: **Arnold Levine, Mark Levitt**
Client: **CBS Records**
Editor: **Susan Jones**
Director: **Arnold Levine**
Producer: **Ken Schreiber/CBS Records**

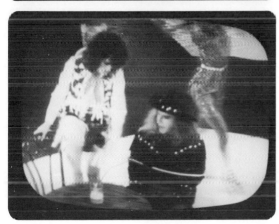

JIM STEINMAN
MUSIC — SFX

REX SMITH/RACHEL SWEET
MUSIC — SFX

1631
Art Director: **Laurence Deutsch**
Photographer: **H.J. Brown**
Writer: **Peter Hassenger**
Client: **Yamaha Motor Corp. of America**
Editor: **Lee Stepansky**
Director: **Michael Klick**
Production Co.: **Laurence Deutsch Design, Inc.**

1632
Art Director: **Arnold Levine**
Designer: **Josephine DiDonato**
Writers: **Arnold Levine, Mark Levitt**
Client: **CBS Records**
Editor: **Susan Jones**
Director: **Arnold Levine**
Producer: **Yvonne May/CBS Records**

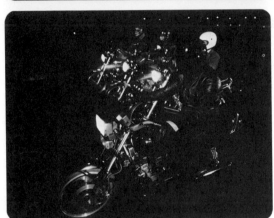

1982 YAMAHA DEALER SHOW
(SFX: URBAN BACKGROUND)
"White noise" of the city, held down and punctuated with sporadic horn-honking, bus brakes, car radios, chatter. Gradually, the sound grows in both volume and intensity, but only mezzo forte.
(SFX: A SIREN RACES THROUGH, IS CUT ABRUPTLY, LEAVING SILENCE.) Everything seems suddenly still.
MUSIC: Electronic tone fades in: long, attenuated, shrouded. An electronic chord is struck, deeper than the first. The chord is held, distorted. We do not hear the sound of the engines.
MUSIC: SURGE
Still no sound of motors, only the hollow, palpable quality of fog.
MUSIC: A pulse begins to build, slowly, rhythmically. Underneath there is an ominous tone of anticipation.

LOVER BOY
MUSIC—SFX

1633
Art Directors: **Stephen O. Frankfurt,
Richard Greenberg**
Designers: **Richard Greenberg,
Stephen O. Frankfurt**
Animation Designer: **Randy Balsmeyer**
Client: **Filmways Pictures**
Editor: **Larry Plastrik**
Director: **Richard Greenberg**
Producer: **Robert M. Greenberg/R.
Greenberg Associates, Inc.**
Agency: **Frankfurt Communications Int.**

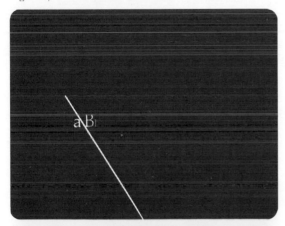

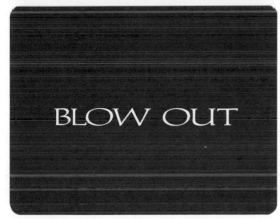

1634
Art Directors: **Stephen O. Frankfurt,
Richard Greenberg**
Designer: **Richard Greenberg,
Stephen O. Frankfurt**
Photographer: **James Szalapski**
Client: **PolyGram Pictures**
Editor: **Larry Plastrik**
Director: **Richard Greenberg**
Producer: **Robert M. Greenberg,
/R. Greenberg Associates, Inc.**
Agency: **Frankfurt Communications Int.**

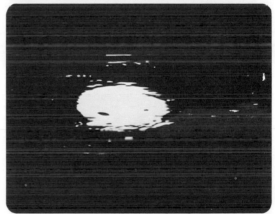

BLOW OUT
1:48-minute
ANNCR (VO): It began with a sound that no one was ever
supposed to hear.
ANNCR (VO): He recorded a murder they say never
happened.
John Travolta
Nancy Allen
A Brian De Palma Film
ANNCR (VO): Brian De Palma's "Blow Out."
Now you hear it . . .
SFX: Fast rewind
ANNCR (VO): now you don't.

AN AMERICAN WEREWOLF IN LONDON
1:22-second
(SFX: MUSIC UNDER THROUGHOUT)
(SFX: MUSIC BUILDS TO PIERCING SCREECH, AS DARK, HAIRY
FORELEG PLUNGES INTO STREAM.)
ANNCR (VO): From the director of "Animal House" . . . a
different kind of animal.

1635
Art Director: **Paul Jervis**
Writer: **Larry Vine**
Client: **Ovaltine Products, Inc.**
Editor: **Morty Ashkinos**
Producers: **Robert Warner, Jody Mellen**
Director: **Tony Mennigner**
Production Co: **Abel Associates**
Music Production Company: **Ciani/Musica, Inc.**
Agency: **Smith/Greenland Inc.**

1636
Art Director: **Alan Weninger**
Artist: **Wayne Becker, Hal Silverman**
Writer: **Scott Ferraiolo**
Client: **Miles Laboratories**
Directors: **Wayne Becker, Hal Silverman**
Producer: **Steve Kelly/Perpetual Animation**
Agency: **Tatham-Laird & Kudner**

CHOCOLATE SHAPES
30-second
(MUSIC UP AND UNDER)
ANNCR (VO): The taste of chocolate. There's nothing in the world like it.
Maybe that's why there are so many ways to enjoy it. But one of the best ways is when it comes fortified with seven essential vitamins and minerals.
And that's when it comes this way.
Ovaltine.
Add Ovaltine flavoring to milk and you turn an . . .
. . . ordinary glass of milk . . .
. . . into an extraordinary treat.
So, if you're looking for a chocolate taste that's nutritious and delicious . . .
. . . look no further.

CAMP ITCHY-OWIE
30-second
NARRATOR: Deep in the dark of the darkest woods was the camp called . . .
KIDS: Itchy owie . . .
NARRATOR: Where things that bite in the day and the night made the children cry . . .
KIDS: Itchy owie . . .
NARRATOR: And every day they'd scratch away 'cause of poison ivy and oak.
KID: Itchy owie . . .
NARRATOR: 'Til by chance, there came to camp new Bactine Hydrocortisone. When they soothed it on, the itchy was gone and it made the owie okay . . . so that night, they slept just right.
KIDS: ZZZZZZZZZZZZZZZZ

1638
Art Director: **Tom Balchunis**
Writer: **Harold Kaplan**
Client: **New York Telephone**
Director: **P. Kimmelman**
Producer: **Steve Madoff**
Agency: **Young & Rubicam**

1639
Art Director: **Paul Collins**
Designer: **Craig Bernard**
Photographer: **George Maus**
Artist: **Boden Fedus**
Writer: **Tom Pedulla**
Client: **New England Bell**
Editor: **Editing Concepts**
Director: **George McGinnis**
Production Co: **Image Factory, Ed Pacio**
Agency: **Cabot Advertising**

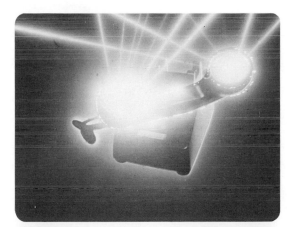

WHAT A DAY
30-second
MAN: What a day!
PHONE: How about a quick pick-me-up?
MAN: Who's that?
PHONE: Me . . . New York's favorite pick-me-up. Pick me up and call . . . ravishing Rhoda in Rockland . . . Gorgeous Gretchen in Greenwich . . . And there's always your mom in Manhattan.
MAN: I know who to call . . .
PHONE: And save 35% by dialing it yourself after 5. Local calls after 9.
MAN: She'll love this. Hello, Mom?
PHONE: Mom?
PHONE: For a quick pick-me-up . . . pick me up.

NEW ENGLAND TELEPHONE
30-second
"This tiny microchip is revolutionizing the way America does business and at New England Telephone we're using the technology in this chip to create a new generation of communications systems.
"In these systems, telephones become communications terminals that you can program like computers to do things no ordinary telephone ever could.
"So call us collect at 617 755 5201. We're New England Telephone."

1640
Art Director: **Rick Marchesano**
Artist: **Steven Oakes**
Writer: **Dennis Coffey**
Client: **PBS**
Production Co.: **Broadcast Arts**
Agency: **Goldberg/Marchesano and Associates, Inc.**

FESTIVAL METAMORPHOSIS
60-second
(CROWD NOISE AND RUSTLING)
VO: Expect the unexpected during Festival Nights on Public TV.
(CROWD QUIETS)
VO: . . . UNEXPECTED SUPERSTARS!
Voice of Paul Simon singing: ". . . Still crazy after all these years." (FADE OUT)
(CROWD APPLAUSE)
VO: . . . VOICES TO THRILL ANY HOUSE.
Voice of Beverly Sills singing, "   "
(CROWD NOISE: "Bravo, bravo!")
VO: . . . UNEXPECTED LAUGHS.
ALLEN'S VOICE: (DELIVERING FUNNY LINE) "Give me three bucks and I'll finish the monologue."

Our profession does not produce lasting celebrities
nor do its members achieve real fame in the sense
of Mozart, Shakespeare, DaVinci or Greta Garbo.
That is as it should be: We are, at best,
inspired craftsmen who work mostly for clients
with given goals and limitations.
And yet the forty-odd members of this Hall of Fame
have had a profound influence on the visual aspects
of everyone's life for at least a half-century.
Most of their work has been seen by more people
than that of even the greatest artists during their lifetimes.
Designers, Art Directors, Illustrators and Photographers
have a large hand in shaping our surroundings.
By setting examples they give content to our dreams.
They often show us how we ought to want to live;
and sell us the artifacts necessary to do it.
The fame is in the results—the work,
often partially anonymous.
The importance of having a Hall of Fame
which is now 10 years old is not the producing
of "Stars" but to provide an on-going
understanding—a diary—of this continuing
development of style for younger talents
to study in future years.
HENRY WOLF, CHAIRMAN
1982 Selection Committee

HALL OF FAME COMMITTEE
Selection
Henry Wolf, Chairman
Gennaro Andreozzi
Saul Bass
William Brockmeier
Ed Brodsky
Bob Ciano
David Davidian
Lou Dorfsman
Lee Epstein
Carl Fischer
Gene Federico
Milton Glaser
Marilyn Hoffner
Walter Kaprielian
Helmut Krone
John Peter
Ernest Scarfone
Eileen Hedy Schultz
Leonard Sirowitz
Bob Smith
William Taubin
Bradbury Thompson
Patron
Gene Federico
Presentation
Arthur Hawkins, Chairman
Managing and Planning
William H. Buckley, Chairman
Jack G. Tauss
Design
Otto Storch

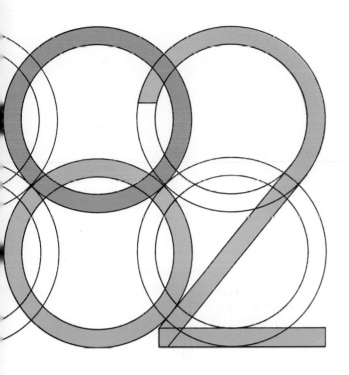

1972	M.F. Agha	1979	W.A. Dwiggins
	Lester Beall		George Giusti
	Alexey Brodovitch		Milton Glaser
	A.M. Cassandre		Helmut Krone
	René Clarke		Willem Sandberg
	Robert Gage		Ladislav Sutnar
	William Golden		Jan Tschichold
	Paul Rand	1980	Gene Federico
1973	Charles Coiner		Otto Storch
	Paul Smith		Henry Wolf
	Jack Tinker	1981	Lucian Bernhard
1974	Will Burtin		Ivan Chermayeff
	Leo Lionni		Gyorgy Kepes
1975	Gordon Aymar		George Krikorian
	Herbert Bayer		William Taubin
	Cipe Pineles Burtin	1982	Richard Avedon
	Heyworth Campbell		Amil Gargano
	Alexander Liberman		Jerome Snyder
	L. Moholy-Nagy		Massimo Vignelli
1976	E. McKnight Kauffer		
	Herbert Matter		
1977	Saul Bass		
	Herb Lubalin		
	Bradbury Thompson		
1978	Thomas M. Cleland		
	Lou Dorfsman		
	Allen Hurlburt		
	George Lois		

HALL OF FAME

RICHARD AVEDON

EDITORIAL
Born in New York City.
Studies with Alexey Brodovitch.
First editorial photographs appear in
Harper's Bazaar in 1945.
Harper's Bazaar photographer until 1965.
Joins *Vogue* in 1966 as fashion
and portrait photographer.
Affiliation continues today.
Other editorial assignments in
Life, Look, Theatre Arts, Newsweek, Time.
In 1976 *Rolling Stone* magazine publishes
"The Family" a special Bicentennial issue
consisting of 76 Avedon portraits,
without text, of the most powerful
people in America.

Visual consultant for the film *Funny Face*,
starring Fred Astaire and Audrey Hepburn.

ADVERTISING
Avedon has photographed and
directed print and television advertising
campaigns for major corporations and
advertising agencies throughout the world.
Client list includes:
First Bank of Boston, Chemical Bank,
Lincoln Mercury, Colgate, Revlon, Chanel,
Max Factor, Clairol, L'Oreal,
Chesebrough-Ponds, Blackglama Mink,
Suntory Liquor, Don Diego Cigars,
CBS Records.
Currently Creative Consultant
and Photographer-Director for
Calvin Klein Jeans, Christian Dior and
Gianni Versace, engaged to develop
world-wide images for print and television.

Nastassia Kinski and the Serpent

Jean Shrimpton   Cher   Robin Williams   John Lennon   Brooke Shields

Dovima with Elephants

Brooke Shields for Calvin Klein

Red Skelton for Don Diego Cigars

Catherine Deneuve for Chanel

Roseanne Vela for Revlon

RICHARD AVEDON

BOOKS
Avedon books include:
Observations, 1959
Nothing Personal, 1964
Alice in Wonderland:
The Forming of a Company,
The Making of a Play, 1973
Portraits, 1976
Avedon: Photographs 1947–1977

EXHIBITIONS
Avedon one-man exhibitions:
The Smithsonian Institution,
Washington, D.C., 1962
The Minneapolis Institute of Arts, 1970
The Museum of Modern Art, N. Y., 1974
The Marlborough Gallery, N. Y., 1975
The Metropolitan Museum of Art, N. Y., 1978
The Dallas Museum of Fine Arts, 1979
The High Museum of Art, Atlanta, Ga., 1979
Isetan, Tokyo, Japan, 1979
University Art Museum, Berkeley, Ca., 1980
Museum project in progress called
The West, a traveling exhibition for the
Amon Carter Museum of Western Art,
Fort Worth, Texas, commissioned for 1985.

Gianni Versace —Italy

First Boston Bank

Famolare Shoes

Blackglama Mink

I Love N.Y. Campaign

Christian Dior

人間は限りなく滑稽な存在なのだ。
だから笑うんですよ。だから厳粛に生きられる。
乾杯！乾杯！そういう私たちに。

PHOTO BY AVEDON

サントリーオールド

Suntory Whiskey —Japan

Johnny and Edgar Winter —CBS

Joan Baez —Vanguard Records

Sly and the Family Stone —Epic

Barbra Streisand —Columbia Records

Amil Gargano

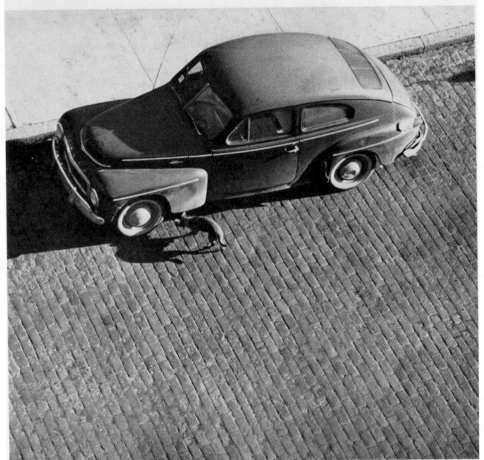

**You can hurt a Volvo,
but you can't hurt it much.**

This Volvo was bought new in Ann Arbor, Michigan, in 1956. Its owner paid $2345 for it, complete. He has raced it, pulled a camping trailer halfway across the country with it, his kids climb all over it, and it's seldom under cover. It has 80,261 miles on it. The head has never been off, the brakes have never been relined, the original tires lasted 55,000 miles, the clutch hasn't been touched, the valves have never been adjusted (much less ground), and it will still top 95 mph. Total cost of repairs exclusive of normal maintenance: One hood latch, $4.50. One suspension rod, $40.00. Not all Volvos will do this. But Volvos have a pretty good average. One enthusiastic owner in Wyoming wrote us that he has driven his Volvo over 300,000 miles without major repair. We think he's exaggerating. It's probably closer to 200,000 miles. See the Yellow Pages for the Volvo dealer nearest you. Overseas Delivery available. **VOLVO**

Volvo 122S compact. Like the Volvo above, it runs away from other popular-priced compacts in every speed range, gets over 25 miles to the gallon like the little economy imports, is virtually indestructible.

CARRY FULL AMOUNT OF BLACK AS INDICATED BY THIS BAR

I was born during the great depression, on June 4, 1932. And, if that wasn't enough, it had to happen in Detroit.

Both my parents emigrated from small towns in central Italy (about sixty miles apart in the province of Abruzzi) and found each other in the City of Wheels.

To my great joy, they are both still alive and well, lucid, energetic, enthusiastic, and loving, and have remained married to each other for the last 60 years.

Although my father never made much money in all the years he worked so hard before he retired, I consider him and my mother to be two of the most successful people I have ever known.

Beyond my family and friends, my next fondest memory of Detroit was a high school called Cass Tech. Thirty years ago, it had to be the finest high school in the country. After graduation, I spent the following two years searching to find a level of teaching in the Arts that came remotely close to what was offered at Cass Tech.

I first enrolled at Wayne University. Had I tried harder, or perhaps transferred to something practical, like hotel and restaurant management, I might have been able to avoid the draft and the Korean War as effectively as my friends did.

I left Wayne University after a year, the Society of Arts and Crafts after one semester, and was drafted in mid-term from yet another art school, which, in turn, left me with no feeling of loss and, in fact, a sense of relief.

In October 1952, at the induction center at Fort Custer, I was told by the interviewing officer that with my academic background, there was little risk of my winding up in the front lines of Korea as a combant infantryman.

In August 1954, upon my return from the front lines of Korea as a combat infantryman, I decided to enroll at Cranbrook Academy of Art. The insulated world of MFA candidates on the small campus of the automobile executive suburbs was too extreme and sudden a change. The cultural shock was more than I could endure. So, restless and impatient, I left after a year to enter the uncertain world of "commercial art".

I spent the spring of '55 pounding on the doors of local art studios in Detroit. My portfolio of drawings, paintings and designs were criticized as not acceptable for newspaper reproduction. Could I render an automobile transmission? Could I work in scratch-board?

Chrysler Corporation, I had heard, was recruiting designers. During my job interview, my prospective employer was intrigued by some typographic designs in my book. I was offered a position that would consist of designing lettering that would eventually appear on either the fronts or backs or sides of Chryslermade automobiles. I declined.

Bitter and disappointed, I took what I thought would be a temporary job in the bullpen of an advertising agency — Campbell·Ewald. After all, how could anyone with brains and talent work in advertising permanently?

My contempt lasted six months.

By December of 1955, I had worked on my portfolio in the evenings to the point where I thought I could finally get a job as an illustrator.

Al Scott, the man who had hired me, was a quiet and thoughtful man. When I told him what I planned to do, he urged me to give advertising a chance. His rationale was convincing: "Would you rather work in a business where you can create ideas or in a business where ideas are created for you?"

For that, I am eternally grateful.

Campbell·Ewald moved me along quickly. After two years, I was promoted to Group Art Director and responsible for five accounts which weren't very large or,

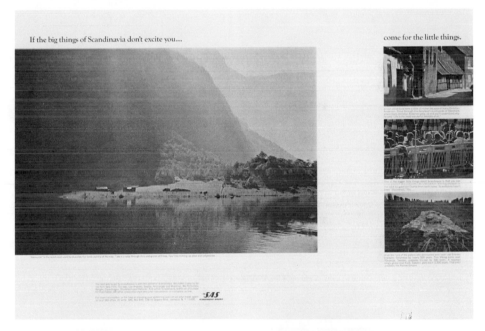

for that matter, very interesting. But I was given encouragement and, more important, support for work I created that was far different from anything previously initiated. I began to enjoy my work enormously.

New York was Mecca. Since adolescence, I had always wanted to be there. In the spring of '59, my dream of working in New York became a reality. Jim Durfee and I were transferred to Campbell-Ewald, New York, to join Carl Ally (who had recently moved there from Detroit) to work on Swissair and to develop new business.

The three of us hit it off together instantly. It took only a few months for us to decide that one day we would have our own agency.

That day arrived on June 25, 1962. We opened our doors with three small offices in the Seagram building with our only account—Volvo.

The ad budget was $300,000. That would yield $45,000 in annual commission. Our combined salaries were $39,000 annually and the rent was $12,600. With our $18,000 of investment capital, we were rock solid for a year, providing we didn't take the client to dinner or use taxis regularly.

The winter following our first year in business, I had the good sense to marry Elaine Pafundi, an art director whom I had met during my brief stay at Benton & Bowles. (Marrying another art director has one real advantage— it automatically eliminates two hours of daily explanations.)

This is the twentieth year of Ally & Gargano and, in retrospect, I believe the goals we established for ourselves back then have been essentially realized: our survival, our commitment to creating and defending good work and, finally, the broad-based recognition we have earned for that effort.

And for that, I am sincerely thankful.

Old Bushmills Irish Whiskey can   do anything, any time, any place.

If you want to know what goes into these holiday drinks besides Old Bushmills (yes, even the pink frothy one is a holiday drink — yes, it is made with whiskey), write to us. We'll send you the recipes.

If we missed your favorite holiday drink, make it with Old Bushmills anyway, then send us your recipe. We plan to do this again next year and we don't want to miss a favorite just because we don't know about it. And we

don't want you to miss Old Bushmills just because you don't know about it. Old Bushmills has burnished Scotch flavor without burnished Scotch smokiness — blended whiskey smoothness without blended whiskey blandness.

And if you're wondering why that whiskey straight, Whiskey Sour, Manhattan, Old Fashioned, whiskey on the rocks, and Irish Coffee are in the picture — well, as we said, Old Bushmills can do anything, any time, any place.

QUALITY IMPORTERS INC., 99 FIFTH AVE., NEW YORK 3, N.Y.

For years, Avis has been telling you Hertz is No. 1.

Now we're going to tell you why.

Hertz

Eddie Anderson had to face up to the truth. She nearly killed him.

The Arrangement

Warner Bros. presents a film Written and Directed by Elia Kazan. Starring Kirk Douglas, Faye Dunaway, Deborah Kerr, Richard Boone, Hume Cronyn. Produced by Elia Kazan, from his novel "The Arrangement." Associate Producer Charles Maguire. Music composed and conducted by David Amram. Production designed by Gene Callahan. Panavision® and Technicolor®

JEROME SNYDER ARTIST WRITER CRITIC GOURMET NOTARY PUBLIC

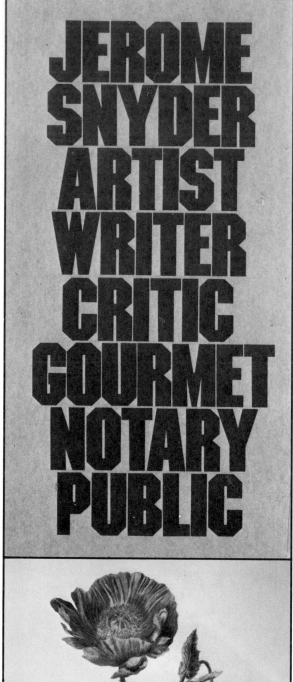

Self-taught and self-made, Jerome Snyder was an artist of uncommonly high order whose extraordinary knowledge and literary abilities were inexorably intertwined and were inseparable from his fanciful visual concepts. In the 50's as first Art Director of *Sports Illustrated,* he introduced contemporary illustration to editorial matter in an arena previously the domain of photography. In the 60's, as Art Director of *Scientific American,* he was well equipped for a job that demanded erudition and comprehension for visual interpretation. Intelligence and multi-faceted skills are reflected in Snyder's paintings and drawings. Larger forms are composed of myriad mosaics of many-colored smaller areas. In the absence of color, his delicate meticulous drawings demonstrate control of line, secure draftsmanship, thoughtful interpretation and a surprising agility for caricature. Later, a new mood evolves—sudden beautiful realism executed with deftness and enormous technical facility.

Although visual efforts were his priority, Snyder was devoted to the written word. His critiques appeared in Graphics, CA, Idea and U&lc. Under the rubric, *Underground Gourmet,* Jerome Snyder and Milton Glaser collaborated to report on low priced restaurants serving well prepared food, in weekly comments and several books of national renown. Seminal artist, writer, teacher, his perceptions at once intellectual and aesthetic, Jerome Snyder's legacy is of picture and word in vibrant unity. His line and language exude clarity and wit, tenderness and vision. He accepted his talents, mined his resources. He used himself for lasting performance.

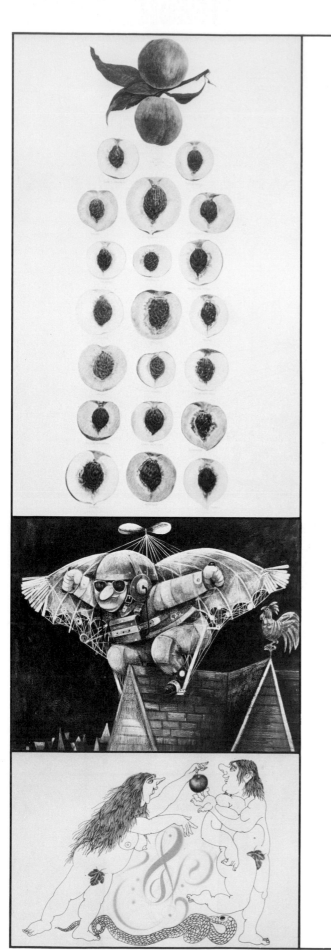

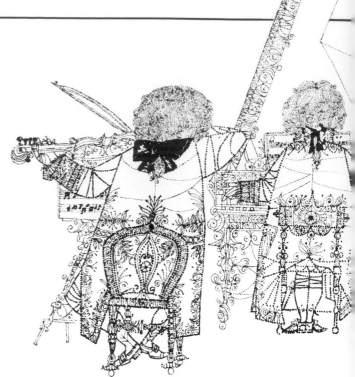

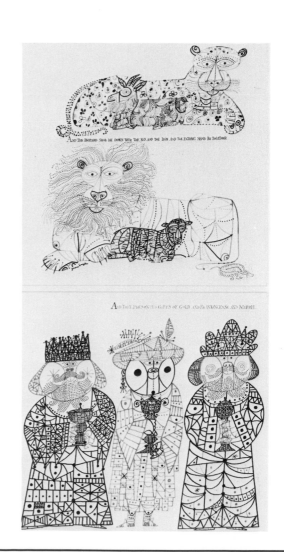

JEROME SNYDER

BIOGRAPHY
1916: Born in New York City
1940: Winner of national competition
for design of mural, Main Post Office,
San Francisco, California.
1941: Winner of national competition
for design of mural, Social
Security Building, Washington, D.C.
1942: Served in U.S. Army—
rank of Captain, Infantry.
1954: Art Director—Sports Illustrated
(the first).
1962: Art Director—Scientific
American.
Member of the Art Directors Club
of New York, American
Institute of Graphic Arts.
Awards from Art Directors Clubs of
New York, Chicago, Los Angeles,
AIGA
50 Best Books, Society of Publication
Designers, Society of Illustrators,
Society of Typographic Arts.
Taught at Cooper Union, The American
University of Biarritz, Pratt Institute,
Parsons School of Design,
Yale School of Fine Arts.
Contributing Editor—Graphics, CA,
IDEA, New York Magazine, U&lc.

Massimo Vignelli

Born in Milano in 1931, he studied architecture there and in Venice, and since then has worked with his wife Lella, an architect, in the field of design from graphics to products, from furniture to interiors.

Based in New York since 1965, their work has been exhibited throughout the world and is in the permanent collections of several museums.

Massimo Vignelli has taught and lectured on design in the major cities and universities in the USA and abroad. Among their many awards: The 1973 Industrial Arts Medal of the American Institute of Architects, and an honorary doctorate from the Parson School of Design, NY.

Following is an excerpt, written by Emilio Ambasz, from the introduction of the catalogue of the exhibition at the Padiglione d'Arte Contemporanea, Milan, Italy, 1980.

. . . For years since 1964, they have been the ambassadors of European design; specifically, the standard-bearers of a Mediterranean brand of Swiss graphic design made more agile and graceful by the traditional Italian flair for absorbing and re-elaborating foreign influence. Almost single-handedly Massimo introduced and imposed Helvetica typeface throughout the vast two-dimensional landscape of corporate America.

His graphic design was always distinct and elegant and, if it is true that as time passed by it began to lose its crisp profile, this was due, in great part, to his having generously taught a whole generation of American designers how to evaluate, organize, and display visual information. By giving away his lucidly elaborated formulas he had allowed them to reproduce his image until it became so omnipresent that it began to become transparent.

There are great comforts in accepting the rewards of having developed an ineffable technique. And in America's Eden, there are even greater rewards for such technical virtuosity provided the exercises take you nowhere. It is to the Vignellis' credit that they did not accept this situation. They have been searching for ways out of such deadening comforts. Admittedly, their probes were at first cautious; but theirs is not blind courage but the lucid sort which presses ahead while fully aware of the risks awaiting. At a crossroads in their careers they valiantly march on. With one hand they hold onto the luminous treasures of their past experiences while with the other they seek, sense, and try for the unknown, hoping for that which daring and risking may bring about.

Flashes of randomness have begun to appear in their work. An invitation to a New York showing of their work was sent to all their friends in the form of a crumpled piece of tissue paper. The paper's color was très chic and the typeface of the most accurate elegance, but the controlled

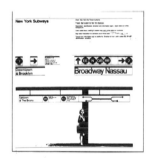

passion that crumpled piece of paper denoted could not be disguised behind its carefully rehearsed throw-away elegance. Massimo and Lella, the professionals par excellence, are now undergoing a subtle but deep transformation. The hand which once followed carefully laid-out patterns has still kept its elegant demeanor, but the gesture is now looser and more openly passionate. Although still tempered by a great amount of self-control, the quest is now after the sheer, inebriating pleasure of questing. Rather than presenting answers in careful doses, it is slowly becoming evident that, in the last period, the designers have been posing questions.

A similar pattern of progress may be observed in their other fields of design endeavor. In the case of furniture design, because of the nature of the production-distribution cycle, the emotional gesture must be a more measured one. It is not, after all, a throw-away item such as a piece of printed paper. But they have traveled from the carefully constructed structural feeling of the seating line "Saratoga" to a more humble acceptance of craftsmanship and manual uncertainty, substituting the round formality and warm textures of the "Acorn" chair for Saratoga's precise geometry and immaculate skin. Thus again, the contingent is accepted and the unique instance tolerated, even welcomed. Wood and leather are chosen as instances of nature, and held together in ways which enhance their physicality. Gradually, the chimera of an eternal system crumbles, or at least lets its internal cracks come up to the surface. A readier acceptance of the temporary, of the accidental, of the one-of-a-kind, seems to emerge from this crisis, an acceptance which is the more laudable if we perceive the existential turmoil these very gifted designers seem to be undergoing. I feel they are entering into a new, even more productive phase. With this exhibition they are taking inventory and evaluating the stock, populating the house they have built in foreign lands.

© **Emilio Ambasz**

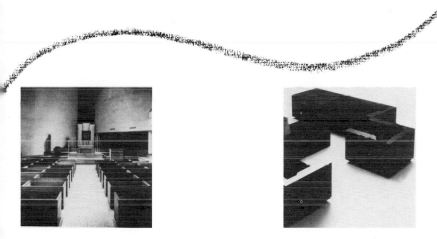

Bill Bernbach
1911-1982

He said,
"The real giants have always been poets,
men who jumped from facts
into the realm of imagination and ideas."

He elevated advertising to high art
and our jobs to a profession.

He made a difference.

Doyle Dane Bernbach

The Art Directors Club reprints the above to honor the memory of a cherished friend.

ART DIRECTORS
1981

While times were tight for most American ventures, the life and times of the ADC were healthy and happy. More programs and more member participation were earmarks of 1981's crowded calendar of exciting events.

John Peter stands by his WWII poster, recipient of the Vermeil medal from France's President.

The 60th Annual Exhibition opened to delighted crowds in Tokyo last fall. It has toured four major cities in Japan every year since '75 as well as to other parts of the globe.

How sweet it is! At the opening of the popular "Valentines" invitational gallery show, here is one of 40 artists—Sheba Emerson with her imaginative work.

Luncheon programs from September to July were S.R.O. Here's Walter Kaprielian introducing representatives of Mainichi Broadcasting to the crowd.

Mary Wells Lawrence presented the Honorable Hugh L. Carey with the 1982 Management Award at the Annual Dinner. They are with Walter Kaprielian and Mrs. Carey, too.

CLUB NEWS

At a memorable Hall of Fame Awards Show inductee and past president William Taubin is congratulated by President Walter Kaprielian and M.C. Arthur Hawkins.

Traditionally a lively new members' party is held at the Club. Lorraine Allen welcomes in Len Sugarman and Arnold Blumberg along with a host of others.

Judging the Annual Show is strenuous, but worth it for Bill Buckley, Jacques Parker, Bill Cadge, Sal Lazzarotti.

Tuesdays the A-Deviates bring the best jazz sounds north of New Orleans to many devoted fans. The players: Flip Philips, Dick Ross (band leader), Jim Collier, Dick Wohlberg, Art Lohman, Bob Pratt, Jim Gribbon, Bob Sparkman

1982

Receptionist Lillian Tong promotes the new ADC sweatshirt.

The 1982 season ended late—in July—because many activities were still going strong. Members were busy, too, creating a new newsletter for the fall, finishing this Annual, and gearing up for next year's Annual Show. Can we top it? We're going to try.

EXHIBIT DESIGN

The Exhibit:

I live in New York City. Many people live here
and love it. Companies live here and love it, too.
But one that recently moved
from NY to Connecticut is Union Carbide.
Too bad for the Art Directors Club —
which had long held its annual shows
at the Union Carbide building.
So we had to look and search
and dig for new exhibit space.
You know it's not likely anyone
would readily cede 3,000 square feet of New York
real estate free for several weeks.
But at the bell, Cooper Union, a public-spirited
(and free! and excellent!) art school came through.
Despite being away from midtown
the show drew well. The hanging itself was
pure simplicity. But our handsome exhibit
system had to remain in storage.
Our Exhibit Design Committee had invested time
and energy and talent to update
that system for use in a space
far different from what Cooper Union provided.
Thus, we must credit designers
Dan Weidmann and Frank Marshall,
whose sensible ideas
we weren't able to use.
Dan handles exhibits and graphics
for the Brooklyn Museum
(which by its very name could never move to CT).
Frank handles graphics and exhibits for GAF
(which is staying put).
Nice try fellas. Wait'll next year.
LARRY MILLER, CHAIRMAN

The Show's Promotion:

The Club was able to coordinate all
show-related graphics thanks to Scott Mednick
of Douglas Boyd Design and Frank O'Blak.
Doug handled the gravy jobs, Frank the drier ones.
Doug volunteered early on to design the
Call for Entries poster and did a stunning job,
showing packages of entries flying
into New York over a symbolic desert
(Controversial? You bet.) We rewarded
Doug—whose firm is in LA, never was in NY—
by also getting him to do the exhibit poster.
It shows the awards flying *out* from NY
over that same desert. Frank O'Blak,
art director at NYC's Robert A. Becker Inc., trans-
lated Doug's visual themes—beautifully, not
dutifully—into many collateral pieces. Result a
homogeneous program. Next year We hope to
integrate the Annual book as well.

Call for Entries   The Exhibition

| "Stormy" | Brian Rushkon | "Stormy" | Leonard Nomes |
| Larry Miller | Daniel Weidmann | Frank B. Marshall III | Frank O'Blak |

AWARDS PRESENTATION

The 61st Awards Presentation was held in the grand ballroom of the Waldorf Astoria, a fitting choice because the hotel has long been the hallmark of New York chic and elegance, and there's a timelessness about the place which matches our show — an event not about fads or fashion but about tradition and an institution in our world. Over 400 people came for cocktails and many stayed to dance until midnight. Winning work was dramatically displayed on three huge screens.

This year's awards show was a team effort of dedicated professionals. Thanking people reminds one of Oscar night because, in fact, there are so many people who helped behind the scenes.

But our special thank you's go to: Frank O'Blak, program and invitation design; Burt Morgan, printing; TypoVision Plus and Ad Agencies Headliners, type; Sterling Regal, printing, paper, separations. The visual presentation was created with the help of Jim Sant'Andrea and Jim Sant'Andrea, Inc., multi-media show producers. Karl Steinbrenner was creative consultant. Judging committee chairman, Harvey Gabor, shared host honors with me; president and immediate past president, Walter Kaprielian and Bill Taubin, gave out the 18 gold and 30 silver awards. While the art, design and copy was the chief attraction, there were extras. Opening and closing the awards segment was a special "New York, New York" A/V show, intercut with fabulous city scenes, with song by the fabulous Liza Minnelli. The "New York, New York" film fit in with a grand scheme—that of presenting the Honorable Hugh L. Carey, governor of New York, with the Club's 1982 Management Award. He was selected for his role in the "I Love New York" TV and print ad campaign. Management Award chairman, Lou Dorfsman, invited Wells Rich, Greene chairman Mary Wells Lawrence, whose agency created the campaign, to make the presentation

This assignment always carries a unique set of problems. First, finding a place with exactly the right ambience for this truly magical night. And second, the site, wine and fine food must come in at an affordable price (no small task in today's money crunch). With the help of so many good people, we succeeded admirably.
DAVID DAVIDIAN, CHAIRMAN

David Davidian

William Taubin

LUNCHEON PROGRAM

It would be difficult to write about the Wednesday lunches without first thanking Diane Moore and her staff at the Club for all their hard work. Jacqueline Little made sure the invitations went out on time, Lillian Tong manned the phone and took the reservations, Debra Woo prepared the wonderful food, Cookie Busweiler helped serve, S.J. Toy tended the bar, Deborah Weathers took our pictures, and Stephen Hendrix made sure the slide projector, video equipment, etc., were in place and in working order every week.

We had a guest speaker almost every Wednesday from September '81 to July '82—the largest crowds anyone can remember.

It was like going to class every Wednesday, except much better. There was no set syllabus. No one except the guests had to do homework and everyone got a gourmet meal. Members brought their clients and friends. Many have since become members of the Club.

One day when I found we were a little shy of guest speakers for the schedule, I called a meeting of the lunch committee. I told them we needed to fill in the line-up, and we began to develop some ideas. The following day the committee members started calling my office, and before the end of the day we had scheduled guests for 16 successive lunches. This not only filled the remaining schedule but gave us a head start on our plans for the next season. The lunch committee people gave me a very good feeling about being a member of the Art Directors Club.

None of this, of course, would have been possible without the people who agreed to be our guests. They came prepared. They brought their notes, their slides, their reels and in some instances, even their own equipment and assistants to run it! Thank you all!

ED BRODSKY, CHAIRMAN

We had a little fun with the picture below—proving the point that each of the hard working members of the luncheon team did the work of two.

Not pictured: Jeff Babitz, Lee Buchar, Jo Ann Goldsmith, Walter Kaprielian, Marie Christine Lawrence, David November, Jacques Parker, Joan Rehak, Herb Rosenthal, Carole Schulter, Jack G. Tauss, Ron Wickham

Beverly Herman   Harriett   Cyd Kilbey

Ed Brodsky   Debra Woo   Ron Coutre   Dan Nelson

Speakers were Tom Carnase below, George Obremski, Saul Mandel, Leon Appel, Lorna Shanks, Syd Hap, Michael

Shall, David Sears & George McGinnis, Isadore Seltzer, Lou Silverstein below, Richard Colligan, the Computer Graphics

Lab of the N.Y. Institute for Technology & Jack Chojnacki, Camila Chavez, David Wagner, Lou Dorfsman below,

Gertrude Snyder, Lou Myers, Sharon O'Neal, Schaedler/Pinwheel, William Wedin, David Moss & Niad & Walter Einsel,

Alberto Gavasci, Prof. Irwin Corey above, Tim Crawford, Gil Cowley, Bill Feigenbaum, Maxine Paetro, and many others.

SCHOLARSHIP

Seventeen lucky kids have been given the chance for schooling and careers which would have passed them by.

Two of these scholarships have been named in memory of past members, the Herb Lubalin Scholarship and the George Krikorian Scholarship. To be able to do this year after year, this committee solicits funds from the community, and year after year the Club has been the happy recipient of Mrs. Lila Acheson Wallace's generosity. Again in 1982 we are grateful to her for her contribution to art education.

Our hats are also off to Dorothy Evans and her staff at the School Art League of New York City, who contribute so much to our effort. Each year they send out a notice for scholarship applications to the school systems in the Tri-State area. Then Dorothy's staff processes the applications, handling the task of requesting portfolios of qualified students and preparing the judging process.

Then we on the committee enter the picture. We reserve a day on our calendars when we will be out of the office, away from the phone, and in the calm of a strange 'hall', we judge a sizable amount of student work.

We were encouraged by the versatility of the talent in people so young, and choosing was difficult. The portfolios offered everything from realistic illustration, graphics and advertising layouts to advanced conceptual communications. Today's students seem to have a good grasp of the current marketplace. There had been a simply wonderful marriage of the "picture and headline" school which I have observed previously. In the last two years there seems also to be a rebirth of graphics coming through in the work. Both graphic design and illustration are leading indicators of this trend.

The students also seem to show more aggressiveness in their desire to move ahead. This could be sensed from the abundance of scholarship applicants.

In their applications they said they wanted to continue with their educations and told us what their goals were about becoming professionals. It gives us all a great feeling to help others progress and enter a profession which has been so rewarding to us.

KURT HAIMAN, CHAIRMAN

The committee:

George Halpern, Charles Dickinson, Zlata Paces, Jo Ann Goldsmith, Ed Suchocki, David Davidian

Kurt Haiman

PORTFOLIO REVIEW

This year 50 art directors and designers critiqued over 500 portfolios.

Reviews were conducted each Monday and Friday from April 5th to May 28th at the ADC for two hours during lunch. These are very intense sessions. One of the initial things we do is to show them that talent is not enough. We explain to them why they should remove extraneous materials from their books—that our business is one of specialization. A designer need not include photography or sketches unless they are excellent (and then only one or two); the beginner with strong selling concepts in his or her book should be directed toward advertising; the young person with a design flair probably shouldn't try for an advertising job. We look for craft in type work and ideas for TV and a host of things. Going beyond the one-to-one portfolio evaluation, we tell the young people about real life in the marketplace. After each day's session an evaluation sheet with comments from the participating art directors is compiled by me and co-chairman, Richard MacFarlane. (Some schools fared well, others not so.) We mail the evaluations to the institutions, complimenting them on their strengths and highlighting weaknesses perceived in their instruction. This personalizes the program and enhances communication between us.

Schools as different in approach as Pratt Institute and the Rhode Island School of Design have written to thank us for the quality of this program, which makes us proud.
JACK G. TAUSS, CHAIRMAN
Richard MacFarlane, Co-Chairman

Students and their teachers make the trip to New York City from as far away as Kent State and the University of Akron in Ohio to have their portfolios reviewed at the ADC—which is a good indication that the program has meaning for them.
As much as the activity means to the students, it also holds tremendous importance for us and is one of the most popular of our programs. I think that each of us feels we're helping to ensure that the young people starting in the field set out with their best foot forward.

Richard MacFarlane   Co-Chairmen Get Together   Jack G. Tauss.

TRAVELING SHOW

We went back on the road again this season making the grand tour of the U.S. As soon as the New York show closed, the exhibit was slipped into crates and the 5,000 pounds of freight hoisted onto a 40 foot trailer truck heading for points west.

For the third consecutive year the ADC show has been exhibited in St. Louis and Portland.
In St. Louis, Missouri, the exhibit was the focal point for an advertising and design seminar entitled "Size Up the Best" with guest speaker Darwin Bahm. The St. Louis people responsible for organizing the

seminar and show were: Barry Tilson, Stan Gellman Graphics; Frank Roth, Frank James Productions; and Larry Pfisterer, Gardner Advertising and the Washington University School of Fine Arts. In Portland, Oregon, ADC member Les Hopkins and the Designers Roundtable held an elaborate opening along with a design seminar, a mini version of the Aspen Design Conference. Featured speaker was John Slaven of Volkswagen. (Mr. Slaven accepted last year's Art Directors Management award for his company from us.)
The exhibits were well attended and considered a complete success by all involved.
The bad news was that due to steadily rising freight charges, it has become difficult to keep costs at a break even point. Next year we hope to get corporate sponsorship to underwrite the traveling show. Meanwhile, a smaller version has become more attractive to sponsors in other cities. This year selected portions of the ADC show were exhibited at: the Art Institute of Philadelphia; the University of Delaware; Northwestern University; the University of Massachusetts.
The show was also seen in Vienna, Austria, thanks to Dr. Gerhard Puttnar, and visited the Philippines, thanks to Nelo Edillon.
Next year we expect to visit more cities here and around the world.
CLUB STAFF
Pictured below (from left to right) Deborah "Stormy" Weathers, Debra Woo, Michelle Morando, Lillian Tong, Diane Moore, Margaret (Cookie) Busweiler, Jacqueline Little, S.J. Toy, Jack Jamison.

Michael Chin   Dan Forte

Daniel Sheehan   Stephen Hendrix

Club Staff

GALLERY

There were six distinctive and exciting exhibits this season:

The Art Director as Artist: The gallery committee kicked off the schedule by giving the entire membership an opportunity to show their own artwork done for their own pleasure rather than assigned work. Every inch of wall space was covered with art ranging from: a wood carving by Jack Jamison; pen and ink drawings by Kurt Haiman, Jerrold Smokler and Jacques Parker; a needlepoint by Jo Ann Goldsmith; and paintings by Martin Solomon, Vincent Pepi, Gladys Barton, Bill Buckley, Art Hawkins, Hal Toledo, Ed Brodsky and Geoffrey Moss, to name a few. So great was the response that we hope this show becomes a tradition at the Club.

Valentines: For the second year, 40 artists were invited to create a valentine. This show gives members the opportunity to see how a variety of illustrators and photographers handle the same assignment. The highlight was the opening party with balloons and an enormous heart-shaped cake enjoyed by over 200 guests.

Photography by Rivka Katvan and Tom Zetterstrom: This show was a delightful mix of black and white photography. Katvan's "Life Backstage," portraits of Broadway performers in captured moments, contrasted with Zetterstrom's landscapes from "Portraits of Trees" and scenes from a moving vehicle in "A Moving Point of View."

A Jerome Snyder Retrospective: The combined efforts of the luncheon and gallery committees gave us a show with a lunchtime opening. Lou Dorfsman and Gertrude Snyder told us about the erudite and talented Jerome. The gallery was filled with his delightful pen and ink and colored pencil drawings and paintings.

Linocuts by Randall Enos and Frances Jetter: These two artists showed us the great versatility achieved by the lino-cut technique. Randy's colorful, satirical images were in sharp contrast with the moody and thoughtful commentaries done by Frances.

The Human Condition, Humorous Drawings by Jo Teodorescu. Last, but definitely not least, this exhibit gave us bright and lighthearted humor (just the thing for July). The work of this Rumanian-born artist combines pen and ink, gouache and bits of collage, showing his very special way of looking at the world.

In addition, we are in the process of arranging a **Bea Feitler Retrospective** for the designer who died this year. We hope a fall showing can be arranged.

NANCY KENT, CHAIRMAN
The committee: Nicki Kalish, co chairman with Linda Stillman

Nancy Kent   Dan Wynn   Nicki Kalish   Randall Enos   Frances Jetter

JAPAN SHOW

It has taken almost ten years to develop the unique relationship that exists between the art directors of our country and those in the land of the rising sun. It is a relationship that is meaningful to both sides. I have tried to tell the brief history of the Japanese and American exhibition tours in the following. What is not included are the hours spent in letter writing, in meeting and planning and the hard work of the committee and others. It is hoped that the international exchange of ideas that we have nurtured with Japan can be enlarged in the future to include other nations because the more that is put into such an exchange the more all of us will get out of it.

Our dialogue with the Japanese started in 1973 and 1974 at the "Inside New York" and EXPO I communication conferences. Leading Japanese designers who were attending the conferences met with our art directors and were greeted cordially.

In 1975, after several stops and starts, we were finally able to send the ADC's 55th Annual show to Tokyo and Osaka for the first Japanese showing. (This was made possible through the cooperation of *Idea* Magazine and Mr. Takeo Yao, president of the Japanese Package Designers Association and a Club member.) Response was gratifying and they have asked for the show regularly every year since then.

In 1975, the Japanese reciprocated by sending us the First Japanese Graphic Idea Exhibition (jointly sponsored by the Japanese Graphic Design Committee and the ADC).

By 1980 our show had grown so popular in Japan that the number of tour cities had grown to 26 (the tour had to be called off near its end because wear and tear from repacking and shipping had damaged the art). Now we have a manageable schedule: the 60th Annual toured four Japanese cities. In March, it was at the Osaka Design Center (sponsored by the Japanese Package Designers Association) and at the Aichi Design Center, Nagoya (the Chubu Creative Club the sponsor); in April, at the Japan Industries Design Hall, Tokyo, (the Japan Industries Design Association the sponsor); and in the fall, at Kanazawa, Fukui (the exhibit has been donated to the Kanazawa Art and Design College).

Meanwhile, we have been fortunate to be able to see a large body of the Japanese work, which is very beautiful. Every three years the Japanese Graphic Idea Exhibition comes here (the second one was in '80 and we are soon to see another one). This show has been viewed by art directors, educators and the general public and tours America under the auspices of the Japanese-American Societies.

SHINICHIRO TORA, CHAIRMAN

The committee: Meg Crane, Jitsuo Haoshi, Eileen Hedy Shultz, Ira Sturtevant, William Taubin

Designer: Shigeo Okamoto

The 60th Annual Exhibition of The Art Directors Club of
N.Y.
第60回ニューヨークADC名古屋展

Tom Yanashi

Shinichiro Tora guided the Japanese Show step by step for a decade.

MEMBERSHIP

Sixty-five new members were welcomed to the Club at the Membership Committee's reception on November 17, 1981.
Those in attendance received a lucite cube to commemorate their membership. They were introduced and urged to participate in the many Club activities.

Membership of the Club stands at 666. A tribute to the value of their membership is the fact that 121 of them are Life Members (25 years plus) and 280 of them have held membership for over 10 years. One of many benefits membership offers is association with professionals from diverse areas of the industry, which includes not only AD's and Junior AD's, but writers, educators and photographers, as well as corporations, colleges and professional organizations.

How one can join is outlined here:
Anyone of the members listed in the back of the book can sponsor a new member, and information and applications are available at the Club, 488 Madison Avenue, NY, NY 10022, or call (212) 838-8140. Below are the qualifications of membership.

Regular: At the time of application the candidate must be a qualified art director with at least two years experience as an AD. Residence or place of business must be within 75 miles of New York City. Regular members have all privileges and may hold any office.

Associate: The candidate need not be a practicing art director but a creative worker in the graphic and industrial arts and professions. The category includes painters, illustrators, photographers, educators, writers, lecturers, journalists, etc. Associate members have the same obligations for dues and assessments as Regular members. They are eligible for election to the Executive Committee but they may not be elected as Officers.

Non-Resident: The candidate must be a qualified art director with at least two years working experience as an AD. Residence and place of business are both outside of the 75-mile radius of New York City. He or she may serve on committees but not as an Officer.

Junior: The candidate must be between the ages of 21 and 25 and have worked in the graphics and industrial arts for at least a year. Residence or place of business must be within 75 miles of New York City.

There also are three classes of Affiliate Membership:

Corporate: This classification relates to corporations doing business in the communications or graphic arts industries.

Institutional: This classification relates to universities, colleges and college level art schools with study programs in the graphic arts or communications, and art museums.

Professional: This classification relates to professional associations in communications or in the graphic arts industries.

Upon acceptance in these classifications, the Affiliate member may nominate three from its staff to attend and participate in Club functions as Associate members.
LORRAINE ALLEN, CHAIRMAN

Lorrainne Allen   Shinichiro Tora   Mike Fenga   Dick MacFarlane   Horst Winkler

Allen Philiba   Sal Lazzaroti   Joann Coates   Tobias Moss   Charles Dickenson

ADVISORY BOARD

The Advisory Board traditionally takes on the job
of running the Awards Presentation.
Additionally, the Board meets throughout the year
to discuss every aspect of Club activities.
The Board is an "Advisory" group in the truest
sense of the word advising on the Hall of Fame crite
on the Constitution,
on matters of education and protocol.
The current Board's personal knowledge
of Club activities extends back to the Presidency
of Stuart Campbell in 1929
and its members have weathered the big depressio
the War Years, the post-war boom.
We have been a part of the many changes
in the advertising, design and communications
business, the growth of TV,
and the enormous changes
that have taken place in the Club.
We bridge the age and the generation gap,
as well, for the ages
of our members range from their 40's to their 80's.
This gives us needed perspective on issues.
But we've noticed that some things
have never changed: the desire to
professionalize the art director was an early one,
to give him (and her) the needed recognition.
The dedication of members towards excellence
in their work and of the officers
in the performance of their duties
or that there is an Advisory Board
around if needed—
not to tell anyone what to do—
but to lend a sympathetic ear. These are constants.
WILLIAM TAUBIN, CHAIRMAN

Every member of the Advisory Board
knows the blood and tears involved in
being President of the Art Directors Club,
for every president, past and present, is a
member.
All of us know what it feels like to make
those hard decisions when, as Harry
Truman so aptly stated, "The buck stops
here."

William Taubin   Art Hawkins   Bill Brockmeier   Garrett Orr

Eileen Hedy Schultz   Bob Smith   David Davidian   Bill Buckley   Jack Jamison

ANNUAL BOOK

This is the fifth annual book we have published through our subsidiary, ADC Publications, Inc.

Just for the fun of it I did some rough calculations as to the number of people who read or, because of pass'along readership, at least look at the Annual in the course of a year. Multiply the 20,000 copies distributed here and abroad this year by ten! Then consider that these Annuals remain on art directors' bookshelves and back issues are borrowed by so many more people during the years and we begin to understand why this book has continued to have the impact it has.

We are enormously proud of the service this collection of best advertising and design always provides.
Despite the advent of other annuals which offer some very stiff competition in the book trade, we have been surprised that our own sales are ever-increasing.

This edition contains more entries and is enjoying a larger print run than any previous issue.

The effort is an enormous one, a fact of which any art director who deals with details and follow-through is well aware. It contains over 1,900 halftones and the same number of captions and a complete cross index of art directors and designers, clients, writers, production companies for ready reference.

We are indeed fortunate this year to have Otto Storch, one of our Hall of Famers, as editor and designer of the book. None of this would be possible, of course, without the job ably handled by the Club staff and we thank Daniel Sheehan, Steve Hendrix, Dan Forte, Michael Chin, who gather the art and credits and handle myriad details under the guidance of Diane Moore. Jo Yanow copy-edited the Club News section. Frank DeLuca of Supermart Graphics is the catalyst in all of this handling the entire coordination, packaging, and all else down to printing and binding.

Distribution of the book is by direct mail and *Print* magazine. Trade distribution in the U.S. and Canada is by Robert Silver Associates. Feffer and Simons handles foreign distribution.

The ADC book division has as its other officers, David Davidian as vice president and Blanche Fiorenza, who replaces Bob Reed, who was secretary of the division since its formation and an individual to whom we owe a debt of gratitude for his book work.

ERNEST SCARFONE, PRESIDENT

Ernest Scarfone   Blanche Fiorenza   Frank DeLuca   Miriam Solomon   Otto Storch

MEMBERS \ INDEX

MEMBERSHIP LIST 1982

Henrietta Abrams
Michael Abramson
Donald Adamec
Gaylord Adams
George C. Adams
Steven Adams
Patricia Addiss
Peter Adler
Charles Adorney
The Advertising Club of NY-PR
Warren Aldoretta
Lorraine Allen
Walter Allner
The Amer. Institute of
    Graphic Arts-PR
The Amer. Soc. of Magazine
    Photographers-PR
Carlo Ammirati
Gennaro Andreozzi
Ted Andresakes
Jack Anesh
Al Anthony
Robert Anthony
Tony Anthony
Clive J. Antioch
Masuteru Aoba
Arnold Arlow
Herman Aronson
The ADC of Boston-PR
Tadashi Asano
Gordon C. Aymar
Joel Azerrad

Jeff Babitz
Robert O. Bach
Ronald Bacsa
Priscilla Baer
Frank Baker
Leslie Baker
Ronald W. Ballister
Robert Barclay
Don Barron
Clyde W. Bartel
Robert J. Barthelmes
Gladys Barton
Matthew Basile
Mary K. Baumann
Allan Beaver
Peter Belliveau
Felix Beltrán
Ephram E. Benguiat
Edward J. Bennett
Laurence Key Benson
David Bentley
John Berg
Sy Berkley
Saul Berliner
Park Berry
Peter J. Bertolami
Barbara Bertoli
Robert Blattner
Robert Blend
Bruce Bloch
David S. Block
Arnold Blumberg
Robert Bode
Ronne Bonder
George Warren Booth
John Milne Boothroyd
William Bossert
Harold A. Bowman
Doug Boyd
Douglas C. Boyd
Simeon Braguin
Joan Brandt
Pieter Brattinga
Fred J. Brauer
Al Braverman
Michael Brock
William P. Brockmeier

Ed Brodsky
Ruth Brody
John D. Brooke
Joe Brooks
Ilene Renee Brown
Cissy Bruce
Robert Bruce
Bruno E. Brugnatelli
Bernard Brussel-Smith
Lee Buchar
William H. Buckley
Aaron Burns
Herman F. Burns
Cipe P. Burtin
Mel Byars

Bill Cadge
Albert J. Calzetta
Stuart Campbell
Bryan Canniff
Tony Cappiello
Cardinal Type Service, Inc.
Thomas Carnase
David E. Carter
Salvatore Cascio
Frank D. Cennamo
C. Edward Cerullo
Irene Charles
John V. Cherry
Kay Chin
Alan Christie
Stanley Church
Seymour Chwast
Bob Ciano
Edmund J. Cleary
Thomas F. Clemente
Mahlon Cline
Mattlyn W. Cline
Robert Clive
Victor Closi
Joann C. Coates
Robert Adam Cohen
Eugene Paul Cohn
Charles Coiner
Michael Coll
David Corbett
Lee Corey
Mark Corvington
Sheldon Cotler
Ron Couture
Thomas Craddock
James Craig
Steven L. Craig
Meg Crane
Brian A. Cranner
Elaine Crawford
Robert Crozier
Richard Cummings
Jerry Cummins
Joe Cupani
Charles Cutler
Ethel R. Cutler

Royal Dadmun
Bilal Dallenbach
Wendy Seabrook Damico
Norman Dane
Stephanie David
David Davidian
Herman Davis
Philip Davis
Robert Defrin
Joe Del Sorbo
Francesca de Majo
M.J. Demner
Marco De Plano
Florian R. Deppe
David Deutsch
Frank M. Devino
Francis DeVito
Madlyn W. Dickens
Charles Dickinson
Arthur Hill Diedrick

Carolyn Diehl
Edward P. Diehl
John F. Dignam
Robert Dolobowsky
Lou Donato
Louis Dorfsman
Marc Dorian
Kay Elizabeth Douglas
J. Wesley Doyle
Nick Driver
Donald H. Duffy
William R. Duffy
Laura K. Duggan
Rosalyn C. Dunham
Rudolph Dusek

Bernard Eckstein
Peter Edgar
William H. Edwards
Don Egensteiner
Antonie Eichenberg
Zeneth Eidel
Prof. Benjamin Einhorn
Stanley Eisenman
Wallace W. Elton
Rod A. Emery
Malcolm End
David Epstein
Henry Epstein
Lee Epstein
Molly Epstein
Suren Ermoyen
Dorothy Evans

Titti Fabiani
Bob Farber
Abe Farrell
Leonard Favara
Gene Federico
Michael Fenga
Lidia B. Ferrara
Lilly Filipow
William F. Finn
Blanche Fiorenza
Don Firpo
Carl Fischer
M.I. Fisher
John E. Fitzgerald
John Flanagan
Ellen Fleury
Donald P. Flock
William H. Ford
Robert Foster
John Fraioli
Stephen O. Frankfurt
Cheryl Freed
Mel Freedman
Frederic B. Freyer
Oren S. Frost
Satoru Fujii
Neil Fujita
Takeshi Fukunaga
Terunobu Fukushima
Michael Fultz
Leonard W. Fury

Harvey Gabor
Leighton D. Gage
Robert Gage
Diana Garcia De Tolone
Gene Garlanda
David Gatti
Joseph T. Gauss
Alberto Gavasci
Charles Gennarelli
Carl H. Georgi
Joseph Gering
Michael Germakian
Victor Gialleonardo
Edward Gibbs
Wayne A. Gibson
Richard B. Gillis
Frank C. Ginsburg

Sara Giovanitti
George Giusti
Milton Glaser
Eric Gluckman
Seymour Goff
Bill Gold
Irwin Goldberg
Jean Goldsmith
Eli W. Goldowsky
Jo Ann Goldsmith
Alan Goodman
Roy Grace
Albert Greenberg
Julie L. Greenfield
Robert L. Greenwell
Richard Gregory
Fred Greller
Jack Griffin
Walter Grotz
Maurice Grunfeld
Nelson Gruppo
Lurelle Guild
Rollins S. Guild

John B. Haag
Hank Hachmann
Robert Hack
Sarah M. Hagerty
Kurt Haiman
George Halpern
Everett Halvorsen
Edward Hamilton
Frances W. Hamilton
Jerome A. Handman
Harriett
Brian Harrod
Paul Hartelius, Jr.
George Hartman
Alan Hartwell
Janet Hautau
Arthur Hawkins
Dorothy E. Hayes
Mark Hecker
Saul Heff
Mary Coyne Heinrich
Shelly Heller
Beverly R. Herman
Wes Heyman
Janice Hildebrand
Jitsuo Hoashi
Ronald Hodes
Marilyn Hoffner
Arnold C. Holeywell
George Holtane
Leslie Hopkins
William Hopkins
Uwe Horstmann
Mitsutoshi Hosaka
W. David Houser
Joe Hovanec
Elizabeth Howard
Mark Howard
Roy Alan Hughes
Jim Hunt
Jud Hurd
Allen Hurlburt
Morton Hyatt

Toshiaki Ide
The Illustrators Guild PR
Skip K. Ishii
Michael Israel
Michio Iwaki

Edward Jaccoma
Robert T. Jackson
Harry M. Jacobs
Lee Ann Jaffee
Moritz S. Jaggi
Jack Jamison
Neilan F. Jenks
Patricia Jerina
D. Craig Johns

Rowan G. Johnson
Bob Jones
Roger Joslyn
Len Jossel
Christian Julia

Nita J. Kalish
Ron Kambourian
Kiyoshi Kanai
Paulette J. Kaplan
Walter Kaprielian
Rachel Katzen
M. Richard Kaufmann
Milton Kaye PR
Nancy Kent
Myron W. Kenzer
Cyd Kilbey
Ran Hee Kim
Judith Klein
Hilda Stanger Klyde
Andrew Kner
Henry Knoepfler
Ray Komai
Robert F. Kopelman
Yoshikatsu Kosakai
Oscar Krauss
Helmut Krone
Eberhard Kruger
Gerard K. Kunkel
Anna Kurz
Norma Kwan

Roy La Grone
James E. Laird
Howard LaMarca
Abril Lamarque
Joseph O. Landi
John Larkin
Pearl Lau
Kenneth H. Lavey
Bonnie Lawrence
Marie-Christine Lawrence
Sal Lazzarotti
Daniel Lee
Don Leeds
Norberto Leon
Dr. Robert L. Leslie
Olaf Leu
Richard L. Levine
Julian Levinson
David Levy
Robert Leydenfrost
Alexander Liberman
Victor Liebert
Beverly Littlewood
Leo Lobell
Vincent Longo
Henry Robert Loomis
Hans Looser
Rocco Lotito
Alfred Lowry
John Lucci
Fred Ludekens
Thomas R. Lunde
Larry Lurin
Robert W. Lyon, Jr.

Lisa MacCallum
Charles MacDonald
Richard MacFarlane
David H. MacInnes
Frank Macri
Sam Magdoff
Louis Magnani
Anthony Mancino
Saul Mandel
John S. Marmaras
Andrea Marquez
Mary C. Mars
Al Marshall
Frank B. Marshall III
William Martin
John Massey

Takao Matsumoto
Theodore Matyas
Marce Mayhew
William McCaffery
Robert McCallum
Gerald McConnell
Kevin G. McCoy
George McGinnis
Fernando Medina
Franz Merlicek
Mario G. Messina
Lyle Metzdorf
Emil T. Micha
Jan Michael
Ann Fairlie Michelson
Eugene Milbauer
Joan Miller
Lawrence Miller
Marcia Miller
Richard V. Miller
John Milligan
Isaac Millman
William Minko
Leonard J. Mizerek
Michael Mohamad
Kenneth E. Morang
Burton A. Morgan
Jeffrey Moriber
William R. Morrison
Thomas Morton
Roger Paul Mosconi
Geoffrey Moss
Tobias Moss
Dale Moyer
Ralph J. Mutter

Yasuhara Nakahara
Makoto Nakamura
Daniel Nelson
NYC Tech. College
Raymond Nichols
Joseph Nissen
Ko Noda
Evelyn C. Noether
David November
C. Alexander Nuckols

Frank O'Blak
Leonard Obsatz
Jack W. Odette
Toshiyuki Ohashi
Joseph O'Hehir
Shigeo Okamoto
John Okladek
Motoaki Okuizumi
A. Robin Orden
Susan Alexis Orlie
Garrett P. Orr
Larry Ollino
Nina Ovryn
Bernard S. Owell

Onofrio Paccione
Zlata W. Paces
The Packaging Design Council PR
Maxine Paetro
Brad Pallas
Nicholas Peter Pappas
Ralph Parenio
Jacques Parker
Paul E. Parker, Jr.
Grant Parrish
Faye Parsons—see Zasada
Leonard Pearl
Alan Peckolick
Paul Pento
Vincent Pepi
Brendan C. Pereira
Victoria I. Peslak
John Pessalano
John Peter
Robert L. Peterson
Robert Petrocelli

Theodore D. Pettus
Stewart J. Phelps
Allan Philiba
Gerald M. Philips
Joseph Piatti
Ernest Pioppo
Peter Pioppo
Melvin Platt
Robert Pliskin
Sherry Pollack
Louis Portuesi
Anthony Pozsonyi
Brenda M. Preis
Benjamin Pride

Charles W. Queener
Elissa Querzé
Anny Queyroy
Mario Quilles
Brigid Quinn
Martin C. Quint
Mike Quon

Uno Alexandre Ramat
Luis Etren Ramirez Flores
Paul Rand
Robert C. Reed
Samuel Reed
Shelden Reed
Patrick Reeves
Joan Rehak
Herbert O. Reinke
Edwin C. Ricotta
Mitchell Rigie
Raymond Robertson
Clark L. Robinson
Harry Rocker
Harlow Rockwell
Peter Rogers
Andy Romano
Lester Rondell
Lloyd M. Rose
Morris L. Rosenblum
Herbert M. Rosenthal
Charles Rosner
Andrew Ross
James Francis Ross
Richard J. Ross
Richard Ross
Warren (Dusty) Rossell
Arnold Roston
Thomas Roth
Frank Rothmann
Iska Rothovius
Mort Rubenstein
Randee Rubin
Robert Miles Runyan
Henry N. Russell
John Russo
Don Ruther
Thomas Ruzicka

Stewart Sacklow
Martin Saint-Martin
Robert Saks
Barbara Stein Salthouse
Robert Salpeter
George Samerjan
Barbara Sanders
Jim Sant'Andrea
John Sargeant
Vincent Sauchelli
Hans Sauer
Sam Scali
Peter Scannell
Ernest Scarfone
Timothy Schaible
Roland Schenk
Paula Scher
Klaus F. Schmidt
William H. Schneider
Carol Schulter
Eileen Hedy Schultz

Rand Schuster
Victor Scocozza
Lisa Scott
Ruth Scott
William C. Seabrook III
Leslie Segal
Fred Seibert
Sheldon Seidler
John L. Sellers
Kaede Seville
Alexander Shear
William Sheldon
Brett D. Shevack
Myron Shipenberg
Takayuki Shirasu
Jerry Siano
Arthur Silver
Louis Silverstein
Milt Simpson
Leonard Sirowitz
Jack Skolnick
O. Paul Slaughter
Pamela Smith
Paul Smith
Robert S. Smith
Jerold Smokler
Edward Sobel
Robert Sobel PR
The Soc. of Illustrators
The Soc. of Publication
   Designers PR
Martin Solomon
Harold Sosnow
Virginia K. Sours
Anthony Spagnola
Nancy E. Spelbrink
Hoyt Spelman
Victor E. Spindler
Leo Stahl
Karsten Stapelfeldt
Alexander Stauf
Karl H. Steinbrenner
Charles M. Stern
Daniel E. Stewart
Richard Stewart
Linda Stillman
Leonard A. St. Louis
Ray Stollerman
Bernard Stone
Otto Storch
Celia Frances Stothard
William Strosahl
Ira F. Sturtevant
Edward Suchocki
Len Sugarman
Seiji Sugii
Amy Sussman
Yasuo Suzuki
Ken Sweeny
Leslie A. Sweet
Michael Sweret
Thomas S. Swimm

Teruaki Takao
Robert Talarczyk
Wendy Talvé
Mazakazu Tanabe
Soji George Tanaka
Tricia Tanassy
Joseph Tarallo
Melissa K. Tardiff
Melcon Tashian
Bill Taubin
Jack George Tauss
Trudie E. ten Broeke
John Tergis
Richard Thomas
Bradbury Thompson
Marion Thunberg
John Hepburn Tinker
Robert S. Todd
Harold Toledo
Gerald Tolle

Yusaku Tomoeda
Shinichiro Tora
Peter Toth
Edward L. Towles
Victor Trasoff
Michael W. Turek

Norio Uejyo
John Urbain
Frank Urrutia

Richard Vasquez
Haydee N. Verdia
Daniel Verdino
Frank A. Vitale
Richard A. Voehl

Dorothy Wachtenheim
Walter Wagener
John Wagman
Charles W. Wagner
Allan Wahler
Ernest Waivada
Joseph O. Wallace
Mark Walton
Robert J. Ward
Laurence S. Waxberg
Warner Amex Satellite
   Entertainmt. Co.
Jessica Weber
Daniel E. Weidmann
William Weinberger
Art Weithas
Theo Welti
Ron Wetzel
Susan F. Whalen
Ken White
Ronald J. Wickham
Gordon M. Wilbur
Richard Wilde
Jack Williamson
Horst Winkler
Rupert Witalis
Cynthia Wojdyla
Henry Wolf
Orest Woronewyck
William K. Wurtzel

A. Hidehito Yamamoto
Yoji Yamamoto
Masakazu Yamashita
Jo Yanow PR
Takeo Yao
Zen Yonkovig
Steve Yuranyi

D. Bruce Zahor
Carmile S. Zaino
Faye Parsons Zasada
Paul H. Zasada
David Zeigerman
Alan Zwiebel

INDEX

Art Directors

Production Company

Photographers

Agencies